BLACK METROPOLIS:

A Study of Negro Life in a Northern City / Volume I

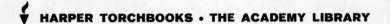

BLACK METROPOLIS

A Study of Negro Life in a Northern City

St. Clair Drake and Horace R. Cayton

Volume I

Introduction by Richard Wright

*Introduction to Torchbook edition by
Everett C. Hughes*

*An Appendix, "Black Metropolis
1961," has been added to this volume
by the authors.*

HARPER & ROW, PUBLISHERS • NEW YORK AND EVANSTON

HARPER TORCHBOOKS ❦ THE ACADEMY LIBRARY
Advisory Editor in the Humanities and the
Social Sciences: Benjamin Nelson

The first edition of this book was published in one volume by Harcourt, Brace and Company in 1945. The authors have added to the Torchbook edition: to Volume I, an Appendix, "Black Metropolis 1961"; to Volume II, an Authors' Preface, a new chapter, "Bronzeville 1961," and "Suggestions for Collateral Reading, 1962." In addition, two new graphs and three new maps have been prepared for the Appendix to Volume I.

First HARPER TORCHBOOK edition published 1962 by
Harper & Row, Publishers, Incorporated
New York and Evanston

Contents

VOLUME I

VOLUME II

List of Tables

VOLUME I

VOLUME II

List of Maps, Charts and Graphs

VOLUME II

Authors' Acknowledgment

MANY YEARS OF RESEARCH AND THE EFFORTS OF A VERY LARGE NUMBER of persons have gone into the formation of this book. The original data were gathered on a series of projects financed by the Work Projects Administration, and referred to in this book as the Cayton-Warner Research. The studies began as investigations of the general social conditions surrounding the problem of juvenile delinquency on Chicago's "South Side." Employing the methods of both sociologists and social anthropologists, the research soon assumed the character of a study of the culture of the entire community, in order to determine the context within which the problem of delinquency could best be analyzed. As is evident from the book, the problem of delinquency ultimately became subordinated to the larger problem of the description and analysis of the structure and organization of the Negro community, both internally, and in relation to the metropolis of which it is a part.

In addition to the Work Projects Administration as a local and national agency, the following members of its administrative staff were particularly helpful: Miss Wilda A. Sawyer, Mrs. Amelia H. Baker, Mr. Frank J. Morris and Mr. Melvin L. Dollar. On the projects themselves, valuable assistance was rendered by Mrs. Mae C. Barnett, in charge of personnel; Mr. Lawrence Langford, who prepared most of the basic maps and charts; and Miss Juanita Simpson, who, for a time, was in charge of the statistical analyses.

Throughout the life of the research project—a period of about four years—approximately twenty research students in specialized fields participated in the collection and organization of material on various phases of Negro life. Through the assistance of the Julius Rosenwald Fund, their work, in the form of monographs, has been made available to the general public at the Parkway Community House in Chicago. The following persons were responsible for the preparation of these individual studies: Margaret Cross, St. Clair Drake, Mary Gardner, John Given, Viola Haygood, Elmer Henderson, Winifred

xiii

Ingram, Elizabeth Johns, George McCray, Mary Elaine Ogden, Lawrence Reddick, Joy Schultz, Estelle Hill Scott, Joseph Semper, Samuel Strong and Elizabeth Wimp. The Work Projects Administration has published three of these monographs in mimeographed form: St. Clair Drake, *Churches and Voluntary Associations in the Chicago Negro Community;* Mary Elaine Ogden, *The Chicago Negro Community: A Statistical Description;* and Estelle Hill Scott, *Occupational Changes Among Negroes in Chicago, 1890-1930.*

From its inception, the research was under the direction of Horace R. Cayton and W. Lloyd Warner, Professor of Sociology and Anthropology at the University of Chicago.

The various projects were sponsored by the Institute of Juvenile Research, the Illinois State Employment Service and the Cook County Bureau of Public Welfare. Individual sponsors were Dr. Earl Johnson and Dr. Louis Wirth, of the University of Chicago.

Various types of assistance were rendered to the research, also, by the Church of the Good Shepherd, the Citizens' Committee on Reemployment, the Chicago *Defender* and the University of Chicago. All of the community institutions studied, although they cannot be listed separately, were most co-operative and helpful.

A preliminary organization of the research materials was made possible by a grant from the Julius Rosenwald Fund. As originally conceived, the material was to have been presented as a research report with emphasis upon methodology in the social sciences. Later, however, the authors, wishing to reach a wider audience, developed the book in its present form. In addition to condensing, rewriting and interpreting the material from the monographs, the authors have, over a period of three years, collected new data with which to bring the book up to date. Since the monographs were used only as primary source material, neither the authors of the individual monographs, the sponsors of the projects, nor the Work Projects Administration can be held responsible for any of the interpretations and conclusions found in these pages.

The basic source materials for this book are the interview documents and newspaper excerpts collected on the Cayton-Warner Research. The most valuable secondary sources have been those publications of the University of Chicago Press referred to throughout the book. The authors wish to express their appreciation to Mr. Joseph A. Brandt,

Director of the University of Chicago Press, for granting them permission to make such generous use of these sources.

The authors wish to acknowledge courtesies extended to them during various phases of the writing by the Parkway Community House, Chicago, and Dillard University, New Orleans, Louisiana. We should like also to thank Miss Arleen Wilson and Miss E. Switzer for their conscientious work in assisting in the checking of sources and the preparation of final copy.

The first six chapters of the book were read critically by Dr. Lawrence D. Reddick, historian, and Curator of the Schomburg Collection. The authors have also, from time to time, received some very valuable critical comments from Mr. Elmer W. Henderson, formerly Director of the Illinois State Commission on the Condition of the Urban Colored Population, and now Midwestern Regional Director of the Fair Employment Practices Committee. Dr. Elizabeth Johns Drake assisted throughout in the preparation of the manuscript for the press, and gave valuable technical assistance at various stages of the work.

The authors sincerely appreciate the unusual interest displayed by Mrs. Elizabeth Moore, who made editorial suggestions, and Mr. Bunji Tagawa, of Graphic Associates, who prepared the illustrations in their present form. Finally, the authors wish to express their appreciation for the sustained interest and encouragement shown by Mr. John Woodburn whose mature understanding of Negro-white relations and Negro life in America has been of great assistance.

ST. CLAIR DRAKE
HORACE R. CAYTON

Introduction

IT IS WITH A SENSE OF KEEN PRIDE THAT I UNDERTAKE TO INTRODUCE *Black Metropolis,* a landmark of research and scientific achievement, to the reading public. I, in common with the authors, St. Clair Drake and Horace R. Cayton, feel personally identified with the material in this book. All three of us have lived some of our most formative years in Chicago; indeed, one of the authors, Horace Cayton, still lives there. Drake and Cayton, like me, were not born there; all three of us migrated to Chicago to seek freedom, life. . . . Drake came from the South; Cayton from the Northwest; and I went to Chicago as a migrant from Mississippi. And there in that great iron city, that impersonal, mechanical city, amid the steam, the smoke, the snowy winds, the blistering suns; there in that self-conscious city, that city so deadly dramatic and stimulating, we caught whispers of the meanings that life could have, and we were pushed and pounded by facts much too big for us. Many migrants like us were driven and pursued, in the manner of characters in a Greek play, down the paths of defeat; but luck must have been with us, for we somehow survived; and, for those of us who did not come through, we are trying to do the bidding of Hamlet who admonished Horatio:

> If thou didst ever hold me in thy heart,
> Absent thee from felicity awhile,
> And in this harsh world draw thy breath in pain,
> To tell my story.

Chicago is the city from which the most incisive and radical Negro thought has come; there is an open and raw beauty about that city that seems either to kill or endow one with the spirit of life. I felt those extremes of possibility, death and hope, while I lived half hungry and afraid in a city to which I had fled with the dumb yearning to write, to tell my story. But I did not know what my story was, and it was not until I stumbled upon science that I discovered some of the meanings of the environment that battered and taunted me. I encountered the work of men who were studying the Negro community, amassing facts about urban Negro life, and I found that sincere art and honest science were not far apart, that each could enrich the other. The huge mountains of fact piled up by the Department of Sociology at the University of Chicago gave me my first concrete vision of the forces that molded the urban Negro's body and soul. (I was never a student at the university; it is doubtful if I could have passed the entrance examination.)

It was from the scientific findings of men like the late Robert E. Park, Robert Redfield, and Louis Wirth that I drew the meanings for my documentary book, *12,000,000 Black Voices;* for my novel, *Native Son;* it was from their scientific facts that I absorbed some of that quota of inspiration necessary for me to write *Uncle Tom's Children* and *Black Boy. Black Metropolis,* Drake's and Cayton's scientific statement about the urban Negro, pictures the environment out of which the Bigger Thomases of our nation come; it is the environment of the Bosses of the Buildings; and it is the environment to which Negro boys and girls turn their eyes when they hear the word Freedom.

Chicago is the *known* city; perhaps more is known about it, how it is run, how it kills, how it loves, steals, helps, gives, cheats, and crushes than any other city in the world. Chicago is a new city; it grew to be bigger in one hundred years than did Paris in two thousand. There are men now living in Chicago whose fathers saw it in its infancy and helped it to grow. Because Chicago is so young, it is possible to know it in a way that many other cities cannot be known. The stages of its complex growth are living memories.

Chicago, it seems, has a way of leaving its imprint upon those who live in it; there have been so many direct, realistic novels and poems and plays written about Chicago by the men who have lived in it that there rose the phrase: The Chicago School. From Chicago have come Sandburg, Anderson, Dreiser, Farrell, Levin, Cohen, Algren, Masters, Conroy; and even Sinclair Lewis lived there for a while. The imaginative expressions of these men have set the tone and pattern of literary thinking and feeling for a large part of the nation for almost two generations.

But the spell of Chicago has invaded more than the literary terrain; the extent to which scientists have relied upon the city for their basic truth of America's social life is no less interesting. It is in Chicago's school of scientific thought that one finds a close affinity among the disciplines of sociology, psychology, and anthropology, and the men most responsible for this, Louis Wirth, Robert Redfield, and the late Robert E. Park, were not afraid to urge their students to trust their feelings for a situation or an event, were not afraid to stress the role of insight, and to warn against a slavish devotion to figures, charts, graphs, and sterile scientific techniques. Scientific volumes brilliantly characterized by insight and feeling are Robert Redfield's *Tepotzlan,* Louis Wirth's *The Ghetto,* Everett V. Stonequist's *The Marginal Man,* Frederick M. Thrasher's *The Gang,* Park's and Burgess's *The City* and Harvey W. Zorbaugh's *The Gold Coast and the Slums.*

Especially has no other community in America been so intensely studied, has had brought to bear upon it so blinding a scrutiny as Chicago's South Side. It was in the University of Chicago's Department of Sociology that such men as E. Franklin Frazier who produced *The Negro Family in Chicago* and *The Negro Family in the United States,* Bertrand Doyle who produced *The Etiquette of Race Relations in the South* and Harold F. Gosnell who produced *Negro Politicians,* were trained and guided. In no other city has the differentiation between groups and races been so clearly shown; nowhere has it been revealed so vividly, for example, how birth rates, death rates, etc., vary as people move out of the center of the city to its outer edges. This, in short, constitutes some of the vast amount of research that preceded Drake's and Cayton's *Black Metropolis.*

But let me bluntly warn the reader at the outset: This is no easy book. In order to understand it, you may have to wrench your mind rather violently out of your accustomed ways of thinking. There is no attempt in *Black Metropolis* to understate, to gloss over, to doll up, or make harsh facts pleasant for the tender-minded. The facts of urban life presented here are in their starkest form, their crudest manifestation; not because the authors want to shock you, but because the environment out of which those facts spring has so wrought them. To have presented them otherwise would have been to negate the humanity of the American Negro.

Black Metropolis reveals (1) the relationship of Negroes to whites in Chicago, (2) the kind of world which Negroes have built up under their separate, subordinate status, and (3) the impact of these twin configurations upon the personalities and institutions of Chicago

Negroes. The fundamental sociological concepts employed are: industrialization, secularization, urbanization, social differentiation, the latter showing the social stratification and the development of social types.

The dominant hallmark of the book is the combination throughout of the disciplines of both sociology and anthropology. The book examines the social structure as though it were frozen at a moment of time, which is the approach of anthropology; and it examines the processes and dynamics which take place in that structure, which is the approach of sociology. In general, the book can be thought of in a phrase that Louis Wirth has used to describe the lives of people who live in cities: Urbanism As a Way of Life; but with this important exception: The Jim Crow lives that Negroes live in our crowded cities differ qualitatively from those of whites and are not fully known to whites.

If, in reading my novel, *Native Son,* you doubted the reality of Bigger Thomas, then examine the delinquency rates cited in this book; if, in reading my autobiography, *Black Boy,* you doubted the picture of family life shown there, then study the figures on family disorganization given here. *Black Metropolis* describes the processes that mold Negro life as we know it today, processes that make the majority of Negroes on Chicago's South Side sixth-graders, processes that make 65 per cent of all Negroes on Chicago's South Side earn their living by manual labor. After studying the social processes in this book, you cannot expect Negro life to be other than what it is. To expect the contrary would be like expecting to see Rolls-Royces coming off the assembly lines at Ford's River Rouge plant! The imposed conditions under which Negroes live detail the structure of their lives like an engineer outlining the blue-prints for the production of machines.

Do not hold a light attitude toward the slums of Chicago's South Side. Remember that Hitler came out of such a slum. Remember that Chicago could be the Vienna of American Fascism! Out of these mucky slums can come ideas quickening life or hastening death, giving us peace or carrying us toward another war.

Can America change these conditions? Or is it hopeless to expect an understanding of this problem? If this problem cannot be mastered, then one thing is fairly certain: The liberals, the intellectuals, the artists, the students, Communists, Socialists, New Dealers, all who hope for life and peace will lose to war. In short, what happened in Europe during the past twenty years will happen here.

I'm not naive enough to believe that many will heed such Cassandra-like warnings, for not many people really believe that any such crisis exists. Hence, at the risk of sounding didactic, I will try to show that there is a problem facing us, a bigger one than even that of the Negro, a problem of which the Negro problem is a small but a highly symbolically important part.

Lodged in the innermost heart of America is a fatal division of being, a war of impulses. America knows that a split is in her, and that that split might cause her death; but she is powerless to pull the dangling ends together. An uneasiness haunts her conscience, taints her moral preachments, lending an air of unreality to her actions, and rendering ineffectual the good deeds she feels compelled to do in the world. America is a nation of a riven consciousness. But from where did the split, the division come?

When man cast off the ancient shrouds of his feudal faith, he had supreme confidence in the natural dignity of man, and believed that reason and freedom could lead him to paradise on earth. Man of Western Europe lunged toward the future, but in the very moment of his acting he committed that error which might well spell his tragedy. Passionately ardent to make his place on earth secure, he snatched millions of black men out of Africa and enslaved them to serve him.

But the white man suffered hang-overs from a feudal morality; he could not enslave others in a confident manner. Having bid for freedom upon the assumption that all men were naturally free, that they possessed in their hearts those impulses that made dignity and nobility a given human right, he could not play the role of master with a singleness of heart. So, to keep what he had and to feel safe with it, he had to invent reasons, causes, explanations, rationalizations, all of which amounted to a declaration of the biological inferiority of the enslaved. Paradoxes and contradictions of thought and feeling became commonplace. It was claimed that white men were "helping" black men by enslaving them; it finally became right to treat black men wrong, and wrong to treat them right. The apex of white racial ideology was reached when it was assumed that white domination was a God-given right.

But another and deeper dilemma rose out of the white man's break with the feudal order, a dilemma more acidly corroding than even that of slavery, one which colored and toned every moment of his life, creating an anxiety that was never to leave him. The advent of machine production altered his relationship to the earth, to his family, to his fellow men, and even to himself. Under feudalism the family had been the unit of production, the nexus of emotional relations, a symbol of the moral order of the universe. The father was the head of the family, the king the father of the state, and God the ruler of the world, and God's priests represented Him in the mundane affairs of man. The eternal and temporal orders of existence coalesced and formed one vivid, timeless moment of meaning, justification, and redemption. Man and earth and heaven formed a unit.

Following the break with the feudal order, philosophers played the role of mediators between the old order and the new, but the facts of machine production proved, in the long run, more powerful in ordering men's lives than even the rationalizations of scientists and thinkers who sought to justify the new dispensation.

Their kinship with the soil altered, men became atoms crowding great industrial cities, bewildered as to their duties and meaning. As Robert Redfield has pointed out: Holy days became holidays; clocks replaced the sun as a symbolic measurement of time. As the authority of the family waned, the meaning of reality, emotion, experience, action, and God assumed the guise of teasing questions. These processes, of course, were realized unevenly in men's consciousness; there were violent jumps and leaps (war) and static periods, lulls (peace); many millions who were daily involved in the processes of change did not realize what was happening until a war came and destroyed some of the lingering, surviving fragments of feudal reality and made a part of the reality that they were *actually, really* living the overwhelming contemporaneous reality. (It was in this way that the fiction that war was an instrument of progress came to find shelter in men's confused minds.)

Men still cling to the emotional basis of life that the feudal order gave them, while living and striving in a world whose every turn of wheel, throb of engine, and conquest of space deny its validity. This dual aspect of living is our riven consciousness, our tension, our anxiety.

The best philosophic energy of American thought has gone into trying to "tell what time it is," how far we have strayed from the feudal home, or how close we have come to making ourselves feel secure in an arid and senseless world. The philosophies of William James and John Dewey, and all the pragmatists in between, are but intellectual labors to allay the anxieties of modern man, adjurations to the white men of the West to accept uncertainty as a way of life, to live within the vivid, present moment and let the meaning of that moment suffice as a rationale for life and death.

But man refuses to behave; having once awakened from the feudal dream and tasted of the sweet fruits of sensuality, speculation, wonder, curiosity, freedom of movement, he will accept nothing less. Stimulated by the pinch of circumstance, he acts irrationally; he won't let well enough alone; he sulks; he broods; he dreams; he revolts; his consciousness spills disdainfully over the banks of pragmatism. Everywhere in the Western world men are rejecting the life of an industrialization which has pounded their lives to meaninglessness, which has reduced them to appendages to machines. Defiantly men hoist up the old slogans of liberty, love, justice, and happiness; and no authority, civil or religious, has yet found a way to divest their minds completely of a belief and trust in these magic signs. (Even Freud, after plowing up man's pleasure-ridden unconscious, seemed to have reeled back in fear and began to babble of a "reality-principle," began to search for some way to reconcile man's inordinate desires with a world that contained no feasible promise of their fulfillment. And even Communists or Fascists, ideologically rigid though they may be, must make use of man's hope-symbols if they want to get a following. And the capitalists themselves contribute campaign funds to politicians whose sworn duty it is to stamp out of the community those very impulses whose existence makes profits possible. Modern man is afraid of himself and is at war with himself.)

Current American thought is so fastened upon trying to make what is *presently* real the only and right reality, that it has quite forgot the reality of the passion and hunger of millions of exploited workers and dissatisfied minorities; it has quite forgot the reality of the impulses that made the men of Western Europe rise and slay the feudal dragon; it has quite forgot the reality of the hot laws of feeling that gave rise to rebellions against oppressive authority. Out of the vast pools of feudal misery, men found the meaning of Revolution; but out of the vaster pools of the misery of industrialization the sons of the men who overthrew the feudal world claim that no new life can spring up, no revolutionary creation can take place. The lives of the dispossessed are not real to them.

America's attitude toward the just-finished war in Europe is an example of how the men who run our industrial world cannot see what really *is*. Locked in the stance of defending the reality they loved, but few Americans believed that the reality of a Hitler was possible; and when, belatedly, they found that he did exist, they naively thought that they could "do business with him." The very conditions of life that nurtured Hitler were not acknowledged for what they were: Seed-beds of revolution. And it is doubtful if a war— which is not yet over—costing 40,000,000 casualties, war with all of its terrible and bloody immediacy, has made what the *real* reality of our time is real for them. It may take yet another war to make them see what really *is*. The hardest thing on earth today for current thought to accept is that we are living through a series of revolutions.

But this has happened before. When the Russians, sick of their feudal prison, smashed out to freedom, the industrial magnates of the West did not believe that Russia could become industrialized, did not believe that Russian peasants had an aptitude for machinery, even when immigrant Russian peasants were operating machines under their very noses in a dozen American cities. It was comforting to believe that only the magical spirit of a God-fearing capitalism could operate machines skillfully.

Hitler saw and cynically exploited the weak spots in our society perhaps more clearly than any politician of modern times. History will no doubt dub the Hitlerites as the most devastating critics of our dis-organized industrial order, not even excepting the Bolsheviks of 1917! Hitler knew his industrial slums, knew the brutalized millions trapped in them, knew their hungers, knew their humiliations, knew the feverish longing of their hearts. Capitalists today hate Hitler for his wholesale, gratuitous murders; but they hate him for another and subtler reason: They hate him for revealing the shaky, class founda-tions of their society, for reminding them of their sundered conscious-ness, for flaunting their hypocrisy, for sneering at their hesitations, for manipulating their racial hatreds to a degree that they had never dared. Gangster of the human spirit that he was, Hitler organized into a brutal army the men who live in those areas of society that the

Western world had neglected, organized those men whose reality the Western world could not see.

Let us disentangle in our minds Hitler's deeds from what Hitler exploited. His deeds were crimes; but the hunger he exploited in the hearts of Europe's millions was a valid hunger and is still there. Indeed, the war has but deepened that hunger, made it more acute.

Today the problem of the world's dispossessed exists with great urgency, and the problem of the Negro in America is a phase of this general problem, containing and telescoping the longings in the lives of a billion colored subject colonial people into a symbol. Yes, when the Negro problem is raised, white men, for a reason which as yet they do not fully understand, feel guilt, panic, anxiety, tension; they feel the essential loneliness of their position which is built upon greed, exploitation, and a general denial of humanity; they feel the naked untenability of their split consciousness, their two-faced moral theories spun to justify their right to dominate.

But the American Negro, child of the culture that crushes him, wants to be free in a way that white men are free; for him to wish otherwise would be unnatural, unthinkable. Negroes, with but minor exceptions, still believe in the hope of economic rewards; they believe in justice, liberty, the integrity of the individual. In the heart of industrial America is a surviving remnant, perchance a saving remnant of a passion for freedom, a passion fanned by their national humiliation.

Black Metropolis is a scientific report upon the state of unrest, longing, hope among urban Negroes, and in writing it Drake and Cayton were working within the compass of the most normal ideas and moral imperatives of the West. A greater claim than that no American can make for the right to be heard.

Sometimes northern white men, seeing the misery of the northern urban Negro, exclaim: "Why do Negroes leave the sunny South to live like this?" When a white man asks such a question, he is either deliberately or conveniently forgetting that white men once left the slumberous feudal world and eagerly took the risks of, as William James phrased it, an "unguaranteed existence." So, too, when the Negro, responding to the cultural hopes of his time, leaves the South and comes to the cold, industrial North, he is acting upon the same impulses that made the men of the West great. The Negro can do no less; he shares all of the glorious hopes of the West, all of its anxieties, its corruptions, its psychological maladies. But, too, above all, like a warning, he shares those tendencies toward surrendering all hope of seeking solutions within the frame of a "free enterprise" society. To the extent that he realizes that his hopes are hopeless, he will embrace Communism or Fascism, or whatever other ideological rejection is offered.

In *Black Metropolis,* the authors have presented much more than the anatomy of Negro frustration; they have shown how *any* human beings can become mangled, how *any* personalities can become distorted when men are caught in the psychological trap of being emotionally committed to the living of a life of freedom which is denied them. The Germans had more than their share of this fundamental frustration, and it was their hopeless hope that Hitler and his murderous legions battened on.

Not long ago I saw one of the greatest documentary films ever made, *Triumph des Willens,* which showed the rise of German Fascism and the "joy" that Hitler gave (while Himmler burned the dissenters!) millions of his duped followers. What vital images flickered across the screen! What limpid faith, what completeness of living! But, as I watched the tragedy of men being cynically betrayed unto death, I wondered if men who love life would lead the next "wave of the future," or would haters like Hitler? I could not answer with certainty.

What would be the reaction if *Triumph des Willens* were shown to a group of American industrialists, law-makers, and college professors with a commentary that said: "Here is what will happen to the millions who inhabit Chicago, New York, Pittsburgh, and Los Angeles, if you and your kind do not lead them to a life compatible with the dignity of their aspirations"? I'm convinced that the professors would say, "Prove it!" The law-makers would say, "Our police force can stop such people from taking power." Our industrialists would say, "The prospect that people will follow such paths is a romantic dream." And their answers would be sincerely given, for they simply do not see the reality of the dispossessed. Their attitude could be described by a phrase which Negroes have coined to indicate the contempt which whites show Negroes: "They play people cheap."

Social discontent assumes many subtle guises, and a society that recognizes only those forms of social maladjustment which are recorded in courts, prisons, clinics, hospitals, newspapers, and bureaus of vital statistics will be missing some of the most fateful of the tell-tale clues to its destiny. What I mean is this: It is distinctly possible to know, *before it happens,* that certain forms of violence will occur. It can be known that a native-born white man, the end-product of all our strivings, educated, healthy, apparently mentally normal, having the stability of a wife and family, possessing the security of a good job with high wages, enjoying more freedom than any other country on earth accords its citizens, *but devoid of the most elementary satisfactions,* will seize upon an adolescent, zoot-suited Mexican and derive deep feelings of pleasure from stomping his hopeless guts out upon the pavements of Los Angeles. But to know that a seemingly normal, ordinary American is capable of such brutality implies making a judgment about the nature and quality of our everyday American experiences which most Americans simply cannot do. FOR, TO ADMIT THAT OUR INDIVIDUAL EXPERIENCES ARE OF SO LOW A QUALITY AND NATURE AS TO PRECLUDE THE DEEP, ORGANIC SATISFACTIONS NECESSARY FOR CIVILIZED, PEACEFUL LIVING, IS TO CONDEMN THE SYSTEM THAT PROVIDES THOSE EXPERIENCES.

Drake and Cayton, in *Black Metropolis,* do not dwell upon these imponderables; but, in writing this definitive study of Negro urbanization, they were conscious of the over-all American problem and they had to assume that white Americans know little or nothing of the Negro, that a mere statement of his problem would go against the grain of American thought and feeling; they had to assume that Negro personality, Negro conditions of life, Negro feelings, and the ardent and ofttimes bitter nature of Negro aspirations constituted an alien realm for white Americans, were unreal to them.

The authors know well that white Americans take it for granted that they know Negroes, and they understand why whites hold to their presumed knowledge with such fierceness. The authors know that the Negro has been on the American scene for some three hundred years, and has been in our society as a more or less free agent for more than seventy-five years. They know, too, that a book like *Black Metropolis* might come as a jolt to whites who assume that their knowledge of the Negro excels the knowledge of Negroes by Negroes. Some whites will feel that the authors were impertinent; others will feel that they had some special ax to grind. Yet nothing could be more erroneous.

What spurred the authors to this task was a conviction on their part that there existed a meaning in Negro life that whites do not see and do not want to see. The authors have an acute concern, not only for the welfare of the Negro, but for the nation as a whole. They willingly shouldered the risks of having gross and fantastic motives imputed to them, for they know that violent events will soon flare forth, prompted either by whites or blacks; and they know that white Americans will stand transfixed in bewilderment at the magnitude and sanguinity of these events. When those events come, the authors want you to know their relationship to you and your life, how to interpret the racial outbreaks that will plague America in the immediate postwar world. This book was written, too, so that Negroes will be able to interpret correctly the meaning of their own actions.

It will be but natural for this honest question to be asked by both whites and blacks: If the racial scene depicted here is true, if the points of view presented here are valid, if the meanings deduced here are real, then why have we not been told all this before?

An honest question merits an honest answer, and that answer lies in the hearts of the white and black readers of this book. The answer is, directly and bluntly: American whites and blacks both possess deep-seated resistances against the Negro problem being presented, even verbally, in all of its hideous fullness, in all of the totality of its meaning. The many and various groups, commissions, councils, leagues, committees, and organizations of an interracial nature have consistently diluted the problem, blurred it, injected foggy moral or sentimental notions into it. This fact is as true of the churches as of the trade unions; as true of Negro organizations as of white; as true of the political Left as of the political Right; as true of white individuals as of black.

The church in America has shied from presenting this problem to the American people from a moral point of view, for fear that it would place itself in a position of having to do something about it. On the other hand, the trade unions, which have so far done more than any other single agency on the Negro front, seek to convert the Negro problem from a complex, race, cultural, and national problem into a relatively simple one of class conflicts and interests. As a result of the trade union attitude, there now exists within the trade union movement many grave problems affecting the Negro people; but there does not exist as yet a satisfactory form of communication by which

Negro trade unionists can make their voices heard as Negroes about their problems.

The political Left often gyrates and squirms to make the Negro problem fit rigidly into a class-war frame of reference, when the roots of that problem lie in American culture as a whole; it tries to anchor the Negro problem to a patriotism of global time and space, which robs the problem of its reality and urgency, of its concreteness and tragedy. The political Right, reacting traditionally, tries to smother the Negro problem as a whole and insists upon regarding Negroes as individuals and making individual deals with individual Negroes, ignoring the inevitable race consciousness which three hundred years of Jim Crow living has burned into the Negro's heart. Both the political Left and the political Right try to change the Negro problem into something that they can control, thereby denying the humanity of the Negro, excluding his unique and historic position in American life.

The powerful Negro press, too, is somewhat afraid of stating the problem of the Negro fully; it is apprehensive lest the concentrated gravity of that problem create such anxiety in whites that they will withdraw what few paltry concessions they are now yielding.

The authors have sensitively studied all of these factors and they have come to the conclusion that any dangers inherent in speaking out boldly and honestly far outweigh adherence to traditional reticences, which strip the problem of its political, moral, spiritual, class, and economic meaning.

But *Black Metropolis* is not a volume of mere facts. The basic facts are assumed. The hour is too late to argue if there *is* a Negro problem or not. Riots have swept the nation and more riots are pending. This book assumes that the Negro's present position in the United States results from the oppression of Negroes by white people, that the Negro's conduct, his personality, his culture, his entire life flow naturally and inevitably out of the conditions imposed upon him by white America. To that extent this book supplements and endorses the conclusions arrived at by Gunnar Myrdal in his *American Dilemma*, that monumental study of race relations in the United States.

The authors have not submitted a total program of action in this book; rather, they have assumed the ultimate aspirations of the Negro, just as Negroes have always assumed them, and just as whites assume theirs. Negroes feel that they are politically and culturally Americans.

The job of the authors was not to quiet or soothe, but to aid white people in knowing the facts of urban Negro life. The authors knew well that there will be many ill-intentioned whites who will seize upon certain sections of this book, lift them out of context, and try to prove their own pet notions of Negro inferiority with them. No attempt was made to forestall such possibilities; it was assumed that the Negro is human, all-too-human.

How can any individual, group, or political party, after reading *Black Metropolis,* bring forth an organizational or ideological program for Negroes without taking into account the durable and sturdy foundation of fact presented here? The decisive and pivotal centers of Negro life in America are to be found in our northern industrial cities, and I would go so far as to say that the measure of sincerity of any individual, group, or political party seeking support among Negroes should be judged by the manner in which it effectively grapples with what Drake and Cayton have so meticulously revealed.

With the bare bones of this problem thus rendered visible, many new ideological excursions, many heretofore unimagined tangents of thought can now be contemplated. For example, what peculiar personality formations result when millions of people are forced to live lives of outward submissiveness while trying to keep intact in their hearts a sense of the worth of their humanity? What are the personality mechanisms that sublimate racial resentments which, if expressed openly, would carry penalties varying from mild censure to death? Does the Negro's tremendous fund of repression affect his speech, his walk, his dress, his music, his health? Why are the highest rates of hyper-tension (high blood-pressure) to be found among the Negro sharecroppers on the plantations of the pastoral South? Is this hyper-tension in any way related to their daily and dramatic rejection by the society in which they live and work and die, the society whose language they speak and whose cultural mandates they try so hard to follow and serve? Why do the personalities of American Negroes show more psychological damage than do the personalities of the Negroes of the West Indies? And is this psychological differential between British and American Negroes in any way derived from their different relationships to the two Anglo-Saxon imperialisms?

There is yet another vista now open for us, a vista of which only artists have so far availed themselves: What new values of action or experience can be revealed by looking at Negro life through alien eyes or under the lenses of new concepts? We have the testimony of a Gunnar Myrdal, but we know that that is not all. What would life on Chicago's South Side look like when seen through the eyes of a Freud, a Joyce, a Proust, a Pavlov, a Kierkegaard? It should be recalled in this connection that Gertrude Stein's *Three Lives,* which contained "Melanctha," the first long serious literary treatment of Negro life in the United States, was derived from Stein's preoccupation with Jamesian psychology.

We know how some of the facts look when seen under the lenses of Marxist concepts, but the full weight of the Western mind has yet to be brought to bear upon this forgotten jungle of black life that lies just across the street or next door or around the corner from white Americans. (How easy it is to leave Chicago and fight and die for democracy in Spain! How soothing it is to prefer to civilize the heathen in Japan when slave conditions exist in Florida! But few white Americans have found the strength to cease being victims of their culture to the extent that they can throw off their socially inherited belief in a dehumanized image of the Negro. Indeed, the whole inner landscape of American Negro life, born of repression, is so little known that when whites see it they brand it "emotionally running amuck" or "psychopathic manifestations.")

What benefits will accrue to our country if this problem is solved? Will it so unify our moral duality as to permit the flowering of our political and cultural expression? (Some politicians have estimated that the presence of rigid anti-Negro feeling in our country has retarded our political development by more than fifty years!) Or will America, when she is brought face to face with the problem of the Negro, collapse in a moral spasm, as did Europe when confronted with the problem of the Jew?

Will the Negro, in the language of André Malraux, find a meaning in his humiliation, make his slums and his sweat-shops his modern cathedrals out of which will be born a new consciousness that can guide him toward freedom? Or will he continue, as he does today, saying Job-like to the society that crushes him: Though it slays me, yet will I trust in it?

In reading those sections of *Black Metropolis* dealing with the wide prevalence of "policy playing" (lottery) among urban Negroes, we can ask with ample justification: What are the limits of individual responsibility for crime? And what is crime, anyway?

And we can ask, after reading the scandalous facts of the low level of literacy among Negro migrants in northern cities, if more education without more opportunity will solve anything. Or will more education merely render Negroes more sensitive and therefore more violently rebellious against whites whom they hold responsible for their degradation?

And, too, perhaps for the first time, we can see how the Negro has had to take Protestant religion and make it into something for his own special needs, needs born of an imposed Black Belt existence. To what extent has racial religion replaced Christian religion in thousands of Black Belt churches? And what is wrong with religion in America that it has turned its back upon the Negro and his problem? And to what degree is religion in America officially and ideologically identified with the policy of White Supremacy?

With the scientific facts of urban Negro life now given in *Black Metropolis,* the way is clear for other workers, black and white, to paint in the shadings, the background, to make three-dimensional the personalities caught in this Sargasso of racial subjugation.

William James,* in discussing the way in which the "social self" of man exists in society, says, ". . . a man has as many social selves as there are individuals who recognize him and carry an image of him in their minds." Then, in speculating upon what a man would feel if he were completely socially excluded, he says, "No more fiendish punishment could be devised, were such a thing physically possible, than that one should be turned loose in society and remain absolutely unnoticed by all the members thereof. If no one turned round when we entered, answered when we spoke, or minded what we did, but if every person we met "cut us dead," and acted as if we were non-existent things, a kind of rage and impotent despair would ere long well up in us, from which the cruelest bodily tortures would be a relief; for these would make us feel that, however bad might be our plight, we had not sunk to such a depth as to be unworthy of attention at all."

There can be, of course, no such thing as a *complete* rejection of anybody by society; for, even in rejecting him, society must notice

* *The Philosophy of William James,* Modern Library edition, page 128.

him. But the American Negro has come as near being the victim of a complete rejection as our society has been able to work out, for the dehumanized image of the Negro which white Americans carry in their minds, the anti-Negro epithets continuously on their lips, exclude the contemporary Negro as truly as though he were kept in a steel prison, and doom even those Negroes who are as yet unborn.

A casual examination of the progressive changes in one phase of Negro cultural expression is sufficient to show how a gradual estrangement has occurred in the Negro over a period of 160 years, an estrangement from complete identification with the nation to atomized and despairing rebellion.

In 1760, a black girl, Phyllis Wheatley, was brought to America from Africa and sold into slavery. By fortunate accident a Christian Boston family purchased her, treated her as an equal, educated her; she became a poet and wrote in the manner of the heroic couplets of Pope. Her *Imagination* * reads:

> Imagination! Who can sing thy force!
> Or who describe the swiftness of thy course?
> Soaring through air to find the bright abode,
> Th' empyreal palace of the thundering God,
> We on thy pinions can surpass the wind,
> And leave the rolling universe behind:
> From star to star the mental optics rove,
> Measure the skies, and range the realms above;
> There in one view we grasp the mighty whole,
> Or with new world amaze th' unbounded soul.

Whatever its qualities as poetry, the above poem records the feelings of a Negro reacting not as a Negro, but as a human being. Then, in the 1920's, when racial hate was at a hysterical pitch, and after the grinding processes of history had forged iron in the Negro's heart, we hear a new and strange cry from another Negro, Claude McKay. In his sonnet, *If We Must Die,* * he seems to snarl through a sob:

> If we must die—let it not be like hogs
>   Hunted and penned in an inglorious spot,
> While round us bark the mad and hungry dogs,
>   Making their mock at our accursed lot.

* *An Anthology of American Negro Literature,* Modern Library, pages 175 and 203.

> If we must die—oh, let us nobly die,
>   So that our precious blood may not be shed
> In vain; then even the monsters we defy
>   Shall be constrained to honor us though dead!
>
> Oh, kinsmen! We must meet the common foe;
>   Though far outnumbered, let us still be brave,
> And for their thousand blows deal one death-blow!
>   What though before us lies the open grave?
> Like men we'll face the murderous, cowardly pack
> Pressed to the wall, dying, but—fighting back!

What has America done to people who could sing out in limpid verse to make them snarl about being "pressed to the wall" and dealing "one death-blow"? Is this the result of a three-hundred-year policy of "knowing niggers and what's good for 'em"? Is this the salvation which Christian missionaries have brought to the "heathen from Africa"? That there is something wrong here only fools would deny.

White America has reduced Negro life in our great cities to a level of experience of so crude and brutal a quality that one could say of it in the words of Vachel Lindsay's *The Leaden-Eyed* that:

> It is not that they starve, but they starve so dreamlessly,
> It is not that they sow, but that they seldom reap,
> It is not that they serve, but they have no gods to serve,
> It is not that they die, but that they die like sheep.

RICHARD WRIGHT

Ile d'Orléans, Québec. July, 1945

Introduction to the Torchbook Edition

BLACK METROPOLIS IS A DESCRIPTION OF ONE OF THE WORLD'S LARGER NEGRO communities, as it was during and at the end of the great depression of the 1930's. It is a history of the labor force of a great, industrially diverse city, and more especially of Negroes as part of that labor force. It is a great social survey, somewhat in the style of Charles Booth's *Life and Labour of the People of London* (17 Vols., published from 1889 to 1903. London), combining history and social statistics with first-hand observation and systematic interviewing. It is a lively monument to the *élan* which, generated by the New Deal, moved artists and intellectuals of all races and ethnic groups to common expression and action. It is, or was, a portent of the future of Negro Americans, a future in which they, like their countrymen of all varieties, would become overwhelmingly urban and would move and be moved toward a middle-class way of life.

Black Metropolis is certainly other things. Richard Wright has said it is a document of the agony of black men in a white world. It has much poetry in it. The authors, in the Appendix, "Black Metropolis 1961," give it still other dimensions. Let me enlarge on the facets I have already mentioned.

In the 1930's Chicago was already an immense gathering place for American Negroes, second only to New York. There were, and are, differences between these two black metropolises, differences which reflect those between the two cities as wholes. It is in the slaughtering houses, the steel mills and the various industries of Chicago, rather than in the light industries and services of New York, that Negro and other rural Americans and aliens get their foot on the bottom rung of the industrial ladder. Chicago's story, in this regard, may give the better clues to what is happening and will happen in other cities, both northern and southern. Some say Chicago is the most segregated city in the country; it may be so. If so, perhaps it is because Chicago is built of larger territorial blocks than many cities. Its Negro district is immense and unbroken. New York is a mosaic of smaller tiles, where the average person, although he may live in a ghetto, is not so many miles from other breeds as in Chicago. Other cities approach one pattern or the other, or lie between. But more and more of them, no matter what their geographic patterns, and especially those requiring a large industrial labor force, have large populations of newly-arrived rural people, predominantly Negro. Many of the processes, many of the institutions described in *Black Metropolis* will be found, in various stages and forms, in all of them.

Every American city has had its own industrial and labor history. To all of them—and to all industrial cities everywhere—new kinds of people have come from time to time to fill the gaps at the bottom of the occupational hierarchy. The new people are generally both rustic and poor. In some sense, then, the story of the labor force of Chicago and the role of the Negro in it is a version of the story of all industrial cities, and of all poor rustics lured to the city by the hope of prosperity or freedom, or driven to it by underemployment, landlessness or technological change. It is the story of a large part of the human race of times recent and to come. The history of every growing industrial city is one of ethnic if not of racial diversity, and of ethnic succession at the bottom of the industrial hierarchy and in the central tenements or peripheral shacks of the slums. It is not always a history of ethnic and racial discrimination, but it is so often enough for *Black Metropolis* to be more universal than the story of a single harsh new city. The themes, in various keys and combinations, are being played out in the cities of all continents.

In the meantime, the balance among the positions and occupations in industrial economies is changing. Advanced industrial economies show an increase in professional and other white collar positions, with a relative decrease in the dirtier and heavier unskilled jobs, and even in the more skilled manual trades. The slaughtering houses which brought Negroes to Chicago are but the shadow of what they were early in the century. The automated steel mill needs no large roving labor gang. As a result, rural newcomers to the city and to its industries will have to make their adjustments more rapidly than in the past; they may easily become part of the pool of permanently unemployed without ever having been fully employed. In the more recently industrialized or still-to-be-industrialized parts of the world such changes may succeed one another more rapidly and catastrophically than in North America. For North America, with its Chicago, is—

industrially speaking—an old country which had more time for its adjustments than the new ones may have.

Black Metropolis is a great social survey, as that phrase was used before the day of statistical surveys of opinion and consumers' preferences. The social survey was a study, undertaken by men who believed that social facts well presented would point the way to reform of the conditions and ways of living at or below the *poverty line*. *Black Metropolis* was produced by the techniques, and with some of the spirit of a social survey, combined with the methods of social anthropology. The anthropologist more than matches the social surveyor in closeness and intimacy of contact and observation, while achieving a far more systematic analysis of social organization than ever dreamt of by the social surveyor. In this study sociologists of the Robert E. Park tradition joined with anthropologists who had worked with W. Lloyd Warner in his series of American community studies. The result is unique; its like may not be produced again. For one thing, it took a New Deal to mobilize the small army of able young social scientists who did the footwork that made the book possible. For another, bright young Negroes do not have to be sociologists and anthropologists any more. A Cayton or a Drake might today, if he chose, become an engineer, an architect or a scientist. Even as late as the Thirties a young Negro intellectual could hardly hope to get work which did not have to do with other Negroes——as clients or as objects of study. Nowadays the social sciences have to compete with other lines of work for Negro talent. The Negro in the New Frontier is not the Negro of the WPA (although he may have been in his youth). Finally, there has been technological change in social science; we now have the survey of opinion.[1] Observation is reduced to the minimum considered necessary to developing a questionnaire yielding answers which can be "coded" or "programmed" for processing by machines. Fewer skilled observers and more standardized interviewers are used. The change is not unlike that in industry. Other styles of gathering and presenting information about various segments of American life may supplant those used in *Black Metropolis*. In the decades since they did this work, the particular people who did it and the two who wrote the book have been moved on by the times and

[1] A questionnaire survey of new migrants to Chicago is being conducted at the University of Chicago by a team of which Donald Bogue is the leader and of which I am a member. Negroes are the most numerous among the newcomers.

by the logic of their own careers to new kinds of work and study. Messrs. Cayton and Drake have become students of racial matters on the world scene; their reputations are also world-wide. They cannot go back and do the same thing over again. The business of reporting on and analyzing the world of Negro and other newcomers to Chicago and the cities of the world, must pass on to others. It is one of the major tasks and adventures before the young people of our time.

Black Metropolis when published was a portent of the future. Negro Americans were rapidly moving to cities; now they are more urban than ever. Urbanization, which used to mean movement to the North, is now proceeding rapidly in the South. In fact, the South is now at last predominantly urban. One-crop agriculture—"stoop" agriculture—is being mechanized and is declining at the same time. We are told that half the people and half the land now engaged in agriculture could be turned to other uses without reducing our national agriculture product. Rural Southerners, Negro and white alike, rapidly being replaced by machines, are streaming into the cities. In Africa, at the same time, there are mass migrations to the cities. It is possible that people of Negro ancestry may become predominantly urban sooner than the peoples of Asia, the East Indies or Latin America—peoples whose ancestors invented cities.

The forms which urbanization will take may vary; certainly the cultures and economies from which the newcomers to cities stem vary greatly. For some the adjustment to city life and industrial work is greater than for others. But the *terminus ad quem* seems much the same in all cases. There is some evidence that all urban and industrial civilizations approach a common occupational structure, require essentially the same kinds of education and technical training, make somewhat the same demands upon people, and produce men of similar mind.[2] Certainly one of the obligations upon us as social scientists is to deploy forces throughout the world to observe and compare the processes of urbanization and to use the knowledge so gained to make the way less dangerous and less costly in human life and pain.

In North America itself one of the developments described in *Black Metropolis* has proceeded so far as to seem a change in kind. We have, in our economy of abundance, become a nation of consumers.

[2] Inkeles, Alex. "Industrial Man: The Relation of Status to Experience, Perception and Value," *The American Journal of Sociology*. LXVI (July 1960), 1–31.

Negro Americans were once looked upon merely as labor. So it has often been in the early phase of industry or industrial agriculture. The consumers were to be found elsewhere. But just as other American workers eventually came to be consumers of the products they made, so also the Negroes. This is the great turning point in any economy. Negro Americans have become consumers to be reckoned with; they were only beginning to become such in the Thirties. The day of the ancient Packard flamboyantly repainted for the Negro trade has gone. In the supermarket of the Hyde Park Cooperative Society thousands of well-dressed (unless happening to choose blue jeans and windbreaker that day) women gather daily to do the family shopping. Most come alone in the shining family car. Many of them are Negro women. Such a woman is the new Negro: the middle-class consumer. It is the Negro consumer who sits-in demanding the right to be served and to consume the products of American abundance and to use his leisure as other Americans do. And, greatest reversal of all, the middle-class Negro, militantly but without violence demanding his right to be served when he has the price, is violently set upon by whites who, by all counts except the caste-symbol of race, are his inferiors. The Chicago race riots of 1919 pitted lower class against lower class. The lynching mob usually found its victim among the poor and the ignorant. In all cases the nice white people stayed at home. *Black Metropolis* gave us a first look at the tastes of the Negro urban middle class, which was not yet militant about its consumption.

Some years ago I cycled off westward toward State Street, Chicago, on one of the streets in the 70's, south of the old limits of the Black Belt. It was a peaceful middle-class area of one-story brick bungalows and two-flat buildings, probably built for second or third generation Irish, Czechs or Poles. Men were washing their cars, mowing the lawn, or painting the back porch on that Saturday morning. Women were coming and going from the shops, or could be seen dusting in the front room. All at once, I saw that one industrious householder had a dark complexion. Then I saw that all were brown or black. It ran counter to all stereotypes; either their faces should have been white or the district should have had a different aspect. Chicago's Negro slums have grown, but so have her Negro middle classes and the districts where they live. The forces which move people toward the middle class American ethos are tremendous among Negroes of American descent. James Conant, in *Slums and Suburbs: A Com-*

mentary on Schools in Metropolitan Areas,[3] declares that the fate of our country depends upon the speed and thoroughness with which we destroy the slum, and the chronic unemployment and unemployability, the crime, the alienation, the hopelessness, the anger which it breeds and fastens upon our body social. It depends also upon the speed with which we make it possible for all Americans to enjoy to the full the opportunities for work, for consumption of goods and services and for participation in social life in their hours of leisure which our economy of abundance makes available. The great, massive crucial case, both as concerns the slum and as concerns full consumption and participation, is with the Americans called Negro. If we do what is necessary to solve their problems, we will have of necessity done it for the rest of us.

Black Metropolis stands as the classic study of urban Negro life. It is not the last word. No living document is. But he who reads it will be well on his way to becoming an understanding and continuing observer of what is and what is to come in our cities.

EVERETT C. HUGHES

Brandeis University
April, 1962

[3] New York: McGraw-Hill, 1961.

BLACK METROPOLIS

Introduction: Midwest Metropolis

Out of the payday songs of steam shovels,
Out of the wages of structural iron rivets,
The living lighted skyscrapers tell it now as a name,
Tell it across the miles of sea blue water, gray blue land:
I am Chicago, I am a name given out by the breaths of
    working men, laughing men, a child, a belonging.

.   .   .   .

Forgive us if we work so hard
And the muscles bunch clumsy on us
And we never know why we work so hard—
If the big houses with little families
And the little houses with big families
Sneer at each other's bars of misunderstanding;
Pity us when we shackle and kill each other
And believe at first we understand
And later say we wonder why.
        —CARL SANDBURG, *The Windy City* *

AMERICA IS KNOWN BY HER BIG CITIES, THOSE AMAZING CONGERIES OF people and houses, offices and factories, which constitute the nerve centers of our civilization, the ganglia of our collective being. America is dominated by her cities as they draw into them the brawn and brain and wealth of the hinterland and give back not only a constant stream of necessities and gadgets, but also a pattern for living. New York, Chicago, San Francisco, New Orleans, Birmingham . . . the impact of each forces itself upon an ever-widening metropolitan region and filters into a host of tributary small towns and farms by radio and newspaper, book and magazine, and the enthusiastic tales of visitors. Each city, too, has its distinctive reputation in the far corners of the earth, distorted and glamorized, but with a basic element of truth beneath the stereotype.

Put your pencil on the map near the southern tip of Lake Michigan and you touch a metropolis (Figure 1) "Queen of the Lakes," "Capital

* From *Slabs of the Sunburnt West* by Carl Sandburg. Harcourt, Brace, 1922.

3

Figure 1

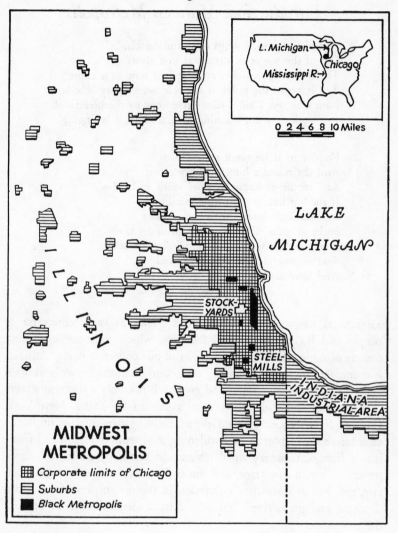

Figure content includes:

Inset map: L. Michigan, Chicago, Mississippi R.→

0 2 4 6 8 10 Miles

LAKE MICHIGAN

ILLINOIS

STOCK-YARDS

STEEL-MILLS

INDIANA INDUSTRIAL AREA

MIDWEST METROPOLIS

Corporate limits of Chicago
Suburbs
Black Metropolis

of the Inland Empire," "Grain Center of the World"—Association of Commerce pamphlets pile encomium upon eulogy, endlessly. And the city is important—CHICAGO, America's second largest in population—MIDWEST METROPOLIS. Approach it by plane and see, sprouting from its center, a spiderweb of railroads swept by a thousand wisps of steam streaking to and fro. Ride into the red glow of steel mills turning out millions of tons of steel a year. Cruise the half-moon border of the lake and you will fly over a multitude of beaches, an impressive skyline, and a beautiful lake front. Ore-boats and cargo vessels creep in and out across the lake, linking the city with five states and Canada.

Swoop low at evening over a forest of water tanks feeding factories set upon the flatness of a prairie, and you will see Chicago's Three Million—her working men and women streaming toward their houses in the inner city, and her white-collar and professional people outward-bound to their homes on the periphery or in the suburbs. The night shift surges through the gates and the city turns into 133 square miles of lighted pin-points clustered about the lake beneath you. This is Carl Sandburg's Chicago:

> Laughing the stormy, husky, brawling laughter of
> Youth, half-naked, sweating, proud to be Hog
> Butcher, Tool Maker, Stacker of Wheat, Player
> with Railroads and Freight Handler to the Nation.*

This is what man has done in a hundred and fifty years, for when New York was over a century old and when Philadelphia numbered 70,000, this spot was still forest and prairie. Less than two hundred years ago, where grain elevators now stand by the lake front and steamers lie against the docks, the canoes of the Pottawattomie and the pirogues of the *coureur de bois* skirted the lake. Midwest Metropolis is a young city.

Chicago's civic boosters have always kept their eyes fixed in friendly rivalry upon New York, the Great Metropolis. Tradition has it that one Mayor, Carter Harrison, on the day of his death by assassination in 1893, "declared that in another half-century London would be trembling lest Chicago should surpass it, and New York would say, 'Let us go to the metropolis of America.'"[1] The fifty years have passed. Present-day local patriots worry little about overtaking the Great Me-

---

* From *Chicago Poems* by Carl Sandburg, Henry Holt, 1916.
[1] Numbers refer to the notes to be found at the end of book.

tropolis in size; rather they claim superiority through uniqueness, be-lieving another declaration made by the same Mayor in a boastful though less prophetic mood: ". . . second city in America in popula-tion and the first city on earth in pluck, energy, and determination."

A thousand American cities and hamlets will immediately rise to dispute this priority in civic virtue, and will substitute a picture of Midwest Metropolis which emphasizes the "pluck" of gangsters, the "energy" of corrupt polticians, and the "determination" of the White Sox and the Cubs to repeat the triumph of nearly forty years ago when each won a pennant in the same season. Despite all that the Chamber of Commerce and local newspapers may do to divert attention to the University of Chicago, Northwestern University, the Field Museum, the Chicago Art Institute, lake-front improvements, and the system of public parks, Midwest Metropolis will no doubt continue to be a symbol, in the popular mind, for none-too-brilliant ball teams, colorful mayors, and gangsters. Hundreds of thousands of Americans will re-member it, also, as the scene of two world's fairs and several disastrous fires, and as the home of Sears, Roebuck and Montgomery Ward, of Al Capone and Samuel Insull. The Second World War tossed it into the news as the fountainhead of Midwestern isolationism; and the antics of a mail-order magnate who defied the War Labor Board, and of two wartime political conventions, drove even the war from the headlines. Chicago has always been good newspaper copy.

Chicago's reputation is primarily the work of newspapermen with an eye for the dramatic. Those indefatigable literary sleuths of a former generation, the "muckrakers," also did their share. Upton Sinclair's *The Jungle,* for instance, not only lent impetus to the passage of a Federal meat-inspection law and resulted in a clean-up of the stock-yards, but also advertised Chicago as Hog Butcher to the World. The complexity and the contradictions, the stark contrasts of Midwest Metropolis, have intrigued many observers as they did Rebecca West who marveled at "an incredible city named Chicago . . . with crime which occasionally takes spectacular and portentous forms, but also an art gallery which alone would make the journey to these parts worth while." And Carl Sandburg, probing it all, passes a defensive appraisal which emphasizes traits other than culture:

> And they tell me you are crooked, and I answer: Yes, it
> is true. . . .

> . . . and I give them back the
> sneer and say to them:
> Come and show me another city with lifted head singing
> so proud to be alive and coarse and strong and cunning.*

Most observers have been impressed by the rapidity of physical growth and the constant change that characterize the city. Lewis and Smith, lively historians of Chicago's "reputation," proclaim that "The city has a daemon—Innovation . . . a passion for tearing up, improving, substituting, enlarging." † A "bareheaded," "shovelling," "wrecking," "planning," "building," "breaking," "rebuilding" city, chants Carl Sandburg as he eulogizes the City of the Big Shoulders. It is perhaps no accident that Chicago's most colorful mayor was known as "Big Bill the Builder" and that the present incumbent stresses a housing program as the keystone of the city's post-war planning.

The collective life of this city by the Lake has been organized and controlled by "The Titans"—the men of the market place, the manipulators of money and people, the fabricators and barterers of things and personalities. Chicago has become a metropolis primarily because men with money to invest discovered early that the site paid dividends. Here money and brains and skill have been conjoined to build a city.

The settling and building of a city requires money and wood and stone and steel; but above all it demands people—by the millions, and in continuous supply, for city births are not numerous enough to keep America's urban population at even a steady level. Midwest Metropolis has drawn upon that general worldwide population movement of the last two centuries which peopled the great American cities. From its birth until the First World War it tapped a seemingly inexhaustible pool of European labor, for Midwest Metropolis has been one of those spots to which people have streamed for more than a century seeking an opportunity to "get ahead," to shake off the past, to "start over." The dynamics of its rapid growth have been the pull of the American Dream and the push of hunger and discontent and restlessness.

* From *Chicago Poems* by Carl Sandburg, Henry Holt, 1916.

† For background material on the history of Chicago, the authors have drawn extensively upon Lloyd Lewis and Henry Justin Smith, *Chicago: The History of Its Reputation,* Harcourt, Brace, 1929, and Centennial Edition, Blue Ribbon Books, 1933. They are also indebted to Bessie Pierce's scholarly and readable *A History of Chicago* (Knopf, 1937). The authors have had access to a mass of primary source data collected as a part of the Cayton-Warner Research, including diaries, life-histories, and newspaper abstracts.

The first great wave of immigration in the Forties brought the Irish, fleeing from a famine brought on by the failure of the potato crop and from the heavy hand of English absentee landlords. Germans, too, in great numbers, found Chicago a welcome haven in the years after the suppression of the democratic revolutions of 1848. By 1850, over half of the inhabitants of Chicago were foreign-born. The Irish ranked first, the Germans second, while the English, Welsh, and Scotch together formed the third largest group.

By 1890, sixty years after its birth, Chicago had become a city of a million persons, and three-quarters of them were either foreign-born or children of the foreign-born. The Germans, the Irish, and the Scandinavians had been arriving by the thousands, encouraged by "runners" in New York, who met the boats and persuaded immigrants to seek their fortunes in Midwest Metropolis. The stream of Northern European immigrants diminished in the Eighties, and Eastern Europeans, particularly Poles and Jews, began to appear in increasing numbers. This "new immigration" reached floodtide between 1900 and 1910, with some 30,000 Italians, 120,000 Russians, 24,000 Hungarians, and 5,000 Greeks pouring into the city during this period.

TABLE 1

POPULATION OF CHICAGO BY ETHNIC GROUP: 1900-1944

Year	Total	Native-white	Foreign-born White and Other Races	Negro
1900	1,698,575	1,081,720	586,705	30,150
1910	2,185,283	1,357,840	783,340	44,103
1920	2,701,705	1,783,687	808,560	109,458
1930	3,376,438	2,275,674	866,861	233,903
1934	3,258,528	2,351,683	670,540	236,305
1940	3,396,808	2,441,859	677,218	277,731
1944	3,600,000	2,642,000	621,000	337,000

The outbreak of the First World War stopped the flow of European immigrants. Simultaneously, war industries in Chicago, as throughout the nation, were expanding. Midwest Metropolis needed manpower, and over 50,000 Negroes poured into the city between 1916 and 1920 from the Deep South. After the war European immigration was resumed, though now it was a mere trickle as compared with its former dimensions. It was composed mostly of small numbers of Italians, Greeks, and Mexicans.

On the eve of the Depression there were still over 800,000 persons of foreign birth in Midwest Metropolis, but the city was in the process of becoming an "American" city, peopled primarily by Negroes and native-whites. (Tables 1 and 2.) The foreign-born whites were dying

TABLE 2

PERCENTAGE OF NATIVE-WHITE, FOREIGN-BORN, NEGRO, AND OTHER RACES, IN
TOTAL POPULATION, CHICAGO: 1890-1944 [2]

Year	Native-white	Foreign-born White	Negro	Other Races	Total
1890	57.8	40.9	1.3	..	100.0
1900	63.7	34.4	1.9	..	100.0
1910	62.2	35.7	2.0	.1	100.0
1920	66.0	29.8	4.1	.1	100.0
1930	67.4	24.9	6.9	.8	100.0
1934	72.1	20.1	7.3	.5	100.0
1940	71.9	19.8	8.2	.1	100.0
1944	73.1	17.1	9.3	.5	100.0

out (and leaving the city) faster than they were being replaced. During the Depression years there was a 20 per cent decrease in the foreign-born population. It was balanced by a 20 per cent increase in the Negro population. The Second World War further depressed foreign immigration, and stepped up Negro migration into the city. Between Pearl Harbor and D-Day some 60,000 more Negroes came to Chicago. As the proportion of foreign-born drops, the proportion of Negroes rises. (Figure 2.) In 1944, there were 337,000 Negroes—almost one person in every ten—living in Midwest Metropolis.

URBAN CHECKERBOARD

The various groups of immigrants who came to Midwest Metropolis tended to congregate in colonies based upon common customs, language, and national origin. Then, as individuals and families learned to speak English, as they acquired an economic stake in the new country and lost their foreign habits and manners, they steadily moved away from these areas of first settlement into more desirable areas of second settlement. Later, they or their children merged with the general population. Today, as one student of the subject has remarked: "By far the largest number of immigrants and their children . . . are no longer distinguishable from the older settlers. The longer they have been here the more widely they are dispersed in the city. Thus, there

Figure 2

PROPORTION OF NEGROES, FOREIGN-BORN AND NATIVE-WHITES IN CHICAGO:1890-1944

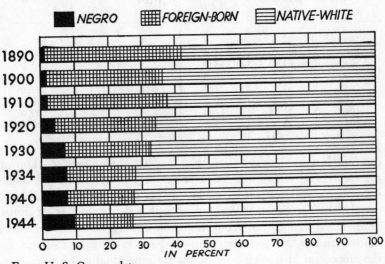

From U. S. Census data.

are practically no English and Scotch-Irish and predominantly German settlements, because these old settlers have amalgamated with the population that was already here and have lost their local and ethnic color."

Only some of the Poles and Italians now live in large, homogeneous communities. The colonies of the other national groups are being rapidly dissolved in the melting pot. (Table 3.) The communities of the foreign-born grow smaller year by year; but, as they shrink and disappear, Negro neighborhoods assume increasing importance in

TABLE 3

FOREIGN-BORN WHITE POPULATION BY COUNTRY OF BIRTH: CHICAGO, 1930 [3]

Country of Birth	Number *	Per Cent of Total Population
Poland...................	149,622	4.4
Germany..................	111,366	3.3
Russia....................	78,462	2.3
Italy.....................	73,960	2.2
Sweden...................	65,735	2.0
Czechoslovakia............	48,814	1.5
Irish Free State............	47,385	1.4
Lithuania.................	31,430	.9
England and Wales.........	27,813	.8
Canada—others............	25,620	.8
Austria...................	24,646	.7
Norway...................	21,740	.6
Yugoslavia................	16,183	.5
Hungary..................	15,337	.5
Greece...................	14,815	.4
Scotland..................	14,264	.4
Denmark.................	12,502	.4
Rumania.................	11,033	.3
Netherlands...............	9,185	.3
Northern Ireland...........	7,404	.2
France...................	4,555	.1
Canada—French...........	4,211	.1
Belgium..................	4,106	.1
Switzerland...............	3,671	.1
Finland..................	2,261	.1
All other nationalities......	15,937	.5
Total—all foreign-born......	842,057	24.9

* Dr. Louis Wirth of the University of Chicago in an address before the Chicago Conference on Home Front Unity in May, 1945, called attention to the changes in foreign-born population that occurred between 1930 and 1940, "The figures showed that somewhat less than 20 per cent of Chicago's population were foreign-born in 1940. The major foreign-born groups in order of their numerical strength were those coming from Poland with 119,000, those from Germany with 83,000, those of Russian origin with 66,000, those from Italy with 66,000, of Swedish origin with 46,000 . . . and so on down the list." A comparison of these figures with those in the table reveals the gradual decline in the number of the foreign-born.

terms of size and influence. Black Metropolis emerges as a significant factor in the life of Midwest Metropolis.

BLACK METROPOLIS

Black Metropolis is the second largest Negro city in the world, only New York's Harlem exceeding it in size. It is a city within a city—a narrow tongue of land, seven miles in length and one and one-half miles in width, where more than 300,000 Negroes are packed solidly— in the heart of Midwest Metropolis. (Figure 1.) Peripheral to this Black Belt are five smaller Negro concentrations which are, in a fundamental sense, parts of Black Metropolis. Of Chicago's 337,000 Negroes a bare 10 per cent are scattered among the white population.

Walk the streets of the Black Belt and you will find no difference in language to mark its people off from others in the city. Only the black and brown and olive and tan faces of Negro Americans seem to distinguish it from any other section of Midwest Metropolis. But beneath the surface are patterns of life and thought, attitudes and customs, which make Black Metropolis a unique and distinctive city within a city. Understand Chicago's Black Belt and you will understand the Black Belts of a dozen large American cities.

Black Metropolis has appeared upon the urban checkerboard during a hundred and fifty years of city growth. The expansion of the Black Belt has been sometimes slow and sometimes rapid; today the Belt has virtually ceased to grow in area, although its population is still increasing. Until the heavy migration between 1915 and 1920, only about one-half of the Negro population in Midwest Metropolis lived in the Black Belt. Today, over 90 per cent of the city's colored population resides there, and this concentration has been taking place while foreign-born communities were disintegrating.

Midwest Metropolis seems uneasy about this Negro city growing up in its midst. In 1919, the Black Belt was the scene of a race riot, and in 1943, when race riots occurred in Detroit and New York, there were fears that a similar calamity might again befall Midwest Metropolis. The anticipated trouble did not materialize, but the fear remains. The basis for this apprehension will be revealed in these pages. Black Metropolis—how it came to be; why it persists; how its people live; what Midwest Metropolis thinks of it; what its people think of themselves and of Midwest Metropolis; whether it, too, will eventually disappear—these constitute the theme of this book.

To understand Black Metropolis, its origin, genesis, and probable destiny, it is necessary first to understand the manner in which Chicago has developed from a small prairie village into Midwest Metropolis.

THE PATTERN OF CITY GROWTH

The National Resources Committee, describing "Our Cities," has observed that "The American city is a motley of peoples and cultures forming a mosaic of little worlds which in part blend with one another but, in part, and for a time, remain segregated or come into conflict with one another."

The two basic facts about the spatial growth of Midwest Metropolis (and of most American cities) are, first, the tendency for people to move steadily outward from the center of the city as they grow more prosperous, leaving the center to business and industry, to the poor and the vicious; and second, the tendency of the foreign-born to settle originally in colonies near the center of the city, with individual families joining the outward stream as soon as they become Americanized in thought and relatively well-to-do. The competition for space among these various economic, social, and ethnic groups, and business and industry, results in strains and stresses. Group attitudes and prejudices are reflected in the rise and fall of land values in various parts of the city and in the economic and social status of neighborhoods. The extent to which these processes have gone on in Midwest Metropolis is plain if one examines a map showing the differences in the proportion of people who found it necessary to go on relief in various sections of the city during the Depression (Figure 3); poverty clusters near the center of the city. It is demonstrated also by the distribution of the foreign-born. (Figure 4.) This sifting and sorting of people through the years on the basis of affluence and social status has resulted in definite "zones of city growth." (Figure 5.) The pattern of concentric city growth is not a perfect one. It is broken by jumps and skips as new businesses or communities based on nationality or class spring up in outlying areas or along arteries of transportation, to be overtaken later by the expanding city.

Chicago began as a collection of settlements upon a prairie with a

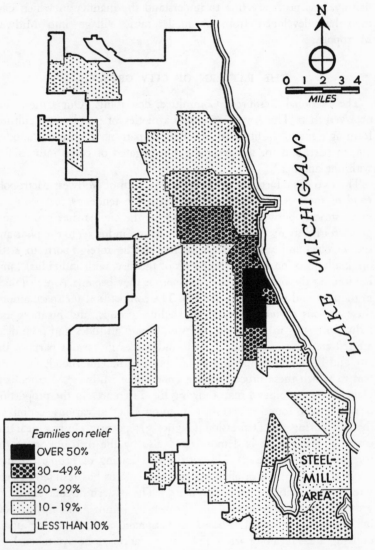

Figure 3
THE DISTRIBUTION OF POVERTY IN MIDWEST METROPOLIS

N

0 1 2 3 4
MILES

LAKE MICHIGAN

Families on relief
OVER 50%
30 – 49%
20 – 29%
10 – 19%·
LESS THAN 10%

STEEL-MILL AREA

Prepared from data given in Louis Wirth and Margaret Furez (eds.), *Local Community Fact Book,* Chicago Recreation Commission, 1938. Data for 1934.

Figure 4

THE DISTRIBUTION OF THE FOREIGN-BORN

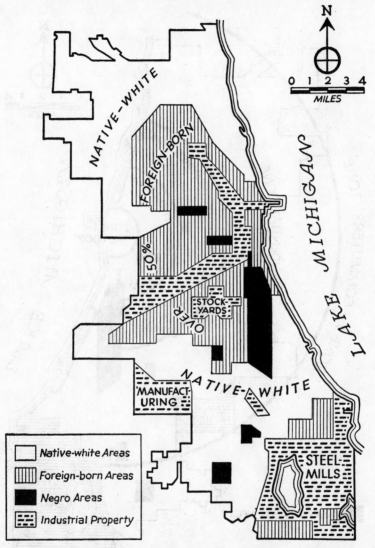

Adapted from map in Robert E. L. Faris and H. Warren Dunham, *Mental Disorders in Urban Areas,* University of Chicago Press, 1939.

Figure 5
ZONES OF CITY GROWTH

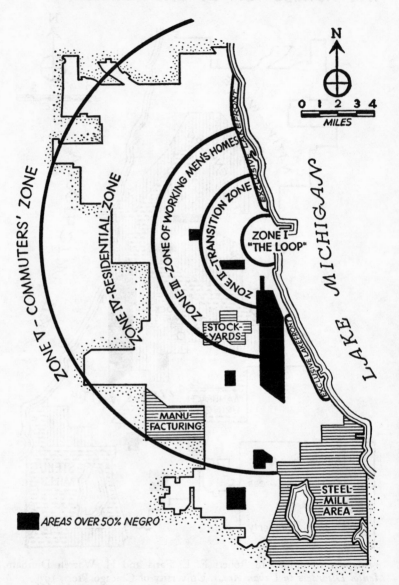

Adapted from map in R. E. Park and E. W. Burgess, *The City*, University of Chicago Press, 1921, and Cayton-Warner Research maps.

lot of room between most of them. In the Forties and Fifties these tended to be ethnic settlements—an Irish community or a German area here, a Scandinavian neighborhood or a Negro settlement there. As these expanded to touch one another they became the first clear divisions of the urban checkerboard, little groups of people each with a common language and customs. As the form of the city became set, new increments of the foreign-born tended to move into the old-established colonies until they got their bearings. Meanwhile, Americanized immigrants or their children filtered out into native-American communities, as individuals or families, and were thus dispersed through the city.

Since the Eighties the areas of first settlement for the foreign-born have been, on the whole, in or close to the so-called slums (Zones I and II of Figure 5), since rents were lowest there and the social pressure against them least. The areas of foreign second settlement were often found in the zone of workingmen's homes, where slightly more prosperous immigrants had moved.

The settlements of the Negroes have followed this pattern with one important difference: Negroes are not finally absorbed in the general population. Black Metropolis remains athwart the least desirable residential zones. Its population grows larger and larger, unable either to expand freely or to scatter. It becomes a persisting city within a city, reflecting in itself the cross-currents of life in Midwest Metropolis, but isolated from the main stream. Black Metropolis as a community is the end result of one hundred and fifty years of intense competition among native-whites, Negroes, and foreign-born for living space, economic goods, and prestige.

The entire history of Chicago from its birth to the First World War was characterized by the struggle, sometimes violent, of the first-comers and native-whites against the later immigrants—the "foreigners." In the Sixties it was everybody against the Irish and the Irish against a handful of Negroes and Hungarians; in the Seventies it was the Know-Nothing native-Americans against the Germans, Irish, Scandinavians, Bohemians, Slavs, and Frenchmen; in the Nineties, the northern Europeans and native-whites against the southern and eastern Europeans, the so-called "new immigration."

However much the native-born and older immigrant groups might dislike the "new immigration," they needed these people in order to maintain their own social and economic hegemony. In the steel mills and packing-houses, in the farm-implement factories and the railroad shops, the foreigners have done that laborious and unpleasant work which permitted the rise of an extensive native-born white-collar middle class and a small leisure class. As the immigrants arrived, the native-born were able to move up in status. By 1910 only one out of every ten native whites was engaged in unskilled labor, while three out of every ten foreigners were so employed. Only eight out of every hundred foreign-born workers did clerical work, whereas thirty out of every hundred native-born workers were doing that. Only a third of the native-born were engaged in industrial production; two-thirds of the foreign-born were so employed. In the railroad shops and on the section gangs, around the blast furnaces and rolling mills, the slaughter-and-packing-houses, the tanneries and lumber yards, wielding picks and mauls and shovels—wherever hot, heavy, or dirty work was to be done—here were the latest batches of immigrants, starting in at the bottom, but planning to get ahead themselves, or to push their children ahead. The children, once they had gone through the public schools, might be expected to move out of the slums, get better jobs, and lose themselves among the older American groups.

Since the First World War, Negroes have replaced immigrants as the primary source of unskilled and menial labor. In the mass, they rest at the bottom of the social and economic pyramid and have inherited the slums. Attracted by the American Dream the Negro residents, in numbers, have entered the city's life at a point almost a hundred years beyond its origin. They have had to compete for a place in a complex pattern already laid down, in a community where the main outlines of activity and tradition had long been set.

THE CHICAGO TRADITION

In the words of Lloyd Lewis and Henry Justin Smith, Chicago is essentially ". . . a hundred years and more of settling arguments on top of the effort to create, on a forbidding shore, a home fit to occupy." The history of the city may be viewed in terms of the continuous conflict between various economic, nationality, and racial groups. The forbidding shore was the marshy rim of Lake Michigan, its air so befouled by the stench of wild garlic that the Indians called it *Chickagou* (garlic) or *Shegagh* (skunk). The first great argument was a thirty-five-year contest to decide whether the Indians or the white men would control the spot—an argument settled by massacre, reprisal, and a shrewd, one-sided bargain just a quarter of a century before the Civil War.

"Why," we might ask, "were either the white men or the Indians interested in 'the place of the evil smell'?" A mistake made by Nature is the answer. Eight miles from Chickagou was a river down which one could sail to the Mississippi and thence to the Gulf. (Figure 1.) Had Nature let her Ice Age glacier-trowel scoop a little more, there would have been a continuous waterway from the Great Lakes to the Gulf; instead, she left a neck of land. The Indians accepted fate, lifted their canoes to their shoulders, and walked from lake to river. For them Chickagou was a convenient portage. But every white man who came there, from the time of Father Marquette and Louis Joliet, dreamed of a canal that would link the Five Lakes with the Father of Waters.

By 1830, a few pioneers had settled on the portage to trade with the Indians and those white men who were seeking farms in the West. A visiting Englishman didn't think much of the human material at the time, and described the settlement as being full of "rogues of every description, white, black, brown, and red . . . half-breeds, quarter-breeds and men of no breed at all. . . ." There was talk of a canal in the air, and a land boom was on throughout the West. In 1833, the town was incorporated—with 200 souls and 243 buildings. Wheat and corn farmers were looking for an outlet to the East, and people with an eye for business gathered in the town by the Lake. A few slaughter-houses and small farm-implement factories appeared. "Chicago was a frontier city in most respects," writes one historian. "The timid feared it; the pious prayed for it; the robust, vigorous, loud, coarse, and irreverent enjoyed it. . . . It is incontestable that a majority of the voters preferred a wide-open town." [4] Chicago had begun to develop a reputation.

During the twenty years between its incorporation and the outbreak of the Civil War, Chicago became a center of speculation in farm lands, canal rights-of-way, railroads, and farm machinery. Nature's mistake was finally rectified when in 1848 the Illinois-Michigan Canal linked the Lake with the Mississippi. Capital from eastern banks, and savings from migrants' pockets and western farmers' socks, poured into the city to finance first "plank roads" and then railroads, McCormick's reaper and George Pullman's machine shop. The town began to fill up with eastern capitalists, Irish laborers, Bohemian, Scandinavian, and German artisans, and a motley crew of sharpers and harpies, their rapid passage to the West aided by the Erie Canal. The countryside was flooded with Chicago "drummers."

In this pre-Civil War period Chicago acquired the reputation of being a "tough" town, and differences of opinion were often settled with vigorous and brutal directness. In the Fifties many of the Protestant, native-born Easterners reacted violently against the customs of their Irish Catholic and German neighbors, particularly Sunday beer-drinking. The city officials, influenced by the semi-secret anti-foreign Know-Nothing Party, eventually succeeded in placing heavy license fees upon saloons and beer gardens and in passing Sunday Blue Laws. The foreign-born responded with a full-scale riot which required a show of artillery to crush it.

This penchant for direct action was carried over into the anti-slavery struggles. Here, however, the lines were drawn in different fashion, with Easterners, Germans, and Scandinavians uniting against the Catholic, proslavery Irish. Again, amid the irritations of the Panic of 1857, the Puritan forces proceeded to clean up "the Sands"—a collection of dives—by purchasing the property and pulling down the houses of the gamblers and prostitutes upon their heads. Pre-Civil War Chicago was a gaudy, dirty, exciting small town, described by a London *Times* correspondent as ". . . an extraordinary mélange of the Broadway of New York and little shanties, of Parisian buildings mixed some way with backwoods life."

The Civil War brought a boom. Then, the war over, Chicago settled down to packing meat, shipping wheat, and making a fortune for Armour, Swift, Pullman, McCormick, Ogden, and Marshall Field. The stench of the stockyards had long since replaced the odor of garlic. "Chickagou" had become Chicago, and its fame spread so wide that Bismarck stated in 1870, "I wish I could go to America if only to see that Chicago." The next year the famous Chicago Fire burned almost the entire town to the level of the prairie.

The city was rebuilt quickly, however, and from the Fire to the turn of the century Chicago-town was busy becoming Midwest Metropolis. By 1890 it had passed the million mark in population, and the scattered collection of settlements and villages had coalesced into a city. It had acquired a national reputation for three things: rapid growth, colorful "wickedness," and frequent labor violence. The World's Fair of 1893 confirmed and advertised this appraisal. Throughout the Eighties and Nineties a few people made money and enjoyed luxuries and leisure. Others had modest security. But the vast masses of laborers were struggling for a living wage and an eight-hour day. Repeated panics periodically drew these economic class contradictions to a head, and the vigor with which labor fought gave the city an international reputation as a center of radicalism.

In the Railroad Riots of 1877, which began in the East and spread to Chicago, pitched battles were fought in the streets and wealthy families fled the city in panic. Nine years later the Haymarket Riot—dynamite, shots, at least seven dead, scores wounded, seven anarchists executed—became America's first left-wing *cause célèbre*. Even mild unionists were entranced by the words of the defiant August Spies: "If you think that by hanging us you can stamp out the labor movement, then call your hangmen. But you will tread upon the sparks. Here and there, behind you, in front of you, and everywhere, flames will spring up!" Artisans who by no means sanctioned the use of dynamite approved when Parsons, the printer, shouted through his gallows hood, "Let the voice of the People be heard!" And Samuel Fielden's words were stirring even if they came from the lips of an anarchist: "I have hated trickery, dishonesty, and injustice. . . . I trust the time will come when there will be better understanding, more intelligence; and above the mountains of iniquity, wrong, and corruption, I hope the sun of righteousness and truth and justice will come to bathe in its balmy light the emancipated world."

Much of the antagonism between capital and labor in the Eighties and Nineties was due to the fact that while the predominantly foreign-born working class fought for immediate labor legislation and talked of Socialism, the Protestant church people and the city's wealthy leaders were interested primarily in moral reform. (The politicians, meanwhile, worked both sides of the street.) The working classes consistently viewed emphasis upon reform and good government as an expression of upper-class and middle-class prejudice, a cover for sophisticated delinquencies, an attempt to beg the more urgent questions of bread and butter. Yet, in the years between the first World's Fair and the First World War, the reform forces burgeoned.

Amid the enthusiasm of the first World's Fair—the Columbian Exposition of 1893—a visiting English journalist, the eminent William T. Stead, uttered a sweeping condemnation of Chicago's municipal life at a public meeting: "You are gigantic in your virtues and gigantic in your vices. I don't know in which you glory the most. . . ." He implemented his criticism with a sensational, red-bound 450-page book, *If Christ Came to Chicago,* giving names and addresses of spots where prostitution prevailed, pilloried the sometimes wealthy owners, exposed the tie-up between police and vice and between the city government and powerful traction interests, and concluded with the observation that the city needed "the application of every known device of sociology or religion to save it." He dressed up his indictment with colorful chapter headings such as "The Boodlers and the Boodled," "The Scarlet Woman," "Casting Out Devils," "Maggie Darling," and "The Conscience of Chicago." On the cover was a sketch of Christ driving the money-changers from the temple, and his last chapter painted a Utopian picture of the future Chicago as "the ideal city of the world." He called for united action, citing Britain as an example: "If these things can be done in London, why cannot they be done in Chicago by the labor unions acting together with the other moral and religious forces of the town?" The book created a sensation.

But labor was in no mood for moral preachments. The panic of 1893 had the city in its grip. Thousands of homeless and hungry transients who had come to the Fair were sleeping in flop-houses and saloons. Wage slashes and unemployment were swelling their ranks. Trouble was in the air. It broke when the workers in the Pullman sleeping-car plant downed their tools. Eugene V. Debs's American Railway Union interceded unsuccessfully for an arbitrament and then ordered railway men not to handle any trains with Pullman cars attached. A paralyzing strike spread rapidly. Violence was rife. For the first time in American history Federal troops were used to crush a strike—on the grounds that the mail must go through. It took artillery to disperse the angry railroad men and the unemployed mobs who fought with bricks and rifles and even turned over a locomotive in their wrath. Eugene Debs went to jail for six months, despite Clarence Darrow's classic defense, and came out America's first prominent native-born Socialist.

Meanwhile a group of one hundred prominent citizens took up Stead's challenge, organized a Civic Federation, and began a clean-up campaign. They put through a civil service law, fought grafting garbage-collectors, broke up a few downtown gambling places, and organized a municipal voters' league. This organization—a coalition of the wealthy-with-a-conscience and the civic-minded of all strata—began a no-quarter fight against crooked politics. Within ten years they had placed ten of their men in City Hall. They trained their big guns upon vice and started a campaign (which lasted eighteen years) to abolish the Red-light District. When in the early 1900's Lincoln Steffens started out to do a "muckraking" job on the city, he was convinced that he would find a "sensationally wicked story" and planned to expose the "rough anarchistic criminality of a wild young western city." He reports that he found "evil . . . obvious, general, bold." But what he considered more significant was a group of cagy, hard-boiled reformers who through the Municipal Voters' League were able to crack the whip over ward politicians.

Another group, including some of the wealthy but spearheaded by the settlement-house workers, the "muckrakers," and the radicals, stressed the need for "trust-busting," increasing wages, shortening hours, abolishing child labor, curbing LaSalle Street and Wall Street, and fighting the traction interests. The people in this group were a part of that general midwestern movement which culminated in Theodore Roosevelt's nomination at Chicago on the Progressive ticket in 1912, with the Square Dealer shouting, "We stand at Armageddon doing battle for the Lord!"—while Jane Addams led the convention in singing *Onward, Christian Soldiers.*

The thousands of laborers in the stockyards and mechanical industries were largely unorganized, and the skilled artisans in the building trades were playing it another way. "Skinny" Madden (father of "business unionism") and his "wreckers," with bare fists, knuckles, and an occasional bullet, were "organizing" the contractors and getting slight wage increases for the workers, a neat pile for themselves, and a "cut" for the politicians. The Socialists were trying to vote in a new society and the IWW was calling for one big union to make all things new. The ward politicians, wise in their worldly wisdom, sat tight and let the winds of reform blow themselves out.

Lincoln Steffens, years later, wrote the epitaph of Chicago's early reformers. They became too interested in "representative government." Powerful interests could tolerate a "good government" movement but not a drive for "representative government." According to him, "They killed it as literally as the gunmen of Chicago now kill one another and as safely."

There have always been two reform traditions in Chicago: one concerned with stopping "vice" and petty political graft; the other with controlling "predatory big business." Sometimes these causes and their spokesmen fuse in a single campaign; sometimes they move along simultaneously; often they clash. And the "gray wolves" of City Hall have been the traditional whipping-boys of both the "good government" and the "representative government" forces.

Throughout the Nineties and early 1900's the church people, the wealthy, and the rising middle class were determined to reclaim the city's reputation and make it "clean"—on the surface, at least. On the eve of the First World War, prostitution had been scattered if not conquered—every old exclusive "resort" and historic bawdy house had been closed. The anti-vice crusaders were still hammering away fruitlessly at the saloon with Frances E. Willard leading her praying WCTU women from grogshop to grogshop.

In 1914, another depression arrived. Chicago was weary of vice crusades and disillusioned by the débâcle of the Progressive movement. War had broken out in Europe. The city turned to an exhibitionist for its mayor, the fantastic Republican playboy, "Big Bill" Thompson with his ten-gallon hat, who proclaimed that he wore no man's halter and promised to make Chicago the biggest city in the world. For the next eight years he ran the city.

The First World War altered the composition of Chicago's population. When it began, the city was two-thirds native-white and one-third foreign-born. When it ended, the proportion of foreign-born had been reduced by six per cent and over 50,000 Negroes had migrated from the South to meet the demands of an expanded industry. This sudden shift in the city's national and racial complexion was accompanied by a devastating race riot in 1919.

A series of labor disturbances occurred during the three years after the war. Neither steel nor packing was effectively organized, despite the bloody strikes of 1919 and 1921 in which Negro strike-breakers played some part. Chicago's attention was now focused on a different field. Before the war, the reformers and the civic-minded had seen their problems as VICE, IMMIGRANTS, and LABOR. Now they turned their attention to GANGSTERS, NEGROES, and LABOR. White labor, particularly, began to visualize Negro workers as a potential threat.

During the lush years between 1922 and 1929 the general population developed two consuming interests: how to share in the wave of prosperity and how to get a drink. The anti-liquor forces had won a Pyrrhic victory during the First World War like that of the vice crusaders who preceded them. They drove evil out of sight and underground, and they got the "alky mob" * as a result. The politicians waxed fat.

Perhaps the most profound change that took place in Midwest Metropolis between the First World War and the Great Depression was a gradual shift in the content of the American Dream as presented by the men of power. During the great agitation for the eight-hour day in the Eighties, the Chicago *Inter-Ocean*, financed by a wealthy restaurateur, had said of the laborers:

The one thing that will confer upon each of them individually the greatest prosperity is to look upon the wages condition not as a necessity for life, but as a temporary stage only in life, from which the wage worker is to emerge into a worker for profits.[5]

Civic leaders emphasized thrift, the establishment of small business, and investment in large ones. But it is doubtful whether this ever represented the American Dream of the average worker. He knew that Midwest Metropolis could not become a city composed entirely of capitalists and small businessmen. To him the American Dream meant something else: a steady job at high wages, and leisure to spend with his family and cronies and in enjoying the diversified entertainment which the city offered. For many, too, it implied the ownership of a home and conveniences. (For most of the foreign-born it also meant the ability to raise a family without the need for their wives to work.) It included savings for old age and for the education of children. With the advent of mass production, automobiles, telephones, radios, plumbing, etc., it grew to include a full and ever-increasing supply of these gadgets. Businessmen of the Twenties, unlike their predecessors, began to encourage the masses to spend rather than to save.

The attitude of a large segment of Chicago's working people throughout the stormy Eighties and Nineties and into the twentieth century seems to have been: "Attain the American Dream under capitalism if we can, and by Socialism if we must." As late as 1920, Eugene Debs drew over 50,000 Socialist votes from Midwest Metropolis, and in 1919 the Chicago City Federation of Labor took the initiative in organizing a statewide labor party, one of whose "Fourteen Points" demanded "public ownership and operation of all public utilities, in-

---

* "Alky mob"—colloquial name for the gangsters who controlled the bootleg liquor business during the Prohibition Era.

cluding grain elevators, warehouses, stockyards, abattoirs, insurance, and banks." The period between the First World War and the collapse of 1929 was, however, one that made the American Dream seem attainable without drastic social change. As increasing numbers of people saw such possibilities, as an older generation of Socialists died off, Socialist tendencies withered and died, and the labor unions concentrated upon immediate demands and upon smart deals with politicians and employers.

Another trend, too, suddenly achieved visible proportions in the Twenties. As industry expanded, the tremendous increase in "paper work" opened up great perspectives that neither radicals nor capitalists of a previous epoch had visualized—a large white-collar middle class. The proportion of capitalists, large or small, had remained relatively constant throughout Chicago's period of rapid industrialization, but the proportion of people doing "clean work" steadily expanded. By 1930 only 60 per cent of the men and 40 per cent of the women in the city were engaged in manual labor or servant work. Almost half the men and over half the women were occupied in some sort of clerical work, and almost half the working population was engaged in either managerial, professional, or clerical work. The vast amount of office work in Midwest Metropolis made it possible for a young woman to work until she made a match, when she could move out and let her younger sister take her place. The native-born, the "successful" foreign-born, and the children of the immigrants left the city's heavy work and dirty work to the rapidly dwindling "new" foreign-born population and to the constantly growing Negro population.

The new middle class of the Twenties was equally unconcerned with vice reform or business reform *per se*. The system was paying off. Chicago was a big city. It had room enough for all kinds of people, and when you had accumulated enough or, if a woman, had married the right kind of man you could clear out of the crowded inner city and get a home in the residential suburbs. The members of the new middle class tried to keep their neighborhoods peopled with persons like themselves, groused about taxes, and tended to enjoy the spectacle of letting the rest of Chicago do as it damned please.

Manual workers saw hope for their children if not for themselves, and those who were organized used their unions to extract what they could without killing the goose that laid the golden egg.

Even the Negroes, last to "muscle in on the racket," weren't faring too badly.

When the crash of 1929 came the city was bewildered but considered the catastrophe just a temporary upset. Chicago's Century of Progress Exposition in 1933 was a sort of defiant gesture in the teeth of economic disaster, and people half believed that enticing enough visitors would restore prosperity. As the city woke up amidst a deepening depression it did so in a typical Chicago fashion. The unemployed took to the streets. Teachers demonstrated for their back pay. Tenants fought bailiffs to keep from being evicted. Midwest Metropolis became a New Deal town, and for the first time achieved something approaching "representative government." A tremendous upsurge of industrial unionism swept the city, with Communists playing an important part. Segments of the new white-collar middle class were drawn into the movement. The CIO organized the harvester plants, and the aged wife of a Haymarket rioter was present at the victory rally as a touch of poetic justice. The steel magnates resisted savagely. The industrialists professed fear of revolution, but the Socialist tradition had been buried with Debs and the Communists were unable to revive it. The politicians swayed this way and that, shooting down the workers in the "Memorial Day Massacre," and then running as "labor candidates" when they saw which way the wind was blowing. The Kelly-Nash machine clutched frantically at the New Deal's coattails and held on for dear life. WPA blossomed. The city limped through the last years of the Depression, a patient of "Dr. New Deal" until "Dr. Win the War" gave it a rejuvenating transfusion.

The Second World War brought new industries and new people— more than 100,000 of them; and over 60,000 of these were Negroes. Tanks, electrical equipment, airplane engines, meat, wheat, began to pour out of Midwest Metropolis in a steady stream. The labor front became quiet, but memories of the past and fears for the future stirred uneasily in the city's subconscious.

"WIDE-OPEN" TOWN

Chicago, as we have noted, has always had the reputation of being a "wide-open" town, whose citizens were never overdisturbed by graft in city government, or by alliances between politicians, the underworld, and/or big-business interests. The vast masses of the factory workers have taken corrupt government as a matter of course, the craft unions have had their own arrangements with City Hall, and the new middle classes, even when temporarily aroused, have never been able to control elections. A scandal breaks now and then, followed by a reform wave—"the heat is turned on." And then things are allowed to settle down to the old routine. The "good government forces" have never had any real strength in Midwest Metropolis. A liberal-labor coalition began to emerge during the Depression but it was closely allied with the Kelly-Nash political machine.

Numerous observers have been impressed, too, with what they call a "sporting tradition" in Chicago life. Lincoln Steffens expressed this most explicitly when he wrote in 1931: "Chicago likes audacity and is always willing to have anybody try anything once; no matter who you are, where you come from, or what you set out to do, Chicago will give you a chance. The sporting spirit is the spirit of Chicago."

A rapidly changing city, wide open, and with a sporting tradition, provides many short cuts to wealth and prestige, politics and "rackets" being the most popular. Young and old know that if you "make a pile" you can become a "big shot"—and that, conversely, if you are a "big shot" you can be expected to "cash in" on it. Sophisticated urbanites develop a cynical approach to every enterprise. "What's his racket?" is a universal Chicago query applied alike to the respectable and to the shady prosperous.

The exigencies of life in Midwest Metropolis, as in almost any rapidly changing community, put a great deal of emphasis upon "luck." Experience teaches that only a few people can get the choicest plums by hard work and frugality, so people tend to set their sights upon a goal of middle-class comfort and to admire from a distance the people who "get the breaks," who "hit the jackpot," and to become sentimental about the casualties who took a chance and lost. Even the people who play the game safe often have a sneaking admiration for the "tough guys," the "smart boys," the "smooth fellows." The tendency to view success in terms of luck is a stabilizing influence amid rapid change and frustrated ambitions; it provides a ready rationalization for those left behind.

This free and easy approach to living, this philosophy of live and let live, the "sporting spirit," is continually being checked and limited, however, by the conflicting drives toward economic security and prestige. Those who have made their pile, those who have attained a modicum of security—the new middle class and the well-organized craft workers—all represent forces of stability in Midwest Metropolis. Their own lives become ordered. Excitement becomes occasional, vicarious, and formalized—the ball game, the races, a convention, a prize fight, or reading about their "wicked city." The philosophy of such people tends to be: "Anything goes so long as it doesn't affect me directly." Let a man feel, however, that his economic security, his prestige in the eyes of his fellows, or his inner core of beliefs is being compromised and he will lash out in defense.

A more fruitful approach to Midwest Metropolis than generalizing about the "spirit of Chicago" in the abstract is to view the city as split into competing economic groups, social classes, ethnic groups, and religious and secular associations, each with its own set of traditions. The violent shifts in public sentiment and action which characterize Chicago history reflect the combination and recombination of these groups when they feel that their interests are menaced. Out of this welter of fears and loyalties and interests have exploded some of America's most bizarre and dramatic incidents—riots, strikes, colorful elections, reform movements, and reactions against reform.

As Midwest Metropolis grows up, its economic and political conflicts become somewhat more simplified in form and more disciplined in expression. There are no longer large blocs of the foreign-born to be organized by enterprising politicians and industrialists. The city gets split into three large economic groups, predominantly white American: the wealthy few, a growing new middle class, and the poorer wage-earners. Among the wage-earners are more than a third of a million Negroes, and predominantly they are the poorer wage-earners—kept apart socially, but sought as economic or political allies at one time or another by competing segments of the white society. It is these Negroes who make up Black Metropolis and who hold a pivotal position in the equilibrium of political and economic power of Midwest Metropolis. Black Metropolis did not emerge until the Twenties, but Negroes were a part of Chicago from the beginning.

PART I

CHAPTER I

Flight to Freedom

THE POTTAWATTOMIE INDIANS WHO RELINQUISHED THE CHICAGO PORTAGE to the white man in 1835 had a saying: "The first white man to settle at Chickagou was a Negro." Frenchmen—trappers, priests, and explorers—had touched this portage from time to time during the seventeenth century; and Louis Joliet and Father Marquette crossed it in 1673. But it was a French-speaking Negro, Jean Baptiste Point de Saible, described by a contemporary British army officer as "a handsome Negro well educated and settled at Eschikagou," [1] who made the first permanent settlement, some time around 1790. At "the place of the evil smell," Point de Saible erected a frontier establishment consisting of a large wooden homestead, bakehouse, smokehouse, poultry house, and dairy; a workshop and a horse mill; a barn and two stables. Here the Pottawattomie came to trade; and the English and French, exploring and fighting for dominance in the back-country, stopped to rest and replenish their stores. Reclaimed from the prairie and wrested from the wilderness, this solitary frontier settlement became the seed-bed of skyscrapers and factories. Its trading post was the progenitor of the wheat-pit and its workshop the prototype of factories and mills. The canoes and pirogues that stopped here foreshadowed the commerce of after-years.

Where he came from originally—this Father of Midwest Metropolis—we do not know. According to one tradition he was from Santo Domingo, and planned to establish a colony of free Negroes near the shores of Lake Michigan. Another story would have him the descendant of a Negro slave and a French fur-trader in the Northwest Territory. We know with certainty only that for sixteen years he and his Pottawattomie wife Catherine, his daughter Cézanne, and Jean Baptiste *fils,* lived at the present site of Chicago. In 1796, for reasons unknown he sold his establishment to one LeMai, who in turn sold it to an Englishman, John Kinzie. Point de Saible then moved to Peoria, where he spent most of the remainder of his life, dying in St. Charles, Missouri. Within the house he had built, so tradition says, Chicago's first marriage was solemnized, the first election held, and the first white child born.

Of Point de Saible one student of early Chicago, Milo Quaife, has written: "He was a true pioneer of civilization, leader of the unending procession of Chicago's swarming millions. Even in his mixed blood he truly represented the future city, for where else is a greater conglomeration of races and breeds assembled together?" [2]

With his departure, only an occasional Negro filtered into the city until the late Forties, when a steady, though small, stream began to arrive.

CHICAGO—CITY OF REFUGE

The earliest Negro migrants to Chicago, like those of later years, were refugees from the bondage of America's cotton kingdom in the South. They poured into the city by the hundreds between 1840 and 1850, fleeing slavery. Some remained; others passed through to Canada and points east.

Chicago gradually became an important terminal on that amazingly ingenious combination of secret trails, mysterious hay wagons, hideouts, and zealous people that was known as the Underground Railroad.[3] Up the Mississippi, across the Ohio River, through the Allegheny gaps, over the western prairie, nearly a hundred thousand slaves were passed from farm to farm and town to town during the seventy years' operation of "freedom's railroad." Secrecy was necessary, even in Chicago, for the Illinois Black Code required every Negro who remained in the state to post a thousand-dollar bond and to carry a certificate of freedom. The federal Fugitive Slave Law of 1793 made it a criminal offense, punishable by a $500 fine, to harbor a fugitive or to prevent his arrest. Yet throughout the Forties and Fifties a few churches and homes in Chicago served as "stations" on the Underground Railroad. The "conductors"—usually church people or political radicals—were recruited mainly from the ranks of white artisans, business people, and Negroes holding free papers. The *Western Citizen,* abolitionist journal, boasted during the Fifties: "We can run a load of slaves through from almost any part of the border states into Canada within forty-eight hours and we defy the slaveholders to beat that if they can." [4]

Furious and frustrated planters in the lower Mississippi Valley fulminated at this lawless traffic in stolen property. They derisively and indignantly dubbed Chicago a "nigger-loving town." One editor in southern Illinois, a proslavery stronghold, contemptuously dismissed Chicago as a "sink hole of abolition." [5] To the slaves, however, it was a city of refuge, and once within its boundaries they jealously guarded their own illegal freedom while helping their fellows to escape.

Chicago's small group of Underground "officials" received its first open support from a wider public when the murder of the famous abolitionist, Elijah Lovejoy, by a southern Illinois mob in 1837 drew sharp protests from a number of church groups. Several antislavery societies sprang up within the next decade. They flooded the city with pamphlets, presented antislavery dramas, sponsored lectures by eminent abolitionists from the East, and tried to organize political support for the Free Soil and the Liberty parties. Gradually the slavery controversy began to affect Chicago as it had numerous other northern communities. Churches and secular organizations alike were riven asunder as radicals and conservatives divided on points of antislavery principle and tactics.

Despite the local political contests of the Forties, however, the general public had not yet become excited over the slavery issue. It was more immediately concerned with proposals for a Galena and Chicago Union Railroad, over which wheat and corn and hogs would flow in abundance, than with the human freight of the Underground Railroad. Yet no obstacles were interposed to curb the abolitionist minority, and Chicago—with a reputation even then for colorful violence—tolerated some rather rough treatment of slave-catchers who came to ferret out fugitives. More moderate antislavery sympathizers were occasionally disturbed by the activities of the Underground; and on one occasion in 1846, when a group of Negroes, armed with clubs and led by white abolitionists, rescued a slave from his captors and "paraded in triumph," they convoked a public meeting to disavow this show of force. The editor of one influential newspaper declared: "Better even is law, enforced by the standing armies of tyrants, than for a community to be the subjects of every handful of outlaws, black or white, who may choose to combine and set the laws at defiance." [6] Just four years later, however, the Chicago city council itself was setting the law at defiance; and, as for returning fugitives to the South, an influential church newspaper was insisting that "no Christian rightly understanding his duties can engage in it."[7]

This crystallization of public sentiment was due primarily to the Compromise of 1850, which gave the southern planters a revitalized fugitive-slave act in exchange for their consent to the admission of California as a free state. The amended act raised the fine for harboring fugitives to $1,000 and added a prison term of six months. A slave-catcher's affidavit became sufficient evidence in court to identify any Negro as a fugitive. Trial by jury and the right to testify in his own defense were denied the suspected slave. Magistrates were rewarded with a ten-dollar fee for ruling in favor of the master, while only five dollars was allotted for decisions in favor of the Negro. Any bystander could be deputized to assist in a capture. Federal officials who let a slave escape from their custody were financially liable for the entire value of the lost property.

A wave of indignation swept through the North when the terms of the new fugitive-slave act were announced. In Chicago, three hundred Negroes—over half the permanent adult population—met in their Methodist Church, organized a Liberty Association, and set up vigilante groups. Seven patrols of six persons each were assigned "to keep an eye out for interlopers." The Association passed a ringing resolution explaining the Negroes' stand:

". . . We do not wish to offer violence to any person unless driven to the extreme, in which case we are determined to defend ourselves at all hazards, even should it be to the shedding of human blood, and in doing thus, will appeal to the Supreme Judge of the Social World to support us in the justness of our cause. . . . We who have tasted of *freedom* are ready to exclaim, in the language of the brave Patrick Henry, 'Give us liberty or give us death.' "[8]

White sympathizers, too, were aroused, and it became evident that some justices would refuse to enforce the law. One famous case, soon after the passage of the Compromise, involved a Mr. Hinch, who arrived in town with a devoted slave to help him catch three fugitives. One day when he and the trusty were standing near Lake Michigan, even this faithful retainer deserted to freedom, by jumping aboard a steamer pulling out for Canada. A group of abolitionists threatened to tar and feather Mr. Hinch, so he appealed to a local justice for the protection of his person and for co-operation in recapturing his property.

The justice advised him that "immediate flight would be his safest course."

Even the Chicago Common Council, the city's legislative body, took formal action condemning the fugitive-slave act as "a cruel and unjust law . . . [which] ought not be respected by an intelligent community." The city police were assured that they were under no obligation to assist in rounding up escaped slaves. At a mass meeting on the night of the Council's vote, a white lawyer made a fiery speech against the fugitive-slave act and closed by "defying the law and trampling a copy of it under his feet, to the delight and admiring cheers of his hearers." [9]

Stephen A. Douglas, Senator from Illinois, had backed the Compromise. He was now so disturbed by this smoldering in the grass roots that he rushed home from Washington to prevent it from becoming a prairie fire. His eloquent and skillful defense of the Compromise won a resolution from his audience condemning the Chicago Council for its "precipitate action." The city fathers would not retreat completely, however. They voted to "reconsider," but refused to "expunge from the record." [10]

But neither Douglas's oratory nor the desire for an orderly community restrained the aroused abolitionists. An official of the Underground Railroad commented in the late autumn of 1850: "This road is doing better business this fall than usual. The Fugitive Slave Law has given it more vitality and activity; more passengers and more opposition, which accelerates business." [11] The Chicago *Daily Journal* had insisted since the early Forties that "every man that wears the image and likeness of his Maker should be treated as a man." Now, it advocated violent action against slave-catchers with a broad, humorous hint: "We have no doubt but those interested are upon their guard and the gentlemen [i.e., slave-catchers] will return with a *flea in their ears.*" [12] The *Democratic Press,* organ of "Deacon" Bross, Chicago's most colorful civic booster of the day, declared that the Fugitive Slave Law could be enforced only "at the muzzle of a musket," and declared that "we have known of many attempts being made to take fugitives away from Chicago, but we have yet to learn the first instance in which the thing has been done." [13]

In case after case during the stormy decade between the Compromise and the Civil War, the Negroes and their abolitionist allies outwitted and outfought the slave-catchers. One of the most dramatic of these episodes involved one Eliza, an escaped slave who had found employment as a maidservant in a house of prostitution. A slave-catcher, discovering her whereabouts, came to claim his quarry, escorted by a local deputy. Eliza and a white girl companion both begged the slave-catcher not to take the girl away. They were silenced by a drawn revolver, while Eliza, kicking and screaming, was forced into a waiting hack. An angry crowd surrounded the carriage, and the captors fled into a nearby armory, dragging Eliza with them.

By this time a large group of colored men, armed with clubs and knives, descended upon the armory. The sheriff then appeared with a warrant for Eliza's arrest on a charge of disorderly conduct—a calculated stratagem to get her away from the slave-catcher. As the sheriff emerged from the armory with Eliza, the crowd wrenched her from his grasp and quickly spirited her away to a station on the Underground Railroad. The mob then proceeded to the house of assignation, threatening to level it to the ground in the belief that the owner had revealed Eliza's identity. The ringleaders were arrested but released the next day. Scant wonder that the Cairo (Ill.) *Weekly Times* was led to complain of the Chicagoans: "They are the most riotous people in the state. Mention nigger and slave-catcher in the same breath and they are up in arms." [14]

Finally, in the spring of 1861, a group of federal marshals threatened to swoop down upon Chicago and other northern cities in one last but futile gesture aimed at appeasing a South on the verge of secession. The Negro community was panic-stricken, and the Chicago *Journal,* leading antislavery daily, in a dramatic admonition advised every Negro without a certificate of freedom to "make tracks for Canada as soon as possible": [15]

Don't delay a moment. Don't let grass grow under your feet. Stand not upon the order of your going but go at once. You are not safe here and you cannot be safe until you stand on English soil where you will be free men and free women. It is folly for you to remain here an instant, for the slaveholders encouraged by their late success are making and will continue to make the most determined effort to reclaim fugitives from bondage. Strike for the North Star.

The Underground was now functioning in the open. Four freight cars were boldly chartered to carry the fugitives to an embarkation point on Lake Michigan. A *Journal* reporter was on hand to describe this exodus: [16]

All day, yesterday, the vicinity of the Michigan Southern depot was a scene of excitement and confusion. After the religious services at the Zoar Baptist Church in the morning, which was densely attended, the leave-taking commenced . . . the fugitives and their friends, going from door to door, bidding each other good-bye and mingling their congratulations and tears.—The colored clergymen of the city were also among the number, and labored ardently in extending encouragement and consolation to those about to depart. . . . In some instances, entire families were going together, in which cases there seemed to be a general jubilation; in others a few members, a wife leaving a husband, or a mother her children, amid tears. . . .

. . . All the afternoon, drays, express wagons and other vehicles were busy transporting trunks, bandboxes, valises and other various articles of household furniture to the depot. The wants of the outer man had been attended to also, and a goodly store of provisions, such as crackers, bread, beans, dried beef and apples, were packed in, and a barrel of water in each car; for the fugitives were to be stowed away in the same cars with the freight, with plenty of fresh air, but no light, and in a crowded unwholesome state.

As the hour of departure . . . drew nigh, the streets adjacent to the depot and the immediate vicinity of the four cars . . . were thronged with an excited multitude of colored people of both sexes and all ages. Large numbers of white people also gathered from motives of curiosity, and stood silent spectators of this rather unusual spectacle. The four cars were rapidly filled with the fugitives, numbering one hundred and six in all, and embracing men, women, youth and infants. In the rear car were two or three sick women, who were treated with the utmost tenderness. . . . The whole business of the transportation was supervised by two or three colored men assisted by several white people.

After all were aboard, . . . the immense crowd pressed up to the cars and commenced the last farewell. . . . Here and there was one in tears and wringing the hands, but the majority were in the best of humor, and were congratulated by their friends lingering behind, that tomorrow they would be free. "Never mind," said one, "the good Lord will save us all in the coming day." . . . [They were] bidding their friends write when they got to "the other side of Jordan," and not forget them in the new country. The minister of the neighborhood church where they had attended, also went from car to car bidding them to be men when they got to Canada.

The larger proportion of the fugitives were stout, ablebodied young men, many of them well dressed and some of them almost white. . . . The elder ones evinced no levity but acted like those who had been hardened by troubles, and were now suffering a lot foreseen and prepared for. . . . Quite a number of children were among the crowd, who, ignorant of the cause of such a commotion, gave the rest constant trouble by getting into the wrong cars and climbing round and between the wheels.

But all were finally stowed away, the bell of the engine sounded and the train started amid lusty cheers, many-voiced good-byes and the waving of hats and handkerchiefs as far as the eye could see. The fugitives heartily responded and the train vanished in the distance. . . .

About one thousand fugitives have arrived in this city since last fall, a large number of whom have left within the past few days.

The Great Canadian Exodus had become another step in the flight to freedom.

FROM CITY STREET TO BATTLEFIELD

Street fights between slave-catchers and abolitionists or between pro-slavery and antislavery crowds were rather common occurrences in northern cities between 1850 and 1860. They were the storm signals of that great political groundswell which culminated in the organization of the Republican party and the election of Abraham Lincoln to the presidency. Both the sporadic violence and the humanitarian agitation of the antislavery movement were gradually merged with and subordinated to political action. Chicago's antislavery forces had tried to elect a mayor in 1841 and failed. Yet, less than twenty years later, the Republican party controlled the city. Migrants from the eastern seaboard, immigrants from England, and German radical refugees from the reaction which followed the European revolutions of 1848 provided the majority which tipped the balance in favor of the Republicans.

In 1856, "Honest Abe" and Stephen A. Douglas, the "Little Giant," both came to Chicago to plead for the senatorial vote. The Democrats roared thunderous assent when Douglas declared that the government of the United States "was made by white men for the benefit of white men, to be administered by white men in such a manner as they should determine."

The next night Lincoln spoke—and with a forthrightness which he seldom assumed in other sections of Illinois. He appealed to the foreign-born, who made up over 50 per cent of the electorate, calling them "blood of the blood, and flesh of the flesh of the men who wrote the Declaration of Independence and pronounced the equality of men."

He took a bold stand against the extension of slavery, declaring that "if we cannot give freedom to every creature, let us do nothing that will impose slavery upon any other creature." He made a stirring plea for national unity: "Let us discard all this quibbling about this man and the other man, this race and that race and the other race being inferior, . . . and unite as one people throughout this land, until we shall once more stand up declaring that *all* men are created equal." One eyewitness reported that as Lincoln finished his address, " 'cheers like blasts of a thousand bugles' came from the throats of his listeners." [17] Douglas won the statewide vote, but Lincoln carried the city of Chicago. He carried it again three years later when he ran for President. He carried it, too, when he sounded his call for volunteers in April, 1861.

Chicago's response to Lincoln's call for troops was immediate and enthusiastic. The native-born volunteered freely. Many of the foreign-born enrolled—in some cases under their national banners. The Hungarians, Bohemians, and Slavs organized the Lincoln Rifles. The German Turner Union Cadets, the French Battalion, and the Scottish Highland Guards marched out to defend the American Union. Even the Irish, Democratic to the core and not too enthusiastic about Republican war aims, now responded to the call of their Colonel Mulligan: "RALLY! All Irishmen. . . . For the honor of the Old Land . . . for the defense of the New!" [18] The street fights of the Forties and Fifties had been transferred to a national battlefield. The flight to freedom had been replaced by a fight for freedom. Only the Negroes were prevented from answering Lincoln's call. Not until 1863 did the Union officially permit them to shoulder arms for their own freedom.

THE COMMUNITY OF THE FREE

For many of the fugitive slaves, the flight to freedom ended in Chicago. When the Civil War began, there were about a thousand Negroes living in the city. Some were "free-born persons of color"; others had been emancipated by kindly masters or had purchased their freedom. The majority were fugitives, without legal certificates of freedom.

In the center of the city, along the banks of the Chicago River, a small community of the free had been growing since 1840. Social life centered around several small Baptist and Methodist churches which also functioned as stations on the Underground Railroad. Three years before the Civil War, the *Christian Times,* appealing to the white community for aid to one of these churches, referred to its membership in laudatory terms:

The colored Baptist church in this city is made up of very excellent and reliable material. Its leading male members are respected and successful business men, and fully capable of directing wisely the financial affairs of the church. . . . The church is small, and though, as intimated above, some of its male members are tolerably prosperous in their business, they are not able to assume the whole burden of these payments.[19]

The antislavery newspapers often referred to the small Negro community with pride, for it seemed to justify their faith in the potentialities of the slaves. On several occasions reference was made to the orderliness of the Negroes and to their interest in literary societies, religion, and education. One editor remarked, with a rhetorical flourish characteristic of the period: "Such evidences speak volumes for the enterprize of those whose fathers dwelt long ago, where the White Nile wanders through its golden sands." [20] There were even occasional hints that certain sections of the white population might do well to emulate these "well informed, and peaceable citizens [who] seldom see any of their brethren grace the police calendar." [21]

That not all the Negro settlers were quiet businessmen or devotees of church and literary societies is obvious, however, from a lurid newspaper account in 1860 of a "Negro Dive in Full Blast." [22] The "excellent and reliable material" within the colored community also had to face other threats to its reputation. Old church records reveal anxious discussion over the question: "If a slave should be separated from his spouse by the master or by escaping into a free state, and should marry another, is he guilty of bigamy?" Sometimes an embarrassing scandal broke, such as the highly publicized account of a "reverend scoundrel" who, caught *in flagrante delicto* with a parishioner's wife, fled into the street, the wrath-maddened husband in hot pursuit. Even the more friendly papers could not overlook the possibilities of such a story, although one journal softened its spicy account of the minister's plight with a sober comment: "The affair has created the most intense excitement amongst the colored population who unanimously take sides against him." [23]

Negro leaders of the period were continually urging their followers to prove that ex-slaves were worthy of the city's hospitality. Typical of those Negroes who had a stake in Chicago's future was one John Jones, spokesman for the Negro community and first colored man to win an elective political office. The *Journal* carried his business advertisement in 1860: [24]

> Go to John Jones' Clothes Cleaning and Repairing Rooms, 119 Dearborn street, and get your clothes neatly repaired and thoroughly cleaned. The oldest and best establishment in the city. Your clothes will not be drawn up by steaming, nor spoiled with chemicals. Give me a trial, my prices are reasonable.

Such men had come to the city to stay.

The antislavery forces in Chicago were united in their opposition to slavery. They were willing to make their city a haven of refuge. They were not of one mind, however, on how to treat the Negroes in their midst. At one extreme were individuals such as the anti-slavery editor who stated frankly: [25]

"I am resolutely opposed to the 'equallizing [*sic*] of the races,' and it no more necessarily follows that we should fellowship with Negroes because our policy strikes off their shackles, than it would to take felons to our embraces, because we might remonstrate against cruelty to them in our penitentiaries."

At the other extreme were a few persons who went all-out for integration and drew the denunciatory fire of southerners for being "amalgamationists" desirous of "mongrelizing" the white race by allowing intermarriage and "social equality."

Throughout the period prior to the Civil War, the laws of the state forbade intermarriage and voting by Negroes. Segregation on common carriers and in the schools and theaters was widespread. The abolitionists regarded these as side issues which should not interfere with the main fight against slavery. Indeed, many abolitionists hoped that once the Negroes were freed, the bulk of them would either remain in the South or emigrate to the West Indies and Africa.

When emancipation was proclaimed, there was considerable discussion in antislavery circles of how Chicago would meet a possible sudden influx of freedmen. The "colonizationists" were hopeful that even those Negroes already in the city would voluntarily leave. When only forty-seven Negroes accepted an invitation from the president of Haiti to emigrate to that island in 1865, and the bulk of the colored population openly declared its intention to remain, the editor of the *Northwestern Christian Advocate* was so incensed at what he called their "impolitic and ungrateful behavior" that he threatened to withdraw his support from a financial campaign of the impecunious African Methodist Episcopal Church.

Most of the former abolitionists and their sympathizers soon became reconciled to the prospect of a small permanent Negro community with its own separate social institutions. A pattern of enforced segregation conflicted with the high sentiments of equality and the brotherhood of man, and that there were some uneasy consciences is evident from the minutes of the Illinois Baptist State Convention of 1865. The impropriety of segregation is suggested in the same paragraph with a statement implying that such separation was to be naturally expected (the italics are the authors'):

". . . We ought to extend fraternal courtesy and kindness to individuals scattered among us *when their numbers are not sufficient to justify the formation of colored churches.* Let them know that all our churches offer them a home and a cordial welcome. *Let them not be tempted to organize churches on the basis of color* rather than of Christian Faith."

While there was outside pressure upon the freedmen to establish a separate institutional life, there were also internal forces at work: a community of interests, a group of educated leaders, and the existence of local Negro churches and lodges with national connections. The ex-slaves were proud to have what they called "something of our own." At the same time they insisted upon the extension of full economic and political opportunity, and access to all public accommodations.

Opposition to an increase in the Negro population was most pronounced among the white laboring classes. It was not the issue of social equality which fundamentally disturbed them, however, but the fear and suspicion that Negro freedmen would be used to depress the wage level. Most bitter in their opposition were the Irish, who, Catholic and poor, were scornfully referred to as "unwashed Dimmycrats" by the Protestant Republican businessmen and artisans who controlled the city and professed to champion the Negro. From time to time during the twenty years preceding the Civil War, Irish workingmen in Chicago rioted against fugitive slaves who secured employment as stevedores, porters, canal bargemen, and general laborers.

In 1864, the Chicago *Tribune* carried a long editorial on "Mobbing Negroes," which probably reflected the antagonism of the Protestant Germans and Easterners toward the Catholic Irish as much as it did sympathy for Negroes. A mob of four or five hundred Irish laborers had beaten a dozen Negroes on the lumber docks, allegedly because "it was degrading to them to see blacks working upon an equality with themselves, and more so, while their brothers were out of employment." The *Tribune* insisted, however, that work was not scarce, and that "if all the black people in the city should leave Chicago tomorrow it would not benefit the condition of the Irish a single dime." Calling them "mobocrats," "raw laborers," and "the most illogical people on the face of the earth," the editor proceeded to belabor the Irish for "biting off their own noses for the benefit of Copperhead demagogues." * "It is a little singular," he observed, "that no class of people in Chicago fear the competition of the handful of blacks here, except the Irish. The Germans never mob colored men for working for whoever may employ them. The English, the Scotch, the French, the Scandinavians, never molest peaceable black people. Americans never think of doing such a thing. No other nationality consider themselves 'degraded' by seeing blacks earning their own living by labor." The editor concluded with a suggestion that "if they must mob anybody, it should be the slaveholders. . . . If they must quarrel with the negroes [*sic*], it should be with the slave negroes. . . . They ought to teach the slave blacks to assert their rights; to 'strike' for wages. . . . By so doing, the Irish laborer would remove the crushing, degrading competition of unpaid labor, and open to himself vast fields of employment now shut out from him by slavery." [26]

The logic of the present was more compelling, however, than this abstract theory of long-run interests. The Irish laborers remained suspicious and resentful against people who castigated them in this fashion, and they made the Democratic party the weapon for their de-

* Chicago suffered from general war weariness during 1863 and 1864. There was widespread dissatisfaction with the draft, and on one occasion Lincoln had to rebuke some of the leading citizens for their lack of co-operation. Treason itself was not unknown, and one plot was discovered which would have resulted in a *putsch* by Confederate soldiers interned in Chicago. Yet throughout the period, except for one mayoral election, the Republicans kept control of the city, and after the war the "radical" Republicans were in the saddle.

fense. Inevitably, local policies were colored by national events, and three years after the Civil War, Irish contingents in a Democratic election parade in Chicago carried signs denouncing Republican reconstruction policies in the South: "LET THE NIGGERS PAY FOR THEIR OWN SOUP"; "NO NIGGER VOTING"; "WHITE SUPREMACY."

Chicago Republicans, their eyes focused upon the growing Irish vote, did not hesitate to openly declare their opposition to any influx of "free and untrained Negroes." There was no such influx, but by 1870 some four thousand Negroes were living in the city—one out of every hundred persons.

Five years after the Civil War the leaders of the Negro community, in conjunction with other Negroes in the state, called a Colored Convention to present grievances and "devise ways and means whereby a healthy opinion may be created . . . to secure every recognition by the laws of our state and to demand equal school privileges throughout the state." [27] The Black Code was still on the books, and, in some of the communities of southern Illinois, Negroes were as thoroughly subordinated as they were in the deeper South. Even in Chicago, as the Negro population increased, colored children were forced to attend the so-called "Black School," and when protests failed, some of the parents resorted to civil disobedience. A colored Old Settler relates the story as her mother told it to her:

"The parents—most of them—objecting to segregation sent their children right on to the nearest schools as before. The teachers declined to assign them to classes or studies.

"The children, however, attended daily, taking their seats in an orderly fashion throughout the controversy that ensued. The school board then determined that any child with no more than an eighth of Negro blood could attend the usual schools; but here again was trouble, for the wide range of complexions in the colored families soon demonstrated the impossibility in such a division. After a short time and a determined fight on the part of the colored citizens who invaded the offices of the Board of Education and the Mayor, the inglorious career of the Black School was done away with and never resumed."

It took twenty years to create a public opinion strong enough to erase all of the discriminatory laws from the state's statute book, but by 1885 this had been accomplished. Lacking political power and appealing solely within the framework of the abolitionist tradition, democratic idealism, and constitutional rights, the community of freedmen were able to mobilize enough support to establish their equality before the law, to secure the right to vote, and to erect a set of guarantees against discrimination in the use of public facilities. To lay the ghosts that stalked in proslavery southern Illinois, the Colored Convention of 1869 explicitly stated that "[we] disavow any and all imputations of, and desire to obtain, social equality." In Chicago, however, neither white persons nor Negroes had any crusading fervor either to espouse or to prevent social relations or even intermarriage. Although Negroes developed their own family and community life, there was considerable friendly social intercourse between colored and white people, and marriages across the color-line were not unknown.

Within a generation after the Civil War the community of the free was accepted as a normal part of the city's life. The tradition became set that Negroes could compete for power and prestige in the economic and political spheres. Yet the badge of color marked them as socially different. Also, the fact that no Negroes rose to the highest positions in the commercial and public life of early Chicago suggests that in a vague but nevertheless decisive sense they were thought of as having a subordinate place.

Before the Civil War the Negro was the protagonist of the abolitionist drama. After Emancipation he was no longer a hero around whom stirring battles were fought in the city streets and the courts. He and his people became just one more poverty-stricken group competing in a city where economic and political issues were being fought out behind the façade of racial, national, and religious alignments. It was a city which for the next thirty years was riven by class conflicts and seared by two disastrous fires—but which was steadily laying the foundations for industrial and commercial supremacy in the Middle West.

CHAPTER 2

Land of Promise

EMERGENCE OF THE BLACK BELT (1865-1874)

AT THE OUTBREAK OF THE CIVIL WAR A HUNDRED THOUSAND PEOPLE LIVED in Chicago. Fifty years later, when the First World War began, the city boasted more than two million inhabitants. The material base for this rapid growth was laid between 1860 and 1890. The city's expanding stockyards and packing plants, farm-implement factories and railroad yards, warehouses and grain elevators attracted the hungry, the ambitious, and the foot-loose from all over the world. Fortunes sprouted in the grain pit. Millionaires were sired in the cattle pens. Reapers, made in Chicago and distributed in the wheat fields, brought prosperity to both countryside and city. George Pullman's sleeping cars, fabricated in its outskirts, carried the city's fame over America's ever-widening web of railroads. There was a magic in the names of Swift and Armour, Marshall Field and Levi Z. Leiter, Potter Palmer and Cyrus McCormick, that turned many a fortune-seeker's steps toward Chicago. Young, boisterous, and busy, the city became a symbol of the vast opportunities which the entire Middle West held for peoples of the eastern seaboard and Europe who were seeking a land of promise.

The Chicago of 1870 was a boom town, its buildings and its people new and rough. Of its sixty thousand structures, forty thousand were made of wood. It was, as one contemporary newspaper said, "a city of everlasting pine, shingles, shams, veneers, stucco and putty." [1] Fires were frequent. In 1871 the Great Chicago Fire destroyed seventeen thousand buildings and left a hundred thousand people homeless—the damage amounted to $200,000,000. The story of Mrs. O'Leary's cow that kicked over a lamp that set a fire that burned a city became an international legend. Local ministers saw the holocaust as an expression of God's judgment upon a wicked city. Southerners and former Copperheads were sure that "God had stricken the Northern city to avenge the 'wanton' destruction which the Union armies had visited upon the South during the Civil War." [2] To most Chicagoans, how ever, the fire was an unlucky but exciting accident—an unfortunate, but in no sense fatal, catastrophe.

The great Chicago fire did not destroy the Negro community, although it consumed the contiguous central business area and the world-famous Red-light District. Since the fire also spared the rows of stately mansions near Lake Michigan, many burned-out businesses were temporarily housed in their owners' fashionable residences. The bulk of the gamblers and prostitutes took refuge in the Negro neighborhood—an area three blocks long and fifteen blocks wide, with some twenty-five hundred residents. When the city was rebuilt, the former Red-light District was taken over by the wholesale trade. The gay underworld remained among the Negroes.

Chicago clergymen again professed to see the handiwork of a persistent and vigilant Deity when in 1874 another conflagration burned out gamblers, prostitutes, *and* Negroes. As a result of this second fire, almost half of the colored families were dispersed among the white residents, but a new Negro community also arose from the ashes of the old. Here, in a long, thin sliver of land, sandwiched between a well-to-do white neighborhood and that of the so-called "shanty Irish," most of Chicago's colored residents and their major institutions were concentrated during the next forty years. The "Black Belt" had emerged.

BETWEEN THE FIRE AND THE FAIR (1875-1893)

In the twenty years between the Great Fire and the first World's Fair (1893), the Negro population increased from five thousand to fifteen thousand. The Black Belt gradually expanded as Negroes took over the homes of white persons who were moving to the more desirable lake-front or to the suburbs. Most of the colored residents were employed as coachmen, butlers, cooks, and maids in the homes of the wealthy; as servants in stores, hotels, and restaurants; as porters on the increasingly popular Pullman coaches; and as maids and handymen in white houses of prostitution. A small Negro business and professional class developed, and by 1878 it had found a mouthpiece in a weekly newspaper, the *Conservator,* whose editor, reminiscing years later, described the general status of Negroes in the Seventies and early Eighties as follows: [3]

. . . There were about five thousand Negroes in Chicago. The *Conservator* was started as a means of expression for Negroes and to aid in the promotion of the welfare of the Negro group.

When the paper was started the behavior of many of the Negroes was characterized by loose living and a lack of proper standards. There were few Negroes of culture and refinement, and only a few jobs of any consequence were held by Negroes. The paper was devoted to the idea of stressing the importance of education, social uplift and correct living. Conflict between the races was not very great at the time the paper was started, consequently there was little space given to the discussion of race relations in the local community. There were, however, occasional clashes between the Irish and the Negroes. When these . . . occurred they were discussed in the paper.

The picture gleaned from the pages of this paper is that of a small, compact, but rapidly growing community divided into three broad social groups. The "respectables"—church-going, poor or moderately prosperous, and often unrestrained in their worship—were looked down upon somewhat by the "refined" people, who, because of their education or breeding, could not sanction the less decorous behavior of their racial brothers. Both of these groups were censorious of the "riffraff," the "sinners"—unchurched and undisciplined. The "refined" set conceived themselves as examples of the Negro's progress since slavery. They believed that their less disciplined fellows should be prodded with ridicule and sarcasm, and restrained by legal force when necessary. They had an almost religious faith that education would, in the long run, transform even the "riffraff" into people like themselves.

The pages of the *Conservator* expressed these attitudes by colorful words of denunciation and applause. One editorial, for instance,[4] inveighed against the seamy side of life with rhetoric and pious sentiments typical of the period:

GOING TO RUIN

We are calling attention to the fact that a number of our girls and boys are on the road to ruin. The boys rioting in the Clark and 4th Avenue dives, laying the foundations for lives of thieves, thugs and murderers, and the girls walking the streets in gaudy attire—attracting notice—exciting comment and rapidly linking their lives, with those whose "house is the gate of Hell, going down to the chambers of death."

How sad it is to see the girls we have known in their innocent childhood, change their lives, just when life's days should be the brightest;

change from piety, virtue and happiness to vice, dissipation and woe. Mothers are you blind? Fathers are you deaf? Christians are you asleep? For the sake of God and Humanity, let someone rescue these young lives from dissipation's perpetual gloom.

As opposed to this pattern of life, the paper held up [5] as pioneering models those young people who were "improving themselves," thereby "advancing the race":

Four colored students graduated last week from the University of Michigan. Two in law and two in medicine. In conversation with colored students during the past year, we were glad to hear that scarcely a vestige of the "caste" spirit is ever seen. They attend, or are free to attend, all meetings, educational and social, and are never made to feel out of place. There has never yet been a colored graduate from the collegiate course. Miss Mary H. Graham whose matriculation in '76 caused such a stir in Michigan circles will be the first to achieve this distinction. . . . Mr. C. Williams, a Sophomore and a young man of rare moral worth, is winning a golden name at the University. . . . He is held in high degree of respect by the citizens and the Faculty. . . . Would there were more such men as he—Ethiopia might well rejoice.

The "young men of rare moral worth," the "girls walking the streets in gaudy attire," as well as plain, ordinary Negroes, continued to come to Chicago throughout the Eighties. By 1890 there were enough of them to sustain twenty churches, a dozen or so lodges, three weekly newspapers, and several social and cultural clubs. Certain individuals had managed to attain some prominence and wealth, and a few possessed well-established businesses catering to a white clientele. John Jones, abolitionist leader, was still tailoring for the city's elite in a building of his own in the heart of the city. Another Negro had invested $60,000 in a downtown office building. Smiley, a caterer, was laying up a small fortune from the lavish affairs he engineered for the Gold Coast—a fortune the remnants of which he was to leave to the University of Chicago.

For these men, the land of promise had been no mirage. None of them had amassed great fortunes or secured key positions of economic control, but they had been financially successful in a modest fashion. A few Negroes of the business and professional classes had also been active in politics since the early Seventies, thus setting the precedent for Negro political representation which subsequently became a part

of the city's tradition. The first colored county commissioner, state legislator, policeman, and fireman all appeared before 1875.[6]

The twenty years between the Fire and the Fair were the turbu-
lent ones for Chicago.[7] On the heels of the post-fire boom, a six-year
stretch of "hard times" ensued, during which there were serious labor
troubles. The political antagonisms of the foreign-born and the native-
whites (evenly divided as to numbers) were organized throughout this
period around such issues as the passage of the Blue Sunday Laws and
the struggle for control of the City Hall. Then came eight years of
continuing prosperity and renewed European immigration, culminating in the panic of 1884-86, which brought in its wake a violent streetcar strike. In 1884, the Illinois State Federation of Labor passed a resolution against the "further importation of pauper labor from Europe."[8]
The Haymarket riot in 1886 resulted in considerable antiforeigner
hysteria.

The small Negro community was barely touched by these political
and economic upheavals. Having adjusted themselves to the economic
competition of the foreign-born by securing employment primarily in
the service occupations, the masses of the Negroes had little reason to
listen to the impassioned oratory of labor leaders who excoriated local
capitalists and eastern bankers. Agitation for the eight-hour day carried no appeal for a colored working population over half of which
was employed in servant capacities. It is significant that the one Negro
preacher in the Eighties who publicly espoused the cause of Socialism
quickly lost his pulpit.[9]

Although unconcerned with the violent struggles of the white workers, Negroes were persistently seeking to widen the areas of political
and economic opportunity for themselves. They found allies among
Republican politicians, civic-minded liberals, and the wealthy for
whom many of them worked. Fighters for equal rights since the days
of slavery, Chicago's Negro leaders resented any attempts to deny political and economic opportunity to themselves or their fellows. The
Illinois Black Code was repealed in 1865. By 1870 Negroes had been
guaranteed the right to vote. By 1874 segregation in the school system
had been abolished. In 1885 the leaders climaxed their efforts by securing the passage of a state civil rights bill designed to protect the liberties of Negroes in the less advanced counties of southern Illinois. They
insisted that every evidence of subordinate status should be eliminated.
They were taking the promises of democracy seriously.

Ostensibly trivial matters sometimes assumed great importance in this struggle for recognition and respect. The *Conservator* on one occasion devoted an entire editorial, humorous in tone but serious in intent, to the use of the lower-case "n" for spelling the word Negro. The editor called the practice "a mark of disrespect," "a stigma," and "a badge of inferiority," and remarked that "the French, German, Irish, Dutch, Japenese [*sic*], and other nationalities are honored with a capital letter, but the poor sons of Ham must bear the burden of a small n." [10]

Colored Chicagoans, like their foreign-born neighbors, cultivated a dual loyalty and pride—allegiance to an ethnic group as well as to America. But they did not feel that race pride should isolate them from the main streams of civic life. The editor of the *Conservator* expressed the dominant philosophy of the Negro community when he wrote in the late Eighties: "As a race let us forget the past so far as we can, and unite with other men upon issues, liberal, essential, and not dependent upon color of skin or texture of hair for its [*sic*] gravamen." [11]

The successful Negroes of the era, many of them former slaves, interpreted their own careers as proof that some day black men would be accepted as individuals and Americans. They visualized the progress of their race in terms of education, personal economic success, judicious political action, and co-operation with powerful and influential white people.

RETROSPECT AND PROSPECT (1894-1914)

In 1893 Chicago decided to show the world how it had survived panic, fire, and class war to become the second largest city in the nation—Midwest Metropolis. Its civic leaders ballyhooed, pressured, and begged until they won from Congress the privilege of playing host to the World's Columbian Exposition—the first World's Fair. For Negroes, too, this was a significant occasion. In 1891 a prominent European historian and traveler had remarked of Chicago that "the severity of the climate repels the Africans." [12] Yet, in 1893, there were fifteen thousand Negroes living in the city. It was only natural that they should wish to display what they and their co-racialists throughout the country had accomplished in the twenty-eight years since slavery. In 1892 a committee met in Quinn Chapel, once a station of the Underground Railroad, and formulated an appeal to Congress for representation at the Fair. A large Negro exhibit was eventually prepared, and colored speakers and singers appeared on various Exposition programs.

For the Negroes, the occasion was a sort of silver jubilee celebrating a generation of freedom. The Prudence Crandall Club, representing the "cultured" elements, entertained the aging but still eloquent Frederick Douglass, famous Negro orator and venerable symbol of the abolition struggle. Commemoration services "in honor of the leaders in the cause of freedom and political equality" were held in historic Quinn Chapel. Frederick Douglass spoke, and when he referred to the stormy Forties and Fifties, he urged the younger generation of Negroes not to forget that "forty years ago there were always here a roof, table, and house for the most abject abolitionist." [13] The night before he left the city, he was, as one daily newspaper reported, HONORED BY BOTH RACES AT HIS LEAVE TAKING.[14]

"The church was filled with an audience of white and colored people. . . . In speaking of the prejudices against men of his race in the South, he said the people of the South had better beware as to how they aroused the strength in the black man's arm. When he made this reference he was cheered."

Before the echoes of Douglass's speech had died away a Negro was burned in effigy in the streets of Chicago. Colored laborers had been imported to break a strike in the stockyards, and the white workers had responded in a style suggestive of the South. But, significantly enough, in Chicago, the victim was burned *in effigy* rather than in person.[15]

There was nothing in the South to lend substance to Douglass's heroic warning. Booker T. Washington's philosophy of compromise was soon to become the holy scripture of southern leaders, white and black. Do not antagonize the white majority. Do not ask for the right to vote. Do not fight for civil liberties or against segregation. Go to school. Work hard. Save money. Buy property. Some day the other things may come.

For ten years after the Civil War, the Republican North had buttressed the southern Negro's franchise with federal power. By 1875, however, Republican ardor had cooled. The Party could now exist without the southern Negro vote, and northern businessmen needed the goodwill of the white South. The ex-slaves had never secured an economic base. Forty acres and a mule might have given them a sort of sturdy peasant independence. As it was, a system of sharecropping replaced slavery, and debt peonage was substituted for legal bondage. It was Booker T. Washington's hope that by hard work and thrift the Negro masses could ultimately establish their freedom by buying the land. But southern landlords, selling their cotton in a world market, had no intention of relinquishing the very source of their power. They used terror and intimidation to keep the former slaves in their place. A rigorous etiquette of race relations was enforced, in which the Negro's role was that of serf, sycophant, and buffoon, bowing and scraping at the throne of white supremacy. An effort was made to straitjacket Negroes into an American version of the caste system. The promises of freedom were harmlessly enshrined in the Emancipation Proclamation and embalmed in the Thirteenth, Fourteenth, and Fifteenth Amendments.[16]

Many ex-slaves who had tasted complete freedom during the few short years of Reconstruction could not adjust to this southern New Order. So throughout the Eighties and Nineties a constant stream of Negro migrants trickled northward to join the larger stream of immigrants from Europe. Chicago attracted a large proportion of those who left the South between 1890 and 1910 in what has been called "the Migration of the Talented Tenth." [17] Among them were prominent preachers and politicians who, for a brief spell after the Civil War, sat in southern state legislatures and in Congress; less distinguished individuals who occupied minor political posts in county and town; and all the restless educated and half-educated, who were not content to live life on southern terms. Many visitors to the first World's Fair who came to look stayed to work. By 1910 there were 40,000 Negroes among the heterogeneous two million inhabitants of Midwest Metropolis. Almost imperceptibly the Black Belt had expanded and absorbed more than 10,000 people within a period of seventeen years.

Upon the narrow economic base of domestic and personal service, Negroes in Chicago had evolved a community life gathering primarily around lodge and church. A few business and professional men, politicians, and ambitious personal and domestic servants constituted a social élite. In the years between the Fair and the First World War, these were the civic leaders, and their wives the social arbiters. A diversified institutional life taking form between 1890 and 1914 included a hospital and training school for nurses, a YMCA, branches of national organizations such as the National Negro Business League, the National Association for the Advancement of Colored People (NAACP), and the Federated Women's Clubs.

Four newspapers were started, one of which, the Chicago *Defender,* is still in existence. A sampling of front-page items from this paper in 1908 reveals the range of interests which made news during this period.

Rev. H. E. Stewart to Preach "Great
Sermon": "Has the Negro Any Reason
To Expect Special Favors from God?"
(9/12/08)

HOPE PRESBYTERIAN CONCERT A HUGE SUCCESS. (9/17/08)

REV. STEWART PREACHES ELKS ANNUAL SERMON;
JUNIOR CHOIR SINGS. (9/17/08)

SECRETARY OF LADY ELKS BREAKS LEG SKATING. (11/14/08)

MANASSEH BALL A GREAT SUCCESS; 1,500 PERSONS—
GRAND MARCH EIGHTH REGIMENT ORCHESTRA.
(11/21/08)

[This club was composed of Negro men and women whose wives or husbands were white.]

AFRO-AMERICAN HISTORICAL SOCIETY
ORGANIZED AMONG GRACE PRESBY-
TERIAN SUNDAY SCHOOL MEN BY MRS.
IDA WELLS BARNETT, PRESENTING PRO-
FESSOR R. T. GREENER, FIRST COLORED
GRADUATE OF HARVARD UNIVERSITY.
(11/21/08)

CHICAGO LADY ELK COMMISSIONED TO SET UP
LODGES IN THE SOUTH. (12/26/08)

LADY ELLIOT CIRCLE, 199, A. D. OF
FORRESTERS ELECT NEW OFFICERS.
(12/26/08)

[A chatty informal article stating, "The order has done much good during the year and besides a neat bank account, they have administered to their sick and needy and have established a record of standing for high morals."]

THE GRAND LADS CLUB GIVES A SOCIAL. (12/26/08)

CHORAL STUDY GROUP ANNOUNCES SUL-
LIVAN'S ORATORIO, "THE PRODIGAL SON,"
TO BE GIVEN AT INSTITUTIONAL CHURCH.
(12/26/08)

THE BASKETBALL LEAGUE ANNOUNCES GAMES FOR 1909. (12/26/08)

"The Triangle Inner Circle Club intend giving the Old Folks' Home a
New Year's present and to make it worthwhile they have combined charity
with pleasure." Plan to hold dance at 1st Regiment Armory, 6th and
Michigan, 50 cents admission. Proceeds for "those dear old folks at 610
Garfield Boulevard." Clubs co-operating in ticket sales were:

Cornell Charity	Des Jeunes Aspirants
I. B. Wells Women's Club	Nogales Club
Centennial Club	Grendenborg Club

[This item (12/26/08) indicates one type of broad community co-operation.]

W. T. Stead's sensational exposé already mentioned, *If Christ Came
to Chicago,* started a battle between the segregationists, who believed
in a legal Red-light District, and the non-segregationists who wished to
abolish it. The struggle went on throughout this period, and engaged the attention of the entire Negro community. The Chicago
Vice Commission reported in 1909 that the growing Negro population
had never managed to keep even one jump ahead of the continuously
expanding Red-light District. It also revealed that the great majority
of the employees in the "resorts" were colored men, women, and children. In fact, some of the most exclusive "houses" were in the Black
Belt. Inevitably the Black Belt became associated in the popular mind
with "vice," and the reformers exhorted the Negro community to
clean house. Some of the conservative Negro leaders accepted the
assignment, but the more militant refused to admit complete blame
for vice in the Black Belt.

One of the most prominent colored ministers declared himself "a
firm believer in the segregation of vice," but accused a prominent white
pastor of trying to widen the boundaries of the Red-light District at the
expense of the Negro community. The white minister was charged
with a desire to push "the boundary lines of vice beyond his own bailiwick" in order to prevent "a large exodus of his parishioners to a local·

ity less honeycombed with dance halls, brothels and saloons." "So like Ajax of old," the Negro minister continued, "all through the long and bitter night, the prayer of this learned divine was for light to see his foemen's fall. And when he did, he gave them no quarter until he succeeded in driving these unfortunates to the very doors of Quinn Chapel, the Olivet Baptist and Bethel churches [colored congregations]. It will be only a matter of time before the churches mentioned will be forced to abandon their present fields. . . . The Negro, like the whites, does not care for his wife and daughter to elbow the Red-light denizens."

Chicago's "vice problem" was not solved by gerrymander, however. In 1912 the reform forces succeeded in abolishing the Red-light District, and the prostitutes were temporarily scattered from one end of the city to the other. The business finally went underground in various parts of the city, including the Black Belt. But the break-up of the segregated vice area did not remove either the reality or the stigma of vice from the Negro community.

Upon one occasion in 1912 when Booker T. Washington publicly urged Negroes in Chicago and other urban areas to wipe out vice from their communities, a colored civic leader retorted: "A good deal of the vice in the 'colored belt' is the white man's vice, thrust there by the authorities against the protest of the colored people. But the thing runs deeper than that. Vice and crime are in large measure the result of idleness, of irregular employment, and even of regular employment that is underpaid and exhausting. It would be fatuous for the white community to deny its responsibility, in very large measure, for the economic conditions under which thousands of Negro men and women struggle right here in Chicago."

The Chicago *Evening Post* supported this position, saying: "While it is a very useful thing to have Mr. Washington preaching free will and full responsibility to the colored people, it would be a very great mistake for the white community to regard this as the last word on the subject. For it is not true in any sense whatever that the colored community is wholly and entirely responsible for the vice and crime which appear now and then in its midst. . . . But these are disagreeable truths and we all shirk them when we can. . . . The colored problem cannot be solved by the colored man alone."

This emphasis upon the interrelatedness of white Chicago and the Negro community had become traditional by 1900. With the passing of the abolitionists, Chicago's wealthy merchants and industrialists had assumed a somewhat paternalistic interest in the Negro community as a part of their general pattern of philanthropy and civic responsibility. Between 1897 and 1906, five of Chicago's most prominent men died— George Pullman, P. D. Armour, Gustavus Swift, Potter Palmer, and Marshall Field I. All except the last were considered "friends of the Negro"—liberal in their contributions to Black Belt institutions and willing to employ them in servant capacities. It is reported that when Potter Palmer died a dozen Negro employees from the famous Palmer House Hotel wept at his bier.

Even after the deaths of these men, Negro leaders maintained their contact with wealthy and powerful whites, but from 1905 through to the First World War, they began to place increasing emphasis upon "racial self-reliance"—the development of political power and a strong business and professional class. They began to urge, too, a diversification of employment and assailed the bars which some labor unions had erected against colored artisans. On the eve of the First World War the pattern of Negro-white relations was one of stable equilibrium. But Negroes conceived of it as a moving equilibrium whose motive force must be "race pride" and unified political action.

Midwest Metropolis was busy absorbing immigrants from Europe between 1890 and 1910—a major "social problem." Because it was American and small, the Negro community was far less of a "problem" to native-white Chicagoans of the Nineties than were neighborhoods inhabited by the foreign-born. For their part, Negroes viewed the influx of European immigrants with mixed emotions. The foreign-born constituted a potential threat to their jobs as butlers and maids, janitors and waiters. They monopolized the skilled and semi-skilled trades. They did most of the city's common labor. Negroes feared them as economic competitors. Yet in the West Side Ghetto and among the Italians of the North Side, these recent immigrants often lived side by side with Negroes, sometimes in the same buildings with them, and fraternized freely.

On the whole, Negroes regarded foreigners with a certain amount of understandable condescension. The foreign-born, in turn, were not slow to adopt the prevailing stereotypes about Negroes. "Foreigners learn how to cuss, count and say 'nigger' as soon as they get here," grumbled the Negroes. Not until the First World War, however, were masses of Negroes thrown into direct competition with the foreign-born in industry.

CHAPTER 3

The Great Migration

BLACK DIASPORA (1914-1918)

IN 1914 THE TIDE OF EUROPEAN MIGRATION WAS SUDDENLY REVERSED.[1] AS country after country was drawn into the First World War, foreign-born men streamed home from Pittsburgh and Cleveland, Detroit and Toledo, from mills and mines, to shoulder arms. Immigration virtually ceased. Chicago, too, lost thousands of workmen.

As the war dragged on, the United States gradually transformed itself into an arsenal and granary for Europe. Farmers laid more land to the plow while industrial plants expanded production. A city whose economic life depended upon the foreign-born to handle its meat, wheat, and steel now experienced a manpower crisis at the very moment when profits were highest and production demands greatest.

Then the great mass of caste-bound Negroes in the South stirred. For several years the cotton kingdom had been ravaged by the boll weevil sweeping up from Mexico. Flood and famine, too, had continually harassed the cotton farmers of the Mississippi Valley. Prior to 1915, however, there had been little to encourage plantation laborers to risk life in the city streets. Now there were jobs to attract them. Recruiting agents traveled south, begging Negroes to come north. They sometimes carried free tickets in their pockets, and always glowing promises on their tongues. For the first time, southern Negroes were actually being invited, even urged, to come to Chicago. They came in droves—50,000 of them between 1910 and 1920. And as each wave arrived, the migrants wrote the folks back home about the wonderful North. A flood of relatives and friends followed in their wake.

A bewildered South had visions of a land left desolate for lack of labor. From every southern state the Negroes came, despite desperate attempts to halt the exodus:[2]

Up from Florida—where the city fathers in Jacksonville passed an ordinance requiring labor recruiters from the North to buy a $1,000 license or take the alternative of sixty days in jail and a $600 fine.

Up from Georgia—where the Macon city council exacted a recruiting license fee of $25,000 and demanded that the labor agent be recommended by ten local ministers, ten manufacturers, and twenty-five businessmen.

Up from Alabama—where fines and jail sentences were imposed upon any "person, firm, or corporation" guilty of "enticing, persuading, or influencing" labor to leave Montgomery.

Up from Mississippi—where agents were arrested, trains stopped, ticket agents intimidated. And at Brookhaven, a chartered car carrying fifty men and women was deliberately sidetracked for three days.

Still they came!

As coercion failed, worried businessmen and planters resorted to conciliation and persuasion in an effort to stem the tide. Leading southern white newspapers began to condemn lynching and the inequitable treatment of Negroes in the courts. Conferences were held in large cities and out-of-the-way southern towns at which Negro leaders were implored to use their good offices with the field hands. The more astute Negro negotiators began to wring promises of more schools, better treatment, higher wages, and other reforms from men who a year before would have scorned to confer with "niggers." Idealistic southern friends of the Negro found their tasks suddenly eased by these economic imperatives. The southern caste system was in the process of profound modification.[3]

The Chicago *Defender,* a Negro weekly edited by Robert S. Abbott, a native of Georgia who had come north in the Nineties and made good, played a leading role in stimulating the migration. It coaxed and challenged, denounced and applauded. It organized a "Great Northern Drive" and succeeded in getting itself banned from many a southern community. It scoffed at the Southerners' reforms under duress:[4]

Turn a deaf ear to everybody. . . . You see they are not lifting their laws to help you. Are they? Have they stopped their Jim Crow cars? Can you buy a Pullman sleeper where you wish? Will they give you a square deal in court yet? Once upon a time we permitted other people to think for us—today we are thinking and acting for ourselves with the result that our "friends" are getting alarmed at our progress. We'd like to oblige these unselfish (?) souls and remain slaves in the South, but to their section of the country we have said, as the song goes, "I hear you calling me," and have boarded the train singing, "Good-bye, Dixie Land."

Eventually America entered the war. More southern Negroes came to replace the men who were drafted. For four years the tug of war between northern industry and southern planters, northern Negro leaders and southern leaders, continued. The migrants kept streaming up the Mississippi Valley, riding the real trains of the Illinois Central over the same route their forefathers had traveled on the Underground Railroad. When the tide slackened in 1920, Chicago had over a hundred thousand Negroes among her population—an increase of 148 per cent in ten years.

Most Negroes visualized the migration as a step toward the economic emancipation of a people who had been tied to the southern soil and confined to common labor and personal service in the North. The Chicago *Defender* expressed this philosophy in an editorial shortly before the United States entered the war. Declaring that "it is an ill wind that blows no one good," Editor Abbott saw the European war not only as "bloody, tragic and deplorable" but also as "opportunity." Coldly realistic, he developed his apologia for encouraging the migration. The European war, he said,[5]

. . . has caused the people of this and other neutral countries to prosper greatly in a financial way. It has meant that the thousands who a year ago were dependent upon charity are today employed and making a comfortable living for themselves and their families. The colored man and woman are, and must be for some years to come, laborers. There is no line of endeavor that we cannot fit ourselves for. These same factories, mills and workshops that have been closed to us, through necessity are being opened to us. We are to be given a chance, not through choice but because it is expedient. Prejudice vanishes when the almighty dollar is on the wrong side of the balance sheet. . . .

Give the best that is in us when we answer the call. It is significant that the great west is calling to the southern black man to leave his old home and come out here where the prospects are bright for the future. Slowly but surely all over this country we are gradually edging in first this and then that place, getting a foothold before making a place for our brother. By this only can the so-called race problem be solved. It is merely a question of a better and a closer understanding between the races. We are Americans and must live together, so why not live in peace?

Negroes were getting the foothold, but the peace and understanding did not follow. White Chicagoans viewed the migrants with mixed feelings. As laborers they were indispensable. As neighbors they would have to be tolerated. Union men were apprehensive. Only "Big Bill" Thompson, the Republican Mayor, and his coterie of politicians truly welcomed them, as they pondered the traditional political loyalties of the Negro people and watched the First and Second Ward Black Belt precincts swell amazingly.

The attitudes of the general public were undoubtedly shaped to some extent by Chicago's newspaper headlines and stories which, day after day, commented in a none too friendly vein: [6]

HALF A MILLION DARKIES FROM DIXIE SWARM TO THE NORTH TO BETTER THEMSLEVES

NEGROES INCITED BY GERMAN SPIES
Federal Agents Confirm Reports of New Conspiracy in South;
Accuse Germans for Exodus from South

2,000 SOUTHERN NEGROES ARRIVE IN LAST TWO DAYS
Stockyards Demand for Labor Cause of Influx

COMMITTEE TO DEAL WITH NEGRO INFLUX
Body Formed to Solve Problem Due to Migration to Chicago
from South

WORK OUT PLANS FOR MIGRATING NEGROES
Influx from the South Cared For by the Urban League
and Other Societies

Negroes were rapidly replacing foreigners as Chicago's "problem."

BLACK LEBENSRAUM

The sudden influx of Negroes into Chicago immediately resolved itself into a struggle for living space. Between 1900 and 1914, the Black Belt and its satellite areas had absorbed over ten thousand Negroes without any serious difficulty. Now the saturation point was reached, and although the migrants had jobs, there were literally no houses to accommodate them. Building construction had virtually ceased with the outbreak of the war. Doubling-up and overcrowding became inevitable. The Black Belt had to expand, and this situation aroused exaggerated fears throughout the city. Where would the black masses, still bearing the mark of the plantation upon them, find a place to live?

As in the case of immigrants, the bulk of the southern migrants during the First World War gravitated first to those areas of their "colony" where rents were cheapest and housing poorest. They took over the old, dilapidated shacks near the railroad tracks and close to the vice area. These neighborhoods had been abandoned in the previous decade by Negroes who became more prosperous and were able to move away. Now their less affluent brothers replaced them.

This tremendous demand for houses resulted in an immediate sky-rocketing of rents for all available accommodations and in the opening of new residential areas to Negroes. There were tremendous profits to be made by both colored and white realtors who could provide houses. And so the spread of the Negro areas of residence began, with the whites fleeing before them. Artificial panics were sometimes created in white areas by enterprising realtors who raised the cry, "The Negroes are coming," and then proceeded to double the rents after the whites had fled.[7]

By 1920 a pincers movement of the Negro population had begun along the two boundaries of the Black Belt, a mile apart, and the pocket in between had begun to close up. (Figure 6.) As Negroes moved in, they bought the synagogues and churches, often at highly inflated prices, took over the parks and playgrounds, and transformed white and mixed communities into solidly Negro areas.

To the west of the Black Belt were the Irish, traditional enemies of the Negroes in Chicago; to the east were native-Americans and the more prosperous Jews, guarding jealously the approaches to the desirable lake front where they had made investments in residential property. The Negroes pressed against both communities, and as they swept southward, the whites in their path moved east and to the outlying areas of the city—but homes were scarce.

The impact of the expanding Black Belt on institutions in white middle-class communities has been vividly described by the pastor of Chicago's oldest white Baptist church, which was eventually sold to Negroes:[8]

. . . In 1915 the cry was heard, "The Negroes are coming." . . . The church reported . . . in 1918, "Our church has been greatly handicapped during the past year by the great influx of colored people and the removal of many Whites." . . . The Negroes coming from the South by tens of thousands, lured by the promise of high wages in the packing houses, mills, and railroad yards of Chicago, swarmed to the blocks surrounding

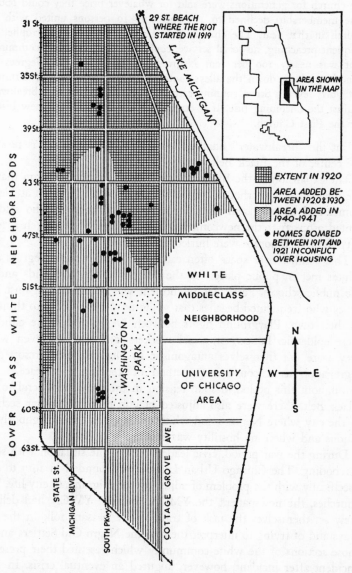

Figure 6
EXPANSION OF THE BLACK BELT

29 ST. BEACH WHERE THE RIOT STARTED IN 1919

31 St.
35St.
39St.
43St.
47St.
51St.
60St.
63St.

LAKE MICHIGAN

AREA SHOWN IN THE MAP

NEIGHBORHOODS

LOWER CLASS WHITE

EXTENT IN 1920

AREA ADDED BE-TWEEN 1920 & 1930

AREA ADDED IN 1940-1941

HOMES BOMBED BETWEEN 1917 AND 1921 IN CONFLICT OVER HOUSING

WHITE

MIDDLE CLASS

NEIGHBORHOOD

WASHINGTON PARK

UNIVERSITY OF CHICAGO AREA

N
W — E
S

STATE ST.
MICHIGAN BLVD.
SOUTH PKWY.
COTTAGE GROVE AVE.

Adapted from map in *The Negro in Chicago*, Chicago Commission on Race Relations, University of Chicago Press, 1922.

the church building. Beautiful homes occupied by families belonging to the church for generations were sold for whatever price they could obtain. The membership declined to 403 and only 10 persons united with the church in that year. The church was face to face with catastrophe. No eloquent preaching, no social service, could save a church in a community that was nearly 100 per cent Negro. . . . Meanwhile the Negroes are steadily pushing down the alleys southward with their carts of furniture, but Forty-seventh Street running east and west still stands as a breakwater against the oncoming tide. If it crumbles there will be some new history for the First Church.

But the "breakwater" finally burst. Forty-seventh Street is now in the center of the Black Belt.

The expansion of the Black Belt developed so much friction that in the invaded neighborhoods bombs were occasionally thrown at Negro homes and those of real-estate men, white and colored, who sold or rented property to the newcomers. From July 1, 1917, to March 1, 1921, fifty-eight such bombs were hurled.[9] (Figure 6.)

This conflict over space often came to a head where Negroes and whites met in public places—at the beaches and playgrounds and in the public schools. Particular resentment was manifested against Negroes who frequented beaches that white people had come to think of as their own. Playground fights between Negro and white children were epidemic. Policemen, social workers, and teachers, even when they were not themselves antagonistic to Negroes, often resorted to segregation as a convenient method of keeping the peace.[10] Yet throughout this period, despite tension in the areas peripheral to the Black Belt, there were also adjusted neighborhoods in other sections of the city where Negroes and whites maintained their neighborly relations and where no hostility was evident.[11]

During the war period, civic leaders viewed the situation with some foreboding. The Chicago Urban League was founded in 1917 to deal specifically with the problem of adjusting the migrants to city life. The churches, the newspapers, the YMCA, and the YWCA had deliberately set themselves the task of training the peasant folk in the city ways and of trying to interpret them to the Negro Old Settlers and to those sections of the white community which resented their presence. Incident after incident, however, augured an eventual crisis. In 1919 it came.

CHAPTER 4

Race Riot and Aftermath

RIOT (1919)

HERE AND THERE THROUGHOUT AMERICA, THE TENSIONS OF POSTWAR RE-adjustment flared into open violence. On the labor front and along the color-line, deep-laid frustrations, uneasy fears, and latent suspicions bobbed to the surface. Group antagonisms suppressed and sublimated by the war effort now returned with doubled fury. For labor, there were the "Palmer raids"; for the Negro, lynchings and riots. The South, particularly, was nervous. Returning Negro soldiers, their horizons widened through travel, constituted a threat to the caste system. They must be kept in their place. A wave of interracial conflicts swept the country involving communities in the North as well as in the South.

Chicago was not spared its measure of violence. The sporadic bombing of Negro homes in 1918 was but the prelude to a five-day riot in 1919 which took at least thirty-eight lives, resulted in over five hundred injuries, destroyed $250,000 worth of property, and left over a thousand persons homeless. For the first time since 1861 the Negro was the center of a bloody drama. Then he was the hero; now he was the villain.[1]

The generally disturbed background out of which the Chicago riot exploded is revealed by a news item in the Chicago *Tribune* for July 4, 1917, reporting a protest meeting against a bloody riot which had occurred in East St. Louis, Illinois. The article, headlined, "LAWYER WARNS NEGROES HERE TO ARM SELVES," quoted one of Chicago's most respected and conservative Negro leaders as saying, "Arm yourselves now with guns and pistols." Another equally prominent leader was quoted as declaring that he "hoped God would demand 100,000 white lives in the War for each Negro slaughtered in East St. Louis." [2]

The Chicago riot began on a hot July day in 1919 as the result of an altercation at a bathing beach. A colored boy swam across the imaginary line which was supposed to separate Negroes from whites at the Twenty-ninth Street beach. He was stoned by a group of white boys. During the ensuing argument between groups of Negro and white bathers, the boy was drowned. Colored bathers were enraged. Rumor swept the beach, "White people have killed a Negro." The resulting fight, which involved the beach police and the white and colored crowd, set off six days of rioting. (Figure 6.)

Pitched battles were fought in the Black Belt streets. Negroes were snatched from streetcars and beaten; gangs of hoodlums roamed the Negro neighborhood, shooting at random. Instead of the occasional bombings of two years before, this was a pogrom. But the Negroes fought back.

Attacks and reprisals were particularly bitter up and down the western and southern boundary between the Irish neighborhoods and the Black Belt. Here youthful white gangs—the so-called athletic clubs—functioning with the tacit approval of the ward politicians who sponsored them, raided the Negro community, attacking the people whom for years they had derided as "jigs," "shines," "dinges," "smokes," and "niggers," and who were now fair game. The rising smoke from burning homes in the white neighborhoods around the stockyards and the railroad tracks, during the next two days, was silent evidence of the embittered Negroes' reprisals.

The reaction of most colored civic leaders was ambivalent. Publicly they were constrained to be conciliatory and to curb the masses who did the actual fighting. Privately, despite a recognition of the horrors of the riot, like Negroes of all classes they justified the fighting as self-defense and as proof that Negroes would not supinely suffer mistreatment. They did not view a riot as unmitigated evil if it focused attention upon injustices. To them it held the same paradoxical elements of good emerging from evil that Wilson saw in the First World War or Lenin in the Russian Revolution.

There were some, however, particularly among Old Settlers,* who viewed the riot as the tragic end of a golden age of race relations. They were very bitter against the southern Negroes, who, they felt, had brought this catastrophe upon them. A group of representative business and professional men met to devise means for ending the disorder. Among the speakers was a lawyer who had come to Chicago

* A term used by both Negroes and whites in Chicago to designate persons who lived in Chicago prior to the First World War.

from Georgia by way of Canada in 1893, studied law, and amassed some wealth. He insisted that "a lot of the trouble is due to Negroes from the South" and called upon "some representative Negroes from the same part of the country [to] do what they can to help quiet things down."

Many Negroes expressed their resentment against one Old Settler who began his address by placing the blame for the riot on the colored population, stating that "One of the chief causes of the trouble is that the colored men have been taught they must act on the policy of an eye for an eye and a tooth for a tooth."

They condemned him as an "Uncle Tom" * when he continued:

"This starts a series of reprisals that is likely to go on until the white man will get mad, and if he does we know what will happen to the man of color. Some of us forget that the white man has given us freedom, the right to vote, to live on terms of equality with him, to be paid well for our work, and to receive many other benefits."

They ridiculed him as a "white man's nigger" for his warning:

"If the white man should decide that the black man has proved he is not fit to have the right to vote, that right may be taken away. We might also find it difficult to receive other favors to which we have been accustomed, and then what would happen to us? We must remember that this is a white man's country. Without his help we can do nothing. When we fight the white man we fight ourselves. We can start a riot but it takes the white man to stop it. We are not interested now in what started the riot, but how to stop it. The Germans thought these same people were so easy-going that they wouldn't fight, and they kept stirring things up until the Americans got mad. That ought to be warning enough! If this thing goes on for three days more there will be no jobs for our men to go back to."

They agreed, however, with his solution, provided it were impartially applied: "If the city cannot restore order then let us with the aid of the militia, have martial law, and take the arms away from the hoodlums." [3]

The bitterness felt by even the more conservative Negro leaders is

* "Uncle Tom," the hero of Harriet Beecher Stowe's famous novel of the abolitionist era, has become for colored people a symbol of the subservient Negro. The term thus serves as a satirical condemnation of any Negro who is thought to be currying favor with white people.

plainly revealed in the tone of the annual report of Provident Hospital for 1919. Proud of the efficiency with which it handled riot casualties, the hospital board detailed its activities as follows:[4]

. . . A crowd of young white toughs from in and near Wentworth Avenue, mainly mere boys, began raids into the colored district, destroying, wounding and killing as they went. On one of these trips the raiders shot into the hospital. That evening fifteen victims were treated at the hospital, one white, the rest colored . . . the majority stabbed or clubbed, and a few shot.

As early as three o'clock in the afternoon on Monday, a mob gathered about the hospital. Feeling was running high. Many of the nurses, worn and tired by long hours of excitement and hard work, found human nature too weak to stand the hideous sights and bloodshed and begged to be taken away . . . but except for short spells of hysteria they were at their posts every minute of the time without sleep and without proper nourishment, for it was difficult from the start to get food into the hospital.

During the twenty-four hours from midnight Sunday to midnight Monday, seventy-five victims were taken care of. A number were taken by friends after having received treatment and a number died. Of these patients nine were white. Cots were placed in the wards and in the emergency room until every available space was occupied; then the victims had to lie upon the floor.

The demand on the hospital surgical supplies and food supplies was heavy; furnishings and equipment suffered; surgical instruments were lost and broken; mattresses were ruined, and furniture was wrecked.

The references to the treatment of white patients were a deliberate build-up for two devastating paragraphs:

It should be borne in mind that the conditions in the colored district were exactly reversed in certain white localities where any offending colored person who appeared was ruthlessly slaughtered, whether man, woman, or baby. From these localities came the raiding parties that caused substantially all the trouble.

The white doctors, of course, were not in attendance during this time and many of the colored staff doctors and the three colored house internes worked day and night; sometimes six operations were in progress at one time.

The daily newspapers headlined the Riot as big news, at the same time editorializing against it. The *New Majority,* organ of the Chicago Federation of Labor, prominently displayed an article, "FOR

WHITE UNION MEN TO READ," reminding the workers of their "hatred of violence on the picket line" and insisting that a heavy responsibility rested on them "not because they had anything to do with starting the present trouble, but because of their advantageous position to help end it." [5] The general public watched and read, but did not participate. Probably its sympathies were divided and its loyalties confused.

The Riot was ended on its sixth day by the state militia, belatedly called after the police had shown their inability, and in some instances their unwillingness, to curb attacks on Negroes.

RECONCILIATION (1920-1922)

One result of the Riot was an increased tendency on the part of white Chicagoans to view Negroes as a "problem." The rapid influx from the South had stimulated awareness of their presence. The elections of 1915 and 1917 had indicated their growing political power in the Republican machine—a circumstance viewed with apprehension by both the Democratic politicians and the "good government" forces. Now the Riot, the screaming headlines in the papers, the militia patrolling the streets with fixed bayonets, and the accompanying hysteria embedded the "Negro problem" deeply in the city's consciousness.

Civic leaders, particularly, were concerned. They decided that the disaster demanded study, so Governor Lowden appointed the nonpartisan, interracial Chicago Commission on Race Relations to investigate the causes of the Riot and to make recommendations. For the next twenty years its suggestions set the pattern of activity for such civic groups as the Urban League, the YMCA, and various public agencies. The Commission's report was the first formal codification of Negrowhite relations in Chicago since the days of the Black Code.

After a year of study the Commission reported that it could suggest no "ready remedy," no "quick means of assuring harmony between the races," but it did offer certain suggestions in the hope that "mutual understanding and sympathy between the races will be followed by harmony and co-operation." It based its faith on "the civic conscience of the community" and opined that "progress should begin in a direction steadily away from the disgrace of 1919."

Immediately after the Riot there had been some sentiment favoring a segregation ordinance. The alderman of one white ward introduced a resolution in the City Council asking for an interracial commission to investigate the causes of the Riot and "to equitably fix a zone or zones . . . for the purpose of limiting within its borders the residence of only colored or white persons." Alderman Louis B. Anderson, Mayor Thompson's colored floor leader, "spoke with acerbity and resentment" [6] against the resolution, and it was referred to the judiciary committee and subsequently dropped. The Governor's Commission, too, was emphatic in its repudiation of such a solution, declaring that:

"We are convinced by our inquiry . . . that measures involving or approaching deportation or segregation are illegal, impracticable and would not solve, but would accentuate, the race problem and postpone its just and orderly solution by the process of adjustment."

The Negro had come to Chicago to stay!

The Commission was very specific in its charges and did not hesitate to allocate responsibility for the conditions which produced the Riot. Even governmental agencies were asked to assume their share of the blame. To the police, militia, state's attorney, and courts, the Commission recommended the correction of "gross inequalities of protection" at beaches and playgrounds and during riots; rebuked the courts for facetiousness in dealing with Negro cases, and the police for unfair discrimination in arrests. It suggested the closing of the white adolescent "athletic clubs." It asked the authorities to "promptly rid the Negro residence areas of vice resorts, whose present exceptional prevalence in such areas is due to official laxity." The City Council and administrative boards were asked to be more vigilant in the condemnation and razing of "all houses unfit for human habitation, many of which the Commission has found to exist in the Negro residence areas." In such matters as rubbish and garbage disposal, as well as street repair, Negro communities were said to be shamefully neglected. Suggestions were made that more adequate recreational facilities be extended to Negro neighborhoods, but also that Negroes should be protected in their right to use public facilities anywhere in the city.

The Board of Education was asked to exercise special care in selecting principals and teachers in Negro communities; to alleviate overcrowding and double-shift schools; to enforce more carefully the regulations regarding truancy and work-permits for minors, and to establish adequate night schools. Restaurants, theaters, stores, and other places of public accommodation were informed that "Negroes are entitled by law to the same treatment as other persons" and were urged to govern their policies and actions accordingly.

Employers and labor organizations were admonished in some detail against the use of Negroes as strike-breakers and against excluding them from unions and industries. "Deal with Negroes as workmen on the same plane as white workers," was the suggestion. Negroes were urged to join labor unions. "Self-seeking agitators, Negro or white, who use race sentiment to establish separate unions in trades where existing unions admit Negroes to equal membership" were roundly condemned.

As to the struggle for living space, a section of the report directed toward the white members of the public reiterated the statement that Negroes were entitled to live anywhere in the city. It pointed out several neighborhoods where they had lived harmoniously with white neighbors for years, insisted that property depreciation in Negro areas was often due to factors other than Negro occupancy, condemned arbitrary advance of rents, and designated the amount and quality of housing as "an all-important factor in Chicago's race problem." The final verdict was that "this situation will be made worse by methods tending toward forcible segregation or exclusion of Negroes."

Not all of the Commission's advice and criticism was directed at public agencies and white persons, however. The Negro workers who had so recently become industrialized were admonished to "abandon the practice of seeking petty advance payments on wages and the practice of laying off work without good cause." There was an implied criticism of the colored community, too, in a statement urging Negroes "to contribute more freely of their money and personal effort to the social agencies developed by public-spirited members of their group; also to contribute to the general social agencies of the community." Negroes were asked to protest "vigorously and continuously . . . against the presence in their residence areas of any vicious resort" and to assist in the prevention of vice and crime.

The Commission expressed particular concern over growing race consciousness, a phenomenon of which the riot itself was evidence. The Negro community was warned that "while we recognize the propriety and social values of race pride among Negroes . . . thinking and talking too much in terms of race alone are calculated to promote separation of race interests and thereby to interfere with racial adjustment." Negro newspapers were advised to exercise greater care and accuracy in reporting incidents involving whites and Negroes and to abandon sensational headlines and articles on racial questions. The investigation had revealed the existence of several small Negro groups, such as the Garveyites and Abyssinians, who were bitterly opposed to any interracial collaboration. The Commission rebuked them indirectly: "We recommend to Negroes the promulgation of sound racial doctrines among the uneducated members of their group, and the discouragement of propaganda and agitators seeking to inflame racial animosity and to incite Negroes to violence." There was, finally, a word of commendation for the work of "the Chicago Urban League, the Negro churches, and other organizations in facilitating the adjustment of migrant Negroes from the South to the conditions of living in Chicago."

In addition to specific recommendations of the type referred to above, the report proposed a long-range educational program grounded in the belief that "no one, white or Negro, is wholly free from an inheritance of prejudice in feeling and in thinking. . . . Mutual understanding and sympathy . . . can come completely only after the disappearance of prejudice. Thus the remedy is necessarily slow."

Social and civic organizations, labor unions and churches, were asked "to dispel false notions of each race about the other," such as "the common disposition, arising from erroneous tradition and literature, to regard all Negroes as belonging to one homogeneous group and as being inferior in mentality and morality, given to emotionalism, and having an innate tendency toward crime, especially sex crime." Prominent among the myths which the Commission sought to explode was one which drew the following comment: "We commend to the attention of employers who fear clashes or loss of white workers by taking on Negro workers the fact that in 89 per cent of the industries investigated by this Commission, Negroes were found working in close association with white employees, and that friction between these elements had rarely been manifested."

In implementing such a program, a frequent interchange of speakers between Negro and white groups was urged. Public-school principals and teachers were asked to "encourage participation by children of both races in student activities as a means of promoting mutual understanding and good race relations in such schools and in the community." The daily press, which had been excoriated by the report, was asked to tone down its sensational treatment of Negro crime and to print more news about Negro achievement. And as a concession to that touchy aspect of Negro-white relations referred to in the Eighties by the *Conservator,* the Commission recommended the capitalization of the word "Negro" in racial designations, and avoidance of the word *nigger* "as contemptuous and needlessly provocative." [7]

OLD SETTLERS AND NEW

When the Great Migration began there were about forty-four thousand Negroes in Chicago. When it ceased there were over a hundred thousand. As has been seen, the impact of this influx upon the white community resulted in a race riot. Its effect on the colored Old Settlers, while less dramatic, was nevertheless disturbing.

The southern migrants reacted enthusiastically to the economic opportunities and the freer atmosphere of the North. But the Old Settlers were far from enthusiastic over the migrants, despite the fact that many of them were eventually to profit by the organization of the expanding Negro market and the black electorate. The Riot, to them, marked a turning point in the history of Chicago. Even today, as they reconstruct the past, they look back on an era before that shattering event when all Negroes who wanted to work had jobs, when a premium was placed on refinement and gentility, and when there was no prejudice to mar the relations between Negroes and whites. As they see it, the newcomers disturbed the balance of relationships within the Negro community and with the white community. From their point of view, the migrants were people who knew nothing of the city's traditions, were unaware of the role which Negroes had played in the political and economic life of Chicago, and did not appreciate the "sacrifices of the pioneers."

Old Settlers still complain that the migrants "made it hard for all of us." Typical of such statements is that of a woman who came to Chicago as a child in the Nineties: "There was no discrimination in Chicago during my early childhood days, but as the Negroes began coming to Chicago in numbers it seems they brought discrimination with them."

Another woman, whose family arrived in 1906, insists that "There's just as much difference in Chicago now as to what it was then as night and day. Why, you could work anywhere. You could even *demand* what you wanted, but you can't do that now. The people wasn't so prejudiced then as they are now."

The theme of these denunciations is usually the idea that the migrants "didn't know how to act" or that they "spoiled things," rather than the mere fact of an increase in the number of Negroes. Occasionally, the remarks are tinged with scorn and bitterness, as in the case of a colored civil engineer who came to Chicago before the Spanish-American War:

"As far as Negroes are concerned, there were very few here then, and the ones that were here had been here for years. They were just about civilized and didn't make apes out of themselves like the ones who came here during 1917-18. We all suffer for what one fool will do."

Old Settlers sometimes cite specific areas of activity in which they insist little prejudice was shown. One of them paints a glowing picture of the "good old days":

"During that time [1912] there wasn't any difference shown in color at all. In the Loop itself they had Negro clerks in the leading stores. So far as professional and businessmen were concerned, the colored doctors had as many white customers as colored. During that time, people would get the first doctor they could, regardless of color. White people didn't pay any attention to your color. In fact, I went everywhere I wanted to go and there was no difference shown me, and you can look at my color and see that nobody'd mistake me for any other nationality. You take the restaurants—you could go into any of them downtown that you wanted to and you would be served courteously."

Another Old Settler, a son of slave parents, came to the city in 1887 from Missouri at the age of nineteen. He mentions the prevalence of miscegenation as an index to the freedom existing at the time:

"In those days Chicago was in its youth. I was a young man and soon got a job waiting table in various restaurants and working in hotels. I made eighteen dollars a month.

"Well, all the Negroes lived down round the Loop. Those were the good old days. There was some colored men that had white wives and they lived good and was respectable. My aunt lived on Twenty-second and Cottage—I lived with her. There was a white family lived there and we all got along fine."

Much of this testimony must be discounted as retrospective myth, but the fact remains that the Great Migration and the Riot profoundly altered relationships between Negroes and the white residents of Chicago and changed the basic economic and social structure of the Negro community. In 1910 Negroes formed a small, almost insignificant part of the city's life. By 1920 there were enough to attract attention, and the rapidity of the influx had excited apprehension.

The bulk of the migrants came to the city from the semifolk culture of the rural South where the daily round was timed by what one eminent anthropologist has called "the great clocks of the sky," [8] and where the yearly rhythm of life was set by the cultivation of the cotton and the cane. Their first task was to adjust themselves to a modern industrial city. Life in the city involved the substitution of the clock for the sun and the discipline of the factory for that of the agricultural cycle. It meant, too, an adjustment to a complex world with a wide variety of associations and churches, a multitude of recreational outlets, and new opportunities in industry and politics.

When the migrants first poured into the city, social agencies and community institutions made a conscious effort to adjust them to city life. But the Negro community as it exists today is not so much the product of any conscious manipulation by social agencies and Old Settlers as it is a natural growth. The migrants were gradually absorbed into the economic, social, and political life of the city. They have influenced and modified it. The city has, in turn, changed them.

The introduction of over fifty thousand new individuals into the Black Belt within a period of ten years swelled the membership of all existing organizations to the bursting point. As groups of migrants found their congenial intellectual and social levels, old organizations accepted new members; additional units of older associations and churches were formed; new types of organizations came into being. Old social patterns, too, were often modified by the migrants who brought their southern customs. Leaders sometimes had to shift their appeals and techniques to deal with the newcomers. New leaders poured up from the South to challenge and supplement or supplant the indigenous leadership. Old Settlers could not isolate the newcomers. They were eventually swamped by them.

The migrants found a functioning political machine in the Black Belt which welcomed their participation. From the South where they were disfranchised they came into a community where the Negro vote was not only permitted but was actually cultivated. The migrants learned quickly, and they were soon incorporated into the First Ward machine in the bailiwick of the news-making bosses, "Bath-house John" Coughlin and "Hinky Dink" Kenna. In the Negro Second Ward they learned that the political life of the community was allied with the world of the saloon and the gaming house. They learned to deal with such influential figures as "Mushmouth" Johnson, the gambler, and "Teenan" Jones, the saloon-keeper, those powerful and almost legendary figures of the Negro demimonde and underworld. It was all new and exciting. The migrants accepted it with gusto and found their place in the pattern, often learning to play the game of politics with skill and daring.

In 1910 Chicago's Negroes were a relatively small group of servants. By 1920 they formed a large segment of the industrial proletariat. Between war's end in 1918 and war's beginning in 1939, over 100,000 more Negroes were absorbed by Chicago's rapidly expanding economy, and the measure of their fate was keyed to the crescendos and diminuendos of the American life during the Twenties and Thirties.

CHAPTER 5

Between Two Wars

GETTING A FOOTHOLD (1919-1924)

THE BLACK BELT BECAME THE BLACK METROPOLIS IN THE TWENTY YEARS between the close of the First World War and the beginning of the Second. The fifty or sixty thousand Negroes who came to the city during the Great Migration had no intention of returning to the South. Despite bombs and riots they insisted upon a place to live within the city, and upon room for friends and relatives who followed them North and for the children who would be born in Midwest Metropolis. By 1925, the city had adjusted itself to the obvious fact that a rapidly growing Negro community was there to stay. Negroes had secured a foothold.

Although Negroes had to fight block-by-block for houses during the war years, they did not have any trouble getting jobs. With the close of the war they found themselves in a precarious position. Returning soldiers wanted their old jobs or better ones. As industries retrenched, Negroes were either fired outright or asked to work at very low wages. White workers became apprehensive over a large pool of unorganized Negroes that could be used to keep wages low. Three years after the war a minor depression wiped out most of the gains which Negro women had made in light manufacturing and in the garment industry. The same year Negroes were used to break a stockyards strike and although they became permanently established in that industry they earned the bitter antagonism of Irish, Polish and Italian workers. In 1924, another recession resulted in widespread unemployment among Negroes. By 1925, however, a boom was under way and racial conflict in industry as well as unemployment subsided. Gangsters replaced Negroes in the civic consciousness as Social Problem No. 1.

THE FAT YEARS

"Behold now the days of super-speed, of super-brilliance, of super-power," wrote Henry Justin Smith, referring to the Twenties in Chicago; "American energy not only had survived the war, but apparently had been redoubled by it. . . . Chicago caught the pace—the amazing, dazzling, even perilous pace of the third decade." [1] This is the Chicago of popular imagination—the Chicago of Al Capone and Jim Colosimo; of Mayor Thompson and Samuel Insull; the Chicago of the great building boom, when the sound of riveting hammers alternated with the fire of sub-machine guns; of skyscrapers and factories thrusting themselves up through a subsoil of slums and speakeasies. People made money in the Twenties and they spent it freely—sometimes with calculation, often with recklessness.

The new white-collar middle class and thousands of frugal skilled and semi-skilled workers rushed to buy or build homes in the suburbs, seeking fresh air and avoiding high taxes. They left the heart of the city to the poor, the newer immigrants, the underworld, the corrupt political machine, and the Negroes. Thousands of other middle-class people stayed within the city limits to stew in bitterness over the foreign-born workers and Negroes who rented and bought the homes of their neighbors who had moved to the outskirts. Among those who stayed within the corporate limits "there arose a diverse community feeling, rather than a civic unity, all up and down the long stretch of city. . . . New centers everywhere—new groups of stores, theaters, churches, garages, and all that the ordinary man needs, with houses clustering about, neighborhood interests developing, improvement-associations, parent-teacher clubs, art and literary societies. More than a hundred Chicagos, there were, within the one Chicago." [2]

And among the "hundred" was Black Metropolis.

The five years from 1924 to 1929 were no doubt the most prosperous ones the Negro community in Chicago had ever experienced. A professional and business class arose upon the broad base of over seventy-five thousand colored wage-earners, and was able for a brief period to enjoy the fruits of its training and investment. Throughout the Twenties, additional migrants from the rural South swelled the size of the Black Belt market. The Fat Years were at hand.

The Negroes spread along the once fashionable South Parkway and

Michigan Boulevard, closing up the pocket which existed in 1920 (see Figure 6, p. 63), taking over the stone-front houses and the apartments, buying the large church edifices and opening smaller churches in houses and stores, establishing businesses, and building a political machine as they went. By 1925 the Black Belt business center had shifted two miles southward, and those who could afford to do so were trying to move from the slums into more stable residential areas. The masses flowed along persistently as the Black Belt lengthened.

Occasionally a white community resisted this expansion violently. In 1921, for instance, the Chicago *Whip,* a militant Negro newspaper, assailed Mayor Thompson for refusing to see a delegation of Negroes who wanted to protest against several bombings. "[He] has only yelped something about five-cent fares," the paper charged almost hysterically, "while our property was blown into smithereens, while our sleeping babes have been torpedoed from their mothers' arms. . . . The City Council laughs at the 'floor leader's' [a Negro] jokes while the poor black people who put him into office toss in troubled slumber with nightmares of bursting bombs." [3]

In one block on Michigan Avenue, a synagogue bought by a Negro Baptist congregation was repeatedly bombed in 1925. (The colored congregation ultimately took out an insurance policy against bombing.) But bombings became rarer and rarer, and finally ceased. To deny living space to Negroes, law-abiding white Chicagoans developed something more subtle than a "pineapple" tossed by a "gorilla" hired by a respectable "neighborhood improvement association." In the spring of 1928, the Hyde Park *Herald,* a neighborhood newspaper, reported a speech [4] proclaiming the efficacy of a new device for locking Negroes within the Black Belt (italics are the authors'):

. . . Judge —— of the Chicago Real Estate Board, before the Kiwanis Club of Hyde Park at the Windemere East, in summarizing the earnest and conscientious work of the Board for the last twelve months . . . proceeded to explain the fine network of contracts that like a marvelous delicately woven chain of armor is being raised from the northern gates of Hyde Park at 35th Street and Drexel Boulevard to Woodlawn, Park Manor, South Shore, Windsor Park, and all the far-flung white communities of the South Side. And of what does this armor consist? *It consists of a contract which the owner of the property signs not to exchange with, sell to, or lease to any member of a race not Caucasian.*

The tensions of the Riot period gradually subsided, but the migration left a residue of antagonism toward Negroes. There were definite restrictions on the activities of Negroes—restrictions due to deeply laid habit patterns which white Chicagoans shared with other Americans. Most Negroes took the matter philosophically, if not fatalistically—unless they were pushed too hard. Then they were likely to direct a storm of invective or blows at any denial of their rights. Usually they avoided trouble spots and enjoyed the city in situations where they didn't have to bother with white folks.

There were stores and restaurants that didn't like to serve Negroes. To walk into certain downtown hot-spots was unthinkable. To run for any state office higher than Senator from the Black Belt just wasn't done. To hope for a managerial or highly skilled job in industry was ridiculous. To buy or rent a house out of the Black Belt precipitated a storm. But after all, Chicago was in America, not in France or Brazil. It was certainly different from slavery sixty years ago, or from the South today. Negroes liked Midwest Metropolis.

There were evidences on every hand that "the Race was progressing." Here were colored policemen, firemen, aldermen, and precinct captains, state Representatives, doctors, lawyers, and teachers. Colored children were attending the public schools and the city's junior colleges. There were fine churches in the Negro areas, and beautiful boulevards. It seemed reasonable to assume that this development would continue with more and more Negroes getting ahead and becoming educated. There were prophets of doom in the Twenties, but a general air of optimism pervaded the Black Belt, as it did the whole city.

On eight square miles of land a Black Metropolis was growing in the womb of the white. Negro politicians and business and professional men, barred by color from competing for the highest prizes in Midwest Metropolis, saw their destiny linked with the growth of Black Metropolis. Negroes were making money in the steel mills, stockyards, and garment factories, in the hotels and kitchens, on the railroads, and in a hundred other spots. "Why," the leaders asked, "should these dollars be spent with white men or wasted in riotous living? If white men are so determined that Negroes must live separate and apart, why not beat them at their own game?"

What did it matter if white men snubbed black men socially? Negroes were building an attractive home life and "society" of their own. They did not need white intimates.

What did Negro ministers care if white Christians sealed themselves off in Jim Crow congregations? They would take the church or the synagogue that white worshipers abandoned as they fled from contact with their black brothers, and turn it into a worthy house of the Lord (when they had finished paying off the mortgage).

Why should Negro doctors and dentists give a damn that most white folks would rather die than let skilled black fingers repair their vital organs? The Negro masses were gradually learning to trust their own professional men and would some day scorn to enrich white physicians at the expense of their own.

Why beg white stores and offices to rescue educated colored girls from service in the white folks' kitchens and factories? Negroes were learning to support their own businesses, and some day colored entrepreneurs would own all the stores and offices in the Black Belt; cash registers and comptometers and typewriters would click merrily under lithe brown fingers.

If Negroes wanted to pay two cents a day for white papers that stigmatized the group as a menace, picturing them as rapists and buffoons, let them do so—but more and more of them were spending an additional dime each week for a colored paper, where they could read about themselves and their own accomplishments and applaud the verbal body-blows that colored journalists slammed at American race prejudice.

Negroes who, a few years before, had been disfranchised, were voting for Negroes to represent them in the councils of city, state and nation. In 1928, Black Metropolis won the acclaim of Negroes throughout America when it succeeded in electing a colored Congressman—the first Negro to occupy a seat in the House of Representatives since 1901. If Negroes used their political power wisely they could bargain for unlimited concessions from the two parties bidding for their votes.

This was the dream of Black Metropolis, not yet fully realized, but on the way—a hope kept alive by press and pulpit.

To some the dream was inspiring. To many it was a makeshift dream, a substitute for the real American Dream of complete integration into American life. To some who watched Negroes inherit the city's slums, crowded together amid squalor and vice, where schemers, white and black, battened on their blood, the dream seemed a fraud and a delusion. "How can we build a metropolis," they asked, "when we do not control the industries that employ the Negro masses? How can we build the good society when we can't get enough decent houses to live in?"

To others, the development of a greater Black Metropolis was a tactical maneuver within the framework of a broad strategy for complete equality. The very preacher, editors, and politicians who did the most to keep the dream of Black Metropolis alive only half believed in its ultimate realization. They knew that unless the ordinary Negro could have a steady income and could share more fully in the wave of prosperity, their own careers would always be insecure. "But," they reasoned, "if Negroes could support their own business and professional class, if they would rally about their politicians, some day their leaders might teach them how to throw their weight in such a way as to win the respect of the white world." Negroes had votes and they were ac-cumulating money. If they used both skillfully, they could force the city to grant them more room in which to live, better jobs and, some day, perhaps, *full* equality. In the meantime, successful individuals would become living examples of what all Negroes could do if they got a chance. Gradually the city would begin to accept Negroes in high places as people, and not as Negroes. The Jews had done it—why couldn't Negroes?

Symbolic of this era of optimism was a colored banker, Jesse Binga, who in 1893 had come to Chicago penniless. Within thirty-five years he had risen from Pullman porter to real-estate speculator and then to banker. A feature writer for a Chicago daily sought him out in 1928 to get his story of Black Metropolis. Binga talked of the forty million dollars which Negroes had to their credit in Chicago's banks; of the four billion dollars' worth of property on which they paid taxes; of the two million dollars they had contributed to charity that year.

He also spoke with pride of "a new generation of business and professional men, coming to the fore"; of the seven big insurance companies "managed by colored people for colored policy-holders—$1,000,000 in premiums a year." He dwelt at length upon the hope which Negro businessmen had of eventually controlling the Negro market and providing jobs for young men and women as clerks, sales-men, cashiers, and managers. He cited as examples the two colored banks, one of them his own. Five years before, these banks had been entrusted with less than a hundred and fifty thousand dollars; now, between them they handled four of the forty million dollars that Chicago Negroes had on deposit.

The Black Belt was experiencing the Fat Years. When Jesse Binga saw an unending vista of progress and profit in the Negroes' future, if only they would support their business and professional men, he was voicing the confident hope of thousands.

THE LEAN YEARS

During the Fat Years, the Negro newspapers "plugged" the dream of Black Metropolis while blasting away at the pattern of white attitudes which created and perpetuated it. Their major thrusts were reserved for those who denied Negroes equal economic opportunity. "Perhaps Negroes could turn their Black Belt into a community of which the city would be proud," they argued, "but only if they were allowed to get better jobs and thus raise their purchasing power and political power." Between 1924 and 1929 the prospects seemed bright.

Then, in 1929, the *Defender* sounded an alarm:

"Something is happening in Chicago and it should no longer go unnoticed. During the past three weeks hardly a day has ended that there has not been a report of another firm discharging its employees, many of whom have been faithful workers at these places for years." [5]

Negroes were advised to "toe the line," work hard and behave decently, in order to impress their employers. By March the paper was thoroughly aroused, and in the mood to find a scapegoat. Its headlines reverted to an old object of attack with a plea for the federal government to "ARREST FOREIGN WORKERS WITHOUT CITIZENSHIP." The paper considered it unfair for "foreigners" to hold jobs while Negroes were jobless, and further charged the foreign-born with being "apt students of segregation" who would not work side by side with Negroes. [6] The Urban League, more sober in its appraisal of the situation, called a conference of leaders in Black Metropolis, after stating that "every week we receive information regarding the discharge of additional Race workers who are being replaced by workers of other races." [7] For the first time in its history, the *Defender* began to advise Negroes to stay in the South.

White papers talked of unending prosperity and were advertising a second World's Fair to celebrate a Century of Progress. But Negroes were a barometer sensitive to the approaching storm. They had reason to fear, while most of Midwest Metropolis seemed to suspect nothing, that the Fat Years were about to end.

Chicago's banking structure broke at its weakest link—in the Black Belt. In July of 1930, Binga's bank closed its doors, while mobs cried in the streets for their savings. Within a month every bank in Black Metropolis was closed. As white housewives balanced the budget, their Negro servants were often the first casualties. When factories cut production, unskilled Negro labor was usually the first to go. Negroes buying homes in the Black Belt and its suburbs suddenly saw their life dreams dissolving. "Past calamities, the grievous incidents bound to afflict an adolescent and quarrelsome city had all been conquered," wrote Lewis and Smith of the early Thirties; "they now appeared easy to overcome compared with the slow crushing movement of a debacle which pulled down one economic edifice after the other. Poverty had spread widely." [8] The Depression had come to Midwest Metropolis and Black Metropolis reflected the general disaster. The Lean Years were at hand.

The first reaction to the Depression was a deep sense of panic and frustration, followed by unorganized demonstrations of frantic mobs. The first organized reaction within Black Metropolis was a movement directed against white men who did business in the Black Belt. A group of ragged pickets walking in front of a Black Belt chain store in the fall of 1929 signalized the beginning of a movement which stirred Black Metropolis as nothing had done since the Race Riot. The attention of Negroes all over the country fastened on Chicago's "Spend Your Money Where You Can Work" Campaign. A Negro newspaper, the *Whip,* risking reprisal from white advertisers, politicians, and mortgage holders, became the aggressive spokesman for applying a boycott against all white business in the Black Belt that would not employ Negroes. The opening shot was fired against a chain grocery which responded to the boycott by hiring three colored girls. (It had never had colored employees before.) The major attack was then leveled against the Woolworth stores, which for a time stubbornly resisted the pressure, but finally hired twenty-one girls, later raising the proportion of colored employees in all stores in Negro neighborhoods to 25 per cent.

Other minor victories convinced the Negro community that the boycott was a useful weapon, and many churches and community organizations united to pay pickets, to hire loudspeakers, to provide bail, and occasionally to supply a detail of members for the picket line.

There was only one loudly dissenting voice, that of the Communists, who insisted that [9]

The triviality of this proposal is obvious on the face of it. It is indeed possible on occasion to kick up a row big enough to force a Woolworth store in Chicago to make a promise. But what has this to do with hundreds of thousands of Negro workers in the coal, iron, steel, oil, automobile and packing industries? . . . There is no substance to the "use of our buying power" proposal; it can only be raised by those whose social vision is bounded by petty industry and petty trade, who see everything not from the viewpoint of the Negro workers—the great mass of the Negro people—but rather from that of the Negro small businessman.

Yet, some people in Black Metropolis branded the boycott campaign itself as Communistic. Others feared that picketing would lead to race riots or to reprisals in the form of more rapid firing of those Negroes who had jobs outside of the Black Belt. But the proposition that stores doing business in colored areas should be forced to hire Negroes was a very popular one.

The boycott campaign opened up a few hundred white-collar jobs. It did not solve the problem of the unemployed thousands. As Negroes watched white artisans coming into their neighborhood to work, or white laborers repairing streets and tracks in the Black Belt, their anger was aroused. On at least one occasion this simmering antagonism exploded with dramatic violence. A mob of unemployed Negroes attacked a group of white laborers who were laying a streetcar track in the Black Belt, chasing them from the site. The Negroes then refused to leave the spot until the Mayor, the colored Congressman, and several traction officials had assured them that colored workers would get a share of the track-laying jobs. Sporadic acts of individual violence against white men working in the Black Belt flared up throughout 1930 and 1931. Some people saw the hand of Communists at work; more careful observers knew that these were merely spontaneous expressions of resentment. Black Metropolis applauded such direct action.

During the first two years of the Depression, hundreds of Negroes faced eviction for nonpayment of rent. Angered by the belief that they were last-hired-first-fired, conscious of their strength since the successful boycott campaign, small groups of young unemployed Negroes formed flying squadrons to resist evictions. The Chicago *Whip* reported such an incident in the summer of 1931:[10]

Declaring their determination to defend the jobless and hungry families which abound on the south side, from eviction by landlords because of their inability to pay rent, a group of young colored radicals . . . restored seven jobless families in the community after they had been evicted by the bailiff's office and their belongings set out in the street.

The first of these cases occurred Wednesday when more than fifty of the group, most of them young men who are themselves sleeping in the Park, restored the belongings of Mrs. K—— W——, a poverty-stricken widow with two small children. . . . The woman, who had been out of work since December, is five months behind in her rent, and had no place to go when she was moved by the officers. A short while after her furniture had been set on the sidewalk, a young radical appeared, and breaking the new lock on the front door, returned her furniture piece by piece, and ordered her to return to the house.

Sometimes the flying squadrons arrived before the police, and directed the family and bystanders to sit on the furniture to prevent its removal. An old spiritual, "I shall not, I shall not be moved," became the theme song of resistance. Landlords and civic authorities again blamed the Communists—and this time they were right.

Throughout the Twenties, Black Metropolis had been hearing new voices talking to the Negro people, voices that spoke strange words: "proletarian," "bourgeoisie," "class struggle," "revolution." They heard the old-line Negro politicians castigated as "misleaders" and "reformists." They saw white men and women standing on street corners with their Negro "comrades," handing out newspapers and leaflets that denounced the "fire-traps" and "rent hogs" in northern Black Belts and painted a Utopian picture of a Negro soviet republic which would arise some day in the South. They had a slogan: BLACK AND WHITE UNITE.

Most of the Negroes in Black Metropolis were too busy enjoying the lush Twenties to pay much attention to these "Reds" or "Communists." But in the early Thirties they began to listen. The Communists' defense of the nine Scottsboro boys stirred the imagination of the Negro people, and thousands of them joined committees and participated in demonstrations. Capitalizing upon this interest, the Communists began a vigorous program of organization in the Black Belt, forming neighborhood Unemployed Councils to demand adequate relief. It was these Councils that led the fight against evictions, and hundreds of non-Communists followed their lead. When eviction notices arrived, it was not unusual for a mother to shout to the children, "Run quick and find the Reds!"

Throughout the spring and summer of 1931 small groups of Negroes under Communist leadership skirmished with the police at the scenes of evictions. Then, one August day, several thousand people decided to march *en masse* to a home in a poverty-stricken neighborhood to replace some furniture. When the police arrived there were at least five thousand people on the spot. The crowd refused to "break it up"; there was some scuffling, and then shooting. Three Negroes lay dead on the pavement when it was over and scores were wounded. Three policemen were badly injured. By nightfall, fifty thousand leaflets had been distributed throughout Black Metropolis, bearing the slogan: DEMAND DEATH PENALTY FOR THE MURDERERS OF THE WORKERS!

The bodies of the dead men were moved to the Odd Fellows' Hall in a run-down Black Belt neighborhood. A guard of honor composed of Negro and white Communists kept vigil, while over eighteen thousand persons viewed the victims. When the funeral procession started for the cemetery thousands of Negroes and white people from all over the city marched in a gigantic protest demonstration. Daily mass meetings were held for a week in a large park adjacent to the Black Belt. The three dead Negroes became the symbol of the city's unemployed masses.

Midwest Metropolis was frightened by this upheaval in the Black Belt. If it had been an out-and-out race riot it would have been understandable. But here was something new: Negroes and whites *together* rioting against the forces of law and order. The Renters' Court immediately suspended all eviction proceedings for an indefinite period. Conservative and progressive Negro leaders went into a huddle with city officials, laying the grievances of Black Metropolis before them and advising immediate action if a "Communist revolution" or a "race riot" was to be averted, and if the ground was to be cut from under the "radicals." The city and the state began to make comprehensive plans for furnishing relief. In fact, the first serious attempts to face the economic crisis in Midwest Metropolis date from this outburst. By demonstrating its discontent, Black Metropolis had set in motion a chain of actions that was to benefit the entire city.

The chaotic turbulence of the early Thirties subsided as various New Deal measures went into effect. Relief and work projects stabilized Black Metropolis. Gradually the Republican grip upon the Negro vote was broken as people began to "vote for bread and butter instead of for the memory of Abraham Lincoln." Organizations of the unemployed, under Socialist and Communist leadership, drew large masses of Negroes into various forms of disciplined petition and protest—against relief cuts, for social security; against discrimination, for housing projects. After 1935, those Negroes who remained in the mass production industries were caught up in the sweeping organizational campaigns of the CIO. The Negro peasants had become proletarians.

New increments of migrants from the South continued to come to Chicago all through the Depression. Between 1930 and 1940 the Negro population increased by more than 43,000. With the collapse of cotton tenancy in the South, and because of discrimination in the dispensing of relief and emergency employment, thousands of Negroes set out for Chicago. Occasionally the Board of Education or one of the daily newspapers would complain that this in-migration was placing a strain upon the city's finances. Negro leaders were quick to remind them that America has no laws against interstate migration, and that, with thousands of white "Okies" and "Arkies" on the road, it was unfair to single out Negroes for attack. Yet, as during the Great Migration, only the politicians really welcomed the migrants—in 1915 the Republicans; in the Thirties, the Democrats, for by 1936 Black Metropolis was a "New Deal town."

The continuous squeezing of Negroes out of industry and the tide of in-migration combined to raise the proportion of Negroes on the relief rolls, until by 1939 four out of every ten persons on relief were Negroes, and five out of every ten Negro families were dependent upon some type of government aid for their subsistence. The Illinois State Commission on the Condition of the Urban Colored Population, reviewing the experiences of the Fat Years and the Lean Years, commented in 1940 that

Given a continuously expanding economy, it is reasonable to assume that Negroes in Chicago would have been able to raise the general level of their skills and to have reduced the disparity between their distribution in industry and that of white workers. But the depression, with a devastating impact, reversed the trend of the Twenties and turned the Negro people from a group with more than its share of the gainfully employed into a population predominantly dependent upon governmental relief.

Between 1935 and 1940, the Negro proletariat seemed doomed to become a *lumpen-proletariat*.

When the first rumblings of the Second World War were heard in Midwest Metropolis, the people of Black Metropolis were living upon WPA and memories. For some, the memories were of the Fat Years. For others the memories were of the chronic southern depression they had just fled. For the former, the Depression seemed a painful, but temporary set-back. For the latter, a $55-a-month WPA check was a net gain when compared with a debt of a bale or two of cotton.

FREEDOM'S WARS

Black Metropolis became aware, long before the city as a whole did, that a Second World War was impending. Negro newspapers were quick to sense the meaning of Fascism and to impart it to their wide reader-audience. A few of the leaders in Black Metropolis were raising money for the Spanish Loyalists at a time when many Americans believed that Franco, Mussolini, and Hitler were doing a salutary police job against Bolshevism. When the Italian legions invaded Ethiopia, the barbershops and street-corners of the Black Belt buzzed with indignation. Haile Selassie became something of a hero to Negroes all over America. A resident of Black Metropolis journeyed to Addis Ababa to become the pilot of the royal family's personal airplane: his exploits were followed with interest. The failure of the Great Powers to halt Italian aggression created widespread distrust of their motives, and in a confused, semi-superstitious sort of way people in Black Metropolis were given to prophesying that those who had sold Ethiopia out would eventually find themselves menaced by the Fascists. When war broke out in Europe few Negroes were surprised, or even very much interested, except in so far as it might stimulate a wave of prosperity in the United States. Anticipation of a war boom reached fever pitch in 1939, and in the years between the inauguration of Lend-Lease and the attack at Pearl Harbor, the main interest of most Negroes was how to get some of the jobs that were opening up.

✦

During the First World War Negroes came into a labor market that needed them. When the Second World War began they were a part of a vast labor surplus. It soon became clear that Negroes were not going to get off the relief rolls until white people had secured jobs in private industry. Black Metropolis seethed with discontent as white men streamed back to work while Negroes generally were being denied employment. Here and there picket lines began to appear around factories on the margins of the Black Belt with signs reading—

HITLER MUST OWN THIS PLANT; NEGROES
CAN'T WORK HERE

IF WE MUST FIGHT, WHY CAN'T WE WORK?

BULLETS KNOW NO COLOR LINE; WHY
SHOULD FACTORIES?

In the forefront of these demonstrations were young people affiliated with the NAACP, churches, and social clubs. Similar demonstrations took place in other northern cities, and in 1940 a militant Negro labor leader, A. Philip Randolph, gave organized form to this widespread discontent by planning the March-on-Washington—a movement that threatened to stage a mass-demonstration in Washington with 50,000 Negroes protesting discrimination in the armed forces and the defense industries. A large contingent from Midwest Metropolis was prepared to participate. But just this threat was sufficient to force the hand of the national administration, which could ill afford such an embarrassment in the midst of a war for the Four Freedoms; and the consequence was the President's Fair Employment Practices Committee, set up as a gesture to avert the imminent March. Black Metropolis, forthwith, began to marshal its cases of discrimination for presentation to the Committee.

Pearl Harbor stimulated a tremendous expansion in the war effort and, as the industries of Midwest Metropolis stepped up production, Negroes were reintegrated into the main stream of industrial life at an accelerated pace. The Fair Employment Practices Committee (FEPC) and the War Manpower Commission took the problem out of the realm of agitation and began to plan for the use of Negro labor as a war measure. By 1944 Midwest Metropolis faced a labor shortage, and a new wave of migration from the South began.

Between 1940 and 1944, 60,000 new Negro migrants arrived in Midwest Metropolis. There were plenty of jobs, but the already trouble-some problems of inadequate housing, congestion, inferior recreational facilities, and overcrowded schools in the Black Belt were aggravated by the influx. Half-forgotten memories of the Great Migration and of the Race Riot and its aftermath were revived among both Negroes and whites. The Negro was once more becoming a "problem" and racial conflict seemed to loom in the offing.

Fear of a racial clash was intensified during the spring and summer of 1943 when serious racial disturbances occurred in Beaumont (Texas), New York, and Detroit, and incipient riots broke out in Los Angeles, Newark, and Philadelphia. In June the Chicago *Tribune,* commenting editorially on the riot of 1919 and the current racial clashes, insisted that "it must not be allowed to happen here again." Upon several occasions it seemed about to happen. A sixteen-year-old colored boy was killed by an over-zealous white policeman and the inciting incident seemed at hand. A white streetcar conductor and a Negro passenger began to fight, and cries of "Lynch him" arose from a few white persons, almost precipitating a riot. A group of white adolescents armed with pick handles and shovels chased a colored boy out of a white neighborhood, and there were rumors that a Negro gang was preparing to march in and "clean up" the white neighbor-hood. The summer passed. Although none of these scattered incidents touched off the riot that everyone expected, the expectation remained, for many people remembered that it was *after* the war that Chicago's race riot of 1919 had occurred.

As soon as word reached Midwest Metropolis in the spring of 1943 that New York's Harlem had been the scene of a riot, Negro and white civic leaders swung into action, intent upon trying to avert a similar outbreak in Chicago. The Negro newspapers, the preachers, and various community leaders urged Black Metropolis to keep cool, to ignore rumors, and to avoid altercations with white people. Depu-tations of Negro leaders, as well as white liberals and union officials, began to petition the Mayor and the police officials to take precau-tionary measures and to assure impartial treatment to Negroes if an outbreak should occur. They also advised the Mayor to appoint a committee to study ways and means of preventing a riot. "During the last war we made a study *after* the riot," commented one Negro poli-tician; "this time let's make the study *before.*" The Mayor was at first reluctant to admit the possibility of a riot. "There is no race trouble in

Chicago," he said; "talk of stopping trouble which is only a myth tends to make trouble." Nevertheless, a few weeks later, at the continued insistence of community leaders, colored and white, he appointed the Mayor's Committee on Race Relations.* With a small grant from the City Council, the Mayor's Committee opened its offices in the central business district, and a Negro economist was hired as full-time executive secretary.

Throughout the summer of 1943 the Committee concentrated its efforts upon preventing a riot. Eight private Committee meetings and two public hearings were held, as well as conferences with police officials, key newspapermen, and various influential persons. The Committee stressed the need to dispel provocative rumors, to counsel patience, and to control adolescent gangs of both races. It appealed to the police officials to lay plans for quickly squelching the first signs of a riot. It also exacted a pledge that if a riot should occur, white policemen would refrain from giving assistance, active or passive, to the whites.

When the summer passed without a riot, the Committee felt that its work had been measurably successful. But it is not easy to evaluate the real efficacy of that work. Undoubtedly the widespread knowledge that the city was prepared to act decisively against rioters had a sobering effect upon would-be disturbers of the peace. It seems less likely, however, that exhortations not to believe or circulate rumors were very effective. That there was no riot may indeed have been due entirely to fortunate accident, since no provocative incident occurred in the Negro community such as the shooting of a Negro soldier which touched off the Harlem riot. Other factors, too, were important. The migration of Negroes into the city during the Second World War did not take on the character of a mass invasion of new and strange people. During the preceding twenty years the city had become used to seeing large numbers of Negroes, and the now large Negro community absorbed

* The Committee had six white members: a banker, a prominent merchant, an outstanding industrialist, a well-known liberal minister, a representative of the Chicago Federation of Labor (AFL), and the president of the Julius Rosenwald Fund who served as chairman. Five Negroes were also selected: the only colored professor in the University of Chicago Medical School, the executive secretary of the Negro branch of the YWCA, the lone Negro member of the national executive board of the CIO, the chairman of the Chicago Housing Authority, and an eminent sociologist—the man who had directed the study of the riot of 1919 and prepared the report for the Chicago Commission on Race Relations.

migrants more easily than the small Black Belt of 1915-19 had done. Also, there was no rapid expansion of the Black Belt in the direction of neighboring white communities to excite fear and stir up violence. Most important, perhaps, were the facts that there were no bitter industrial conflicts involving the use of Negroes as strike-breakers, and that few disturbances occurred over the upgrading of Negroes such as those that took place in Detroit at various times in 1942 and 1943. In fact, the rate of upgrading was relatively slow, and although large masses of Negroes appeared in new industries, the bulk of them were employed in new plants where a tradition against Negroes had not been set and where CIO unions were deliberately preparing white workers to accept Negroes. Finally, there was no wholesale influx of white workers from the South with intense anti-Negro attitudes, as in Detroit.*

The Mayor's Committee may not have been solely responsible for preventing a riot in the summer of 1943, but its activity did focus attention upon the danger of a battle along the color-line. As an expression of the will to prevent a riot it deserves some study. The Committee was primarily concerned with police measures and with appeals to Negroes and whites for mutual forbearance. Yet, from the beginning, it accepted the premise that race riots are symptomatic of deeper-seated social maladjustments. It initiated a search for the cause and cure of racial tension—that latent uneasiness which occasionally bursts forth into violence. Early in 1944, the Committee sponsored the Mayor's Conference on Race Relations to air the underlying sources of trouble in Midwest Metropolis. A Negro sociologist, addressing the first session, suggested that "racial tensions arise when people have not been allowed to participate in the American process and where they have been slowed down in their drives to be like any other group. . . . Tensions have developed in part over the slogans of the country mobilizing itself for war, stimulating the individual to demand the Four Freedoms. . . . Tension has developed in white people who think the Negro is moving too fast or who do not want him to move at all." These were the roots of tension during the Second World War.

* Sporadic incidents involving Negroes and whites tend to snowball into a riot when there has been a period of tension raising the general level of excitability. Normally, they remain isolated conflicts between individuals or small groups. Other Negroes and whites simply view such incidents as spectators and do not pitch into the fray.

The overcrowded northern Black Belts are highly sensitized areas of discontent whose inhabitants are keenly aware of the treatment of Negroes throughout the country. The advent of the Second World War heightened this race-consciousness, for Negroes were not only segregated from whites in the armed forces, but were also Jim-Crowed at post exchanges and theaters in many camps and sometimes humiliated and attacked by civilians in the South. In the early stages of the war, the Marines barred Negroes; the Navy relegated them to the role of messmen; and the Coast Guard was not too enthusiastic about using their services. (The Waves and the Spars did not condescend to accept Negro women until the eve of the 1944 presidential election.) All of this was common knowledge, discussed in the Negro press, on street-corners, and in barbershops. Every rumor of discrimination against Negro soldiers or sailors sent a tremor through Black Metropolis.

Increasing the tension was the fact that when the country emerged from the Depression colored workers had to wait until the pool of white unemployed workers was soaked up before they could get jobs on a large scale. Even when their services were eventually utilized they had to face opposition to their use as skilled workers and foremen, or in clerical pursuits. Thus, in addition to all of the minor irritations incident to a war—rationing, long hours, crowded streetcars and buses, high prices, congested living quarters *—Negroes were confronted with discrimination on the home front and in the armed forces. Yet, at the same time, the war was advertised as a crusade for the Four Freedoms! Apathy and irritation, cynicism and resentment were widespread. The Negro's nerves were on edge.

The outburst in Harlem, the bloody melee in Detroit, and other interracial clashes here and there about the country all had their effect upon Black Metropolis. This identification with the fate of Negroes in other communities was reflected in a rumor which gained currency during the Detroit riot—that several hundred carloads of Negroes from Chicago were on the way bringing arms to aid their racial compatriots. It was against this generally disturbed national background that the Mayor's Committee set itself the task of trying to pluck up the roots of racial tension in Midwest Metropolis. The proceedings of

---

* The congestion within northern Black Belts is in itself conducive to violent outbursts, which can be rationalized in terms of *racial* protest. A rabbit-warren existence results in frayed tempers. This congestion is, as we shall see, a result of a color-line which prevents Negroes from renting houses in the open market.

the Mayor's Conference on Race Relations were published by the City of Chicago in a booklet, *City Planning in Race Relations,* and widely distributed. (The quotations and excerpts that follow are from this booklet.)

It was obvious that much of the tension originated in conditions outside of the control of anyone in Chicago, and one participant in the Mayor's Conference emphasized this point by stating that "so long as there is one single law on the statute books of any state or municipality which deprives Negroes of a single constitutional right, so long will there be racial tensions which at any time [may] lead to racial conflict. America on the national level, therefore, must move swiftly toward the abolishment [*sic*] of all forms of discrimination." Being recent migrants, it was inevitable that Negroes in Black Metropolis would be keenly interested in conditions in the South from which they came and where their friends and relatives still lived.

It was equally evident, however, that there were tension points within Midwest Metropolis itself. Negroes were accusing the city of denying them a square deal. White people were becoming alarmed at the truculent mood of the Negroes. The Mayor's Committee, aware of these circumstances, pledged itself to "work with city officials and civic groups to bring practical improvements in basic conditions that will mean a definite step toward its goal—justice and equal opportunity for all people of Chicago, regardless of race, creed or color." One white speaker posed the problem in concrete terms: "Chicago's mission is not to solve the race problem, but to do certain direct and tangible things that will insure equal access to jobs, to good housing, to health, and to welfare for all groups within the community."

The whole conference proceeded upon the assumption that doing these "direct and tangible things," making these "practical improvements in basic conditions," would reduce dangerous tensions within the Black Belt and diminish the chances of a riot. It was evident from the discussions, however, that most of the participants realized that widening the areas of Negro participation in the life of Midwest Metropolis, while reducing the tension on the Negro side, might actually excite tension among white people. Therefore, throughout the conference, the more conservative white participants placed their emphasis upon "goodwill," "education," and "gradualism." They were opposed to quick and drastic revisions of the Negro's status upward. They feared resistance from the white side. All of the Negro speakers, on the other hand, and some of the whites, called for speedy adjustments to prevent the Negro's frustrations from erupting in violence.*

The proponents of a rapid tempo of change advocated strong government action to insure equality of opportunity. The most outspoken Negro participant, a prominent attorney and former city alderman, referring to an AFL leader's plea for "goodwill" and education to erase the color-line in craft unions, said frankly: "We will not wait, but we are pressing hard to integrate the Negro into all phases of life in this and other communities. Education is not the only answer. The whites also must show some forbearance and co-operation. They must recognize that Negroes are part of America, they are giving their lives and sustenance in this great battle and they are entitled to recognition."

The Negroes were particularly annoyed at the evasions of the representative of the Board of Education who, in defending the city against the charge that Black Belt schools were neglected, had prepared a pamphlet to prove that Negroes were at least better off in Chicago than in the South. One colored speaker said flatly, "I recommend very strongly that we gather up every one of those pamphlets and burn them."

The Executive Secretary of the Mayor's Committee, a prominent young Negro economist, sounded this same note of urgency in his summary of the entire conference: "No one defined exactly how gradual gradualism is, or just exactly what this education is. Those of us who belong to minority groups, however, have been hearing about it for an awfully long time!"

One white speaker, a well-known journalist, attempted to raise the discussion to a higher plane than riot-prevention by reminding the conference that "obviously the purpose of this Committee is something far more than merely to prevent riots or to preserve the outward semblance of order. . . . Because it is right; because it is a democratic imperative; because we in Chicago share the national commitment to the total destruction of fascism in all its forms—let us then build a Chicago which is worthy of the democratic foundation on which it stands."

✦

* The riots in Detroit, New York, and Philadelphia were characterized by intensely aggressive action on the part of Negroes—particularly against white stores. In fact, these riots may be interpreted as violent mass protests by Negroes rather than as attacks upon Negroes by whites. In only one of these cities did any large number of white persons participate—Detroit.

The remaining chapters of this book constitute a study of Black Metropolis during the Depression and the early period of the Second World War. These years cover a crisis period in the history of Western Civilization. They mark the culminating point of sweeping processes set in motion centuries ago: industrialization, nationalism, imperialism, urbanization, secularization. The dominant motif of the period was the search for conscious social controls, for methods of "social planning." Politics was becoming a profession of problem-solving. An eminent Negro scholar, W. E. B. Du Bois, once remarked that "the problem of the Twentieth Century is the problem of the color-line." At first glance this seems like a very narrow, ethnocentric approach to world affairs. It contains, however, a large element of truth.

The pre-eminence of the white western European powers has been based upon the four-hundred-year-old political and economic subordination of the colored peoples of Asia and Africa. It is only within the last hundred years, however, that the color-line has become a problem. The cumulative effect of exposing millions of exploited colored people to the democratic traditions of liberty, equality, and fraternity, and to the revolutionary tradition of international socialism, while at the same time educating them, and arming them to fight in white men's wars, has begun to tell. China, Africa, India, Indonesia—within each land there are the stirrings of revolt.

The color-line in America is merely a specialized variant of this worldwide problem. For over two hundred years, Negroes were imported from Africa as slaves. But slavery never had *complete* moral sanction in America, nor were the slaves ever completely reconciled to servitude. The history of the Negro in Midwest Metropolis, like the history of the Negro in America, is the story of a conflict between the principles of American democracy and the existence of a color-line.

PART II

CHAPTER 6

Along the Color-Line

FOR OVER A HUNDRED YEARS MIDWEST METROPOLIS HAS BEEN A MAGNET drawing Negroes from the plantations of the rural South and from the streets of southern small towns and cities. Some were adventurers, carefree and curious. Others were the ambitious, burning with a desire to "get ahead." Most of them were ordinary "poor folks" who had heard that there was steady work in Chicago paying wages high enough to let them live comfortably. And when the wages failed there was adequate "relief." All were bent upon escape from a section of the United States where their freedom was limited by a rigid color-line and where equality of opportunity was denied them.

Over 80 out of every 100 Negroes in Midwest Metropolis were born in the South. Most of them came to the city as adults during the thirty years after the outbreak of the First World War. This tide of mass migration was, as we have seen, set in motion by the manpower needs of that war, and its basic impetus has remained economic. But economic drives do not tell the whole story. That there were other important motivations behind the migration from the South to Midwest Metropolis is suggested by the answers which a large and representative group of migrants gave to a question asked by the Commission on Race Relations in 1920: "Do you get more comfort and pleasure from your higher wages?" Typical of the responses were the following replies:[1] (The italics are the authors'.)

1. Yes. Living in better houses, *can go into almost any place if you have money,* and then *the schools are so much better here.*
2. Yes, I live better, save more, and *feel more like a man.*
3. Yes. I can buy more. My wife can have her clothes fitted here, she can try on a hat, and if she doesn't want it she doesn't have to keep it; *go anywhere I please on the cars after I pay my fare;* I can do any sort of work I know how to do.

4. Yes, *Go anywhere I please,* buy what I please; ain't afraid to get on cars and sit where I please.

5. Well, I make more money. I can't save anything from it. *There are so many places to go here.*

6. Yes. *More places to go,* parks and playgrounds for children, *no differences made between colored and white.*

7. Have money to get whatever is desired. Live in a better house and *can go places denied at home.*

8. *Don't have to look up to the white man.*

9. *Don't have to go to the buzzard roost* * *at shows.*

10. *No lynching; no fear of mobs; can express myself and defend myself.*

Such statements show exhilaration over feeling "free," over the release from subordination and fear. This sense of "freedom" was even more explicit in the answers to the question, "What do you like about the North?"

1. Freedom in voting and conditions of colored people here. . . .

2. Freedom and chance to make a living; privileges.

3. Freedom and opportunity to acquire something.

4. Freedom allowed in every way.

5. More money and more pleasure to be gotten from it; personal freedom Chicago affords, and voting.

6. Freedom and working conditions.

7. Work, can work any place; freedom.

8. The schools for the children, the better wages, and the privileges for colored people.

9. No discrimination; can express opinions and vote.

10. Freedom of speech and action. Can live without fear. No Jim Crow.

11. Liberty, better schools.

12. Like the privileges; the climate; have better health.

The subsequent experiences of the early migrants dissipated much of the élan with which they embraced their new home, for the Race Riot of 1919 and the depressions of 1921 and 1924 suggested that Midwest Metropolis was not the Utopia which many of the more naive had envisioned. The prolonged depression of 1929-39 further disillusioned them. But Negroes continued to come, and those who were there stayed.

Other factors than the economic cycle helped to disillusion the mi-

* Semi-humorous colloquial name for the Jim-Crow balcony in southern theaters.

grants. They found that though Midwest Metropolis was "less prejudiced" than the South, it, too, drew the color-line. They were freer
than in the South, but not completely free. They found equality, but
not complete equality. As we saw in Part I, Midwest Metropolis has
always been somewhat uncertain about what place Negroes should
have in the city's life. The result is a color-line which marks Negroes
off as a *segregated* group deemed undesirable for free association with
white people in many types of relationships. The color-line also serves
to *subordinate* Negroes by denying them the right to compete, as individuals, on equal terms with white people for economic and political
power.

This present chapter includes a brief discussion of the color-line in
Midwest Metropolis, beginning with those situations where it is drawn
least sharply and concluding with those in which it is most rigid.
Throughout, an attempt is made to ascertain whether these situations
are tension points or whether both Negroes and whites seem to accept
the implicit segregation and subordination. The remaining chapters of
Part II will analyze some of these situations in greater detail.

Why, it might be asked, do Negroes continue migrating to Chicago
in the face of a color-line? The answer is simple: "That line is far less
rigid than in the South." It will be seen too that although Midwest
Metropolis has a color-line, the Negro masses are not deprived of an
education and are actually encouraged to vote. The color-line is not
static; it bends and buckles and sometimes breaks. This process results
in tension; but the very existence of the tension—and even of the violence that sometimes results—is evidence of democracy at work.

FREEDOM AND EQUALITY—LIMITED

Freedom to Come and Go: In the South, Negroes are constantly
reminded that they have a "place," and they are expected to stay in
it. In Midwest Metropolis, they have a much wider area of "freedom
to come and go." The city is not plastered with signs pointing
COLORED here and WHITE there. On elevated trains and streetcars, Negroes and whites push and shove, sandwich themselves in,
and scramble for seats with a common disregard of age, sex, or color.*

---

* At certain periods, however, crowd situations can become a source of potential conflict. During the Great Migration there was frequent friction between

At ball-parks, wrestling and boxing arenas, race tracks and basketball courts, and other spots where crowds congregate as spectators, Negroes will be found sitting where they please, booing and applauding, cheering and "razzing," with as little restraint as their white fellows. This same absence of segregation prevails in virtually all of the city's theaters and movie houses.*

The retail stores of the city, too, as a general rule, treat Negroes like any other customers with money to spend. Negroes may handle the goods, try on hats, gloves and shoes, and generally exercise the prerogatives of consumer choice. Eating in the larger chain restaurants is a mass activity as impersonal as shopping, and Negroes freely utilize these facilities, as they do most of the cheaper small restaurants throughout the city. Certain stores and restaurants discriminate against Negroes, but these are in the minority and constitute exceptions to the general rule. They will be discussed later in this chapter.

In most situations where Negroes find "freedom to come and go" without being Jim-Crowed, they are in close bodily contact with white people and are associating with them as equals. But all are essentially *public* rather than private situations, and in none is there any implication that the persons involved are friends or even acquaintances. They are simply isolated, atomized individuals who happen to be sitting, standing, looking, watching, pushing, shoving side-by-side. Each minds his own business and is under no obligation to be friendly or even courteous to others. People are lost in the crowd. This is the equality of anonymity.

Negroes in Midwest Metropolis expect free and unhampered access to all facilities operated by the municipal, state, or national government. White people in the city are not ordinarily disturbed by their

Negroes and whites on streetcars and elevated trains. Then for a period of fifteen years there was little friction on public conveyances. During the Second World War, incidents on crowded vehicles once more became fairly common.

* Access to places of amusement is guaranteed by a state Civil Rights Law, but within the last fifteen years Negroes have seldom found it necessary to invoke it. Yet, as late as 1920, the Commission on Race Relations reported with respect to theaters that "there are petty evasions of the law, disagreeable encounters, and small but insistent snobberies. . . . Reports of investigators indicate that the managers of movies are convinced that their main floors at least should be guarded against Negroes." By 1935 discrimination against Negroes in downtown theaters was virtually non-existent and only a few neighborhood houses tried to Jim-Crow Negroes. Successful prosecution of theaters during the Twenties was partly responsible for this policy.

use of libraries, museums, or the city junior colleges, but there are public situations where an attempt is sometimes made to draw the color-line. For instance, objections are frequently expressed to the presence of Negroes in certain elementary and high schools, and to their use of parks, beaches, and swimming pools in various sections of the city. These objections are usually voiced by residents in white middle-class areas. The very existence of a Black Belt leads the public to feel that Negroes should have their own schools and public recreational facilities, and should not "invade" those in other sections of the city. When Negroes do use such facilities outside of the Black Belt, attempts are sometimes made to segregate them or to limit their activities. In some areas of the city this community opposition is reflected in children's gang fights. Occasionally, too, a policeman or a park official may take the initiative in putting Negroes "in their place." Thus, the National Association for the Advancement of Colored People reports one case as follows:

At a children's party sponsored by the City Park District at Sanford Park, a park official rushed forth and tried to separate the colored children from the white. Only by the intelligent action of the group leaders was a riot averted. Protesting to the Mayor and other city officials, the NAACP was assured that no racial discrimination was intended.

Sometimes a park official finds himself in opposition to community sentiment when he tries to carry out a policy of no-discrimination. In speaking to an Irish interviewer in 1937 the director of a park in an Irish neighborhood contiguous to the Black Belt described such a situation:

"In the last few months I've noticed they [the Negroes] don't come in here so often. Well, the only reason I can give is the community just won't stand for it. In the summer there were quite a few, but the younger fellows just rebelled about them. They came to me about it and I told them that I couldn't do anything about it. One of the leaders said that *they* would see about it.

"I cannot say that we have had much trouble with the different races. The Negroes just stopped coming here. The recent outbreaks didn't happen in the park, from what I understand; they happened out on the street. If I find that any one of the people working here had anything to do with keeping them away from this park, I would do all in my power to get him fired. I don't believe in any prejudice whatsoever. In college I learned a lot about mixing with different races, and I think if they taught more about it in the lower schools there would not be any prejudice."

In Midwest Metropolis bathing beaches and swimming pools are among the primary tension points. The Race Riot of 1919 began with a bathing-beach incident, and during the subsequent quarter of a century the beach question has continued to plague Chicago authorities.* In 1931, a Negro newspaper commented editorially:

Once again there is the threat of interracial strife emanating from the bathing beaches along the lake shore in the Hyde Park district. Several cases have been reported to this office where groups of colored bathers have been insulted, molested, or threatened by bands of white hoodlums who resented their presence at the public recreation places. In at least two cases, it is reported that South Park police officers, stationed to keep order and to protect all decent citizens from annoyance or danger, have shown a disposition to treat the complaints of the colored bathers lightly or to signify their agreement with their white annoyers.

Two years before, Negro civic leaders and politicians had expressed their determination to fight out the battle of the beaches. The Chicago *Tribune* had headlined their stand: COLORED LEADERS ASK EQUAL RIGHTS AT CITY BEACHES; SEEK POLICE PROTECTION FOR NEGRO BATHERS. A Negro newspaper, reminding its readers that ". . . it was just such circumstances in 1919 which resulted in race riots," went on to add that "no one wants a repetition of these outbursts and the responsibility for keeping down these interracial conflicts rests, in the final analysis, upon the shoulders of those officers of the law who are stationed at the beaches." Negroes were urged to continue using the beaches, and it was announced that "the officials of the South Park board have promised full co-operation in maintaining peace and protection of ALL citizens at the beaches which are maintained for the pleasure and benefit of all." At the same time, however, community leaders suggested the establishment of more adequate beach facilities near the Black Belt in order to relieve the "pressure" on beaches frequented by white people.

---

* There seem to have been some beach incidents even before the Riot of 1919. As early as 1913 investigators for the Juvenile Protective Association reported that "even the waters of Lake Michigan are not available for colored children. They are not welcomed by the white children at the bathing beaches, and late last summer one little colored boy who attempted to bathe at the Thirty-ninth Street beach was mobbed and treated so roughly that the police were obliged to send in a riot call."

The continued expansion of the Negro community finally brought all of the beaches along a ten-mile lake-front stretch within walking distance of some part of the Black Belt, and at some of them indirect patterns of segregation began to appear. At one park, for instance, Negroes and whites used separate sections of the beach with an imaginary line dividing them. Later a fence was erected to mark the line, and this act so enraged one prominent Negro politician that he threatened to tear it down with his own hands.

This pattern became so well known that in 1935 a group of white boys were observed chasing a Negro boy away from a *less* exclusive "white beach," telling him to "make it down to your own beach in Jackson Park"—a *more* exclusive park, but with a segregated Negro bathing area. During the same summer a conflict at this beach was reported in the Negro press: POLICE OBJECT TO MIXING OF RACES ON BEACH; ARREST 18. SAY THEY ARE TRYING TO PREVENT RACE RIOT. The paper commented cynically:

According to information given the Chicago *Defender,* the arrests came as a direct result of the efforts of a group of white youths, led by some University of Chicago students, to test the meaning of that fence which the South Park board erected during the beach season last year. At the time the fence was built, it was charged that the purpose was to separate the Race bathers from the whites on the beach. This the Commissioners denied, declaring that the fence was to enclose a "private" beach which anyone could enter by paying a small fee. But the completion of this "private" beach has been delayed, the only noticeable result being to separate the races, the whites, for the most part, going to the south of the fence while members of the Race stay on the north side.

The University of Chicago students who tested the meaning of the fence were forthwith accused by the police of being Communists.

Between 1935 and 1940, several other incidents of this type occurred. In one case a colored woman and four girls were denied a locker at a park pool; white children in the neighborhood then cut up their clothes. In another instance, at a lake-side beach, thirty Negro and Mexican children under a WPA recreation director were driven away by a group of white children. A policeman refused to make an arrest, stating that he had received orders to "put all colored off the beach." The General Park Superintendent would not admit that such an order had been given, but did blame "Communist agitators" for the presence of Negroes at a beach that they had not previously frequented.

Several liberal organizations, Negro and white, as well as the Communists, joined in the protest, and one Negro clergyman in the neighborhood was quoted as saying that "the discrimination will be met with no compromise." The trouble finally subsided, and Negroes and Mexicans continued to use the beach without further incidents.*

Most Negroes do not wish to risk drowning at the hands of an unfriendly gang. Therefore they swim at all-Negro beaches, or in the Jim-Crow sections of mixed beaches, or in one of the Black Belt parks. The NAACP, however, defends those who wish to stand upon their rights, and its files for the years 1936-38 record one "victory." In the wording of the record, the NAACP "forced the use of swimming pool for Negro youth at Armour Square Playground."

As we have pointed out earlier in this chapter, the color-line is seldom drawn in theaters or at large athletic events. But in amusement places such as roller-skating rinks, bowling alleys, and public dance halls there is a rigid line. All these are recreational situations that emphasize active participation rather than merely looking on, and in which men and women participate together. The significance of this distinction will appear after our discussion of "social equality." It is sufficient at this point to note that such centers of commercial recreation seldom become tension points, since Negroes generally avoid them.

As mentioned previously, Negroes use the city's popular-priced restaurants freely and without embarrassment. There are restaurants, however, as well as taverns, night clubs, cocktail lounges, beer parlors, and similar spots that do not welcome colored patronage. During the five years preceding the Second World War, numerous cases were verified of restaurants' and taverns' refusing to serve Negroes. Some drew the color-line openly. Others resorted to subterfuge. Some proprietors or employees, for instance, would not turn Negro customers away, but just tried to make them so uncomfortable that they would never return. They were curt to them, or they overcharged, or they made the meal unpalatable by oversalting the food or by unorthodox concoctions.

---

* The Chairman of the Mayor's Committee, a white man, commenting in 1944, seemed to feel that a firm stand by the city on the beach question was desirable. He complimented the Park District on "doing a good job in race relations" and said that bathing beaches "now serve the total population in a way formerly regarded as impossible. The very firmness of the interracial stand of the Park officials has quashed most of the mutterings of Nordic mothers and white youths who have tended to feel that they have the exclusive rights to such public facilities."

Such discrimination was prevalent in establishments on the margins of the Black Belt and in places where the management was anxious to maintain an "exclusive" atmosphere. A few cases will suffice to illustrate these practices: [2]

A Negro man walked into a tavern in a Polish neighborhood and was refused service by the owner. The Negro reminded him that there was a state Civil Rights Law. The owner said he didn't give a damn; he just wasn't going to serve any Negroes.

A bartender in an Irish neighborhood contiguous to the Black Belt boasted to a white interviewer of the "Mickey Finns" that he prepared in order to discourage Negroes who came in and ordered drinks.

Two colored schoolteachers and several white friends attended a luncheon at an exclusive coffee shop. The Negro women were allowed to sit down, but the waitress ignored them and served the white women. One of the colored women protested and was told that she could eat in the kitchen.

A wealthy Negro real-estate dealer, active in civic affairs, went into a downtown cocktail lounge after an evening at the theater. The waiter told him that a bottle of ginger ale would cost $10. The Negro proffered the money without complaint. The waiter, angry because his dodge had not worked, called the proprietor. The proprietor summoned a policeman. The Negro, citing the Civil Rights Law, demanded that the policeman arrest the proprietor. The officer refused on the ground that he didn't believe the Civil Rights Law made failure to serve Negroes a misdemeanor. Several city officials also subsequently refused to issue a warrant. The Negro took the case into civil court and won his suit—though the affair cost him more than the amount he received in judgment.

The city's hotel managers, by general agreement, do not sanction the use of hotel facilities by Negroes, particularly sleeping accommodations. When the issue is pressed, however, as in the case of visiting conventions or athletic teams, the barriers are sometimes relaxed. Most of the hotel cases in recent years have resulted from attempts to discriminate against Negroes who were attending meetings, or visiting guests in the hotels. A number of such cases have reached the courts in recent years. One of the most unusual was the case of a Negro labor leader who, en route to a meeting in a downtown hotel, was told to use the freight elevator. He sued the hotel. The manager settled the case out of court by paying a lump sum and giving the defendant a written promise that such incidents would not recur.

Not all hotel owners capitulate so easily. Some pay their fines and continue to draw the color-line. On the other hand a few hotels are considered "friendly to Negroes" and are frequently used by mixed groups for banquets, meetings, or dances.

Though the situations described above are possible tension points, the actual occasions upon which conflict arises are few, for Negroes tend to avoid "embarrassment." In the years immediately following the Riot, the Chicago *Tribune* actually published an editorial sanctioning violations of the Civil Rights Law and commending Negroes for not pressing more insistently for its enforcement: [3]

He [the Negro] is not Jim-Crowed by law. A line is drawn by usage. The law in fact forbids what actually is done. It is a futile law because it encounters instinct.

Legally a Negro has a right to service anywhere the public generally is served. Wisely he does not ask for it. There has been an illegal, non-legal, or extra-legal adjustment founded upon common-sense which has worked in the past, and it will work in the future.

There are many Negroes, however, who defy these "illegal," "non-legal," and "extra-legal" barriers, and who show little respect for the dictates of "instinct" and "common-sense." Others, while not seeking a show-down, sometimes bump into Jim Crow unwittingly. When confronted by such discrimination in public places, the individual Negro is likely to react with an eruption of verbal violence. (The less restrained have been known to smack a waitress or proprietor or to break up chinaware and furniture.) Persons acquainted with the Civil Rights Law, and with the functions of organizations such as the National Association for the Advancement of Colored People and the National Negro Congress, sometimes report these cases and seek legal aid. The NAACP reported, for the period 1930-40, "Judgments well over $7,000 secured from Chicago restaurants." Midwest Metropolis offers Negroes "freedom to come and go," but it is Freedom—Limited.

Equality Before the Law: To Negro migrants, fresh from the South, Midwest Metropolis presents a novel experience—a substantial measure of equality before the law. Here, they can expect a reasonably fair trial in the courts, with a choice of colored or white counsel. There are no lynchings. They can vote for those who make and administer the law. They can aspire to office. The right to cast a ballot without molestation and to vote for Negroes as well as whites is a particularly convincing evidence of freedom as Harold F. Gosnell points out in his study of "The Rise of Negro Politics in Chicago": [4]

When a Negro migrates from the South to the North, he goes through a transformation. . . . One of the badges of his changed life is the ballot-box. . . . To some of the race-conscious Negroes, the ballot-box is the symbol of emancipation, a guaranty of equality of opportunity.

Although a few prominent Negroes were active in Chicago politics before the Great Migration, the "Negro vote" did not become an important factor until there was a large Black Belt electorate. After 1915, both the Republican and the Democratic machines began to compete for the large bloc of Negro votes that could be used to swing a close election. Black Metropolis was a Republican stronghold throughout the Twenties. By 1936, however, the Depression had swung it into the New Deal ranks. Then, with the beginning of the Second World War a shift back to the Republicans became evident. But in the crucial presidential election of 1944, the Negro vote was once again in the Democratic column. The possibility that Negroes may vote as a bloc whenever they feel that their vital interests are affected means that they sometimes hold the actual balance of power.

Within a decade after the Great Migration, Black Metropolis had elected two Negro aldermen, one State Senator, four State Representatives, a city judge, and a Congressman. This political activity led Gosnell to comment in 1935 that "the Negroes in Chicago have achieved relatively more in politics . . . than have the Negroes in other cities of the United States." [5] Wielding such political power, Negro politicians have been in a position to demand appointive positions for a few hundred individuals and equitable treatment in the courts for the masses (as well as dubious "benefits" from the great Chicago enterprise of "fixing" and "rigging" everything from traffic tickets to gambling dens). They have also been able to expose and check discrimination in the administration of the civil service laws and in the enforcement of the Civil Rights Law. They have created, among influential white politicians of all parties, an awareness of the Negro's desire for

equal opportunity. The appointment of the Mayor's Committee on
Race Relations, to which we have frequently referred, was as much an
evidence of the political power of the Black Metropolis as it was an
expression of spontaneous civic foresight and virtue.

At times the political activity of Negroes can become a tension point.
There is some evidence, for instance, to indicate that the passions
aroused among Democratic politicians and the anti-Thompson faction
of the Republican party contributed to the riot of 1919. Some months
before the Riot, the Black Belt vote had accounted for three-fourths of
the plurality by which Thompson won at a time when he was fighting for his political life.* The black newcomers were accused of thwart-
ing the will of the city. The *Property Owners' Journal* called its readers' attention to the fact that there were 40,000 Negro voters in Chicago:

> their solid vote is the Negroes' great weapon. . . . When both our prin-
> cipal political parties are split, and when each of them has two or more
> candidates in the field, this solid block of 40,000 becomes a possible
> power and might be able to defeat or elect a candidate. This vote situation
> is the foundation of the Chicago Negro's effrontery and his evil design
> against the white man's property. He feels that he holds the balance of
> power. . . . He therefore becomes arrogant, insulting, threatening. . . .
> The Negro should be consistent. As he segregates his vote and casts it
> all together in one block, so he should live altogether in one block.

Such attacks were not confined to small neighborhood papers. The
Republican, but anti-Thompson, Chicago *Tribune* felt it necessary to
warn the Negroes in 1920:[6]

---

* Some of the fiercest rioting occurred along the boundary between the Black
Belt and some Irish neighborhoods. The Commission on Race Relations discovered that adolescent gangs organized as "athletic clubs" were particularly active, and that most of these athletic clubs were sponsored by precinct and ward
politicians. Interviews with "old-timers" in this area of the city suggest that politicians and policemen aided and abetted these adolescent gangs. It is perfectly
understandable why the Irish politicians saw the Negro as a "menace." Between
1840 and 1910 the Irish, as a group, had raised their socio-economic status, and
had been particularly active in Democratic politics which supplied an occupational base for a lower middle class by providing clerical jobs in the municipal
bureaus, jobs as firemen, policemen, inspectors, etc. Now, with a new ethnic
group coming into the city and voting Republican, this whole stratum of the
Irish community seemed in danger. Negroes would demand the jobs which had
traditionally gone to the Irish. This antagonism was undoubtedly a contributing
factor to the Riot. For a fictionalized version of the Irish-Negro antagonism of
the Twenties and Thirties consult James T. Farrell's *Studs Lonigan* trilogy.

The Negro has had political equality. There has been an attempt to give him a fair representation in public affairs and not to resent his presence there. . . . We admit frankly that if political equality had meant the election of Negro mayors, judges, and a majority of Negroes in the city council the whites would not have tolerated it. We do not believe that the whites of Chicago would be any different from the whites of the South in this respect.

No such blunt definitions of the Negro's "place" ever occur in party pronouncements. After the first excitement of the Great Migration wore off they also ceased to appear in the press. But a color-line in politics remains. The most ambitious Negro politician would not think of running for Mayor or Governor. He would not have a chance if he sought to represent an area outside of the Black Belt in the state legislature or in Congress. It is definitely not the custom for white voters to select Negroes to represent them, administer their affairs, or pass judgment upon them. Whites do not balk, however, when an occasional Negro, elected from the Black Belt or appointed by the Mayor or the Governor, occupies a position of considerable power and prestige. The appointment of a Negro to head the Chicago Housing Authority in 1941, for instance, excited no organized opposition and very little comment.

The color-line in politics is also reflected in the types of political plums that go to Negro politicians and their henchmen. The big contracts and the heavy graft are reserved for whites. Negroes get the petty "cuts" from gambling and vice protection. In fact, a tradition has developed that Negroes will not demand big political rewards. Also, in matters of street-cleaning, garbage disposal, and general city services, Negro areas are neglected. During the period of the Depression, however, when vast Federal funds were at the disposal of the machine in power, the Black Belt was able to secure some expansion of social services. Political leaders in Midwest Metropolis, balancing the pressures of ethnic, economic, and religious blocs, are forced to grant some of the demands of Negroes, and Negro politicians shrewdly demand all that they think the traffic will bear.

THUS FAR—NO FARTHER

Negroes in Midwest Metropolis experience a degree of "freedom to come and go" and a measure of political equality denied them in the

South. Discrimination in public places is not widespread and, being illegal, can be fought. Yet there are two areas in which the color-line is tightly drawn—employment and housing.

The Job Ceiling: Individual Negroes have never been allowed to compete on absolutely equal terms for jobs in Midwest Metropolis. Before the Great Migration, custom relegated the majority of them to servant occupations, and trade-union barriers reinforced the custom. Between the First World War and the Depression, the bulk of the Negro population became concentrated in the lower-paid, menial, hazardous, and relatively unpleasant jobs. The employment policy of individual firms, trade-union restrictions, and racial discrimination in training and promotion made it exceedingly difficult for them to secure employment in the skilled trades, in clerical or sales work, and as foremen and managers. Certain entire industries had a "lily-white" policy—notably the public utilities, the electrical manufacturing industry, and the city's banks and offices. Then, the Depression squeezed the masses of the Negroes onto the relief rolls. With the outbreak of the Second World War, they began to filter back into private industry and by 1944 they were beginning to appear in a wide variety of skilled technical and clerical jobs.

During the Second World War there was little organized opposition to the use of Negro labor, but the nightmare of postwar reconversion haunted Negroes even more insistently than it did white people. The Mayor's Subcommittee on Employment reported in 1944, after a study of Negro employment problems: "The one concrete opinion that came out of the survey was that unless maximum employment continued, the operation of seniority contracts would work heavily against Negroes, who for the most part are recent employees." The CIO representative at the Mayor's Conference prophesied that "the alternative to full employment is chaos, civil war, and a third world war." The AFL spokesman warned that "if a great crash comes after this war men will fight and die to hold or get a job. The worst of passions will be unleashed. Without jobs there will be increased racial tension." The chairman of the Mayor's Committee summed the matter up as follows: "The big question is what will happen after the present emergency is over. If we cannot keep up full employment, earlier patterns of discrimination are almost certain to return. The all-important question facing Negroes is: can they hold in industry and organized labor a fair part of the gains of the past four years?" Negroes continued to wonder whether they were fated to spend another period as beneficiaries of a WPA.

Economic competition between Negroes and whites has been, as we have seen, a source of irritation and bitterness since the days of the Flight to Freedom. The two World Wars resulted in the temporary lifting of the Job Ceiling, and raised hopes among Negroes that the gains would be permanent. There is a note of fatalism, however, in the good-humored report of a Chicago newspaperman who, discussing his meeting with some Negroes from Midwest Metropolis hauling supplies on the Western Front in the autumn of 1944, said:

Chatting with these engineers around locomotives, you hear them say what good jobs these would be back home and how it would feel to be pulling into Chicago Union Station at the throttle and whether after victory they would be driving these big engines . . . just as they drive them here in France.

Both the reporter and the men, however, know that not even a war has been able to budge the Brotherhood of Locomotive Engineers from its constitutional requirement that members must be "Caucasians of good moral character."

The Black Ghetto: The Job Ceiling *subordinates* Negroes but does not *segregate* them. Restrictive covenants do both. They confine Negroes to the Black Belt, and they limit the Black Belt to the most run-down areas of the city. There is a tendency, too, for the Negro communities to become the dumping ground for vice, poor-quality merchandise, and inferior white city officials.* Housing is allowed to deteriorate and social services are generally neglected. Unable to procure homes in other sections of the city, Negroes congregate in the Black Belt, and what the Mayor's Committee discussed as "the Problem of Congestion" arises.

Although Negroes know that residential segregation has implications of inequality and inferiority—that it implies *subordination*—they

* This is not necessarily a deliberate assignment of inferior city personnel to Negro areas. In the case of schoolteachers, for instance, it is known that white teachers begin to ask for transfers when a community is "going colored." This results in the definition of schools in Negro communities as "undesirable," and retention in such a post is interpreted as "punishment." There is also some evidence to indicate that teachers have been actually "banished" to the Black Belt as a disciplinary measure.

do not oppose residential segregation with the same vigor that they display in attacking the Job Ceiling. In fact, the insistent housing demands that arise from Black Metropolis are essentially demands for more room, for a larger Black Belt, one not confined to the deteriorated slum areas of the city. White people, however, usually interpret the attack upon restrictive covenants as the expression of a wish to scatter about the city, and they are disturbed by the prospect. But the most aggressive political leader in Black Metropolis, a man personally opposed to all forms of segregation, explained the nature of the mass pressure for the abolition of restrictive covenants, in a speech to the Mayor's Conference (the italics are the authors'): [7]

"Out in my district just a few days ago a pamphlet was passed around among the citizens. This pamphlet, signed, among others, by the Vice President of the Drexel Bank, called upon all the citizens of that section to stop the infiltration of Negroes into the community. They say, by the way, that there is a studied plan of Negroes to move one Negro family into every block in the city of Chicago. This is being circulated by white people, not by colored people, to stir up among white people throughout the South Side a feeling of resentment against Negroes. Now, everybody with common sense knows that there is no studied plan of Negroes to move one family into every block. *Negroes want a normal development in their housing problem—a normal expansion; to be able to move as they need to; to move farther and farther in extension of the area where they live.* They want restrictions put out of the way so that they can make a normal infiltration into these areas [i.e., areas contiguous to the Black Belt]."

The conflict over living space is an ever-present source of potential violence. It involves not only a struggle for houses, but also competition for school and recreational facilities, and is further complicated by the fact that Negroes of the lowest socio-economic levels are often in competition with middle-class whites for an area. Race prejudice becomes aggravated by class antagonisms, and class-feeling is often expressed in racial terms.

Residential segregation is not only supported by the attitudes of white people who object to Negro neighbors—it is also buttressed by the internal structure of the Negro community. Negro politicians and businessmen, preachers and civic leaders, all have a vested interest in maintaining a solid and homogeneous Negro community where their clientele is easily accessible. Black Metropolis, too, is an object of pride to Negroes of all social strata. It is *their* city within a city. It is something *"of our own."* It is concrete evidence of one type of freedom—freedom to erect a community in their own image. Yet they remain ambivalent about residential segregation: they see a gain in political strength and group solidarity, but they resent being compelled to live in a Black Belt.

Social Segregation: Negroes in Chicago express unqualified opposition to a Job Ceiling, and they are ambivalent about residential segregation. In the matter of "social segregation," however, they are seldom articulate. Yet, it is in the "social" realm that their segregation from white people is most complete: in voluntary associations, church congregations, and in clique relations and family life.* Black Metropolis has its own set of institutions, bound by innumerable ties to similar Negro groups all over the United States. This web of social relationships between colored people is sharply marked off from the corresponding "social" world of white people—marked off in the South by law and in the North by custom.

THE SPECTER OF SOCIAL EQUALITY

During the period of the Great Migration there was a widespread expression of fear that the color-line might not hold. While the fear applied to every aspect of Negro-white relationships, its most intense form was that of the "social-equality scare." In 1920 the Chicago *Tribune,* reflecting this general uneasiness, lashed out at "sociological transcendentalists" and "misguided sentimentalists," charging them with "spreading propaganda for *social equality."* Their activities were dubbed "even more vicious than Red propaganda among Negroes" (a reference to the activities of the IWW). Conceding that "agitation for *social equality* may have every support under the law and under what

---

* The term "clique," which will appear frequently in this book, is used in the specialized sense of an informal grouping of people on the basis of common interest or personal congeniality. It has here none of the sinister implications popularly associated with it, but rather is synonymous with "set," "gang," "crowd," or "bunch." In many respects, as Professor W. Lloyd Warner has demonstrated in his studies of modern communities (e.g., *Yankee City,* Yale, 1943), the clique is one of the most important social units in modern society, since it controls the behavior of its members even more rigidly than do family, church, or formal associations.

ought to be human justice," the *Tribune* vowed that social intermingling would never be sanctioned in Midwest Metropolis.[8]

The real promoters of this social-equality scare were several property owners' associations, intent upon preventing the infiltration of Negroes into middle-class white neighborhoods. Speakers at public meetings appealed to all "red-blooded, patriotic, loyal, courageous citizens" to bar Negroes from white neighborhoods, insisting that "you cannot mix oil and water. You cannot assimilate races of a different color as neighbors along *social* lines." One issue of the *Property Owners' Journal* carried the following diatribe:[9]

Keep the Negro in his place amongst his people, and he is healthy and loyal. Remove him, or allow his newly discovered importance to remove him from his proper environment, and the Negro becomes a nuisance. He develops into an overbearing, inflated, irascible individual, overburdening his brain to such an extent about social equality that he becomes dangerous to all with whom he comes in contact.

"Social equality" is a scare-phrase exciting fear and distrust of the Negro. In the North, however, nervousness about the Negro's social aspirations is sporadic—it is not the ever-present incubus that hangs over the South. A social-equality scare is sometimes fomented deliberately, as in the case of the real-estate interests mentioned above. Occasionally it will arise from excitement over the appearance of a Negro in some unusual context, as when he takes a supervisory position that no Negro has ever held before; or when a Negro man is seen talking and laughing with a white girl; or a colored family moves into an all-white neighborhood; or a Negro party enters a restaurant or night club hitherto frequented by whites only.

WHAT IS SOCIAL EQUALITY?

When a Southerner says that he is against social equality his meaning is usually clear. He doesn't believe in addressing a Negro as Mr. or Mrs. or Miss. He will not permit Negroes to call him by his first name. He doesn't approve of shaking hands with Negroes, or of eating or sharing sanitary facilities with them. He draws the line at sitting beside them in public places or allowing them to attend the same schools and churches. He definitely objects to intermarriage, and while he is not too censorious of sexual excursions across the color-line by white men, he keeps a ready rope for any Negro male who may dare to turn the tables.

A great deal of what the South would call "social intermingling" takes place in Midwest Metropolis without exciting apprehension or antagonism. In fact, lack of color-consciousness is the rule in most of the day-by-day contacts between Negroes and whites. Members of the two groups treat each other as individuals and react in terms of occupational roles, individual personality traits, or socio-economic and cultural attributes rather than in terms of race.

Chicago Negroes and whites are thrown together in large numbers in work-situations where maintaining a rigid color-line would not only be a nuisance, but would sometimes be economically unprofitable. With no compelling tradition of separate cafeteria facilities or sanitary arrangements, the large industrial plants of the region have maintained a general pattern of unsegregated facilities. On the whole this pattern has been accepted as normal.* Some "semi-social" extensions inevitably arise from these contacts. Employees eat lunch together, call each other by their first names, play and joke with one another, share intimacies, gossip and news. In general both Negro and white workers, unless facing a crisis situation, exhibit very little color-consciousness on the job.

Color-distinctions are also minimized by the demands of economic necessity and political expediency. The white man doing business with Negroes, the salesman trying to close a deal, the labor leader rallying his followers, the politician seeking votes—all such types not only extend the ordinary courtesies to Negroes, but sometimes find themselves joking, back-slapping, dining, and otherwise fraternizing with them.

When white people in Midwest Metropolis express fear that Negroes will demand social equality, they do not mean these semi-social acts of courtesy, friendliness, and informal social intercourse. *They mean, rather, the prospect of Negroes' becoming members of white cliques, churches, and voluntary associations, or marrying into their families.*

* The Subcommittee on Employment of the Mayor's Committee on Race Relations reported, in 1944, that unsegregated cafeteria and dressing-room facilities were the rule in the factories of the Chicago metropolitan region, but that "in hiring and assigning new workers . . . the greatest difficulty arose from adjustment of white workers to unsegregated facilities." Yet, "if the proper groundwork is laid, it is the general experience in this area that a non-segregated pattern can be followed in locker-rooms, lunchrooms, toilet facilities and work relationships."

The last-mentioned possibility is most "frightening" because it raises the prospect that Negro men *generally* may begin to flirt and seek dates with white women.* Any gesture on a Negro's part that can be interpreted—even remotely—as a bid for such relationships will excite apprehension. Weakening of the color-line in employment or political activity is often opposed, or viewed with alarm, lest it lead to social equality as defined above.

But the pattern of social segregation, although general, is not absolute. There have always been a few church congregations with both Negro and white members. A few Negroes have always lived in "white neighborhoods." Here and there, the semi-social contacts of Negroes and whites slide over into firm and fast friendships. There are even a few whites and Negroes who are married! Midwest Metropolis not only tolerates these deviations from the general pattern, but actually seems to accept them as a normal part of city life—not enthusiastically perhaps, not without some head-shaking—but generally in a spirit of "live and let live." This tolerance of deviations is due in part to the fact that the average person is unaware of the extent to which such intermingling occurs. Being scattered and diffuse, the evidences are not general or obvious enough to excite apprehension. Isolated examples of full social equality do not seem to threaten the general pattern of segregation, and so long as they do not involve a given person's friends and relatives they do not necessarily disturb him. This acceptance of deviations is revealed in a statement which appeared in the *Property Owners' Journal* [10] in 1919 at a time when a social equality scare was being assiduously whipped up in areas contiguous to the Black Belt. Since the statement was part of a bitter attack upon Negroes,† the following excerpt is a significant index to the rather

---

* A social-equality scare arose during the Depression years when public attention became focused upon the activities of the Communist Party. That organization was widely accused of stirring up Negroes to demand social equality. The presence of Negroes at picnics, dances, and demonstrations sponsored by left-wing groups was cited as irrefutable evidence that the "Reds" were planting ambitions in the Negro's mind that would not stop short of the Caucasian nuptial bed.

† So widespread was the accusation that Negro leaders were advocating intermarriage that the most aggressive Negro leader of the period, Dr. W. E. B. Du Bois, editor of *Crisis,* felt it necessary to read the following statement into the record: "The *Crisis* . . . most emphatically advises against race intermarriage in America . . . because of social conditions and prejudice and not for physical reasons." The editor asserted, however, that his magazine would defend "the moral and legal right of individuals who may think otherwise." (Quoted from

wide limits of tolerance in Midwest Metropolis (italics are the authors'):

The Negro is unwilling to resume his status of other years; he is exalting himself with idiotic ideas on *social equality*. Only a few days ago Attorney General Palmer informed the Senate of the nation of the Negroes' boldest and most impudent ambition, sex equality.

From the Negro viewpoint sex equality, according to Mr. Palmer, is not seen as the equality of men and women; it is the assertion by the Negro of a right to marry any person whom he chooses regardless of color. *The dangerous portion of their outrageous idea does not consist in the accident that some black or white occasionally may forget the dignity of their race and intermarry. This has happened before; doubtless it will recur many times.* Where the trouble lies is in the fact that the Department of Justice has observed an organized tendency on the part of Negroes to regard themselves in such a light as to permit their idea to become a universal ambition of the Negro race.

As a corollary to their ambition on sex equality, it is not strange that they are attempting to force their presence as neighbors on the whites. . . .

Such tolerance of occasional "accidents" denotes a far less intense devotion to maintaining the color-line than is evident in the South. In the final analysis, the individual's tolerance of such deviations is apparently limited primarily by how close they approach, or seem to approach, his own intimate circle, his family, cliques and voluntary associations. Midwest Metropolis is a large city; it has wide social as well as spatial distances. That some Negroes and whites associate as intimate friends, or even court and marry, can be viewed with a certain amount of detachment so long as the incidents remain remote. But if a man is made to feel, by propagandists or by some personal experience, that *his* sister or *his* daughter might marry a Negro, or that Negroes might appear as members of *his* social club or church, the specter promptly arises. In the South, every white man feels impelled to protect *every* white family, clique, and church from Negro "contamination." In Midwest Metropolis, each person is concerned only with his own.

That social-equality scares are not more frequent is partly a function of greater "tolerance," but this tolerance is undoubtedly due to the small proportion of Negroes in the city, to the inconspicuous nature of

the *Crisis* in F. G. Detweiler, *The Negro Press in the United States,* University of Chicago, 1922, p. 145.)

the little social intermingling that does occur, and to the habit of interpreting much of the social contact as "not really social," but as "semi-social" activity dictated by political or economic ends. Despite the periodic outbursts by property owners' associations, most of the white people in Midwest Metropolis do not seem to feel that there is any "danger" of Negroes attempting to cross the color-line *en masse* by seeking membership in white families, cliques, voluntary associations and churches. Sometimes, however, they seem to have their doubts. Then the specter of social equality rises to haunt them.

DO NEGROES WANT SOCIAL EQUALITY?

Ask a Negro civic leader in Midwest Metropolis whether "his people" want social equality, and he's likely to answer: "If you mean the right to procure goods and services anywhere—yes, absolutely. We don't call that social equality. If you mean the right to rent or buy a house anywhere in the city—why, of course. Is that social equality? If you mean a *yearning* to .visit white people in their homes and to be visited by them—nonsense! But, as for the privilege of doing even that if both white and Negro individuals desire it—why not? This is a free country. Intermarriage? Well, it takes two to get married, and if one of them is white, what right has the law to interfere? But why should Negroes seek to marry whites? They have all colors within their own race [punctuated with a nervous laugh]. What Negroes *really* want is equal economic opportunity and enough room to live in. If you give us that, and just leave people alone, these social problems will work themselves out. Why raise the question of social equality, anyhow? Nobody's pressing that issue. You can't legislate social equality, and it's certainly not democratic to legislate against it."

This is the "advanced view" of most northern Negro leaders. There are many Negroes in Midwest Metropolis, however, who, as a matter of either expediency or sincere conviction, will proclaim the philosophy of Booker T. Washington: "In all things purely social we can be as separate as the fingers, yet one as the hand in all things essential to mutual progress." * These are reassuring words, and most white people

---

* Booker T. Washington's great popularity and influence among southern white people was due in part to the fact that he seldom failed to lay the specter of social equality when addressing either a Negro or a white audience. Yet a careful reading of the very speech in which he stated the famous five-fingers-of-

seem to appreciate hearing them. In fact, many "friends of the Negro" seem to regard it as *lèse majesté* when a responsible Negro leader publicly sanctions social intermingling and intermarriage. To do so, they argue, may alienate the less emancipated whites who could be won over to support the more limited goals of political and economic equality for Negroes. White sympathizers with the Negro's struggle for status treasure any handy quotation that seems to prove that Negroes do not want social equality. Nevertheless, colored leaders today in Midwest Metropolis do not find it necessary to announce ostentatiously, as did the Colored Convention of 1869: "We explicitly disavow any and all imputations of social equality."

Yet, in so far as social equality is defined to mean intermarriage and integration into white cliques, churches, associations, and families, Negroes exert no pressure for it and manifest very little interest in it. What some people choose to interpret as a clamor for social equality— demand for equal access to public facilities, opposition to segregation in public places, and defense of the right to compete on the open market for houses—these things constitute, from the Negro's viewpoint, a demand for *civil* rights and not a bid for social acceptance. When such situations involve close contact between Negro men and white women (as in dance halls or bathing beaches) or when "exclusiveness" is an issue (as in certain hotels and restaurants), the presence of Negroes is often interpreted as a threat to the stability of the "social" color-bar. Negroes are generally indifferent to social intermingling with white people, and this indifference is closely related to the existence of a separate, parallel Negro institutional life which makes interracial activities seem unnecessary and almost "unnatural."

Since the eighteenth century, a separate Negro institutional structure has existed in America. Through the years it has been developing into an intricate web of families, cliques, churches, and voluntary associations, ordered by a system of social classes. This "Negro world" is, his-

the-hand "Atlanta Compromise" will reveal at least one sentence which sounds a little like "double-talk": "The wisest among my race understand that the *agitation* of questions of social equality is the extremest folly, and that progress in the enjoyment of *all privileges* that will come to us must be the result of severe and constant struggle rather than of artificial forcing." (Italics are the authors'.) There is just a hint in this sentence that Washington was denouncing *agitation* for social equality rather than social equality itself as an ultimate goal. In an article published posthumously, Washington attacked all forms of segregation, labeling them an insult to Negroes. In the popular mind, however, he is still thought of as the great leader who defended segregation.

torically, the direct result of social rejection by the white society. For Negroes, however, it has long since lost this connotation, and many white people never think of it as such.* It is now the familiar milieu in which Negroes live and move from birth till death. It is accepted as "natural" and is psychologically satisfying. Negroes do not usually think of their institutional life as something "inferior." In fact, they express considerable pride in it, viewing it as evidence that they, as well as whites, can create a collective life. Thus, they do not "agitate" for social equality, because they do not ordinarily experience their social separateness as oppressive or undesirable. Black Metropolis is the world of their relatives and friends. They know no other.†

Despite this almost complete adjustment to social segregation, there are situations in which resentment against the pattern is openly expressed. A Negro may have no desire to marry a white person or to make sexual excursions across the color-line; but he usually gets boiling mad at any attempts to break up mixed couples in a public place or to legislate against intermarriage. Negroes generally do not display the least interest in joining white churches, but when a white pastor preaches a "goodwill" sermon in a Negro church, there is likely to be a great deal of grumbling about "insincerity," and some biting comments about "white Christianity" with its "Jim-Crow churches."

There are certain border-line situations, too, in which Negroes feel

* This attitude toward Negro institutions is evident if we examine religious denominations. There are separate conferences, conventions, associations, and synods paralleling those among whites. Few Negroes or whites think of these as "protest" organizations. The present generation accepts them as a natural part of the social environment. Yet separate Negro churches came into being as a protest against the Jim-Crow seating of Negroes in mixed churches, against the inability of Negro leaders to rise to the top, or against being considered wards of white "home mission" boards. This process is still at work in some denominations. For instance, the African Orthodox Church was organized in the Twenties as a protest against the unwillingness of the Roman Catholic Church in America to ordain and assign Negro priests.

† This subjective acceptance of institutional segregation by most Negroes must not be confused with some important objective facts, viz., (1) that white people, in general, have a tendency to view the separate Negro institutional life with a certain amount of amused condescension and patronizing curiosity; (2) that under present conditions, segregated institutions are actually inferior in economic and social power; (3) that social isolation results in distorted perspectives and personality development. There are some gains to the total culture resulting from segregation—distinctive contributions to the arts and to literature; but against these superficial gains must be set the cost in ignorance, poverty, and resentment.

that they should be accepted for participation, but which white people often define as "social" or "private." Thus a Negro who does not interpret separate cliques, families, churches, and voluntary associations as "unfair" or "unjust" might expect to be included in a dance sponsored by a store where he works, a school that he attends, or a union to which he belongs.* In the planning of dances, picnics, or parties the question arises as to how the Negroes should be treated. Whenever Negroes in such a situation are ignored, barred, or subjected to "special arrangements" they usually resent it. Nobody likes to feel "left out" or to be regarded as a "problem." Sometimes Negroes will put up a fight for inclusion in such activities. More often they will withdraw and mask the snub by feigning a total lack of interest in the proceedings or by professing a preference for the company of Negroes. Those who elect to fight usually make it clear that they consider the issue one of "civil" or "economic" rights rather than one of *social* equality. Those who decide to withdraw accept the definition of the situation as *social* and disavow a desire to participate.

When a white person does make friendly overtures, these are often viewed with suspicion—"he must have something up his sleeve," or "she doesn't really mean it." Negroes assume *prima facie* that even the friendliest approaches are hedged about with reservations and hesitancies, if not actual insincerity. The disavowal of interest in social relations with white people is partly a protective device against actual embarrassment, since "socializing" across the color-line usually takes place in an atmosphere of constraint and uneasiness. Both Negroes and whites in such situations are constantly exposed to expressions of disapproval by both races, and it seems much simpler for each to stay on his own side of the color-line.

* The authors have had access to several hundred interviews with Negro students of Chicago's high schools, junior colleges, and universities. Many colored students, although attending mixed schools, reported a preference for all-Negro schools because they offer a more satisfying social life. In some of the mixed high schools, Negroes were not welcomed at school dances, and therefore had organized their own clubs to sponsor proms. In a few cases, discrimination against Negroes was practiced in extracurricular activities, especially dramatics and swimming. Negroes on athletic teams stated that they felt uncomfortable because they never knew when the whole team might be embarrassed by opponents who would refuse to accommodate them when they were on tour. It is difficult to make any generalizations about the dominant attitudes. A large proportion of the students were aggressively determined to demand complete integration. A very few colored students preferred to transfer to all-Negro schools. The majority seemed resigned to a certain amount of Jim-Crowism.

The vigor with which many Negroes deny any interest in being friendly with white people, any desire for social relations with them, also reflects annoyance at the widespread charge that Negroes are "pushing" for full social equality. The average Negro does not give social intermingling a second thought unless he is brought face to face with a gratuitous snub, or until he sees the specter being used to limit his civil rights, his economic opportunity, or the expansion of Black Metropolis. Negroes may not agitate for social equality, but they certainly express resentment at being reminded that they can't have it.*

Whether there is some suppressed *active* desire for social acceptance on the part of Negroes is a question that cannot be answered by sociological analysis.† There is certainly no *overt* pressure in that direction. Nevertheless, some psychologists suspect that, beneath the surface, all Negroes desire to be completely accepted and integrated into American life with no barriers of segregation—social or other—erected against them. Such drives, however, must be deeply repressed.‡ An eloquent expression of this view was made in 1944 by Lillian Smith, distinguished white southern novelist and educator, in an article in *The New Republic*, "Addressed to White Liberals." She states:

* In order to preserve their sense of self-respect, whether or not they personally desire association with white people, Negro leaders feel impelled to defend the abstract right of Negroes to be accepted as social equals. Thus the editors of the Baltimore *Afro-American* make their position clear: "Anybody who says he doesn't believe in social equality is an advocate of the Hitler theory of superior and inferior races." A well-known colored lawyer from Midwest Metropolis, writing in the Pittsburgh *Courier*, was caustic in his attack upon conservative Negro leaders: "Shrewd diplomatic colored folks do not always desire to make definite commitments as to their views on this subject. . . . They indulge in double talk. . . . Whatever the indefinable and illusory thing is that we style 'social equality,' all other enlightened people on earth desire it. . . . How can the colored American expect to be a first-class citizen as long as he is regarded as a social leper and an American untouchable?"

† Perhaps the most adequate answer to this question would come from the discipline of psychoanalysis. However, relatively few Negroes have been analyzed and there is no published body of literature to which one can refer. However, a recent article by Dr. Helen V. McLean, "Racial Prejudice," published in the *American Journal of Ortho-psychiatry*, Vol. XIV, No. 34, October, 1944, indicates that author's belief that Negroes are resentful of their humiliation and frustration at the hands of white people. The implication of the article is that Negroes do desire social acceptance and are resentful at not receiving it.

‡ Horace R. Cayton, in an article prepared for the magazine *Twice A Year*, "Frightened Children of Frightened Parents," suggests the manner in which ordinary childhood fears are deepened and intensified in the case of Negro children.

I understand the desperate fear that causes certain Negroes to deny their hunger for things that make men human. I understand also the fear in the white man's heart that makes him more willing to work for specific, short-range goals such as the vote, better jobs for Negroes, than to change his own attitude about himself and the white race. . . . We must break the conspiracy of silence which has held us in a grip so strong that it has become a taboo. We must say why segregation is unendurable to the human spirit. We must somehow find the courage to say it aloud. For, however we rationalize our silence, it is fear that is holding our tongues today.

Since there is no mass demand for social equality defined in terms of segregated cliques, families, clubs, and churches, many conservative Negroes and white people decry any tendency to discuss the issue. There is, however, a growing awareness in Black Metropolis of a fact which thoughtful students have long recognized, and which has been stated clearly by the Swedish economist, Gunnar Myrdal, whose monumental study of Negro-white relations in the United States, *An American Dilemma,* is accepted as definitive: [11]

Social discrimination is powerful as a means of keeping the Negro down in all other respects. In reality it is not possible to isolate a sphere of life and call it "social." There is in fact a "social" angle to all relations. . . . The interrelationships between social status and economic activity are particularly important. . . . As long as Negroes, solely because of their color, are forcibly held in a lower social status, they will be shut out from all middle-class occupations except in their own segregated social world. . . . Social segregation involves a substantial element of discrimination.*

The specter of social equality will no doubt continue to haunt the scene so long as social segregation is forcibly imposed upon Negroes. It becomes a source of tension, however, only when it is actively evoked by white interest groups, or when there is a wide difference of opinion as to what constitutes social equality. An examination of the analysis

* The South has organized Negro-white relations upon the juridical fiction of "separate but equal" accommodations for Negroes. It has been repeatedly demonstrated that segregation in the South is accompanied by inequality of school facilities, of accommodations in public places and on common carriers, and in the areas of the cities where Negroes predominate. Despite this fact, the Supreme Court of the United States has consistently refused to rule that segregation of Negroes is a form of discrimination. In cases involving this question, the Supreme Court never goes beyond a demand that separate accommodations must be "substantially" equal. In the North, too, although in less pronounced form, segregation of Negroes tends to be associated with a high degree of inequality.

below will reveal that there are some things which whites call social equality, but which Negroes do not think of as such. Around these critical foci tension arises. (Note situations marked by asterisk.)

AREAS OF AGREEMENT AND DISAGREEMENT BETWEEN NEGROES AND WHITES AS TO THE MEANING OF SOCIAL EQUALITY

Area of Agreement Between Negroes and Whites	Area of Uncertainty	Area of Disagreement
(No pressure from Negroes against the color-line.)	(Some Negroes exert pressure against the color-line. Some whites resist. Others accept situation as semi-social.)	(General pressure from Negroes who do not interpret these situations as "social," although white people have a tendency to do so.)
1. Intermarriage	* 1. Negro residence throughout the city.	* 1. White-collar employment outside of Black Belt.
2. Membership in white cliques, churches, and social clubs.	* 1. Use of commercial recreational facilities outside of Black Belt.	2. Membership in business and professional associations.
3. Visiting and entertaining across the color-line.	3. Use of sanitary facilities, elevators, etc., in hotels and apartment houses outside of Black Belt.	3. Use of hospital facilities outside of Black Belt and in all city hospitals.
	4. Attendance at social affairs of unions, professional and technical societies, or at place of employment.	* 5. Unrestricted use of beaches and parks throughout the city.
	5. Interracial dancing at affairs listed in (4).	

There is continuous pressure from the Negro side to have white people accept a more restricted definition of social equality—to include only intermarriage, and familial, church, and associational relationships.* Some of the relations that Negroes would define as "non-

* Occasionally a Negro leader will approach the problem the other way around. He will say, "Yes, we *believe* in social equality, but we exclude intermarriage

social," however, are those in which racial attitudes of white people are reinforced by considerations of economic interest or social prestige (as in the situations marked with asterisks). Tension will continue so long as disagreement in the evaluation of these contacts exists.

The next three chapters constitute brief case studies of the forces that keep Negroes segregated and subordinated in Midwest Metropolis. Segregation, as we have pointed out, is fundamentally a reaction against the specter of social equality. It is the way Midwest Metropolis has of saying: "We do not wish to have Negroes in our families, cliques, associations, and churches. They are not our *social* equals."

Social segregation is maintained, in the final analysis, by endogamy— the rule that Negroes must marry Negroes, and whites must marry whites—and by its corollary that when an intermarriage does "accidentally" occur, the child must be automatically classed as a Negro no matter how white his skin color. Chapter 7, "Crossing the Color-Line," describes what happens to that small minority of persons who do intermarry. It suggests the strength of those *informal* social controls among both Negroes and whites which keep the number of such marriages small despite the fact that there are no legal prohibitions against them. The chapter also deals briefly with "passing," a practice by which a few Negroes with white skin and Caucasoid features and hair do cross the color-line.

Almost as rigid as the taboo on intermarriage is the practice of resi-

and intimate social relations from the definition of the term." Thus, when Dr. W. E. B. Du Bois of the NAACP was under fire during the Twenties for advocating social equality, he answered as follows: "We believe that social equality . . . means moral, mental and physical fitness to associate with one's fellowmen. In this sense the *Crisis* believes absolutely in the Social Equality [*sic*] of the Black and White and Yellow races, and it believes, too, that any attempt to deny this equality by law or custom is a blow at Humanity, Religion and Democracy. No sooner is this incontestable statement made, however, than many minds immediately adduce further implications; they say that such a statement and belief implies the right of black folks to force themselves into the private social life of whites and to intermarry with them. This is a forced and illogical definition of social equality. . . . Social equals, even in the narrowest sense of the term, do not have the right to be invited to or attend private receptions or to marry persons who do not wish to marry them. . . . On the other hand every self-respecting person does claim the right to mingle with his fellows if he is invited and to be free from insult or hindrance because of his presence." Dr. Du Bois was thus able to *advocate* social equality without becoming an advocate of intermarriage or of acceptance of Negroes into white cliques, associations, and churches.

dential segregation. In Chapter 8, "The Black Ghetto," an attempt is made to trace the tie-up between the specter of social equality and economic interest that results in the concentration of Negroes within the Black Belt. An understanding of the forces that result in a separate Negro community is essential to an understanding of Part III of this book.

Chapter 9, "The Job Ceiling," examines the mechanisms by which Negroes are subordinated in the economic life of the city, for while segregation is not the rule in industry and commerce, Negroes are prevented from rising, in the mass, above a certain occupational level. Job discrimination, like residential segregation, reflects the specter of social equality as well as fear of the economic competition of Negroes.

It is significant that Negroes exert pressure against the color-line in the reverse order from our presentation. They feel most resentful about the Job Ceiling, are ambivalent about residential segregation, and are generally indifferent to the taboo on intermarriage. These attitudes emerge in the following chapters from materials gathered by participant-observers during the Depression when the economic insecurity of Negroes had intensified their race-consciousness. The Second World War made no change in the order of these demands for equality but increased race-consciousness even more than did the Depression.

CHAPTER 7

Crossing the Color-Line

WHEN A WHITE MAN IN THE SOUTH CASTS A ROVING EYE UPON A LIKELY colored girl, the culture permits him to engage in any type of affair that stops short of marriage, be it flirting, discreet consummation, or concubinage.* For the Negro man who might be foolhardy enough to display a similar interest in women-folk across the color-line there is a standing prescription—the noose. For the white woman, there is social ostracism. The preservation of "the honor and purity of southern womanhood" is the most sacred duty of the white gentleman. Just to make sure that there shall be no accidents, all intermarriage of Negroes and whites is made a criminal offense. Sexual excursions across the color-line must proceed in one direction only, and even these must not be dignified with benefit of clergy or of law.

In Midwest Metropolis, marriage between Negroes and whites is not illegal. Also, clandestine relations occur in both directions. In general, however, both Negroes and whites frown upon those who venture across the color-line. While some defenders of "white supremacy" might welcome the aid of the rope in keeping things straight, violence is rarely visited upon those who do cross the line. Yet Midwest Metropolis most definitely does not approve of intermarriage.

The fear of intermarriage plays a dominant role in keeping Negroes "in their place." † It may be the justification for not hiring Negro men

---

* One of the most popular novels published in 1944, *Strange Fruit,* by Lillian Smith, dealt with some of the complications arising from this old southern custom.

† Closely associated with the fear of intermarriage is fear of "passing." Because some Negroes have enough Caucasian traits to make them look like white, there is always the "danger" that they may cross over into the white society. Both types of situation involve overt acts of crossing the color-line, and are generally resented by the white society. The difference between intermarriage and passing lies in the fact that in the former case it is immediately obvious to the general public that the color-line is being crossed, whereas "passing" is, in its very nature, a surreptitious act.

Curiously, the white community in Midwest Metropolis does not seem to fear

as elevator operators or busboys, or an excuse for residential segregation. The ultimate appeal for the maintenance of the color-line is always the simple, though usually irrelevant question, "Would you want your daughter to marry a Negro?" To many white persons this is the core of the entire race problem.

SEX AND COLOR

Any discussion of intermarriage should be placed within a wider framework of general sex relations. Pre-marital and extra-marital affairs between colored and white people not only are much more frequent than intermarriage, but may be the first steps leading to it.

Lord Bryce, in his famous study of America, remarked, "Whoever examines the records of the past will find that the continued juxtaposition of two races has always been followed either by the disappearance of the weaker or by the intermixture of the two." * Race mixture takes place in Midwest Metropolis—just as it does in Mississippi. In Midwest Metropolis, the forms of miscegenation vary along a continuum ranging from the most casual sexual relations to permanent marriage unions, and from commercial relations devoid of any sentiment to those of great emotional involvement.

It is difficult—in fact, almost impossible—to estimate the amount of miscegenation in a city like Midwest Metropolis. Yet from the interviews conducted for this study it would seem that there was hardly a colored man who did not claim knowledge of some Negro male who

or resent "passing" so much as it does intermarriage, although the former is much more common and involves many more persons. Perhaps this is because passing leaves intact the fundamental principle of segregation, and at the same time provides a method of escape for those who have arrived at a state of biological whiteness which to some extent actually embarrasses the maintenance of racial barriers. Intermarriage, on the other hand, represents a flagrant and obvious breach of those barriers. The fact that it involves relatively few persons does not mitigate the tensions to which its occurrence may give rise.

* James Bryce, *The American Commonwealth*, New York, 1911, p. 532. For concrete data on racial intermixture consult J. A. Rogers, *Sex and Race*, volumes 1-3, Rogers Historical Researches, New York, 1943. Rogers, an industrious free-lance Negro journalist, has compiled three volumes of anecdotes, travelers' tales, excerpts from diaries, abstracts of laws, newspaper items, and pictures dealing with racial mixing throughout the world. Some of his interpretations seem forced, and his use of the sources is often uncritical, but since he presents his documentation, these books form an invaluable source of information on a subject about which there has been a conspiracy of silence.

had had sexual relations with a white woman. Interracial sex experiences were much less frequently reported by Negro women and varied greatly according to social class.* Negro women of the lower class sometimes boasted of "having white men," while middle-class and upper-class women were almost unanimous in denying any such experiences. Thus, a lower-class Negro girl, a semi-prostitute, related her early experiences in the South and her current escapades in Chicago as follows:

"I hadn't had nothing but white men until the Depression came, outside of my husband. I have usually worked around doctors' offices, and as a rule you 'go' with them. When I was in the South, that is all I had. They were the best that the city had, such as judges, justices of the peace, presidents of different railroads, and rich farmers. I wouldn't think of letting a poor sap 'go' with me, for that is when you ruin your reputation, but as long as you deal with rich white men, a soul will never know it. Up here it is hard to find a white man that is in love with you.† I suppose I am lucky, at that [referring to a northern white man with whom she was having an affair], for I didn't know, myself, this would end up like it did; but to my surprise he fell for me in a big way. The only thing I hate is he is not a rich guy. I could even take him away from his wife if I wanted to, but I feel like it would be too much of a sin to take him away from his children. If it was just his wife, I wouldn't care. I would just figure, let the best lady win."

The attitudes expressed by this girl are typical of a fairly large number of women of the disorganized lower class. Although a middle-class girl might be rather promiscuous, only in rare cases would she indulge in, and almost never would she admit to having had, sex relations with white men. Such an admission would disgrace her in the eyes of her associates. It would also seriously depreciate her value in the Negro marriage market; and, of course, there is almost no chance for her to marry a white man.

* Complete descriptions of the various social classes within the Negro community are given in Chapters 19, 20, 21, and 22.

† This expression implies that it is easy to find white men in the South who *are* in love with their Negro paramours. The extent of "permanent sexual relationships involving white men and Negro women" in a Mississippi town has been discussed at some length by Allison Davis and Burleigh and Mary Gardner in *Deep South,* University of Chicago Press, 1941, pp. 33-38. They report and describe several such unions, on a common-law basis, in a state where intermarriage is prohibited by law.

Negro men of all classes were open in discussing their affairs with white women. In Midwest Metropolis, as in most northern cities, there is much more sexual freedom across racial lines than many persons suspect. Flirting on the job between workers—colored and white—is not at all unusual.* Frequently, a white girl will flirt, play, and banter with a Negro lad without self-consciousness, or a second thought, even when she refuses to accept a date. A young packing-house worker relates some of his experiences with white girls on the job:

"I've been working at the stockyards. I was the only colored in a group of white girls. They treated me the same as if I was white. One gave me ice cream and candy. I says to her, 'Why don't you let me take you out sometime and show you around?' She says that she is told that policemen will beat her up if she is caught with colored.† I told her there ain't nothing to that. People would see us together and stare at us. But they wouldn't know who we were. This girl was not prejudiced. She was just afraid. There are a lot of people like that.

* Colored men, when they are sure of their ground, will often initiate such flirtations. In general, however, Negro men, even in a northern urban community, are hesitant about flirting with or dating white girls. Men recently from the South sometimes express fear that white women will "trick" them, i.e., voluntarily indulge in flirtation, and then, if observed by other white persons, accuse the Negro men of being the aggressors, or even charge them with attempted rape. Youngsters raised in the North are less likely to exhibit this particular type of fear, but are more apt to be afraid of losing their jobs should a white employer or fellow employees become aware of the flirtations. It is widely believed in Black Metropolis that Negroes have been dropped from employment in several large Chicago hotels and restaurants because they were too friendly with white girl employees. Negro men also occasionally have the experience of misinterpreting the gestures of a white woman, who is simply being playful without any thought of dating, and who draws the color-line sharply if the man takes her behavior too seriously.

† The fear of molestation by the police may have a basis in actual experiences. Between 1938 and 1944, in Chicago, there was ample evidence to indicate that individual policemen sometimes considered it their civic duty to break up mixed couples appearing in public. The authors know of half a dozen cases in which policemen intimidated mixed couples on the street or in cabarets, both within the Black Belt and in white neighborhoods. In one case, a policeman forced the white girl into a squad car, lectured her for "going out with a nigger," and called her a Communist. In another case, the Negro man was threatened with arrest on the charge of contributing to the delinquency of a minor although the girl was 22. These seem to be the acts of individual policemen, undertaken on their own initiative, but they reflect two widespread beliefs about Negro-white couples: (1) the parties are probably Communists, or (2) the white woman is either a prostitute or an innocent victim of a rapacious Negro.

"At the yards, me and another colored boy was coming down a dark hall with a colored and a white girl. He put his arms around the colored girl and I put mine around the white girl. The door opened and the foreman saw us. He didn't say anything. But the matron told the white girl not to have too much to do with Negroes."

Deterrents to Intermarriage: Although there is considerable interracial sexual play, actual sex relations are most frequently either commercial or casual. Only a small proportion of these contacts finally leads to intermarriage. A number of instances were known in which white girls had sexual relations with Negroes but would not appear with them publicly or marry them. And, of course, this pattern of secrecy is the rule when white men have relations with Negro women.*

When flirtation arises between a Negro and a white person in Midwest Metropolis—as it easily does, especially where the individuals are working together—the casual play may grow into romantic love. There then comes a time when the couple must face the necessity either of marrying, with all of the disadvantages which might accrue to both parties, or of breaking off the affair. This may involve an emotional crisis, for there are pressures in the Negro as well as the white society against intermarriage. The Negro community, in response to the prejudices of whites and with the rise of "race pride," has developed a reciprocal feeling of disapproval which in its extreme form borders on abhorrence. Negro women, for reasons which will be made clear later, are likely to be particularly caustic, as in the following interview statements:

"I don't think that people should intermarry. I feel that there are enough people in our own race to marry without going out of the race for husbands and wives. People get along better when they marry their own race."

* The clandestine nature of most interracial sex relations in both the North and the South indicates the strength of social controls over individual behavior. There are undoubtedly scores of individuals on both sides of the color-line who have no feelings of revulsion against such relations, and who in varying degrees are attracted toward one another. But if they are to maintain the social approval of their associates, they cannot be seen publicly associating with a person of the opposite sex and race in a situation that carries sexual overtones. Few white girls in Midwest Metropolis would be willing to risk the contumely or actual ostracism that might be visited upon them if they were accused of having intimate relations with Negro men.

"I think intermarriage is degrading to both races. If a white girl marries a colored man, her people won't open their door to him, like his people will accept her. Then, too, a white woman who is married to a Negro will never be accepted by all of his friends. In fact, the man himself will lose some of his friends."

"Why should Negro men marry white women? White men don't want to marry us. They just *use* us when they can."

There is also a widespread tendency for Negroes to deny any opposition to intermarriage on principle, but to express skepticism of the motive of a white person who marries a Negro. Thus, another woman states:

"I'm not against intermarriages, and I think everyone should satisfy themselves. But here is the thing I can't understand. Why, if they look down on us as inferior, will they come out of their race with all the superior advantages and marry one of us? I don't think the better class of white people and the better class of Negroes will seek intermarriage."

A few—a very few—Negro women, and a larger proportion of men, will make comments like the following:

"I think it is all right, because social equality will exist some day. This old idea must be done away with that people should just marry their own race."

Certainly the thought of the antagonisms they will meet from members of both groups plays an important role in preventing many interracial marriages and makes very apprehensive those who do decide to marry. A young Negro factory worker related this story, replete with rationalizations of his fears, and revealing the normal reactions of a young fellow who didn't want to "get hooked."

"I went with a white girl for five years. She was Polish, and very nice; she was really a swell kid. She wanted me to marry her, but I like brown-skinned girls. Her name was Mamie. We were both working at the same factory on Halsted Street, and she worked right across from me. The first week I was there I noticed her staring at me every time I looked up. I looked off whenever I saw her looking at me. One day after I had been there about two weeks she said that she liked the materials I gave her to work on because they were fixed so well. Then later that day she asked if I ever went any place for pleasure, and if so, she would like for me to take her out sometime, if I would. Just like that, no stammering or anything. One thing I can say about white girls is that they are outspoken.* Then we began to go out together all the time.

"But one night when we were alone, she asked me if I would marry a girl if the girl was in love with me. I told her, 'Yes, if I was in love with the girl.' Then she waited a long time and asked me if I would marry her if something should happen to her. So I said, 'Yes—if it should.' She asked me if I wanted her to be a girl of bad reputation, and I told her, 'No,' and that if I had to marry her I would. She told me she loved me and wanted to marry me, and wanted me to come and tell her father that we were to be married. Now, I knew that would only start trouble, and anyway, I didn't care enough for her to marry her.

"Well, for about two weeks I didn't go out with her, and avoided her as much as possible. Then, as things happened, my part of the work was discontinued. So I didn't go back out there. The other fellows who went with the other two white girls still worked there, and Mamie used to send me messages by them. She continued it for about two weeks, and then she came over to my house. She 'pitched a fog' (made a scene). She raved about the fact that I didn't love her and that I played a dirty trick on her. I finally quieted her down and explained things to her.

"I didn't tell her that I wouldn't marry her because she was white. I just said I didn't go around her any more because I didn't think we should get married; because sometimes she would want to go places I couldn't go, and that after a while she would get tired of my company, and that I thought after a few months she would find someone she really cared for and would marry him and it would be better for

* There is a widespread folk belief among Negro men that if white women are interested in a Negro man they will be both direct and persistent about the matter. This is partly a sort of defensive reaction, an unconscious assertion by Negro men that they do not pursue white women; that the women are always the aggressors. There are other widespread beliefs, too—that if a white woman really loves a Negro man, she will exhibit an unusual intensity of passion; that "opposites attract"; that foreign white women prefer Negroes to American white men. That at least one of these myths is occasionally shared by white women is suggested by a note which a young white man showed one of the authors, from a girl he was courting. The girl, apparently teasing him, wrote, "A nice colored fellow sat across from me on the 'El,' and winked at me. What would you say if I'd dated him? Opposites attract each other, you know."

her future. She said she was willing to go any place that I wanted to and would work with me, if I would only marry her. But I couldn't do that. We finally drifted apart, and although that has been over six years ago, she was still asking about me the first of this year. This is the way I feel about it. If anyone else wants to marry out of their race—that is, if they are really in love—I say go ahead and follow your love. But personally, I wouldn't marry a white girl because I can't forget what the white people have done to my race. I was born in the South and I have seen them do awful things to women and men of our race." *

The most important deterrent and cause for apprehension, however, is the attitude of close friends and relatives. A white woman who was a domestic in a white family recalled the pressure that was put on her by her employers when it was discovered that she was going to marry a Negro who worked for the same family:

"My employer saw the notice about the marriage license in the *Daily News*. He told me he had seen it and asked if it was true. I was feeling nervous and told him it was true. He said, 'You are new here. You don't know what it is like here. Do you know what will happen if you marry this man? You will be ostracized. No one will want to have anything to do with you.' I said, 'I'm going to do it.' He said, 'You have a friend in Texas. I'll get you a ticket and you can go there till it blows over.' He tried to get me to go, but I didn't."

During the period of courtship it is difficult for mixed couples to meet openly, and although the validity of Negro-white marriage is established by state law in Illinois, couples sometimes encounter difficulty both in obtaining a marriage license and in finding a person to perform the marriage ceremony.†

It Does Happen Here: In spite of the fact that intermarriages are relatively infrequent, and that in all probability the rate has been de-

---

* The authors were acquainted with a Negro man, married to a Polish girl, who occasionally beat her when drunk. Both partners reported that when this happened, he would also curse her for all of the ills which whites had visited upon Negroes, implying that this justified his behavior in beating her.

† Some couples report that they were refused licenses in Chicago. But the authors know of at least one case within the last three years in which both partners appeared at the City Hall, and were granted a license without question. The judge who performs marriages there, however, refused to marry the couple, and expressed disapproval in a very obvious manner.

clining since the beginning of the present century, a student at the University of Chicago who made a study of Negro-white marriages in Midwest Metropolis in 1938 was able to locate 188 mixed families. He reported that he knew of an equal number of couples who either could not be located, or refused to grant interviews.*

In 147 of these 188 cases of intermarriage, the Negro partner was the husband. That so few white men marry Negro women may be partly accounted for by the fact that such marriages endanger the economic position of the white wage-earner even more than that of the Negro. Furthermore, the Negro women most likely to attract white men are at a premium in the Negro community. Also, since it is the male partner who plays the more aggressive role in contracting marriage, and since white women are "forbidden fruit" to Negro men, it is not surprising that more Negro men than white marry across the color-line. It is this one-sided aspect of intermarriage that irks Negro women.†

* This study, "Negro-White Marriages in Chicago," by Robert Roberts, was prepared as a master's thesis from materials gathered for the Cayton-Warner Research. Roberts's field notes and interviews indicate that in many cases where he had conclusive evidence that he had found an intermarried couple, the white partner insisted upon being called a Negro, and denied any identity with the white race. In other situations, the door was simply slammed in his face by couples who refused to be interviewed. It was his opinion that there were perhaps several hundred other couples who were living in common-law. Almost all of the 188 families included in this study granted extensive interviews and talked freely about the circumstances leading up to their marriage, as well as their experiences since marriage. The authors have supplemented the Roberts interviews with first-hand knowledge of eight or nine cases of intermarriage. No statistics by race of applicants for marriage licenses are kept in Chicago. Roberts interviewed officials at the marriage license bureau, and it was the impression there that less than three per cent of the colored bridegrooms married white women, and that an even smaller percentage of colored women married white men. There was general agreement that the proportion had declined during the last thirty years. Two students of interracial marriages, George Schuyler and J. A. Rogers, reported over a thousand mixed couples in Chicago during the Twenties.

† One of the authors overheard a discussion in 1939 among some Negro Communists in which the whole question of intermarriage was being aired. A young colored Communist woman was protesting because a prominent Negro artist had married a white woman. She was rebuked by her husband for uttering sentiments unbecoming to a Communist Party member, and was threatened with "party discipline" for giving vent to "nationalistic deviations." In self-defense, she flashed back with the charge that the white men in the Communist Party seldom married colored women, and that they should therefore be accused of "white chauvinism." Her critics were disconcerted, for no one could name a single male Communist in Midwest Metropolis who was married to a colored

Proportionately fewer Negroes of high social status, except intellectuals and "Bohemians," marry white persons. Both the social controls of the Negro community, which make it difficult for a person occupying a responsible position to make such a break, and the satisfactions that come with being at the apex of a social group (even though it is a subordinate one) deter such persons. Among "Bohemians" and intellectuals, however, intermarriages are tolerated by the Negro group just as eccentric behavior by their white counterparts is tolerated by the general society. But a Negro professional man, businessman, or politician would, under ordinary circumstances, endanger his position of leadership and responsibility by marrying a white woman, regardless of her status.*

There is practically no intermarriage within the present-day Negro

girl, although there were a number of cases in which Negro men had married white women. The general community pattern prevailed even within this radical sect. A very intelligent white Communist man sought to explain the matter privately to one of the authors by observing that attractive colored girls, on the whole, steered clear of the Party, and moreover, white men hesitated to make overtures to colored girls in the Party, because all colored girls seemed distrustful of any white man's sincerity.

George Schuyler, in a Haldeman-Julius Little Blue Book, *Racial Intermarriage in the United States,* claims that of 1,100 mixed marriages reported in Cleveland, 60 per cent were of white men to Negro women, while in New York and Chicago only a fifth of the intermarriages were of this type. It is probable that a surplus of foreign-born men at some period of Cleveland's history accounts for the difference.

* Prominent Negroes married to white women are always open to the charge that they have "deserted the race." There are no "respectable" Negro leaders in Midwest Metropolis who have white wives. One very prominent man was married to a very light woman and it was widely believed that she was white; but the couple always denied this.

Communist leaders report that within their circles, although intermarriages are not frowned upon, they have observed Negro women, upon some occasions, voting against measures proposed by certain Negroes who had white wives. It was difficult not to suspect that this behavior was either a conscious or unconscious expression of disapproval of interracial marriage. In northern urban areas other than Midwest Metropolis, there are isolated Negro community leaders who have not forfeited their position of leadership by acquiring white wives, but such cases are very rare. Frederick Douglass, the famous abolitionist leader, married a prominent and wealthy white woman after the death of his first wife, who was colored. He was widely criticized but answered his critics with a jocular reference to his own illegitimate infusion of white blood: "I spent the first half of my life with my mother's people. I'm spending the second half with my father's people." In general, it may be observed that when Negro leaders married to white women have found it possible to retain their positions of influence, it has been in spite of their marriage; a white wife never strengthens their position *vis-à-vis* Negroes.

middle class, which is even more conservative than its white counterpart. Members of the Negro middle class have fewer social contacts with, and opportunities for meeting, white people than do lower-class or upper-class Negroes. In most instances their self-contained world gives them enough satisfaction so that they have scant interest in the world of white society, and little tolerance for those who have. The same is true, though to a lesser degree, of the respectable lower class. Before the Great Migration, however, intermarriages were more frequent among ordinary, relatively stable, working-class individuals, particularly servants. Some of these families are still intact, and most of their children and grandchildren, now adults, have merged with the general Negro community.

There are, however, two groups in the general society which not only tolerate but, by their social philosophies, tend to encourage intermarriage. One is the Bahai movement, a religious group, while the other is made up of "left-wingers"—various groups of Communists, Socialists and other political radicals.

If not identified with one of these deviant groups, the white partner in a Negro-white marriage is not infrequently a foreign-born person, who is not completely assimilated into American culture and does not fully realize the implications of intermarriage or did not at the time that the marriage occurred. A case in point is that of an Italian, whose Negro wife described their courtship as follows:

"The white people I worked for were Italian and I met my husband through them. He hadn't been here in this country very long and didn't speak very good English. We started going out together, and in a short time he asked me if I would marry him. He said he wanted me to meet his family. I was surprised! My parents were dead, so I wrote and asked my uncle what to do. He said it was okay, and for me to quit worrying.

"Then I went over to my husband's house to meet his family. They were drinking wine and eating spaghetti, and everybody was talking in Italian. His dad told me that he didn't care what color I was so long as I was a good woman. He then told me that he wanted me to marry his son. Al, my husband, said we could get married in the City Hall; we didn't need to be married in the Catholic Church. So we were."

Statistical data on the occupations of Negroes and white people who intermarry are very scarce. There are none for Chicago, and only for Boston is such information available over a period of years. The Boston data, however, may provide some insight into the situation in Midwest Metropolis. The record shows that, in Boston, Negro-white marriages, more frequently than others, take place between persons of differing occupational levels. The white partners, both men and women, are, on the average, in lower occupational levels than the white population as a whole. Negro husbands of white women, on the other hand, are generally higher in the scale than the average Negro and often higher than their wives. Among the Negro brides of interracial marriages, however, unskilled workers (including domestic servants) predominate.

In Midwest Metropolis, the most common initial contacts leading to intermarriage were found to be of an occupational character. Often couples met while serving as chauffeur and maid for the same household, as cook and waitress in a restaurant, or as fellow-workers in a factory. Others became acquainted as neighbors, living in the same district, or met through a common friend. Very few mixed marriages resulted from contacts made in schools or religious organizations. Even the Bahai movement brought together only two of the intermarried couples interviewed, although it is the authors' belief that there have been additional marriages among the Bahai group, and certainly there have been couples who, after marriage, have turned to this movement to find the fellowship denied them by the society in general. Association in "left-wing" political groups has been somewhat more productive of interracial marriage, but most intermarried couples now living in Midwest Metropolis, despite popular belief, are not affiliated with radical groups.

The Trials of the Intermarried: Intermarried couples have their problems. One of the primary difficulties is keeping a job, and here both partners usually find (or feel) it necessary to conceal their marriage from white employers. Most of the intermarried couples interviewed talked rather freely about themselves, but when the subject of their employment arose, they did not like to give any information. "That's one subject we're both reticent about, because he would lose his job as soon as I would lose mine if they found out that his wife is white," a wife remarked. "Yes," the husband said, "I am sure of that." The wife continued:

"I stayed home from May to August when he was sick. I couldn't let it be known that I was his wife. I was supposed to be in New York.

I had to be careful that nobody from the office saw me while I was supposed to be away. I had to step about the house quietly, because the people from his [railroad] line came to visit him. I had a colored woman here and I went to the kitchen when visitors came. We have to be careful because we're buying our home and can't afford to lose our jobs. If we had enough money to be independent, we wouldn't care who knew we were married."

Another white office worker, asked if she associated with the girls from her office since her marriage to a Negro, answered: "I go out with them all the time. They don't come here because they think I'm rooming. Occasionally I entertain people from the office on the North Side, at the home of a white friend."

Fear of economic reprisal seems least pronounced among civil service employees, and within recent years a few interracial couples seem to have worked out a satisfactory adjustment in this type of employment without the necessity of concealing their marriages. In one of these cases, both partners (a white man and a colored girl) had previously been fired from the same private social agency when they were married, but the husband subsequently acquired a good Federal civil service appointment. If one of the partners to an interracial marriage has an independent business, there is even more security. Perhaps the two Chicago interracial couples most secure financially were one in which the white husband of a Negro girl was a wealthy real estate operator, and another in which the Negro husband of a white wife was a labor leader with a firm grip on his union. In some northern communities, Negro physicians seem to be among those best able to escape economic reprisals for a mixed marriage.

Mixed couples also often experience great difficulty in securing a place to live. In most cases, except where the Negro partner is light enough to pass, it is necessary for them to live in a Negro community. The exceptions to this rule seem to be rather old, established mixed couples who have been living in mixed Negro-white neighborhoods for many years. Such families report little opposition from neighbors who have known them over a long period of time. They may experience difficulty, however, if the composition of the community changes. Within the Negro community, many of the better apartment houses and hotels will not rent to intermarried couples for fear that they are not really married, and therefore are not "respectable." Certain hotels within the Negro community have the reputation of catering to common-law mixed couples and to white prostitutes and their Negro pimps. "Respectable" couples are continually complaining that the existence of such establishments makes it hard for them to convince rental agents and neighbors that they are legally wedded and law-abiding.* One wife reported that when she first moved into the Black Belt, she found notes in her mailbox saying, "We don't want poor white trash in this neighborhood." She remarked, "At first I was worried, but then I thought that I wasn't trash and shouldn't be concerned. I ignored the notes after that."

(Of course, housing is at a premium in the Negro community and any family has difficulty in obtaining living quarters. At most, inter-married couples are only especially disadvantaged.)

Even when they are able to keep their jobs and find suitable homes, intermarried couples suffer in a greater or lesser degree from social ostracism. Not only society in general but also their close friends and relatives usually disapprove of their marriage. To avoid injuring the feelings and social standing of his family, the white partner often commits "sociological suicide" and buries himself in the black community. In other cases, it is only years after the marriage that he or she will inform parents or other close relatives. One woman said: "I may tell the family some day. I'm not in a hurry. I have two sisters working in Chicago. They don't know about it. They don't know where I am." Another woman told her relatives:

"Some of my sisters and some of my brothers disapproved, but they still wrote and visited me. My other relatives don't approve at all. I have a brother in St. Louis who is very good to me. However, he doesn't approve of my marriage and is ashamed for people to know that his sister is married to a colored man."

On the other hand, a Negro who met his white wife at a university

* A recently married mixed couple experienced some trouble in finding accommodations. Yet their experience reveals the contradictory and unpredictable nature of attitudes in Midwest Metropolis. They went to the rental office of an exclusive apartment in the Black Belt and apologetically announced that they were "mixed but respectable." The rental agent, a white woman, said: "Oh, that's all right. We have five mixed couples in here and they're all fine people. At first the owner didn't want mixed couples because he thought it would ruin the reputation of the building. But I've picked some fine people." Since accommodations in this building were not suitable, they finally rented an apartment from a white Latvian couple marooned in a Negro neighborhood, and subsequently sustained neighborly relations both with this couple and with Negroes living in the building.

in Midwest Metropolis reported that he sustains friendly relations with the girl's six sisters and brothers (and the sisters- and brothers-in-law), all of whom were college students, and natives of a Midwestern city. One of the sisters, although friendly, at first seemed embarrassed by her sister's choice of a husband. The source of her difficulty, as she frankly stated, was her own boy-friend, concerning whose attitudes on race she was very uncertain. She subsequently married another man (an easterner) who apparently was without racial prejudice, and the former embarrassment seemed to disappear. The parents, in this case, were moderately well-to-do, and "liberal" in their general socio-political orientation. But the father, in addition to whatever personal objections he may have had, was probably irritated by his daughter's marriage to a Negro because his job depended somewhat upon the goodwill of numerous white southerners. The mother, however, took the marriage in her stride, accepted the Negro man as a son-in-law (although she had not seen him), and indicated by her letters that she intended to play the role of "approving parent." About two years after the marriage, she met the Negro who had married her daughter, and surprised him by the matter-of-fact manner in which she acted. This is an atypical case, but indicates the flexibility of the social structure in Midwest Metropolis. The ironic twist to this story is that the Negro man's mother, who lived in a small southern town, was seriously per-turbed by the marriage, because she feared the social disapproval of acquaintances who might accuse her son of "deserting the race," and the possible hostility of local whites should they discover what her son had done.

The reaction to intermarriage in lower-class white families is some-times very violent. The following conversation took place between two white men who knew of two white girls who had married Negroes:

"Are the girls' people still living?"

"Sure, but they are barred from their parents' home. Last summer one of the relations died and Willie [the girls' brother] said he would kill the nigger-lovers if they dared show their faces around. They didn't show up at the wake or at the funeral, neither."

"Do you think Willie would really start trouble if they wanted to pay their parents a visit?"

"Christ, yes. Whenever he gets a couple of shots under his belt he goes out looking for any nigger. As soon as he spots one it means trouble. He got cut up about fifteen different times, but he just keeps on looking for trouble. Some day he will get a good cutting and he will learn his lesson."

"I wonder if the parents are the same way about the thing that Willie is?"

"I don't know, but they are ashamed for what the girls done. Once the father was going to get them arrested, but he figured that if one of the newspapers got hold of the story it would be in print and everybody would know about it then, so he just disowned them and let it go at that.

"Ethel was quiet and good-looking and she was well built. She could of got herself some nice white fellow if she wanted to, but I suppose that after she got in with her sister's crowd, they went on parties with colored people, and then she teamed up with one of them. You know, that thing called love is great. But I don't think I ever could marry a boogie [Negro]."

It is ordinarily difficult for the white partner in an interracial marriage to maintain steady friendships with other white people. A white woman married to a Negro related this:

"I still have a dear friend that works downtown. She doesn't ever come to see me since I was married, but she always calls me and whenever I am downtown I go in and see her. You know how they feel toward me. They look at my husband as some kind of beast. He has made me a better husband than most of theirs have."

"Interracial couples have to watch out for themselves," commented another woman. "If they are in trouble, they can't count on help from anybody but themselves."

One of the most annoying problems that intermarried couples must face is that the white woman (for the white partner is usually a woman) will not be considered respectable by Negroes or whites. Nearly all couples interviewed expressed fear of such censure. Even women who had been married for years and had raised families still felt defensive about this prevalent attitude.* One woman, quite ad-

---

* In one case, a white mother had raised her three colored children in a mixed neighborhood without difficulty. One day she was walking down the street with her teen-age son, and passed a drugstore, before which a white crowd was congregated. Someone in the crowd yelled, "Now just look at that nigger walking down the street with that old beat-out whore." The woman was so shocked that she went home and cried. It was the first time, so she reports, that she became really aware of the "vice" label sometimes placed upon mixed couples who appear on the streets of Midwest Metropolis.

vanced in years, stated: "The colored don't like white women married to colored men. They say they are white trash. My sons won't let anybody say that about their mother." A young Negro girl coming to the defense of the white wife in an interracial marriage, whom she knew, revealed this general opinion:

"I knew a white lady who was married to a colored man. They owned their own home and he had a business. They had three girls and one of the girls and I were pals. I was in their home a great deal. I called her 'Mother,' and she was a wonderful woman. It makes me mad when I hear anyone say, 'When you see a white person marry in the Negro race, they are poor white trash.' I know 'Mother' wasn't any trash."

The widespread feeling that a white person who marries a Negro is necessarily of lower social status has some basis in reality. It also reflects the fact that Negroes (unconsciously) accept their assigned status as "inferiors." They find it hard to conceive of a "sane" or "decent" white person giving up higher status to marry a Negro. It indicates, too, a reciprocal and defensive "racial prejudice" on the part of Negroes.

Compensations of the Intermarried: In the face of so many disadvantages, how then do intermarried couples find their existence endurable? How do they justify their behavior to themselves and others? In what social milieu do they move?

The peculiar social position of intermarried couples in Chicago at one time led to their banding together to form the Manasseh Club. This club had a motto—"Equal Rights for All"—which suggests that the members sought a supporting ideology. The original Manasseh Club seems to have been founded in Milwaukee some time after the turn of the century, and shortly thereafter a branch was established in Midwest Metropolis. The members of the Manasseh Club were stable, working-class couples, who scrutinized all new candidates for membership carefully, in order to bar common-law unions and shady characters. The group was organized as a fraternal benefit society, owned a cemetery plot and had elaborate initiation and burial rituals. The organization engaged in many social activities, including an annual picnic and dance. By 1910 it had become an established part of the associational complex in the Negro community. Its annual ball, presented at the Eighth Regiment Armory, was one of the high spots of the social season. The club disintegrated in the late Twenties, but the surviving members still retain a measure of informal solidarity.*

The existence of such a club indicates that before the Great Migration, mixed couples, although not ostracized by Negroes, felt themselves to be sufficiently unusual to need some sort of mutual psychological reinforcement. They elevated intermarriage into a virtue, and the Negro community, while not accepting this valuation of their behavior, definitely did not consider them an undesirable group. One Old Settler, when asked why such a club existed, remarked: "As for the Manasseh Club, I don't know why, but they kept to themselves. I don't know if it was them or us. Our family, I know, had no prejudice. But they had their own affairs and dances."

A former member described certain service activities of the club:

"The men looked out to see if there were any Manasseh couples who needed help. The men looked up interracial couples to see if they were in any kind of need. During this Depression, sometimes we helped them get on relief. If any baby needed milk, we'd see that it got milk. If any children needed clothes to go to school, we'd see that they were clothed. We took up a collection and turned it over to families in need. I was secretary when the club broke up."

The Manasseh Club is no longer in existence; perhaps, indeed, its potential role has become less important. In recent years there has been a greater tolerance of interracial association among intellectuals, artists, and professional persons in the field of civil service, both Negro and white. Intermarried couples can find a circle of friends among these tolerant groups. Within recent years, too, the Bahai and Communist movements, advocating complete racial equality, including intermarriage, have attained some slight, though appreciable, influence. By identifying themselves with such groups and embracing their doctrines, intermarried couples not only find a suitable social milieu, but also

* The club took its name from Manasseh, who, according to a Biblical story, was the son of Joseph, the Hebrew, and Asenath, the daughter of an Egyptian priest, Poti-pherah (Genesis 41:44-52). Manasseh members were especially solicitous about their reputations during the period of the Great Migration when illicit miscegenation was apparently widespread and all mixed couples were suspect. (See Rogers, op. cit., volume II, p. 288. The author claims that "a great wave of miscegenation swept that town [Chicago] in the early fall of 1917." He made first-hand investigations of many black and tan cabarets, buffet flats and resorts in order to document this claim.)

gain a *raison d'être* and a philosophic justification for their behavior. In fact, the social pressures against intermarriage are so severe that those who have violated the taboo invariably seem to find it necessary to develop counter-rationalizations to those contained within the dominant mores, even when they do not embrace philosophies that justify or exalt their position. For instance, a rather unsophisticated white wife of an interracial marriage said:

"I don't see why people should make any distinction between white and colored. A black and a white horse together look plenty good to me. I don't see any difference with people. It's just an opinion that has been handed down. A lot of people think in their hearts that intermarriage is all right, but they haven't the courage to express themselves before the public."

"No," declared another white wife, appealing to religion for her justification, "color doesn't mean a hill of beans to me. God made us all. I don't care about color. Some people think I'm crazy, but when they get to glory, they'll see there's no color there."

A third said, defensively: "My child looks about as good as any child on the street, black or white. So what's wrong if a person chooses a colored man as a husband? Had I married a Jew, a Dago, or some other nationality, not a word would have been said. But as soon as you take on a colored man, the world begins to think you're insane, or else low-class."

Some Negroes justify intermarriages on the basis of the sexual behavior of white men toward Negro women:

"A white man doesn't want colored to have his woman, but he will go with anybody he wants to. I am speaking of the South now. It was the white man who broke the colored race. He was the first to mix with colored women." (I.e., "turn about is fair-play.")

Some intermarried persons think of themselves as crusaders in solving a social problem or in working toward a new society. A woman who was deeply religious said:

"I think that interracial marriage will solve a lot of our problems. I think the relations between the races will be improved by interracial marriages. The right sort of marriages, I mean, because if they are interracially married, people learn to live better than other couples."

The World of the Intermarried: Many of the older intermarried couples live in the past, romanticizing the pre-Migration days when the Manasseh Club was a respected institution and when "the inter-racials" cut quite a figure in the community. Most of them have raised their families in an atmosphere of middle-class respectability, and are now spending their declining years quietly among a small circle of friends from the defunct Manasseh society, their immediate neighbors, or the members of their churches.

The new crop of mixed couples falls into four broad groups: (1) the intellectuals and "Bohemians," (2) the religious and political radicals, (3) the "sporting world," and (4) the stable middle class. In the last group are fewer than a dozen couples, who live a rather normal exist-ence. Typical of these is a Negro woman married to a white man, both of whom attend fraternity and sorority dances in the Negro community, have a small circle of friends (of equivalent social status), and are rais-ing a family. The husband is a civil service employee in the profes-sional category. Within the "sporting world" are one or two well-known, moderately wealthy couples, and a larger number of rather "shady" individuals. Stresses and strains are perhaps least pronounced within this group, which exists upon the fringes of "respectable" society anyway, and whose members derive their prestige from within their own closed circle. The intellectuals and "Bohemians," too, exist in a milieu in which people who are different and individualistic often gain prestige rather than win disapproval. The status of mixed couples within Communist circles fluctuates somewhat with the shifts of the party line. In the early days of the Depression, there was probably encouragement of intermarriage, for then the Communist Party was emphasizing revolutionary action. With the elaboration of the Popular Front ideology, more stress was placed upon conformity to the general mores. Mixed couples still find a congenial atmosphere within left-wing circles, but there is a definite feeling that prominent Communists would do well for political reasons to avoid intermarriage, since it might reduce their influence among both those Negroes and those whites whose confidence has yet to be won. The Bahai religious move-ment, however, not only sanctions but encourages intermarriage, to the end that amalgamation may occur, and, in time, a "cosmic race" emerge.*

* Miscegenation among musicians and stage people is perhaps as widespread as among any social types in Midwest Metropolis (as in other northern communi-ties). Formal intermarriage is virtually non-existent, however. People with their careers on stage or screen at stake cannot afford to risk alienating the

The following case has been selected as illustrating how a mixed couple which begins as an ordinary middle-class family may be attracted to a group such as Bahai, to obtain social reassurance amid the vicissitudes of a world that can be rather rough on the intermarried.

Mr. and Mrs. Brown live in a new two-story brick building in one of the better Negro residential districts. Their house is very attractively furnished, and the whole atmosphere is one of middle-class respectability. Mrs. Brown works in a downtown office in a supervisory position. Her husband is a railroad waiter. Their combined income makes it possible for them to maintain a standard of living comparable to that of most middle-class white couples. They are about forty years of age, and have been married for about twenty years.

Mr. Brown was born in Kentucky, the son of one of the wealthiest farmers in that section of the state. Both of his parents had been slaves. He has Negroid hair and light brown skin. Probably he has as much white as colored blood. He went through prep school, and then attended a small Negro college for a time. Later he came to Chicago, and there met his future wife. They became acquainted through a Negro girl who was passing for white in the office in which Mrs. Brown worked. After the two young women had been intimate friends for some time, the Negro girl told Mrs. Brown her secret, and invited her to her home. At that time, Mrs. Brown was engaged to a white man who lived on the North Side in Chicago. Mrs. Brown said: "When I went to this girl's home, Mr. Brown was often there. I don't know what attracted us to each other, but music was one common bond. After I had seen Mr. Brown for some time at this girl's house, we became very fond of each other. We decided not to see each other any more, and didn't for four months. But after my brother left town, we did see each other again and finally married."

One of the first problems that faced Mrs. Brown was informing her relatives of her marriage. "I was married three months before I decided to tell my sister," she recalled. "On that day we saw a hard-looking blonde woman with a dark Negro. My sister remarked, 'Isn't that terrible?' I didn't tell her of my marriage then, as I had planned, but I told her a week later. She said, 'Sis, are you happy with him?'

public by having a mixed "affair" formalized. Persons in the theatrical world have stated that they feel the American public will tolerate rumors and gossip about the interracial "affairs" of their stars, but couldn't "take" a bona fide marriage.

I told her that we were very happy together, and she said, 'That's all that matters.'"

Mrs. Brown did not, however, tell her other relatives of her marriage for a long time—not until it became necessary for her to support them:

"I rented an apartment for them on University Avenue [in a white neighborhood]. That's when I told my mother about my marriage. But I didn't tell my brother, even then. For a while I was the only one that was working in the family, and it became necessary for my mother, sister, and her three children to live with us. My sister didn't like it because the baby used to climb all over Mr. Brown, but she got over it after she had gotten to know him. My brother, who was in the Army, disapproved strongly of my marriage when he found out about it. He was in the Philippines and I know that while he was there he lived with a Filipino woman. Yet he thought it was terrible that I married a Negro. He said it was terrible, but he sent my husband and me cards on Christmas and on our birthdays. I told my sister that if she saw him, she should tell him I thought it was terrible that he lived with a native woman without marrying her, and then left her heartbroken when he returned to America. He said later that he would like to see me six feet underground. I wrote him a letter and told him that I still loved him, no matter what he thought. Then I told Mother never to mention me to him, as if I were dead.

"About two years later my brother 'phoned. I asked him to come over and he came. I put him and Mr. Brown together in the parlor. They talked and became acquainted. Mr. Brown told him that I was not supporting him, that he had always worked, and that I was working because I wanted to. My brother saw that my husband was not a bad fellow. For a year and a half after that, until he left town, he didn't miss a Sunday with us."

A major problem which Mrs. Brown faced from the first was the problem of keeping her job. She did not tell any of the office people about her marriage, and was constantly in fear of being discovered. A number of embarrassing incidents occurred, and she tells how she handled them:

"One day my husband called to drive me home from work. Just as he was about to start the car, I saw my boss. I told my husband to stop and asked my boss if he was going to the station I was going to. I was in the back seat and Mr. Brown was in the front. I introduced Mr. Brown to my boss, but didn't say who he was.

"Another time my husband was teaching me how to drive the car. I must have been talking about something intimate because we were both laughing. We were both sitting in the front seat. One of our salesmen drove right up next to our car and saw me. I told Mr. Brown to stop. I talked with the salesman and told him I was trying to learn to drive, but wasn't having much success. I always make it a point to stop and talk whenever I am with my husband and someone I know from the office sees us, else they might wonder what we are doing together and tell others what they have seen."

The Browns assert that this subterfuge is carried on only for economic reasons, for both feel that they would lose their positions if it were known that they were married. "We have to be very careful in going out," they said. "We have a car and go together often. The only thing that bothers us is that we can't introduce each other as husband and wife." Outside of Chicago, where there is no fear of detection, they have made many trips, including several cross-country expeditions, and while on these, they ate in white restaurants and stayed in white hotels. "If Mr. Brown's skin were a little lighter," remarked his wife, "we could go anywhere together."

In summarizing her attitude toward interracial marriage Mrs. Brown said:

"I think that anyone is foolish to plunge headlong into an interracial marriage without careful consideration. My sister married a Negro she had met in our home. We were all opposed to it for it was a foolish marriage. I wouldn't have wanted my sister to marry that man if he had been white, because he wasn't at all worth while, but it makes it even worse to marry a man like that who is colored. If I weren't married to a Negro and had a daughter, I wouldn't like her to make a point of intermarriage. I wouldn't want her to marry just *any* colored man."

Although the Browns have no children, they have these observations to offer about the offspring of intermarriage:

"Don't you think the children of interracial marriages are finer people than most people? I think they are generally more intelligent than either white or colored. I think the white race needs a little mixture of the Negro. The Negro is more carefree and easy-going than the white person, and the whites can use some of this characteristic."

Mrs. Brown continued:

"Don't you think that, if a good friend of a white person married a Negro, that person would think more of colored people? They would think that some colored people would be worth while or their friend would not have married one. I know one girl at the office whom I finally told of my marriage. She didn't like colored people and thought interracial marriage was terrible. Since then she has come to my house and met Mr. Brown, and she thinks he is a fine man."

Mrs. Brown does not, however, minimize the difficulties involved in interracial marriage:

"If you do make an interracial marriage, you have to think a lot of each other. We like each other enough to forget the world. The high-class colored person doesn't care to mix with white. Many people have the idea that any colored man would like to marry a white woman. That isn't true."

The majority of the Browns' friends are white and are connected with the Bahai group. It is with these people that they spend most of their leisure time:

"We go to the Bahai meeting as often as we can. I'd say we go three or four times a month. We drive to the temple in Winnetka every Sunday in the summer and go to the downtown meeting twice a month. We go to their homes and they come to ours. We have white and colored friends here together."

Their membership in the Bahai church seems to be the great stabilizing force in the lives of the Browns. It gives them a circle of associates which allows them to defy the mores of the general society and helps them to circumvent some of the difficulties of their marriage. In talking about her religion, Mrs. Brown contrasts the attitude of the Episcopal Church, to which she formerly belonged, with that of Bahai:

"I used to belong to the Episcopal Church. One day I met a bishop whom I used to know well. He asked me why he didn't see me at church any more. I told him that I went to the Bahai Temple on Sundays. He said that I was getting away from the Christian church. I said that it is simply the Christian religion brought up to date. Then the bishop said, 'There is something in your life that you are not telling me.' I said, 'Yes, there is. I'm married.' 'There is nothing unusual about that,' the bishop said. I said, 'No, but my husband is colored.' I asked him what he thought about it, and he said, 'I'm shocked.' Then he asked me if I was happy, and I said that I was. Then I asked the

Bishop if I could go to his church with my husband. He said that as an individual he would have no objections, but that the congregation would object. I told him that was the difference between his church and the Bahai."

Mrs. Brown's religion has not only acted as a means of justifying her behavior, but has fired her with a sort of crusading zeal to think of intermarriage as the solution to the problem of color. "I think interracial marriage will do a lot to break down prejudice," she said. "I can truthfully say we've been very happy. Other interracial couples that I I know have also."

Like most of the wives of interracial marriages interviewed in this study, Mrs. Brown was sensitive about her respectability:

"I think that the truth is what will help us interracial people. Of course there are some we can't speak highly of. They are the ones that get in the news. Everyone knows about Jack Johnson's wives. But if you see an interracial woman like Mrs. Sampson, who has raised a family and has always led a quiet, decent life, it never gets in the newspaper." *

It Doesn't Always Work: Intermarriage—like marriage—does not always work. Few data are available concerning interracial couples who subsequently secured divorces.† There is, however, no evidence to in-

---

* Perhaps the most highly publicized case of a Negro man's interracial "affairs," in the history of American journalism, was that of Jack Johnson, the pugilist, who married and divorced two American white women, and then married a French woman. Interracial "affairs" and marriages make the daily press when they are sensational enough to be "news" or have some human interest twist. In 1930, for instance, several Chicago papers carried the story of a millionaire who had married his colored housekeeper in 1927. The man's sister had haled him into court on the charge that he was demented and that "a scheming Negro woman" was after his fortune. Three years later a similar story appeared involving another very wealthy Chicagoan. In 1934, the biggest "interracial" story involved the daughter of a former National Commander of the American Legion who had married a Negro Communist, and whose father attempted to have her declared psychopathic. In 1938, the marriage of Mary Dawes, wealthy Boston socialite, to a prominent Negro social worker, Julian Steele, was carried as straight news.

† It is not easy to trace persons who were formerly partners in interracial marriages after the marriages are dissolved. Nor are such persons likely, even when they can be traced, to be willing to grant interviews. Rumors circulate in the Negro community about many interracial couples who have "busted up," but the difficulty is in knowing whether they were ever really (i.e., legally) married in the first place. It has not been possible to secure much information on common-law marriages—even when such unions are permanent—because the persons in-

dicate that the divorce rate is higher among the intermarried than in the population as a whole; indeed there is reason to think that the reverse may be true. The fact that they have violated a taboo together may well act as an additional bond between interracial couples. There is also, of course, another factor that would operate in the same direction: the difficulty which the white partner faces in securing another spouse.

Furthermore, when intermarriages do not go smoothly, it is almost impossible to ascertain whether the racial factor is ever directly or even indirectly involved, except very superficially. If a white wife quarrels with a Negro husband over his drinking, and in the process calls him "good for nothing," he may interpret the insult as a "racial" slur, and react accordingly. In fact, some interracial couples report the use of terms such as "nigger" and "poor-white trash" in family arguments. But such derogatory jousting implies a desire to "hurt" rather than any basic racial prejudice. One elderly white woman who regarded her marriage as a failure (although she had no intention of ever leaving her Negro husband) remarked: "Color hasn't nothing to do with it. He'd be just as no-good if he was white."

WHAT ABOUT THE CHILDREN?

"Broad-minded" white persons sometimes say, "I don't disapprove of intermarriage, but what about the fate of the children? For their sake, perhaps, intermarriage is unwise." Although there have been cases in which intermarried couples have refrained from having children for fear they would prove embarrassing to the white partner, or would not find a comfortable existence either in the white or in the Negro community, these are exceptions. While interracial parents may worry, particularly about how their children will be received by relatives, an examination of a large number of cases indicated that intermarriage is not a very serious deterrent to raising a family. Most of the interracial couples studied in Black Metropolis have children. They are, of course, *Negro* children.

It is difficult, but not impossible, for the children of interracial marriage to make a social adjustment. Nor are such persons invariably

volved are not likely to grant interviews. More common-law marriages in the lower class than on other social levels may explain the apparent low incidence of legal intermarriages in this group.

unhappy. The child of an intermarried couple is usually not accepted by the white community unless he passes. In the Negro community, on the other hand, while there is some stigma attached to having a white parent, it is not very strong. Some of the most popular "leading" young matrons of a generation ago in the Negro community were children of interracial marriages. Often the community completely forgets the interracial background. Some children of intermarried couples are even slightly boastful of the fact. Any stigma arising from white ancestry which may exist among Negroes can extend only one generation back. *No* light-complexioned Negro can trace his ancestry far without running into white blood. The product of an interracial marriage is always in the position to insinuate that at least *his* white blood was acquired *legally*. The usual light color of the offspring of an intermarried couple actually places the child among the preferred physical group in the Negro community.*

There are instances, however, in which parents have worried about the possible color of the children. One woman said:

"The thing that worries me is that the baby is so white. I'm afraid it will not get brown. Do you think it will? The doctor said it would be the color of its ears. If that's true, he will be white, and his hair is very light. My husband is a dark brown-skinned man. He says the baby looks like me and took everything from me. I'm worried too, on the other hand, that if the baby grows dark, he may resent the Negro blood. The social worker told me that. I don't care; he's my baby and I love him, and I'll never let no one take him from me."

The presence of a child in an intermarriage does, however, create a number of problems. One of these is the attitude of the parents and relatives of the white partner. To them, the Negro spouse is a difficult enough problem to adjust to, but still is not a blood relative. The child of the intermarriage, however, is a blood relative, and must be either accepted or rejected. This can be a real emotional crisis. Some couples reported that they had not informed white relatives of the existence of children for this reason.

A woman who had recently had a child by her Negro husband was asked if she were going to tell her family. "Maybe some day," she replied; "but I am not in a hurry." This fear on the part of the white spouse is usually well founded, for it is seldom that the relatives, even though somewhat tolerant of the intermarriage, will welcome the

* (See pp. 495-506.)

natural products of it. The white wife of a Negro commented, "One of my sisters visited me one day and she knew that Joe Junior was my child, but she just couldn't kiss him." * In another case, the Negro husband had died, leaving his wife with a number of children. It was necessary for her to return to her father's home. Although he accepted her, he had reservations about the children:

"My dad's crazy about my children, since we've been living here at home with him. Of course, whenever he gets drunk, he argues with me about having married a colored man. He doesn't like for me to have anything to do with colored people now. I tell him he married who he wanted and I married who I wanted. He objects mildly to my naming my son after my husband, but he's pretty good most of the time. You know—so far as you would expect a white father to be after his daughter had married a colored man."

How the Children Adjust: Most interracial couples realize that their children will be classified as Negroes and must adjust to life in the Negro world. One white mother, not only accepted this fact, but claimed to be proud that her children would have nothing to do with white people:

"One of my boys can pass for white, but he prefers colored. My boys wouldn't marry a white woman. They all married colored. No, they never went out with white girls."

Another white mother did all that she could to strengthen her son's position in the Negro world:

"My boy is recognized and belongs to all the best colored societies and organizations. He is a member of a tennis club composed of lawyers, doctors, and such men. It costs us a lot to keep him in these organizations, but we want him to be in with the best people."

A third white woman, however, could not quite see how her chil-

---

* On the other hand, a Negro serviceman from Chicago who is married to a white woman relates the following episode: "My wife's sister came to New York with her baby to visit her husband, who was in an embarkation camp. When they left, my wife and I accompanied them and my mother-in-law, who had come with them, to the station. The baby kissed my wife good-bye. I wondered what would happen next, but did nothing. Finally my sister-in-law said, 'Your niece wants to kiss you good-bye. See how she's wrinkling up her nose?' The station was crowded. Curious stares were already being focused in our direction. I reached over and pecked at the baby, acutely self-conscious. It was interesting to note that apparently it was only I, the Negro, who was self-conscious—and not my sister-in-law, my mother-in-law, my wife—or the baby."

dren would be able to adjust to either the white or Negro community. She observed: "I hope by the time they are grown up, America will not be so prejudiced. I think in ten years this country will be something like Russia."

Usually if the child of an intermarried couple tries—either owing to encouragement from the white parent or on his own volition—to associate with white people, he encounters many difficulties. (This, of course, is true only where the family cannot or does not pass for white.) The story of two very light-skinned girls who attended mixed high schools, reveals the special problems of such children. A neighbor of one of the girls related one incident:

"Her mother was very kind to her and they were a high type of family. But in some ways the mother was brutal, too, because she didn't have any real insight into the situation. The girl didn't want to go to school and said that the other kids were mean to her. When the mother left the room, I had a chance to talk to the girl alone. She said that she was neither white nor black, and got to crying. She tried to make friends with white children at school and succeeded very well. When she was alone with them after school and wasn't afraid they would discover about her home, she was much happier. She was fifteen years old, and very well developed. The white boys liked her and she went out with them quite a bit. But she had difficulties because, as she said, they fell in love with her and after a while she'd tell them she was a Negro. She was going to run away as soon as she finished high school. There had been occasions when she stayed away from home for a week end. She said she was just staying at the home of white girls, and I think she really was. She was planning to get a job as soon as she could when she ran away. I couldn't talk her out of it, but I didn't really try, because that would probably be the best adjustment for her." In this instance, the white mother encouraged her daughter to be white, and apparently the girl intended to be—by leaving her family and passing permanently into the white group.

In the other case, the girl "identified" closely with her colored mother, but could not work out an adjustment in a mixed high school, where she was thrown into contact with both white and Negro students. She said:

"I live in a colored neighborhood and I feel closer to the colored teachers because of the fact that my mother has colored blood. I would prefer associating with whites, but I have found that it is difficult to do so. They are all right until they find out that I am colored, and then they show prejudice. It is very hard to be friendly with whites and not be invited to their homes. Of course, I could never invite them to my house.

"The colored students accept me until I act as if I am interested in becoming friendly with a white girl. Then they act funny with me. I guess that I feel that I am colored, but when I tell white people that I am, they don't believe me. I think that I have an advantage that most people don't have in being able to associate freely with both races. There are some colored that are just like white, but there are some that are lowering their race. I don't tell the white students that I'm colored—but some colored students here know I am because I live around them, and they make it their business to tell the others. Some of the colored students have a funny attitude toward me when I am with whites, and I guess they think I feel myself superior to them."

Most children of this type usually solve their problem ultimately by passing over into the white group. Some leave their parents while they are very young; others wait until their education is completed, or even until their parents die. With no strong family ties, and with few roots in the Negro community, "passing" is the logical way out of a difficult situation for the very light children of a mixed marriage.

If the child of an interracial marriage wishes to be white but cannot "pass," he may suffer severe maladjustment. He does not feel at home with either group, and often considers himself neither Negro nor white. Robert, the sixteen-year-old son of a white woman and a Negro man, represents a case of this type. He is light brown in color, with black, very wavy hair and regular features. He is just too dark to be able to pass under ordinary circumstances. When questioned about whom he associated with, he answered: "I don't go out with any colored people at all. Around here they don't like me so much. But I get along all right. Once in a while I have an argument and then they say, 'You think you're smart because you're half white.' I play ball with colored, but I never pal around with colored fellows." Asked what race he thought he belonged to, he replied, "I never thought of it. I like to get along with one as well as the other, but that is kind of hard to do. Colored people don't like people who are mixed; but that's just the lower class of colored people. I know a lot who are educated and they are not like that." To the direct question, "Do you consider yourself colored?", Robert answered in the negative. In explaining the fact that he attended a certain white Catholic school, however, he remarked, "They don't allow colored in that school. But, you see, the nuns there knew my mother."

Robert also maintained that he had never gone out with a colored girl, but that he went with lots of white girls, and was going to marry one; that he would not consider marrying a Negro. "I think intermarriage is all right if they can get along together," he said. "But to tell you the truth, I don't like to see it very much. It's all right with me —I don't care about it—but I don't like to see it. No, I can't give you any reason for not liking intermarriage. I just don't like it, that's all."

But such "in-betweens" constitute a very small proportion of the children of mixed parents. The majority make a successful adjustment in the Negro community, as Negroes—or they pass completely over into the white group. It should be emphasized, also, that only a negligibly small proportion of the Negroes who can pass for white are the offspring of intermarriage. The problems of the children of interracial couples in the Negro community are, from an objective standpoint, exactly the same as those of the children of two Negro parents who look as though they were white. A child of an intermarried couple may, however, have a different attitude toward his color. If his parents are isolated, the child may identify with the white parent, and consequently find it more difficult to become completely integrated into the Negro community.

A ROSE BY ANY OTHER NAME

"Passing" is one of the most prevalent practices that has arisen out of the American pattern of race relations. It grows from the fact that one known drop of "colored" blood is sufficient to make an otherwise completely white person a Negro. As there are thousands of Negroes whom neither colored nor white people can distinguish from full-blooded whites, it is understandable that in the anonymity of the city many Negroes "pass for white" daily, both intentionally and unintentionally. But, should white people become aware of their remote colored ancestors they would, in all probability, treat them as Negroes.*

---

* The authors have interviews which suggest that some white people in the North are willing to overlook a small infusion of Negro blood provided the person who is passing has no social ties with Negroes. Several persons when questioned on this matter said that they knew of white people who were

There are few figures on the amount of passing which takes place in the United States. Estimates of the number of people who permanently leave the Negro group and are assimilated into white society each year vary from 25,000 to 300,000. These are only estimates, and no conclusive body of statistical data is or ever could be available, especially on those who pass only temporarily or occasionally. There is not, however, a single Negro family known to the authors that has not been aware of instances, sometimes of scores of instances, in which friends, acquaintances, or relatives have crossed the color-line and become white—"gone over to the other side," as Negroes phrase it.

There are various degrees of passing, accompanied by different degrees of estrangement from the Negro group and emotional identification with the white community. Thousands of Negroes pass unintentionally daily. In a large city such as Midwest Metropolis, light-skinned Negroes who go into restaurants, who seek choice seats at a theater, or who are hired in certain jobs are mistaken for white without their being aware of it. A very light woman recently went to an exclusive photographer to have her picture taken. She returned at a later date with her daughter, who was obviously a Negro. The photographer refused to take the daughter's picture and told the mother that he did not care for colored patronage. Only then did she realize that she had been unconsciously passing for white.

Often, when caught in a situation in which he or she is taken for white, a Negro will carry through the bluff even when challenged, in order to avoid embarrassment. A young lady who did not approve of passing related the following incident:

"Speaking of passing—a strange thing happened to me this summer. When I went down to visit my father in Kentucky, I had to change trains at a station on the other side of the Mason-Dixon line. The porter took my bags and escorted me to the coach. I wasn't paying any attention to him. I just took it for granted that he was taking me to the correct coach. When I stepped into the coach, I immediately knew that he had made a mistake. All of these white people were seated and there I was! I said, 'Listen, porter—' and that's all the further I got. He said, 'That's all right, miss, the conductor will call your stop.' He

suspected of having Negro blood and that it was a joking matter. In one case everybody, including the suspect, saved face by saying it was perhaps *Indian* blood.

passed my bags overhead and tipped his hat and walked away. So I sat down and was so ill at ease.

"I noticed several of the white people glancing at me and then after the second look, they looked off. I had had my hair freshly done, and when it is fresh it looks dark brown and wavy, and I did look decent because I was wearing my best. I took a magazine and began reading. After a bit, the conductor came up and after removing his hat and apologetically clearing his throat said, 'I know this is highly irregular, miss, but—uh—pardon me—may I ask you what nationality you are? Uh—are you Jewish?' I could have kissed the conductor for giving me that lead, because as soon as he started talking, I knew what he was going to say. I knew that if I said I was a Negro and tried to explain that I wasn't trying to pass, he wouldn't believe it. Also, to have to go back into the Negro coach with the conductor leading the way would be quite embarrassing to me. The Negroes would think I was trying to pass and got caught. So I decided to play up to the situation. 'After all,' I said, 'this is highly ridiculous. Yes, I am a Jewess, and I consider this a grand insult.' I wore my haughtiest expression, and I was scared to death. By this time several of the white people had turned around and were listening to us.

"The conductor flushed and was very much embarrassed. I just know how he must have felt. He apologized again and then walked away. I was scared. I didn't enjoy the ride at all, and but for the company of a little eight-year-old white child, I talked to no one. It was lucky for me that I hadn't told Father I was coming. Suppose he had been at the station to meet me—then I would have been in a mess. I told Daddy about it and he just laughed. He thought it was a joke! And that's why I couldn't be bothered with trying to pass. I'd rather be colored and not be bothered. That's why I hate the South."

As the above incident suggests, passing in the South can often lead to serious trouble—it violates both custom and law. There are numerous stories about the dashing young man who comes to a southern town, cuts quite a figure, perhaps becomes engaged to a socially prominent local girl, and then suddenly and mysteriously disappears, never to be spoken of again. It is discovered by accident in such instances, so the tales go, that the man, though he appeared to be white, had Negro blood. In the North, however, where the population is not so sensitized, and in the crowded and impersonal atmosphere of the big cities, little thought is given to the possibility that someone might be passing, and no punitive action is taken by the society even when a person who is passing is discovered. In Midwest Metropolis, many Negroes pass merely for convenience. A light-complexioned girl remarked to one of the authors, "Whenever I am downtown alone I always go to one of the better restaurants. They think I am white, I guess; I never ask them. I wouldn't think of going with my husband, who is dark, for they might refuse us and we would be humiliated. Of course I never speak about this to him, as he is so sensitive about his color." It is common practice for very light women to patronize white beauty parlors where, according to them, they can get better service cheaper and without waiting. Often, too, a light person will purchase theater tickets for darker persons so that the latter will not be Jim-Crowed with other Negroes in the theater, or refused seats on the main floor.

From the initial state of passing unintentionally or passing for convenience, there often develops, in more adventurous persons, a practice of passing for fun. This behavior, too, can be engaged in without any feeling of guilt or disloyalty to the race; it is looked upon as having fun at the white folks' expense. Couples, and sometimes parties, will go to white cabarets and exclusive dancing places just to see what they are like and to get a thrill. Even in these cases, however, the persons involved are rather careful about relating these escapades to their friends for fear of censure from the darker persons. "I wouldn't tell everyone this, but you get around and would understand," said a light-complexioned girl. "The other night I was out with Harry—you know he can pass for white—and after we had seen a show in the Loop he said, 'Let's go over to the Pump Room.' We did and had a glorious time and it wasn't any more expensive than the Rhumboogie. No, I wasn't in the least nervous. How could they tell we were colored? There were no colored waiters who might have recognized us. After this I am going to places like that any time I am out with him." Light-complexioned people who go out with white persons of the opposite sex frequently prefer to go to white places, for there is less fear of detection on the part of the Negro community, which in the case of a woman is a matter of some concern.

A fourth type of passing arises out of economic necessity or advantage. Negro girls have had difficulty in obtaining employment in white-collar jobs. Positions as stenographers, telephone operators, receptionists, and clerks are usually closed to anyone who is known to be colored. As there are many Negro girls of superior ability and training who wish such jobs, it is not unusual for some of them to pass, if they can, in order to obtain such work. There is no way of knowing how frequently such passing occurs, but there are few upper- or middle-class Negroes who do not claim knowledge of persons who have passed for economic reasons. Men in this category usually pass to obtain technical positions, and there are verifiable instances where eminent positions as scientists, physicians, and public administrators are held by these "white Negroes."

Usually the individual returns to the Negro community for all of his social contacts and uses his light skin color simply as a method of circumventing economic discrimination. Friendships with whites are generally avoided, as they would lead to complications. One girl reported:

"My mother is very fair and passes for white on most of the jobs she has had, but she doesn't like to do it. It always brings about so much trouble. She makes friends and soon they want her to come to see them and they want to come to see her. One friend that she had had for over a year used to invite Mother to her apartment. This woman knew Mother had two children, and she would say, 'You'll just have to bring those children over so I can see them.' We would have fun talking about it. Well, she finally had to quit; the girl was becoming too chummy."

The final stage of passing—crossing over completely to the other side of the color-line—involves passing in order to associate socially with white people. For a Negro to pass socially means sociological death and rebirth. It is extremely difficult, as one loses in the process his educational standing (if he has gone to a Negro school), intimate friends, family, and work references. People well established in the Negro world and older people seldom pass socially and completely. There is too much to lose and too little to be gained.

Who Can Pass? Scholars have speculated about the amount of Negro blood which a person must have to pass. One concludes that persons with an eighth or less of Negro blood are frequently able to pass as white in a society that is not highly discriminating. Another believes that individuals with one-sixteenth colored ancestry are always able to pass as white. In Midwest Metropolis, a person with still a greater amount of Negro blood can no doubt pass. In other parts of the country, where there are many Mexicans, Puerto Ricans, and

South Americans, it is even more difficult to detect persons with considerable Negro blood.

Passing is dependent on many factors other than skin color. Many fairly dark persons with sharp features are taken for Indians, East Indians, Egyptians, or members of other dark groups. The texture of the hair in many borderline cases plays an important role. But no single factor is so important as the general configuration of skin coloring, texture of hair, and facial characteristics in determining whether a person may be "taken for white." Because of the large admixture of Indian blood among Negroes, many have a Mongolian cast to their features. These individuals, if they have straight hair, can pass for non-Negro, even if quite dark. Then there are many subtle characteristics such as dress, general deportment, mannerisms, and degree of self-assurance which all play their parts.

Quite apart from all these factors and from any objective analysis of the individual's physical make-up is the factor of the social situation. In instances where Negroes are out of the conventional role, whites who have stereotyped notions of what Negroes should do, where they might be found, and how they should act are led to mistake obvious Negroes for white or other racial stock. A young Negro student entered a cab at the railroad station and asked to be taken to the University of Chicago. Although he was brown-skinned and had woolly hair, the cab driver asked if he was not Argentinian. A prominent Negro went to an exclusive night club with a white party, and even though he was introduced to the manager as a Negro, the manager refused to believe his eyes or the statement of the white members of the party. This sort of mistake is also sometimes made by Negroes. At a high school where all the students were colored, but it was the custom to have a white speaker for the commencement exercises, a light brown-skinned Negro addressed the audience and was thought by the majority of the student body to be white. Americans, white and black, see with their emotions as well as with their eyes, and actualities are colored by stereotyped expectations.

On the other hand, any white person—including the lightest blond can, if he wishes, pass for colored. Dr. Robert Park, the eminent sociologist, on two occasions passed for a Negro in order to obtain a room in a Negro hotel. A white girl who worked at a social agency in the Black Belt found out to her amazement, after working with Negro people for a year, that almost all of them not only thought she was a Negro, but refused to believe that she wasn't joking when she said she was white. Some white persons married to Negroes habitually pass for Negro in order to gain some advantage or to avoid embarrassment. The white wife of a Negro railroad waiter related the following incident:

"I have an annual pass with the railroad company my husband is with. I used it a couple of times. Yes, I was questioned when I used the pass and I said that although you might not think so, I have colored blood. I was telling the truth because I have red blood in my veins, and that's colored. The man who questioned me was a southerner and I told him that if he doubted my identity he could wire my husband at my expense."

Many persons, especially white southerners and Negroes, believe that they are so sensitized to Negro racial characteristics that they can detect persons who are attempting to pass for either white or Negro. The following incident illustrates a belief in this special ability. Speaking of her mother, who was passing for white for economic reasons, an informant said:

"She used to hold a nice position at a hotel here. One day a man called her name and said, 'You remind me of a little colored girl.' She thought the most suitable answer was, 'You remind me of a little colored boy.' He said, 'Maybe I am.' It turned out that he was colored and lived on the South Side. It is kind of funny how colored people know one another almost ten times out of ten."

The authors found, however, that among the staff of the Cayton-Warner research, one dark-complexioned white girl was constantly mistaken for colored and one very light Negro girl was identified by most visitors, both white and Negro, as not being colored. Mixed parties have been held in the Negro community where white girls have passed for Negro and Negro girls for white, to the utter confusion of all of the guests. Although persons particularly sensitized to racial differences may be a bit more astute in identifying racial characteristics, a point is reached where it is impossible with even the most refined anthropological measurements to distinguish Negroes from whites. The racial identification of such marginal persons is sociological rather than biological; and what really determines their "race" is how much the public knows about their ancestry.

✦

Passing as a Process: Few people, regardless of how light they may be, grow up as Negroes and then suddenly make an intellectual decision to pass for white. Those who pass over the color-line do so step by step until the emotional ties which bind them to Negroes are severed, on the one hand, and new relationships with members of the white community achieved, on the other hand. The first step, as has been indicated, is usually unintentional passing, where a Negro with a light skin suddenly realizes that in going about the city, outside of the Negro community, he is taken for white. Later the individual becomes more adventurous and begins to pass for some minor convenience, such as obtaining a Pullman when traveling in the South. The individual then may find a subtle pleasure in fooling white people and going places where he knows he would not be welcomed as a Negro. Still later he may seek employment in the white community with every intention of keeping all social relations among Negroes. But as intimate friendships are established with white fellow-workers, in many cases the individual is gradually drawn farther and farther away from his emotional attachment to members of the black community. For such an individual the final break comes when the irritations of trying to remain colored and the attractiveness of the white world outweigh his trepidation.

For one who is not firmly anchored in the Negro community emotionally, there is much temptation to take such a step. At first he finds that the color-line in Midwest Metropolis seems to disappear for him. There is no close scrutiny by his new-found white working companions and friends. There is no fear of any more reprisal than being fired from a job or losing some new acquaintances. Then more and more difficulties begin to arise. He begins to dread meeting old Negro friends while out with the new white ones. There are cases where daughters have refused to speak to their mothers on the street and sons have looked the other way, when accompanied by whites, upon encountering their Negro fathers. As the new job and the new friends become of more emotional importance, the individual has a constant, haunting fear of being discovered. There is the possibility that an old Negro enemy may turn him in, or that some white person may accidentally discover him and work vengeance on him.

Then there arises a moral crisis. On the one hand, it is hard to continue to live in two worlds; but on the other hand, there is a sense of guilt over being unfaithful to the Negro world with which he and his family have been identified. Then it is that many an individual either announces to a startled office manager, foreman, or fiancée that he is a Negro and would prefer to be known as such, or commits sociological suicide, to be reborn on the white side of the color-line.

An individual who makes the latter choice is not operating in a vacuum. There is the constant and disturbing pressure of the Negro community which both pushes and pulls him. Many very light men, especially, feel uncomfortable in the Negro community. They are very conspicuous when out with Negro groups except when all are as light as they. This is the push which exerts itself on them from birth. They are always suspect—the community feels that in most cases they are only looking for a chance to escape the confines of color. Passing episodes are carefully concealed from most of their Negro friends, for the community would in most cases censure them; and even when they pass solely for economic reasons, only a partial and begrudging sanction is given them. Finally, the condemnation of the Negro group itself operates in the same way as the attractiveness of moving freely in white society, to allow them to make a moral decision to cross over the line. Although there is far from unanimity on the subject, many Negroes would agree with a young woman who said:

"Well, I don't see anything wrong with it, if the person can get something out of it. But personally, I don't like it. I think if for commercial reasons it is done as Mary Malone is doing [she named a well-known Negro girl who passes for white on the stage], that's not so bad; but I wouldn't want to deny my race otherwise. And then I would associate with colored people after I was finished work. What I mean is that I would pass only for business purposes and not because I didn't want to be colored."

There is a widespread belief in the community that Negroes protect other Negroes who are passing. One white woman married to a Negro stated:

"Some people would try to prevent a person from holding a job if they knew he wasn't entitled to it because of color. My husband knows a man who is colored and who is working as a white man, but my husband never recognizes him. There is a sort of code of honor among colored people not to reveal the identity of a person who is working as white."

Although there are occasional instances of Negroes exposing others who are passing, in general there is great tolerance on the part of

Negroes if they know they are not being slighted or are being slighted for economic reasons only. The difference in attitude of two colored girls who worked in a downtown department store illustrates this point:

"Mary and I got a job working at Field's one Christmas. Mary had had much more practice at passing than I. But she was scared to death that someone—some colored person—would see her and recognize her. They put her in the costume jewelry section right on the first floor. Negroes would come in and she would try to avoid them and turn her back. Then they made a point of trying to speak to her. Finally she became a nervous wreck and had to quit. They put me in the handkerchief section on State Street, and people were coming in all the time that I knew; but I always spoke to them and would wait on them if they came to my counter. So I got along all right. Lots of people who sensed that I was going to speak to them would just nod and move away quickly. They weren't resentful. I really needed the money; but it wasn't a life-and-death matter, so I couldn't think of not speaking to someone that I knew."

The practice of passing for economic reasons is so frequent and the Negro's economic position is so desperate that some years ago the Chicago *Defender* gave partial sanction to this behavior in an editorial [1] mainly slanted toward poking fun at the attitude of whites:

In our big department stores in the Loop can be found many sons and daughters who come back "home" at the close of the day, and by the same token would come back home to stay if their identity was found out. They are not as fair as lilies but the fact that most of the stores are "manned" by Jewish girls whose complexion and hair is swarthy helps the situation out materially. It is a shame and a disgrace that we must be forced in order to make a livelihood, to live this life each day, but there is not another way. We pour thousands of dollars, hard earned, into the coffers of the storekeepers and yet we are denied recognition or a chance to earn some of it back except we apply for some menial position like running an elevator or janitorship, and in many places we are even denied this class of employment. That our men and women are superior in every way to the average wage-earner found in these stores is without question, but worth doesn't count when prejudice creeps in, so we must fight fire with fire, and those that are able to "get by" peace be with them and it is our duty not to hinder them in any way. Last Monday was the Jewish New Year and all of that faith were given a holiday—without pay—by the store managers. This, of course, made a number of our young ladies who were Jewish pro tem take two days off. "There are tricks to all trades," said one of them laughingly, "and we had it to do to allay suspicion." So even with the serious side of it there comes something in the lighter vein. But it does seem with a concerted effort this situation could in a measure be changed for the better, patronize the store that offers the most to you and yours and you will be aiding materially in the movement.

A Rose Is a Rose Is a Rose: Although thousands of Negroes are lost to the Negro race each year by passing, scores of thousands have passed for a while only to return to the—for them—warmer and more comfortable milieu of the Negro community.

A prominent colored physician reported that for some years after he left college he passed for white in practicing medicine. He could never feel quite comfortable and was particularly concerned about his relationships with his family. After having established a successful practice, he suddenly decided to return to the Negro group and there achieved a position of prominence which he could never have attained in the larger society. Another well-known Negro businessman for a number of years lived on the North Shore, but he too returned to the Black Belt and, with the capital he had accumulated and the insight into white business practices he had obtained, was able to establish one of the most successful enterprises in the community.

In both of these instances, as in many others, passing was profitable at one period of the individual's life, when he had no money and little experience, but it was equally profitable later on to return to the Negro community. Usually the fact that he has passed is a guarded secret, for it would indicate that at one time he had severed his emotional identification with the community and he would be suspected of demonstrating a similar disloyalty again. Men pass for noneconomic reasons more frequently than women; it is also more common for men to return to the Negro group. Once a light girl has passed, she would be considered disloyal—sullied, and not to be trusted—and would not be able to make such an advantageous marriage were she to return to the Negro group. While it is common knowledge that thousands of Negroes pass, cases of those who return are relatively infrequent. In the lives of many prominent Negroes, however, are gaps which can be explained only in terms of a temporary passing over the color-line.

Passing has been described as a process where one gradually relinquishes his social relationships and emotional identification with the Negro community. It should not be thought, however, that every person who passes completely goes through each step of this process; it is merely the pattern generally followed. Many people are never successful in breaking their ties completely with either group, and severe maladjustment often results.

Passing is one way of crossing the color-line. It does not challenge the mores of the society, for it is surreptitious. It does, however, bring with it miscegenation, introducing a constant stream of Negro blood into the white population. In fact, as Louis Wirth and Herbert Goldhamer state, "One southern state legislator, in speaking against an especially severe bill restricting Negro-white intermarriage, is reported as saying that if the definition of Negro incorporated in the bill were accepted there would not be enough white people in the state to pass it." [2]

Midwest Metropolis is not aware of the volume of passing nor disturbed enough about it to take punitive action. Nevertheless anyone discovered is usually considered a Negro. If such an individual has attained a position of great importance, however, the episode is often hushed up. Negroes claim to be aware of many cases of this kind, and numerous stories on the subject circulate throughout the community.* It is even widely believed that there has been at least one "Negro" president of the United States.†

A Two-way Passage: In Chicago people do occasionally cross the color-line. And when they do, they may encounter difficulties. But hundreds of Negroes have lived and are living as white, and a small group of whites have become sociological Negroes. It can and does happen here—but not with the frequency which would warrant the irrational fear of "amalgamation" held by many white people.

What does this race crossing mean? More Negro blood than most suspect finds its way into the white population—not enough, however,

* Such stories are hard to verify. Occasionally, however, an incident becomes a matter of public record. Just before the First World War, for instance, a wealthy Chicago publisher, always considered white, was found to be a "Negro" when his darker relatives showed up at his funeral. A similar case appeared in the neighboring state of Indiana in 1940 when a leading businessman and philanthropist was revealed as colored at his funeral.

† J. A. Rogers marshals an impressive array of evidence to substantiate this claim, including a statement from S. H. Adams, *The Incredible Era,* to the effect that the President in question not only did not deny his Negro ancestry but simply said, "How do I know? One of my ancestors might have jumped the fence." (See J. A. Rogers, *op. cit.,* pp. 254-258.)

to change the physical characteristics of that group at all. Passing is of much more serious import to Negroes. Yearly a number of "white Negroes" pass over the line. This perhaps robs the Negro group of possible leaders and well-trained persons who could add immeasurably to the welfare of the group. But it should be noted that a relatively small proportion of those who can pass really do cross over completely, and there are some who have passed completely but who "return to their race" with capital and experience which allows them to become leaders. It's a two-way passage in many instances.

Intermarriage, on the other hand, operates to introduce more white blood into the Negro group, modifying to an extent that physical type. The study of the "American Negro" is not merely the study of Negroes so designated because they are culturally distinct from the Negroes of Africa, but is also the study of the formation of a relatively distinct physical type." [3] Intermarriage (though nonlegal miscegenation is much more important in this connection) is one of the means by which this new type—the brown American—has come into existence.

THE "BLACK BABY" BUGABOO

Mixed couples usually express a desire for either light brown-skinned children or children who can pass for white. People who oppose passing often cite the "danger" of a "black baby"—a "throwback"—sometime cropping up should the Negro who has passed, or his descendants, marry a white person. Negroes who are passing occasionally hesitate to get married or to have children for fear that "Negro blood will out." This emphasis upon the "black baby" arriving to embarrass its parents has a dual significance. On one hand it reflects the general attitude of the dominant white American culture toward "typical" Negro physical traits—the definition of black skin, thick lips, and kinky hair as "ugly." On the other hand, it expresses a desire that children shall not look so different from the parents as to excite embarrassing stares or malicious gossip.*

* Esthetic standards vary from culture to culture. Many Central African groups think that thin lips, white skin and straight hair are ugly. And among white people there are many who can recognize "black" beauty or "yellow" beauty as well as white. There are people, too, who in choosing a mate do not put such standards in the primary place. Students of Latin American countries have frequently called attention to the fact that the marriage of whites to very Negroid types is not unusual, and that the white partners feel no shame in such

The "black baby" bugaboo is often cited as the primary objection to passing. Edward M. East, the geneticist, has discussed the probable origin of such black babies as do appear in the following passage:

"A favorite short-story plot with which melodramatic artists seek to harrow the feelings of their readers is one where the distinguished scion of an aristocratic family marries the beautiful girl with telltale shadows on the half-moons of her nails, and in due time is presented with a coal-black son. It is a good framework, and carries a thrill. One waits shiveringly, even breathlessly, for the first squeal of the dingy infant. There is only this slight imperfection—or is it an advantage?— it could not possibly happen on the stage as set by the author. The most casual examination of the genetic formulae given above demonstrates its absurdity. If there ever was a basis for the plot in real life, the explanation lies in a fracture of the seventh commandment, or in a tinge of negro [*sic*] blood in the aristocrat as dark as that in his wife." [4]

The genetic formulae referred to by East, and generally accepted by geneticists and anthropologists, support the following conclusions: *

1. In the case of two persons both theoretically white but having, whether they know it or not, some Negro blood, an accentuation of some Negro characteristics may occur in their offspring, but in all probability the offspring of such unions will be able to pass for white.

2. It is impossible for the offspring of a recognizable Negro and a *pure* white person to be any darker than the Negro partner, and in all probability it will be lighter.

3. The offspring of two mixed-bloods (e.g., mulattoes or quadroons) may be darker than either, but in all probability would not be black.

Even a widespread knowledge of these facts will not dispel the "black baby" bugaboo, for what white person can be sure that he has no Negro blood, or what Negro who is passing that he will not

cases. Yet, often, very devoted couples of this type want children who are blends and consider a dark child unfortunate. (See Donald Pierson's *Negroes in Brazil,* University of Chicago Press, pp. 111-76, for an interesting discussion of these patterns as he observed them in Bahia where intermarriage is not frowned upon, and in many ways is actually encouraged.)

* In detailing these conclusions we have used the expression "Negro blood" instead of the more precise formulation in terms of genes that govern characteristics such as skin-color, hair form, shape of nose, etc. Obviously, however, blood has nothing to do with heredity, but it is probable that the colloquial use of the term "Negro blood" will remain long after the general public is aware that it really refers to "genes for Negro traits."

marry a "white" person who has a few drops from way back? The chances of such marriages producing a "black baby" are extremely remote—but it could happen. "In all probability" is not a very reassuring phrase. So long as "blackness" of skin is considered a misfortune, the bugaboo will remain. Even if the habit of stigmatizing people because of their skin-color were to disappear, a "black baby" would still be considered a misfortune until everyone knew that an occasional dark child born to lighter parents did not constitute *prima facie* evidence of interracial adultery.

WHAT OF THE FUTURE?

The specter of social equality is enough to seriously limit the competition of Negroes economically, politically, and socially in Midwest Metropolis. But it is unlikely that, given our present form of government and the Negro's present political strength in Chicago, any stringent legal action will be taken to keep people from crossing the color-line. The majority of the people in Midwest Metropolis may not like intermarriage, but it is not a burning issue and therefore does not evoke formal legal action. Such action would, of course, be fought by the Negro citizens of Chicago. Although their feeling of race pride leads most of them to disapprove of intermarriage, its legality is important to them as one manifestation of their equal civil rights.

Many whites will continue to exploit the fear of intermarriage as a means of retaining economic dominance, and as a devastating question to be raised in connection with any concessions, no matter how small, which the Negro community requests. A few intermarriages will no doubt continue to take place, as well as clandestine "affairs," but "crossing the line" is not uppermost in the minds of the Negroes. Relaxation of the taboos against intermarriage is something white people are most reluctant to grant. It is also the "concession" which Negroes, as a group, are least likely to request. That it looms so large in the white mind is the irony of race relations in Midwest Metropolis.

CHAPTER 8

The Black Ghetto

THE STRONGEST VISUAL EVIDENCE OF A COLOR-LINE IN MIDWEST METROPOLIS is the existence of a Black Belt. Of the city's 337,000 Negroes, over ninety out of every hundred live in areas predominantly Negro.

It is not unusual for a language, nationality, or racial group to begin life in the city as a "colony." The distinctive thing about the Black Belt is that while other such "colonies" tend to break up with the passage of time, the Negro area becomes increasingly more concentrated. By 1940, this area in Chicago had virtually ceased to expand in size, but new migrants to the city were pouring into it, and very few Negroes were trickling out into other parts of the city.

The persistence of a Black Belt, whose inhabitants can neither scatter as individuals nor expand as a group, is no accident. It is primarily the result of white people's attitudes toward having Negroes as neighbors. Because some white Chicagoans do not wish colored neighbors, formal and informal social controls are used to isolate the latter within congested all-Negro neighborhoods.

The native-born, middle-class, white population is the group that sets the standards by which various people are designated as desirable or undesirable. The attitudes of this middle-class group are probably decisive in restricting Negroes and other groups to special areas of the city. These attitudes become translated into economic terms, and though the kinds of people the white middle class desires as neighbors do not affect property values adversely, their dislike and fear of other groups is reflected by a decline in the sales value of residential property when such people begin to penetrate a neighborhood. In Midwest Metropolis, such ethnic groups as the English, Germans, Scotch, Irish, and Scandinavians have little adverse effect on property values. Northern Italians are considered less desirable, followed by Bohemians and Czechs, Poles, Lithuanians, Greeks, and Russian Jews of the lower class. Southern Italians, along with Negroes and Mexicans, are at the bottom of the scale of middle-class white "desirability." *

The areas in which these groups are concentrated become stigmatized as "slum neighborhoods," and there is a tendency to blame the group for the condition of the area. One factor that complicates this whole matter of land-values—for the areas in question *are* predominantly slums—is the fact that the "undesirable" groups usually inherit sections of the city that the older, more well-to-do inhabitants have abandoned and thus "the undesirable racial factor is so merged with other unattractive features, such as proximity to factories, poor transportation, old and obsolete buildings, poor street improvements, and the presence of criminal or vice elements, that the separate effect of race cannot be disentangled." [1]

Given the definition of an area and the people in it as "undesirable," the expansion of the area will be resisted. If, however, individuals within it are able to change the telltale marks of poverty, name, foreign language, or distinctive customs, they may move out and lose themselves in middle-class, native-born white neighborhoods. This, Negroes wearing the badge of color, cannot do. Negro areas must either expand as parts of a constantly growing Black Belt, or stagnate as deteriorating slums.

EVOLUTION OF A BLACK BELT

The Negro area of Midwest Metropolis has been expanding for almost a hundred years—sometimes slowly, sometimes rapidly; occasionally with serious disturbances, but usually as a peaceful process. The expansion has taken two forms—a gradual filtering-in of Negroes among the white population, and mass invasion. Before the Great Migration, the usual process of filtering-in seems to have been one in which a few Negroes would move out of the Negro colony into surrounding areas. As others followed them, small nuclei of Negroes were formed. Then, when the proportion of Negroes to whites became large, the white population would move, leaving the areas all-Negro.

Before the Great Migration, over half of the Negro population lived

* Most social-distance scales indicate that native-born Americans tend to arrange people in a rank-order of desirability as neighbors which places Northern Europeans at the top, and Negroes, Mexicans, and similar colored groups near the bottom.

outside of the then small Black Belt.* Some of these were servants living near the white families for whom they worked. Others were families who had bought property on the outskirts of a city that eventually grew out to meet them. Still others were moderately prosperous people following the general residential trend away from the center of the city.

Old Settlers have a tendency to romanticize this period, but it is evident from their comments that sporadic, unorganized resistance to Negro neighbors was sometimes encountered. One woman, referring to her experience in the Eighties, indicates that antagonism toward Negroes was strong enough to permit a person to annoy a neighbor by renting a house to a Negro:

"There has always been race prejudice here, but not so strong as it is now. The owner of this house was a German and he was mad at his neighbor. He was tickled to death to rent it to colored, just in order to spite Mrs. Richmond. Later I bought the house."

Occasionally a light-skinned Negro would move into a neighborhood and it might be some time before he was "discovered." One very light Negro, reporting such an episode, said:

"In 1904 or 1905, I moved in here. I bought in 1907. There were white neighbors on both sides at first. I rented the house the first time I moved in it. The man I rented the house from talked to me about the place, and rented it to me, and he thought I was a white man. The neighbors made complaints about it. He said, 'The man has a lease and he'll keep it until it is up.' After the lease was up, I bought the house for a price reasonable at that time. The fellow was a Scotchman."

The experiences of individual Negroes during this filtering-in process depended on many factors, including the social-class and ethnic composition of the area, as well as the class and skin-color of the Negro. When only a few Negroes were involved, and they were of equivalent social status to the whites, or when the whites were of lower class position than the colored people, initial hostility usually gave way to toler-

* In 1910 there were no communities in which Negroes were over 61 per cent of the population. More than two-thirds of the Negroes lived in areas less than 50 per cent Negro, and a third lived in areas less than 10 per cent Negro. By 1920, 87 per cent of the Negroes lived in areas over half Negro in composition. A decade later 90 per cent were in districts of 50 per cent or more Negro concentration. Almost two-thirds (63.0 per cent) lived where the concentration was from 90 to 99 per cent Negro!

ance or even friendliness. But when large numbers of Negroes followed, antagonisms were aroused, and eventually the white population would move away. Old Settlers frequently refer to the relative ease with which they made adjustments, once they had filtered into some types of white neighborhoods. The following two statements summarize the experiences of scores of pre-migration Negro families. One woman states:

"I came to Chicago in 1903. I lived on Lincoln Street—there were foreigners there. My children used to go to white kids' parties, for where we lived there was nothing much but foreigners. There was only one other colored family in that block. The white people never used to call my children names."

Another woman suggested that while relations between children and adults in such areas were often friendly, the social barrier stiffened during the critical adolescent period:

"I was raised on the Near North Side and at that time we were the only Negro family over there. I didn't know so much about color until I was about eleven or twelve years old. In fact, I hadn't given it a second thought. My playmates were all white. I used to go to their parties and they would come to mine; but after I was old enough to go into high school, that was where the trouble started. I never did have any serious trouble, but it wasn't so pleasant as it had been when I was a child."

This woman also blamed an increase in the *number* of Negroes for changes in white neighborhood sentiment:

"As long as there was just one colored family over there it was all right, but after the neighborhood began to have an increase in the number of colored families, the children started to making trouble among themselves, and, of course, that brought the older people into it."

Concurrently with the filtering-in process, the Black Belt itself was expanding in these pre-Migration years. As whites moved out of areas adjacent to the Black Belt to seek better homes farther from the center of the city, Negroes moved in. So long as Negroes were but a minute percentage of the population, they were easily accommodated. It was only after 1915, when 65,000 migrants came into the city within five years, that resistance became organized. Negro migrants were then compelled to spill over the margins of the Black Belt, and their search for homes in other parts of the city was eventually interpreted as a "mass invasion." Yet even the Negroes who streamed into the city during the first three years of the Great Migration had little difficulty in renting or buying property near the small Black Belt, for middle-class white residents were abandoning these areas. Real-estate agents and property owners of both races promoted the expansion of the Black Belt, and there was little friction.

But when the United States entered the World War in 1917 building operations were suspended and a housing shortage quickly resulted. Property owners' associations began to talk of re-establishing neighborhoods adjacent to the Black Belt as exclusively white. This meant that the Negroes who had already moved in must be forced out if possible, and that no others must be allowed to enter. Before the housing shortage, these adjacent white communities had been willing to absorb a few Negroes and then to relinquish the community to them as they became too numerous. Now they were disposed to stay and fight.

Several property owners' associations which had been originally organized for neighborhood improvement, now began to focus their attention upon keeping out Negroes. They sponsored numerous mass meetings to arouse the citizens to the peril of "invasion." They published scathing denunciations of Negroes branding them arrogant, ignorant, diseased, bumptious, destructive of property and generally undesirable. A wave of violence flared up and between July, 1917, and March, 1921, fifty-eight homes were bombed—an average of one every twenty days. Two Negroes were killed, a number of white and colored persons were injured, and property damage amounted to over a hundred thousand dollars. The victims of the bombings were Negro families that had moved into white neighborhoods, as well as Negro and white real-estate men who sold or rented property to them. Feeling was particularly strong against real-estate men who were suspected of renting to one or two Negroes in a block in order to frighten the white residents away so that the realtors could move Negroes in at higher rents.

The most widely publicized bombing case was that of Jesse Binga, the Negro banker and real-estate dealer mentioned earlier. Binga was of relatively high social and economic status, and could hardly be accused of not knowing how to care for property. In fact, the property owners' associations attacked him precisely because he *did* represent a higher-status Negro. When he bought a home in a white middle-class area, the *Property Owners' Journal* denounced him for having "wormed his way into a white neighborhood," characterizing him as one of the "misleaders of the Negro, those flamboyant, noisy, witless individuals, who by power of superior gall and gumption have blustered their way into positions of prominence amongst their people." [2] Since verbal threats failed to dislodge him, bombs were tried. These also failed.

The property owners' association never admitted complicity in these bombings, and responsibility was never definitely placed by the police. Indeed, individual groups of property owners warned against violence, one such group declaring that the *moral* onus rested on the associations if the bombings continued, even though the associations were not actively involved.

By 1925, the wave of bombings had ceased. Since that time the major device for controlling the expansion of the Negro community has been the restrictive covenant—an agreement between property owners within a certain district not to rent or sell to Negroes. Although their constitutionality is being questioned, the covenants have been recognized as legal by the courts, and property owners' associations continue to use the pressure of public opinion to secure signatures from white owners who may be reluctant to enter into them.

As early as January, 1920, the Chicago *Tribune* reported [3] under the caption, "United Action Keeps Negroes Out of 57 Homes," that

The Chicago Real Estate Board extended felicitations to the Grand Boulevard branch of the Kenwood and Hyde Park Property Owners' Associations yesterday, when the association proclaimed that in sixty days it had forestalled Negro occupancy of fifty-seven houses south of Thirty-ninth Street.

In May of the following year, the same paper noted that the Chicago Real Estate Board was as ready to penalize those who sold to Negroes as to felicitate those who would not: [4]

Immediate expulsion from the Chicago Real Estate Board will be the penalty paid by any member who sells a Negro property in a block where there are only white owners. This was voted unanimously at a meeting of the board yesterday, following an appeal by Col. V—— H. S——, a former president of the organization, that the board take a definite stand on the Negro question. He called the Chicago Real Estate Board cowardly, and declared it had always sidestepped the issue. His motion followed a plea by the Grand Boulevard Property Owners' Association for co-operation of the realtors in settling the property ownership problem.

PATTERNS OF ADJUSTMENT

As a result of competition for space, four main types of neighborhoods have developed: (1) mixed, unadjusted neighborhoods; (2) mixed, adjusted neighborhoods; (3) contested areas; and (4) neighborhoods that are entirely white or Negro.*

There are certain mixed, lower-class neighborhoods which have a tradition of hostility toward Negroes; in others, hostility arises only occasionally. In most of these, Negroes are living among the foreign-born. The equilibrium is easily disturbed in these areas, and a trivial incident may precipitate a crisis. In recent years the problem has arisen whether Negroes and whites are to be segregated in Federal housing projects in these areas. This, in turn, has repercussions on the larger community.†

There are other low-status areas where Negroes and whites live side by side as neighbors in proportions of from one-fourth to two-thirds Negro. In such situations Negroes are in intimate contact with foreign-born groups. Relations seem to be most harmonious with Italians, Mexicans, and Jews, and least with the Irish and Poles. Although there are occasional fights among the children, there is on the whole little friction. The social life is generally separate, and Negroes in such areas often look down on the foreign-born. One colored woman, for instance, said: "We're not segregated here. Who are these 'hunkies' to segregate you? Most of them are as black as I am." ‡

Other Negroes who live in mixed areas not only tolerate their neighbors but sometimes become friendly with them:

* This system of classification was used originally in the study of the Riot, by the Chicago Commission on Race Relations.

† There are three Federal housing projects in which Negroes and whites live without any official segregation. In each of them there have been minor racial difficulties, but, on the whole, the various ethnic groups sustain neighborly relations with one another.

‡ Another woman, who does not live in a mixed neighborhood, expressed the same feeling: "Being a southerner, I've always lived in a Negro community, and I didn't come this far to live among the Polacks, Dagoes, and other low-class white trash. I prefer living among my own group."

"I have been in this neighborhood twenty years. I think Italians get along better with colored than other whites."

"I went to a mixed school. Two of my closest friends were Japanese, fully Americanized and friendly. We visited in each other's homes. We were friendly with Jews and Italians, mostly Italians."

"Over here there are only seventeen or twenty colored families. Most of the people are Jewish, some are Polish. The Polish are rather prejudiced. Our next-door neighbors are Irish. They visit me, but I have an excuse and never visit them."

"All of the old white settlers of this community are dead. But most of the children I went to school with still live in the community. All of the girls I grew up with are still my friends. This might seem a funny statement to make, but really I know nothing about Negroes, but I know all about white people. These white people in this community are all my friends. A Polish family moved just a few doors from me. They weren't here a week before they started trying to get my neighbors to sign petitions to get me out of the community, but they refused to sign against me and next month I saw a sign for rent in the flat the Polish people rented."

Because of the general difference in cultural background, Negroes and foreign ethnic groups have little in common, and some mutual suspicions and occasional antagonisms are inevitable, as revealed in the following statements by residents in mixed areas:

"I remember how I used to fight with the white children, especially the Dago children. They would call out to us colored children, 'Nigger, nigger, never die, black face and China eye,' and when I would catch one and get through with him he would think *he* was black."

"The Italian boys were so low morally. They made several attempts to rape some of the girls . . . used to gang us . . . We were always able to have a good fight and have some blood shed. The intense feeling lasted till now. The friendships were not lasting."

"I used to live on the North Side as a school kid. Two colored boys went to school with me. An Italian girl liked one of these boys.

Her family sent Bill one of their famous black hand warnings. All us colored fellows were scared to death."

"Over here, there is not much mixing among the grown-ups. Small children play together at times all right. Dagoes call the children 'niggers' once in a while. These Dagoes over here is rotten. They think they is better than you, especially the young women. On Clark in some of the restaurants they are not particular about serving you."

"This place is ruined. Nothing is around here but these old Italians from New Orleans. You will hear one telling his neighbor, 'Don't visit niggers in their houses.' I would send them all back to Italy where they belong. I hate them folks."

There are a few areas in which lower middle-class Negro and white families have lived harmoniously over a long period of time. A few Negroes are scattered among white families, and there is some adult family visiting and friendly contact between children below teen-age. Negroes in such neighborhoods usually go into the Black Belt for church services and recreation. Public schools and neighborhood movies in such areas seldom discriminate against the Negroes they know. This equilibrium is disturbed when the number of Negroes begins to increase appreciably or when larger numbers of lower-status Negroes filter in. Signs of trouble usually appear first in school situations. Tension between white teachers and the new Negro students arises. The older colored population is torn between "race loyalty" and antagonism toward the newcomers. Conversations between parents are reflected in the playground squabbles of the children. And the adjusted area becomes a "contested area" if the proportion of Negroes continues to mount.

RESTRICTIVE COVENANTS AND CONTESTED AREAS

It is in middle-class white neighborhoods adjacent to Negro communities, when a mass invasion is feared, that antagonisms become most highly organized. Such spots become "contested areas." There were several such areas in Midwest Metropolis on the eve of the Second World War. (Note the areas east and south of the Black Belt in Figure 7.)

Figure 7

TYPES OF RESIDENTIAL AREAS:1934

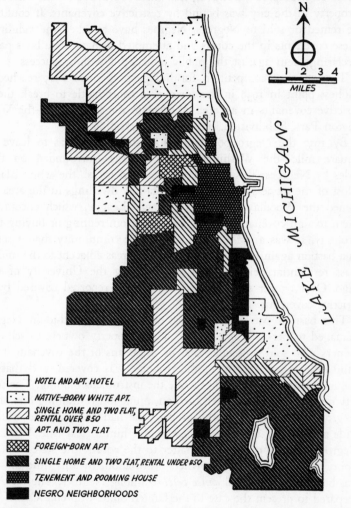

HOTEL AND APT. HOTEL

NATIVE-BORN WHITE APT.

SINGLE HOME AND TWO FLAT, RENTAL OVER $50

APT. AND TWO FLAT

FOREIGN-BORN APT

SINGLE HOME AND TWO FLAT, RENTAL UNDER $50

TENEMENT AND ROOMING HOUSE

NEGRO NEIGHBORHOODS

Prepared by combining a group of maps in Faris and Dunham's *Mental Disorders in Urban Areas*. The "hotel and apartment hotel" and the "native-born white apartment" areas east of the Black Belt, and the "single home and two flat" areas to the south are "middle-class" white neighborhoods.

The Commission on Race Relations had warned in 1920 against the enforced segregation of Negroes, By 1930, such measures had become so widespread, however, that three-fourths of all the residential property in the city was bound by restrictive covenants. It could not be rented or sold to Negroes. Negroes have attacked the validity of these covenants in the courts and attempted to have state laws passed declaring them against the public policy, but without success.

Tension over competition for living space since 1925 reached its highest point in 1938 in the form of a court battle to break the restrictive covenants in an area adjacent to the Black Belt—the Washington Park Subdivision. The story is revealing.

By 1937 the Negro population had so expanded as to leave one square mile—the Washington Park district—surrounded on three sides by Negroes; this district was referred to as "the white island." Most of the owners of one- and two-family dwellings in the area had joined the Woodlawn Property Owners' League, which encouraged them to sign covenants barring Negroes from renting or buying their property. It was a point of pride with the community that it served as a bastion against the Negro influx into areas adjacent to the middle-class residential neighborhoods surrounding the University of Chicago. Over 95 per cent of the frontage was reported covered by restrictive covenants.

This bastion was first breached when several well-to-do Negroes managed to persuade one or two white property owners to sell. The owners who sold contended that by the terms of the covenant it was valid only if 95 per cent of the frontage was covered, and that not enough owners had signed to make the instrument binding. The property owners' association then filed an injunction restraining one of the Negroes from occupying the property he had bought. The Chicago Title and Trust Company refused to give him a clear title. When the Negro purchaser carried the matter to the courts, the state Supreme Court upheld the property owners' association. By this time the case was becoming a national *cause célèbre* among Negroes. The NAACP prepared to present the case to the United States Supreme Court. The lines were tightly drawn. National real-estate magazines declared the case would set a precedent for all northern communities and called on member organizations to watch it with care. Money-raising campaigns were opened in the Negro community, and Negro newspapers all over the country began to comment on the significance of the case.

Meantime some of the larger white real-estate companies with an eye for business began to break the covenants. They moved Negroes into one or two apartment buildings, immediately raising the rents by from 20 to 50 per cent. In 1940 there were many cases of whites and Negroes living in the same building, the latter paying—for equivalent accommodations—rentals much higher than those paid by the whites; in such cases the realtors were urging the white families to leave so that their apartments could be rented to Negroes at a higher rate.

The smaller property owners were then pressed to sell their property to the realtors because "the neighborhood was going colored and the value of their investments would fall anyhow." Some owners, seeing the economic advantage, preferred to sell or rent to Negroes directly. But these owners were in a dilemma: If they sold to Negroes and broke the covenants, the property owners' associations would challenge the transactions; whereas, if they did not sell to Negroes, either they would find themselves stranded in all-Negro communities, unable because of the covenants to rent any portion of their property to Negroes, or they would have to sell at a loss to the larger real-estate companies.

As they became aware of this dilemma, the Small Property Owners, Associated, Inc., came into being.[5] The organization described itself as "a mutually incorporated body . . . organized solely for the express object of seeking immediate relief from the present existing impractical and now highly injurious exactions of the so-called 'Restrictive Covenant.'" It did not attack restrictive covenants on principle, nor indicate that the members wished to live in Negro neighborhoods. Covenants were now considered economically disadvantageous, and their espousal was simply called "blind loyalty" to a losing cause. In fact, the officers hastened to assure reluctant owners that the organization was

. . . composed entirely by WHITE property holders . . . and was instituted for the purpose of legally petitioning by exhaustive court procedure, relief from the glaring inequity of this existing "restrictive agreement" upon the undeniable grounds of repeatedly proven Abandonment, Impracticability [*sic*] to further Enforce, Public Policy and to reassure our members the restoration of their inherent American right to again freely exercise, within their discretion, adequate safeguards toward the vital protection of their financial investments herein.

Antagonism was focused on "high-priced East End attorneys" (a reference to the University of Chicago area) sponsored by funds from a "non-resident property owners' league" which allegedly

... during the past several years has been actuated solely by a motive to assure the maintenance of white residential supremacy ... regardless of the great financial detriment, mental anguish and impracticability of those owners within said subdivision to further withstand the devastating losses sustained through the vainly impotent racial rental restrictions exacted by that non-residential body.

The shoe was pinching!

The NAACP, which had been preparing the case for the United States Supreme Court, enlisted the aid of this white small-property owners' group. A brief filed by the white lawyer reveals how the white supremacy dogmas disintegrated under the pressure of economic necessity: [6]

Your plaintiffs further allege that in view of the large Negro occupancy in said area ... there are only a certain class of the poorer white people that desire to remain there; that they are poor rent payers; careless with the upkeep and care of property; and will pay only very low rentals, and that said property cannot be operated at a profit.

Your plaintiffs further allege that the Negro tenants pay substantially larger rentals and permit the buildings to be maintained from the income of said property; that the buildings now classed as white properties are not maintaining themselves and will result in ultimate financial ruin and loss of property.

When the case was carried to the Supreme Court, a ruling was handed down which, in effect, constituted a victory for the Negroes. The court did not rule that restrictive covenants were invalid, but it did state that each parcel of property in the area constituted a specific, individual case and that no decision against one owner for renting or selling to a Negro constituted a precedent binding others. The cost of fighting several hundred cases through the courts every time a violation occurred would have bankrupted the Woodlawn Property Owners' League.

The editors of national real-estate journals were quick to point out that this was no clear-cut victory for opponents of restrictive covenants. The business manager of the Woodlawn association, in an article in one of these magazines, commented [7] (the italics are the authors'):

The Lee versus Hansberry case and the decision in connection with it are so important to Chicago real estate that they deserve a correct and complete discussion, free from racial prejudice and mysterious legal technicalities and phrases—with emphasis on the import to the city, to realtors, and owners of real estate. The United States Supreme Court *did not touch upon the constitutionality or legality of restriction agreements originally upheld by it in previous cases, nor did it rule upon the validity or sufficiency of the particular Washington Park restriction agreement before it in this case.*

The validity and sufficiency of this restrictive agreement is yet to be determined and the Woodlawn Property Owners' League stands back of a number of cases which have been filed in the courts which will determine the validity and sufficiency of the agreement not passed upon by the United States Supreme Court in the Lee versus Hansberry case.

Before such "a number of cases" were heard, however, the bastion collapsed. In 1940 the area was 80 per cent Negro. By 1945 there were practically no white families in the area.

The first "official" attitude of property owners in such a contested area is one of unqualified opposition to Negro residents, and this view is usually voiced by the property owners' associations on behalf of its members. It has been shown, however, that the divergent economic interests of small and large property owners may cause a new organization to develop, stressing the economic interests of the smaller owners. When such a crisis has arisen and Negro invasion is imminent, the residents must face the choice of remaining in the area with Negroes, of selling at a low rate to the larger real estate companies, of selling to Negroes in violation of the covenant, or of fighting the covenants.

During the period of tension, a white interviewer talked with a representative group of *property owners* living in the "white island." (Absentee owners and tenants were not interviewed.) It was found that a few of these people were very bitter toward Negroes, and a few were apparently willing to live beside Negroes as neighbors, while the largest number expressed no hostility toward Negroes as such, but wanted to sell to them at a profit and move. These attitudes may be summarized in relation to what the persons who made them planned to do in relation to their own property—i.e., whether they planned to move, or to remain in the area, or were undecided.

Most of the extreme antagonism toward Negroes was expressed by people who definitely planned to leave. But the anti-Negro die-hards were a minority, even within this group. The following statements are typical of those made by persons planning to move:

"I'm not prejudiced, but I'd burn this building down before I'd sell it to any damned nigger."

"I don't want to bring my children up among Negroes, but where can people go in this city to keep away from Negroes?"

"There are just too many colored people here now."

The last quotation represents the reason most frequently given by persons planning to leave the neighborhood. The comments of the few individuals who planned to remain in the area were more varied:

"Why move? Negroes will be in all neighborhoods after a while."

"I don't mind some colored neighbors so long as the neighborhood isn't *all* colored."

"We've owned this house for years. I think the Negroes in here should be allowed to stay, but no more should come in."

"The people in here just fear intermarriage, that's all. And they're crazy! We need more government housing for Negroes."

The largest group—the "undecided"—provided an even greater variety of reactions:

"The rich Negroes get along all right in this neighborhood."

"Before the mob started coming, the Negroes in here were good neighbors. I'm not prejudiced against them, but a Negro man held me up the other day. I'm scared to stay here."

"I don't know about covenants. It doesn't seem worth all our time and money to fight for them. We can make good money by dealing with Negroes."

"We struggled hard to get this home. I'm going to stay as long as I can, but if Negroes move in all over the place, everything we worked for will be lost."

"It isn't logical to keep restrictive covenants if the only way some people can make money is to rent to Negroes. There's nothing to do but stay here and face the problem. I think real estate is a better investment here than in the suburbs."

"I'd rather have good Negro neighbors than some of the white trash that's coming in as the Negroes come. But I feel lost in this neighborhood now."

The last quotation is of particular interest because it contains two sentiments that were widely prevalent among the white residents of the neighborhood. The first was the feeling (and it seemed to be a fact) that the area was deteriorating irrespective of the influx of Negroes—i.e., in terms of new, undesirable white residents, and of the physical appearance of the community, The second sentiment, even more universal, and present among persons who were going to move out of the neighborhood as well as those who planned to remain or were undecided as to their course of action, seems extremely significant. Most of the white people did not object to the presence of a few Negroes, but they were very much afraid that they, as individual white families, would become completely isolated in a Negro area.

Gunnar Myrdal, Swedish social scientist previously referred to, has analyzed the way in which the fear of becoming isolated in an all-Negro neighborhood operates to reinforce other aspects of the struggle for living space:[8]

". . . [the] situation creates a vicious circle, in which race prejudice, economic interests, and residential segregation mutually reinforce one another. When a few Negro families do come into a neighborhood, some more white families move away. Other Negroes hasten to take their places, because the existing Negro neighborhoods are overcrowded due to segregation. This constant movement of Negroes into white neighborhoods makes the bulk of the white residents feel that their neighborhood is doomed to be predominantly Negro, and they move out—with their attitudes against the Negro reinforced. Yet, if there were no segregation, this wholesale invasion would not have occurred. But because it does occur, segregational attitudes are increased, and the vigilant pressure to stall the Negroes at the borderline is kept up."

As to how much objection white people would have to living in neighborhoods with a few Negroes of similar socio-economic status there is no certain evidence. As we have seen, there are such mixed neighborhoods in Midwest Metropolis. Yet in an opinion poll taken by *Fortune* magazine for the Carnegie-Myrdal study of "The Negro in America," from 77 to 87 per cent of the informants in various sections of the country declared themselves in favor of residential segregation. Such uniform expression of opinion throughout the country suggests that the *thought* of having Negroes as neighbors is very distasteful—though experience shows that many people, who in answer to a direct question will oppose Negro neighbors, would not use violence to evict them, and might ultimately come to accept them.

RACIAL NO MAN'S LAND

One consequence of the pattern of residential segregation is that an area of potential conflict has been created all around the boundaries of the Black Belt. Even during a period when the Belt is not expanding there is always the possibility that an invasion may begin, and this is reflected in periodic "scares," as well as in the policy of business places on the margins of the Black Belt. Proprietors of taverns, drugstores, restaurants, and neighborhood theaters are keenly sensitive to the moods of their clientele, and business places close to the Black Belt are likely to disapprove of colored patronage. This, in turn, antagonizes the Negroes and creates an additional source of friction. From 1936 through 1940 the NAACP handled a number of court cases involving establishments on the edge of the Black Belt. As restaurants and taverns became conversant with the demands of the state Civil Rights Law, they sometimes resorted to the strategem of declaring their establishments to be "clubs." White patrons were given "membership cards," and when Negroes sought service they were asked to produce their cards. This was particularly infuriating to Black Belt residents when the enterprise was on the *Negro* side of the residential dividing line.

The intensity of feeling about Negro patronage, and the manner in which a white businessman can help to crystallize anti-Negro sentiment, are revealed by the following conversation between a white interviewer, working incognito, and a white man who had run a tavern for fifteen years on a corner now marginal to the Black Belt.

Interviewer: "Do you have much Negro trade in here?"

Owner: "No, and I don't want any of the black bastards hanging around here. All they can do is to cheapen the tavern's name."

Interviewer: "Supposing a few colored people came in right now, how would you act towards them?"

Owner: "The way I feel right now I could grab one by the ass of the pants and throw him out on the street. I hate them all, all of them."

Interviewer: "But after all, you are in this place for business, regardless of the color of people, aren't you?"

Owner: "I am in it for a living, but if I have to depend on a black son-of-a-bitch for it, I'll turn the key in the door first."

Interviewer: "Why is it that you feel that way about the Negro people?"

Owner: "I'm from the South, and I'm telling you, when I came to Chicago and saw the way some of them acted I thought I was in a different world."

Interviewer: "Do you mean to say that there was that much difference in them?"

Owner: "As much difference as between day and night."

Interviewer: "But if one or two came in, wouldn't you serve them?"

Owner: "Yes, I would, but that is not saying *how* I would serve them. I don't even like to ride on the same streetcar with them."

When the neighborhood actually seems to be "going colored," white merchants and owners of restaurants, drugstores, and taverns must face the problem of Negro patronage. As has been explained, restaurants and taverns resort to a number of devices if they feel they do not want or need Negro patronage, or that they will lose more white patrons than will be replaced by Negroes. One tavern-keeper in a marginal area, who has run his business for thirty years without Negro patronage, revealed some methods of discouraging such patronage. He indicated "how" *he* would serve them:

Interviewer: "Do you have much Negro trade?"

Owner: "No, and to tell you the truth I don't want any of it."

Interviewer: "Do you refuse to serve any of them?"

Owner: "No, I serve them all right. You see, if I have any white customers I wait on them first, and I might clean the bar and fool around for five minutes or so, then I'll go up to the Negroes and ask, 'What can I do for you?' If they call for a beer, I give them a snit [a four-ounce glass]. They might look at me and grumble to themselves and pick up their change and walk out. Most of them will bang the door. If any of them ask for a shot of whiskey, I give them this [showing a bottle of very cheap whiskey]. If they put down a quarter, I ring it up and walk away from them [the price of a "shot" of whiskey being ten cents]."

Interviewer: "Did any of them ever call you on it?"

Owner: "Some of them said something and I told them that that is what it costs and if they don't like it, stay out of here."

Interviewer: "Do you think that by coming in they spoil your trade?"

Owner: "I don't think it—I know it, and I don't want any part of them. Why, two years ago I was down South, and I'm telling you it did my heart good to see them being put in their place. They run wild in Chicago as compared to down there."

Interviewer: "You have a colored porter, haven't you?"

Owner: "You mean Bill? Sure, he's a nigger, but a good worker. Of course, I keep him in his place, though. I believe in keeping them in their places, and Chicago lets them go too damn far."

Some proprietors in these marginal areas adjust themselves to a changing clientele and occasionally reinforce their decision with myths about the *superiority* of Negroes as customers. Thus an Irish bartender who had been asked point-blank for an opinion, said:

"My experience with colored people has been that they're easier to get along with than the majority of other people. It wouldn't bother me any if our whole trade were colored. Working people and some clerks make up most of our colored trade now; a few, a very few, of the top guys—insurance men and those running the policy games. I'd a lot sooner have the workers; the top guys are just smart enough to think they own the world. No, I never made any particular friends with any of the colored people; just business, that's all.

"We never have had anything anyone could call trouble in here. White and colored fellows in here drinking every night and never a fight or a serious argument in all that time. You know, yourself, that's a lot more than most of these clubs and hotel bars in the Loop can say. You just have to let the fellows know who's running the place, that's all; no need to get tough.

"You say none of this will be used for anything? Well, by God, buddy, it better hadn't! If my name comes out, you'd better skip town. I'll be out looking for you."

In the "dives," too, the problem of a mixed clientele arises. The proprietor of a "joint" located on the dividing street between an Irish-Polish and a Negro area, detailed his contribution to harmonious race relations as follows:

Owner: "You won't see any trouble. You see, most of these girls are hustlers, and if they start any trouble they get put in jail, and you know they don't like that at all."

Interviewer: "I've been in some taverns where a mixed group causes trouble. Can you give me a lead?"

Owner: "Sure, I've been around here for six years and I've never had any trouble yet. I am not in the 'game' any more. You see, all I do now is rent rooms to the girls, and if they cause trouble here, I don't let them rent any rooms."

Interviewer: "Do you rent rooms to the white girls here, too?"

Owner: "Sure, some of the colored boys want to give a white girl a play. It's all right with me, and sometimes a white boy wants a colored girl. It's just the same thing. I'm here for money, and if they want to pay me, I'm satisfied."

Interviewer: "Do the police ever bother you or your rooming house?"

Owner: "No, I get along all right with them. You see, Sergeant —— is a silent partner in this place, and him and I get along all right, and it helps all of us. You know the old saying, 'Don't bite the hand that's feeding you'?"

Interviewer: "That's a good motto if you live up to it."

Owner: "Well, in our business we make it a point to make everyone live up to it, and if they don't we just shun them in the tavern."

The following conversation with a Jewish tavern-keeper indicates the reactions which can be expected when a proprietor decides to cater primarily to colored trade:

Interviewer: "All your trade is Negro, isn't it?"

Owner: "Yes, and I dare say the colored people are the best-natured crowd in the city."

Interviewer: "Do you have any white trade at all?"

Owner: "Yes, I have a few fellows that I made friends with over at 39th and Wentworth."

Interviewer: "Do you ever have any trouble when there are the two races together?"

Owner: "No, I am over here quite a while and I haven't had a fight in this place since I've been here."

Interviewer: "Are your bartenders white or Negro?"

Owner: "They are colored. I have to have them, because all of my trade is colored."

Interviewer: "Do your white friends that come in ever complain to you about the bartenders?"

Owner: "No, and if they did it wouldn't get them anywhere at all. I feel that if they come in this place I accept them as my friends, and I show my feeling that way. In business you've got to cater to everybody, and if Negroes spend money with me, I am their friend."

Interviewer: "Supposing your tavern was in a different location in the city, would you feel the same way about them?"

Owner: "I wouldn't even care if I owned a tavern across from the City Hall. If they wanted to spend a dime with me I would give them the same consideration that I would give you, and I know you for about five years, don't I?"

Interviewer: "Yes. Would you feel the same way about your help?"

Owner: "That would be different. If you are in a Jewish neighborhood, naturally you would have to have some Jewish people working for you."

Interviewer: "Well, Harry, it looks as if you weren't prejudiced at all."

Owner: "No, I'm not. I'll tell you one thing—if you ever make friends with a colored person you can always depend on him. One night this place was broken into and the door window was all broke.

One of my colored friends called me up on the 'phone and stood guard at the door until I came. When I got here I couldn't find a thing missing. Now I ask you how many of my white friends would do a thing like that? When you got friends like that you don't care what color they are, just as long as they are true. That's what I think about the colored people. I don't think I can say that I have one of them what I could call an enemy of mine."

RESIDENTIAL SEGREGATION AND NEGRO-WHITE CONTACTS

The dominant type of community is the "all-white" or "all-Negro" neighborhood. (The term "all-white" is less precise than "all-Negro," for there are proportionately more Negroes scattered about in white communities than there are white people living in Negro communities.) This results in a pattern of relations which reduces to a minimum any neighborly contacts, school contacts, or chance meetings in stores, taverns, and movie houses between Negroes and whites of approximately the same socio-economic status. Yet Negroes and white people are not completely isolated within their respective neighborhoods.

Negroes in White Communities: Hundreds of Negroes find it necessary to go into white communities daily in order to earn a living. Midwest Metropolis is used to seeing Negroes all over the city in the roles of domestic and personal servants, of unskilled workers in restaurants and stores, and of mechanics and car-washers in garages. They are accepted as a normal part of the workaday population, and sustain friendly occupational relations with white employees and employers.*

An occasional Negro may be found occupying some position of minor importance in a white community. Negro postmen work all

* Some of the craft unions have made attempts to bar Negroes from working outside of the Black Belt. In 1940, testimony before the Illinois State Commission on the Condition of the Urban Colored Population indicated that the steamfitters' and plumbers' union had made the Negro craftsmen sign a pact not to work outside of the Black Belt. When they crossed the line they were subjected to violence, their work was damaged "mysteriously," and other unions were called out on sympathetic strikes against them. The musicians' union (an AFL affiliate) has also attempted to dictate the specific spots in the city at which colored musicians may play. While restricting Negro competition in this fashion, the white craftsmen reserve the right to work in the Black Belt!

over the city, as do social workers. Colored schoolteachers, firemen, librarians, and policemen are usually assigned to Negro areas, but here and there Negroes hold these types of jobs in white neighborhoods. In 1934 there were 803 teachers in areas 95 per cent Negro and over. Of these, only 272 were colored (33.9 per cent). These 272 colored teachers made up 88 per cent of all colored teachers in the city, only 12 per cent being in more mixed neighborhoods. Harold Gosnell, who presents these figures, reports that he found 31 Negro teachers in some twenty schools which were almost entirely white.[9] Some of these were no doubt "passing" either by design or accident, as in the case of a teacher who said:

"I have been at a near West Side school for all the ten years that I have been a regular teacher. I have never been particularly race conscious. . . . I have never had any trouble with the pupils or the parents.

"There was just one colored substitute during the time that I have been there. I remember her because she proved something that I have been thinking a long time, namely, that the children don't think of a teacher as colored unless she has a black skin. I remember one of my children came in late and when I asked him the reason he said that he had been showing the 'nigger' teacher her room."

There seems to be little opposition to Negro teachers in foreign-born neighborhoods, but Gosnell reports that "in the more prosperous neighborhoods inhabited largely by native whites we did not find Negro teachers who were recognized as such." Interviews with city employees and Federal employees working in white neighborhoods reveal that most of them met initial hostility but were subsequently accepted.

Negroes make little use of the educational, religious, and recreational facilities in white residential areas. The few who do move about the city to theaters and churches or who attend neighborhood institutions meet with little discrimination. Most Negroes who attend churches outside of the Negro areas do so in rather specialized relationships— for example, a visiting group of singers, a special speaker, or a Negro preacher exchanging a pulpit with a white pastor.* These "good-will" activities are not extensive, however, and involve very few Negroes.

* The one exception would be Catholic churches. At the present time, Negroes are allowed to join the nearest parish church and to send their children to the parochial school. This is a recent development, however. In 1940, one of the authors made a study of the Catholic Church in Chicago and found that three Black Belt Catholic churches had been set aside as "Negro" churches and that

In general, the pattern of residential segregation results in habits of thought which characterize certain parts of the city as "white" and others as "Negro." Negroes are expected to remain in their areas unless they have "legitimate" business outside of them. Thus, when Negroes visit friends in some white neighborhoods they are viewed with hostility or suspicion, and may be asked to use back doors and freight elevators. In areas close to the Black Belt, when tension is high because of a threatened invasion or some alleged crime, the police have been known to adopt a policy of stopping Negroes at night and questioning them. Sometimes children's gangs will chase Negroes out of such neighborhoods. These waves of suspicion and antagonism tend to appear and disappear and seldom become set as traditional.

White People in Negro Communities: As an area is "taken over" by Negroes, only those white people remain who have sentimental associations or economic interests. Janitors of apartment houses, businessmen living on their commercial property, prostitutes, priests and nuns at Catholic churches, a few partners in mixed marriages—these are the types of white persons who reside permanently in the Black Belt. Their presence is not considered unusual and they are generally not resented by their Negro neighbors.

Although few white people reside in the Black Belt a host of them come into the area daily—merchants, laborers, social workers, schoolteachers, salesmen, agents and collectors, policemen—and all are the objects of considerable resentment. They are competing with Negroes and exercising some degree of dominance and control over them. The Negro rationalizes his antagonism to such occupational types on the ground that it is unfair for them to hold such positions in Negro communities when Negroes are not allowed to exercise similar functions in most white communities. Expressions of antagonism are usually confined to grumbling or individual discourteous acts. Occasionally, however, a movement arises designed to focus attention upon the "exploiters" in the Black Belt. The two most dramatic of these within recent years are treated elsewhere in this book: the "Spend Your Money Where You Can Work" Campaign of the early 30's, and a

colored Catholics, no matter where they lived in the city, were forced to hold membership in one or the other of these churches. They could attend Mass at other churches, but deaths and marriages were to be solemnized in the Jim-Crow churches. There were several cases of Negro children who were refused enrollment in the nearest parochial school, although this was a violation of canon law.

violent anti-Semitic campaign in 1938. Antagonism is always latent toward "white people who take money out of the Black Belt."

Not all of the white people who come into the area "take money out," however. The cabarets and other "hot spots" have become famous, and many white people come into Black Metropolis for entertainment of varying degrees of respectability. Negroes who profit by this trade naturally do not display resentment toward the "good-timers" and the "slummers." But Negro civic leaders and many middle-class people protest against the tendency to regard Black Metropolis as an exotic rendezvous for white pleasure-seekers.

The pattern of residential segregation inevitably gives rise to an intense community consciousness among Negroes. They begin to think in terms of gaining control of their own areas, and the struggle for this control is the dominant motif of economic and political action within Black Metropolis.

BLACK BELT—BLACK GHETTO

The deep-seated feeling that Negroes are, in the final analysis, somehow fundamentally different from Poles, Italians, Greeks, and other white ethnic groups finds its expression in the persistence of a Black Belt. Midwest Metropolis seems to say: "Negroes have a right to live in the city, to compete for certain types of jobs, to vote, to use public accommodations—but they should have a community of their own. Perhaps they should not be segregated by law, but the city should make sure that most of them remain within a Black Belt." As we have suggested previously, Negroes do not accept this definition of their "place," and while it is probably true that, if allowed free choice, the great majority would live as a compact unit for many years to come, they believe that *enforced* segregation is unjust. They do not always clearly see the full implications and consequences of residential segregation, but they are generally resentful. A sampling of comments made at a time when discussion was widespread about restrictive covenants in Hyde Park will reveal the nature of this resentment. Thus, one prominent Old Settler, the daughter of a German father and a Negro mother, was vitriolic in her denunciation of residential segregation:

"I don't think we would need any housing projects on the South Side if Chicago wasn't so full of this silly old race prejudice. We ought to be able to live anywhere in the city we want to. What the government should do, or somebody with money, is to fight these restrictive covenants and let our people move where they want to. It's a dirty shame that all types of foreigners can move anywhere in the city they want to, and a colored man who has been a soldier and a citizen for his country can live only in a Black Belt. What's the use of fighting for a country that treats you that way?"

A colored "wringer man" in a laundry came to Chicago in 1921 because he had heard of "the good wages and grand opportunities." Now, having become well-adjusted, he resents residential segregation:

"Residential segregation is a big mistake. When I came here, there were white and colored living in the same neighborhood and the people seemed to understand each other. But since this neighborhood is colored only, everything is different. There are less jobs, and the neighborhood is not kept as clean as it used to be. I cannot offer any way to break down segregation. When I was married, I tried to rent houses out of the district, and the real-estate agents wouldn't rent to me. Yes, if Negroes can get houses in Hyde Park, or anywhere else, they ought to take them—for the housing condition for colored on the South Side is rotten."

Another laborer from Georgia who has been in the city nearly thirty years was also heated in his denunciation:

"Racial segregation is rotten. When white and colored both lived in this section, the rents were not so high and there seemed to be a better understanding. I have often wondered if segregation has not had a lot to do with the lack of employment, for there are certain white people that try to prove that all Negroes are bad. When they come over here, they go to the worst part of the section to prove their point."

Somewhat more moderate in his disapproval is a colored chauffeur who came to Chicago in 1912 as a Pullman porter:

"Racial segregation is something that I am not sure is a blessing. The housing proposition is serious, for the rents are very high, and the houses are not kept up as they are in white neighborhoods. On the other hand, if we were scattered among the white people there would be far less work, for by being close together we get a lot of work from the stores owned by white people that are doing business in our neighborhood. I have thought of ways to break down this segregation, but when I think that anything you do makes you a lawbreaker, you then cease to fight individuals, for then it becomes a war with the law. Remember that the police, the judges, and the strongest lawyer groups are all white and they stick together. I have seen one case of a fight between the police and the colored citizens and know that it was far from being an equal fight."

Many other Negroes, however, express a willingness to risk trouble in attacking this form of segregation. A skilled worker, a respectable church member, was very emphatic on this point:

"Hyde Park is no more than any other place in Chicago. The Negroes ought to move into Hyde Park or any other park they want to move into. I don't know of anything on earth that would keep me out of Hyde Park if I really wanted to move into it. Personally, I don't care anything about the good-will of white people if it means keeping me and my people down or in restricted neighborhoods."

A minority defends the existence of enforced residential segregation. This is done not on principle, but as a matter of expediency, or for fear of racial clashes, or because such persons feel that the time to attack segregation has not yet come. Thus, a colored waiter who blames most of the discrimination against Negroes on the Great Migration, partly defends segregation:

"I myself believe segregation is good, for if the white and colored lived together there would be fights constantly. About the only business benefit we derive from a Black Belt region is from a political standpoint, for there are a lot of people working that have gotten their appointments from their power as a voting factor. I think segregation is caused by the Negro's failure to try to get out of the district. In fact, I have never tried to live out of the district. There is no reason—I just have not thought of it."

Occasionally the opinion is expressed that Negroes are not "ready" to move into better neighborhoods, that they must first prove their worth by making the Black Belt a cleaner, more orderly, better-kept area. Thus one man states:

"Our duty to ourselves and to those with whom we come in contact is to show the world that we are an advanced people, that we are law-abiding and respectable and that we are able to care for the property we control or occupy. You can bet your bottom dollar that when we do this, we will be welcome wherever we care to live."

This theory that individual Negroes must wait until the whole group improves itself before they can get out of the Black Belt is not at all popular with ambitious Negroes.

Most Chicago Negroes feel that the right to rent or buy a house offered to the public should be inalienable. Yet Negro businessmen and politicians will sometimes state privately that they prefer keeping the Negro population concentrated. During a campaign against restrictive covenants, one prominent Negro leader confided to an interviewer:

"Sure, I'm against covenants. They are criminal. But I don't want Negroes moving about all over town. I just want to add little pieces to the Black Belt. I'd never get re-elected if Negroes were all scattered about. The white people wouldn't vote for me."

Most Negroes probably have a similar goal—the establishment of the *right* to move where they wish, but the preservation of some sort of large Negro community by voluntary choice. But they wish a community much larger than the eight square miles upon which Black Metropolis now stands.

At one session of the Mayor's Conference on Race Relations in 1944, the Chairman of the Chicago Housing Authority stated [10] of the Black Belt that

"In 1939 there was an excess population of 87,300 persons, measured by citywide standards of density. Since then an estimated 60,000 or more persons have moved into the area to accentuate an already bad condition.

"The race relations problem of Chicago resolves itself around the question of living space for Negro citizens. A major revision in public opinion on race relations must be effected before private or public agencies can make any substantial contribution to the solution of this problem."

Negro newspapers and civic leaders unanimously oppose enforced residential segregation and bitterly attack the forces that have created an overcrowded Black Belt. To them, the area is a Black Ghetto, and they insist that "new areas should be opened to break the iron ring which now restricts most Negro families to intolerable, unsanitary conditions. Restrictive-covenant agreements and the iron ring creating a Negro ghetto must be smashed." [11]

Even the Chairman of the Mayor's Committee accepted the characterization of the Black Belt as a "ghetto," and there was general agreement among the participants in the Mayor's Conference in 1944 that most of the social problems within the Black Belt were fundamentally related to the operation of restrictive covenants. (Only the spokesman for the Chicago Real Estate Board disagreed.*) The conference listed among the "ghetto conditions" high sickness and death rates; † a heavy relief load during the Depression; inadequate recreational facilities; lack of building repairs; neglect of garbage disposal and street cleaning; overcrowded schools; ‡ high rates of crime and juvenile delinquency; and rough treatment by the police.

The ghetto characteristics of the Black Belt are related, in the first instance, to the poverty of its people. Here, the proportion of families on relief during the Depression was the highest for the entire city. (Figure 8.) The restricted economic base of the community was also

* The real-estate interests in Midwest Metropolis insist that a general scarcity of houses is the primary problem, and that, if there were enough houses or a building program in process, middle-class white families would move away from areas close to the Black Belt and Negroes could then take over the abandoned houses. They blame New Deal restrictions and the Federal housing program for the housing shortage, charging that private capital has been made reluctant to invest. The Chicago Real Estate Board refuses, unequivocally, to sanction the abolition of restrictive covenants. Yet plenty of houses would not solve the basic question of the *quality* of housing available for Negro occupancy. Negroes would still be concentrated in areas of the city that have begun to deteriorate.

† In 1925, Chicago had the lowest death rate for any American city of 1,000,000 and over, but the Negro death rate was twice that for whites. (H. L. Harris, Jr., "Negro Mortality Rates in Chicago," *Social Service Review*, v. 1, no. 1, 1927.) The average standard death rate for the years 1928-1932 was 9.2 for native-whites, 10.4 for foreign-whites, and 20.0 for Negroes. (Elaine Ogden, *Chicago Negro Community*, WPA, 1939, p. 201.) Differences in infant mortality are reflected in the fact that 3 Negro babies die before their first birthday to every 2 white babies. Social disorganization in the Black Ghetto is reflected in deaths from homicide—six Negroes die from violent assaults for every white person who is killed.

The striking differentials in morbidity rates are those for tuberculosis (see Figure 9) and venereal diseases. The Negro tuberculosis rate is five times the white rate and the venereal disease rate is reported as 25 times that for whites. Both diseases are closely related to a low material standard of living and widespread ignorance of hygiene. *It should be borne in mind, however, that we are dealing with rates, not absolute numbers.* The actual number of Negroes who have venereal disease does not warrant the common belief that "the Negro race is eaten up with syphilis and gonorrhea." About 75 venereal disease cases were reported among every thousand Negroes in 1942, and 3 among whites.

‡ Civic leaders are most bitter about the double- and triple-shift schools in the Black Belt. In 1938, thirteen of the fifteen schools running on "shifts" were in Negro neighborhoods. Pupils spent half of the day in school and were "on the streets" for the rest of the day. In 1944, the School Board alleged that this system had been abolished, but Negro leaders disputed the claim. The Board of Education consistently refused to give the authors any data on overcrowding in the schools. A building program has been projected which may relieve the situation in the future.

Figure 8

POVERTY AND SOCIAL DISORGANIZATION

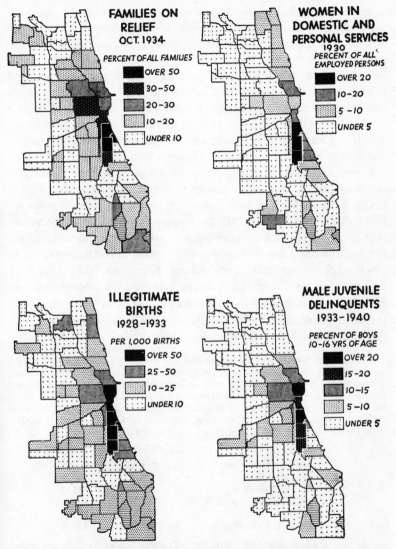

The rates for families on relief and for women employed in domestic service are from Wirth and Furez, *Local Community Fact Book.* Insanity rates are from Faris and Dunham, *Mental Disorders in Urban Areas* and juvenile delinquency rates were compiled by the Institute for Juvenile Research. (The Black Belt community areas are those outlined in white.)

evident in the high proportion of women doing domestic service. As a low-income area, the community was unable to maintain a high material standard of living. This poverty was aggravated by the housing problem which caused overcrowding. Given these factors, and the lack of widespread health education among Negroes, it is not surprising that the tuberculosis death rate is five times higher than it is for whites, and that the Negro areas have the highest sickness and death rates from tuberculosis. Chicago has the highest Negro death rate from tuberculosis of any metropolitan city in the United States.*

The Black Ghetto also suffers from a type of social disorganization which is reflected in high illegitimacy and juvenile delinquency rates † and a high incidence of insanity. (Figures 8 and 9.)

Restrictions upon free competition for housing, and the inability of the Black Belt to expand fast enough to accommodate the Negro population, have resulted in such a state of congestion that Negroes are living 90,000 to the square mile as compared with 20,000 to the square mile in adjacent white apartment-house areas. Since they entered the city last and are a low-income group, Negroes, in the aggregate, have inherited the worst sections of Midwest Metropolis. They have been able to "take over" some fairly decent housing in neighborhoods that were being abandoned by white residents, but these were no longer prized as residential neighborhoods. Negroes have thus become congested in undesirable residential areas.

---

* These high tuberculosis morbidity and mortality rates among Negroes may reflect the fact that Negroes as a recently urbanized group have not developed immunity to the disease. But the wide differentials also reflect the well-known fact that the care of tuberculosis demands bed rest with plenty of nutritious food. (Rates from Dorothy J. Liveright, "Tuberculosis Mortality Among Residents of 92 Cities of 100,000 or More Population: United States, 1939-41," U. S. Public Health Reports, July 21, 1944, pp. 942-955.)

Cities of 1,000,000 and Over Population	Tuberculosis Death Rates: 1939-41	
	For Whites	For Negroes
Chicago, Illinois	45.4	250.1
New York, New York	40.4	213.0
Philadelphia, Pennsylvania	44.3	203.5
Detroit, Michigan	36.5	189.0
Los Angeles, California	49.7	137.3

† In 1944, the Superintendent of the State Training School for Girls at Geneva, Ill., reported that Negro girls made up 36 per cent of all girls at the institution. Frazier has noted a steady rise between 1919 and 1930 in the proportion of Negro boys brought before the juvenile court. In the latter year 21.7 per cent of the boys brought before the court were Negroes.

Figure 9

DISEASE AND DEATH

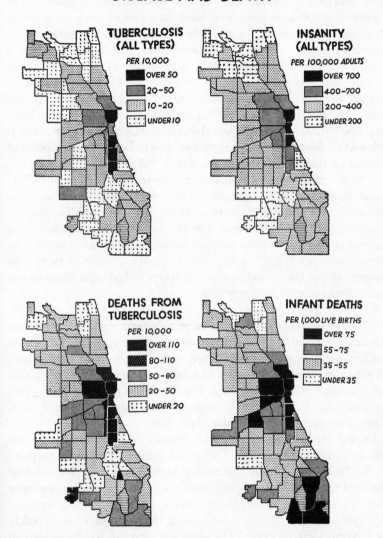

Tuberculosis morbidity rates and infant mortality rates are from Wirth and Furez, *Local Community Fact Book*. Tuberculosis mortality rates are from the records of the Municipal Tuberculosis Sanitarium. Map showing insanity rates adapted from Faris and Dunham, *op. cit.* (The Black Belt community areas are those outlined in white.)

Over half of Black Metropolis lies in that area which the city planners and real-estate interests have designated as "blighted." The "blighted areas" have come into being as a part of the process of uncontrolled city growth, for as Midwest Metropolis has grown, spontaneously and in response to economic utility, its center has become a citadel of imposing office buildings surrounded by an ever-widening belt of slums. As the city expands, this slum land becomes valuable as the site of future wholesale establishments, warehouses, transportation terminals, and light industries. No one wishes to invest in new housing upon these potentially valuable spots. Housing already there is allowed to deteriorate and is then torn down. From the standpoint of residential desirability, this entire area is "blighted."

The superficial observer believes that these areas are "blighted" because large numbers of Negroes and Jews, Italians and Mexicans, homeless men and "vice" gravitate there. But real-estate boards, city planners, and ecologists know that the Negro, the foreign-born, the transients, pimps, and prostitutes are located there because the area has already been written off as blighted. The city's outcasts of every type have no choice but to huddle together where nobody else wants to live and where rents are relatively low.

Black Metropolis has become a seemingly permanent enclave within the city's blighted area. The impecunious immigrant, once he gets on his feet, may—as we have mentioned several times—move into an area of second-settlement. Even the vice-lord or gangster, after he makes his pile, may lose himself in a respectable neighborhood. Negroes, regardless of their affluence or respectability, wear the badge of color. They are expected to stay in the Black Belt.

During the last twenty years the Negro's demand for housing has always exceeded the supply. The rental value of residential property in the Black Belt is thus abnormally high. The speculative value of the land on which the property stands is also high, and—even more than the restriction of supply—this has a tendency to drive rents up. A prominent real-estate operator, during the Depression, said frankly to a Negro social worker: "There are two ways to handle residential property in the Black Belt. Figure on amortizing the investment in twenty years and scale the rent accordingly. Plan to amortize your investment in ten years and double the rent. If this section is doomed for residential purposes anyhow, the latter is a better business practice for us." Houses in Black Metropolis pay off now. The land they occupy will do so in the future.

Midwest Metropolis does not intend to keep on growing haphazardly. City planners and the larger real-estate interests hope some day to control its growth, and Chicago's master plan calls for the eventual reclamation of the inner city, with a garden belt of privately financed, medium-rental apartments replacing the slums. Here, it is hoped, members of the new middle class will make their homes, close to the Loop where they work, and well within the city limits. The blighted areas will thus be reclaimed. Low-cost housing nearer steel mills and industrial plants in the suburbs will be constructed (also, for the most part, with private funds) to attract the skilled and semi-skilled workers. But some question marks remain.

"What," asked an official of a Negro civic agency, "do the Chicago Real Estate Board, and the city, plan to do with the Negroes who now live in the blighted areas? Will restrictive covenants be relaxed so they, too, can move to the suburbs and near-suburbs?" This was during the Depression, when Negro labor was not in demand, and the answer of a member of the Real Estate Board was crisp: "We have no plans for them. Perhaps they can return to the South."

The realtor's remark reflected the rather general antagonism of Chicago taxpayers toward the 40,000 Negroes who migrated to Black Metropolis during the Depression. There was a tendency during this period to feel that Midwest Metropolis had no responsibilities toward an unwanted population which was crowding into the already saturated Black Belt. Vacancy rates for the entire city were low, and no new areas of occupancy were opened to Negroes until near the eve of the Second World War, when one square mile was added to Black Metropolis. It is ironic that the lone Federal housing project within the Black Belt actually displaced sixteen more families than it accommodated. The Second World War brought 60,000 more Negroes to the city—this time a welcome addition to the labor market. Over 1,500 units of war housing were made available, but at least 10,000 more were needed. Wartime controls froze Black Belt rents at their already high levels, and overcrowding mounted to an almost intolerable point.

Some private real-estate groups have become interested in the possibilities of investing in Negro housing, but the question still remains: "Where shall it be situated?"

Negro civic leaders in Chicago were quite pleased when Newton

Farr, a former president of the National Association of Real Estate Boards and one of Chicago's most intransigent defenders of restrictive covenants, conducted a survey of "hundreds of the best posted real estate men in eighteen large cities" on their opinion of Negroes as renters and potential home owners. The questions and replies are summarized below: *

(1) Does the Negro make a good home buyer and carry through his purchase to completion?...... 17 of the 18 cities reported YES.

(2) Does he take as good care of property as other tenants of a comparable status?...... 11 of the 18 cities reported YES.

(3) Do you know of any reason why insurance companies should not purchase mortgages on property occupied by Negroes?...... 14 of the 18 cities reported NO.

(4) Do you think there is a good opportunity for realtors in the Negro housing field in your city?...... 12 of the 18 cities reported YES.

To a double-barreled question, "Is the Negro good pay as a tenant or are more frequent collections necessary and losses greater?" six cities said the Negro tenant is "good pay," seven said "no," and two reported conflicting experiences. On the second half of the question ten cities reported more frequent collections are necessary, while two disclaimed this.

A majority of cities commented that Negroes maintain neatness and repairs on new property as well as whites, but underscored that relatively few properties in good condition are sold to Negroes.

Some weeks later, Newton Farr, as determined as ever to "hold the line," reiterated to Negro leaders that he was interested in providing *Negro* housing, not in mixing whites and Negroes within neighborhoods. He felt that *Negro* housing might be a paying investment in the post-War world, but segregation must be maintained.

The city faces a dilemma—a sort of social paralysis. Midwest Metropolis doesn't want to let Negroes stay where they are, and it doesn't want them to scatter freely about the city. It doesn't want to rebuild the inner city to house them, nor does it wish to provide homes elsewhere. And all the time Black Metropolis—a big, stubborn, eight-square-mile fact crammed with over 300,000 people—grows more and more congested.†

* The quoted material and summary are from the New York *Herald Tribune,* November 19, 1944.

† The Chicago Plan Commission has divided all residential areas into five types, as of 1942, and made plans for the future status of each. Thus, "blighted

These Negroes, upon whom the city depends for much of its un-skilled and semi-skilled labor and for a large part of its domestic service, continue to pile up upon one another within these congested areas. As they do so, morbidity and mortality rates rise out of all pro-portion to those in the rest of the city. Crime and juvenile delinquency rates, too, indicate that serious maladjustments are present in the Black Belt. Black Metropolis acquires the reputation of being a "slum area," and the bare statistical record and surface impressions seem convincing evidence that Negroes make undesirable neighbors. This estimate of Negroes is reinforced deliberately by the real-estate interests and inci-dentally by the press and radio. Rumor and chance impressions further confirm the reputation of Black Metropolis as a "rough" neighborhood.

During the fifteen years between the Great Migration and the De-pression, the Black Belt gained the reputation of being a colorful com-munity, "wide-open" and rough. It was also considered "easy picking" for the Republican machine. Yet most of the city paid little attention to Black Metropolis for ten years after the Race Riot of 1919, except dur-ing the excitement of an election campaign or an occasional "vice cru-sade." Its immediate neighbors, however, feared it because it was steadily expanding and pressing upon them.

The Depression made the entire city conscious of Black Metropolis. In the first place, the area became the scene of the eviction riots and the "Spend Your Money Where You Can Work" Campaign. Then it

and near blighted" areas are to be eliminated, becoming *rebuilt* areas; "conserva-tion" areas are those which will, in the future, become *ripe for rebuilding;* those which are, at present, "stable" are expected to become *conservation* property; present areas of "arrested" or "progressive" development and "new growth" will some day be *stable.* "Vacant" areas will gradually become ripe for *new growth.*

Two-thirds of the main Black Belt area has been classified as "blighted" or "near-blighted" and a third as "conservation" property.

Of the 250,000 people in the Black Belt, the Commission estimated that at least 87,000 persons should be moved out in order to thin the population down to the optimum in conservation areas and to a level of health and decency upon re-building the blighted areas with a combination of walk-up apartments and row-houses. At least 16,000 should move even if three-story walk-up apartments replaced all the present housing in the blighted areas.

The Commission favored intensive new building within two small Negro communities outside of the Black Belt and the creation of a new segregated community on the edge of the city limits. These three Jim-Crow communities could accommodate 30,000 or 40,000 people from the main Black Belt.

(Cf. booklet *Design for Public Improvements,* by the Chicago Plan Commis-sion and mimeographed memorandum, "Population in South Side Negro Areas.")

reversed its political tradition of fifteen years and went Democratic. Throughout the Depression period Black Metropolis was good copy for the white press. The Chicago *Tribune,* for instance, professing alarm at the high proportion of Negroes on the WPA, occasionally made snide comments on the waste of the taxpayers' money. The militant demands which Negroes raised for better housing and more relief were sometimes hysterically interpreted as evidence that Black Metropolis was turning "Red," and on at least one occasion a Hearst paper headlined a revolution in progress. (The incident was merely a tenant strike in a single building.) All the daily papers rediscovered the presence of a widespread gambling syndicate, and devoted columns to the life and works of Negro racketeers. Though the *Times,* a liberal tabloid, tried to be helpful and ran several feature stories with appropriate pictures emphasizing the dirt and squalor and ramshackle housing in the area, it rounded off the series with a sensational exposé of Black Belt "rackets."

Whenever an institution in the Negro community launched a drive for funds, the evidences of community disorganization were emphasized in the press in order to stimulate charity. On one occasion, a citywide drive against syphilis involved the uncritical publication of statistics and maps which suggested that the Black Belt was a "cesspool of disease" (the actual words of one newspaper).* Such publicity

---

* Negro civic leaders are very ambivalent about the matter of publicizing health statistics on Negro communities. They point out that persons unfamiliar with statistics confuse high *proportions* with high *absolute* figures. For instance, only 5 Negroes in a 100 may have syphilis, but if the fact is publicized that the Negro *rate* is 40 times that for white people, the public will begin to view every Negro as a potential paretic. Yet, in order to focus the attention of the larger white world upon the Negro's plight, it is necessary to emphasize poverty and disorganization, to display the sores of Black Metropolis like a beggar seeking alms. One civic leader pointed out that this approach sometimes boomerangs and quoted the words of an industrialist that he had approached about hiring some Negroes: "Mr. Smith was over here recently soliciting money for that Negro hospital. He showed me a lot of charts and graphs on tuberculosis and syphilis. I can't put your people in my factory using the same rest-rooms and cafeterias that the other workers use."

The following sampling of editorial appeals in daily papers during a money-raising drive for a hospital in Black Metropolis suggests the manner in which the white public's fears are aroused and the unsavory reputation of Black Metropolis reinforced, in order to stimulate charity. The editorials of three daily newspapers, in addition to presenting factual material, stressed the imminence of some disaster originating in the Black Belt. The *Times* stated: "We must at once remedy our dereliction or, with the growing consciousness of the Negro of his political

helped to fix the reputation of Midwest Metropolis during the Depression. A new liberal daily, the *Sun,* appearing in 1941, inaugurated a less sensational approach to Black Belt problems, but the reputation of the area was already fixed.

The existence of these conditions has become a convenient rationalization for keeping Negroes segregated. The University of Chicago (with properties tangential to the Black Belt), neighborhood property owners' associations all around it, and the Chicago Real Estate Board have visualized restrictive covenants as a permanent *cordon sanitaire.*

Community leaders in Black Metropolis, as well as professional and businessmen generally, are worried about the area's reputation in the larger white world—a world which identifies each of them with the Black Ghetto. Throughout 1938, one Negro weekly newspaper ran a symposium, "Is the South Side Doomed?", encouraging discussion of community improvement. The series of articles revealed general agreement on the necessity for abolishing restrictive covenants if doom was to be averted. Community leaders devote much of their time and attention to petition, protest, and legal.action designed to abolish restrictive covenants. (They have been doing this for twenty years, without success.) While aware of the economic and social forces which create the ghetto, they also cling tenaciously to the possibility of reducing life within the area to order and neatness. This hope has resulted in "clean-up campaigns," drives for increased police protection and health facilities, and the constant stimulation of community morale. These efforts are frustrated, however, by the necessity for trying to improve living conditions within an area too small to accommodate the population, given the present amount and quality of housing.

As it becomes increasingly crowded—and "blighted"—Black Metropolis's reputation becomes ever more unsavory. The city assumes that *any* Negroes who move *anywhere* will become a focal point for another little Black Belt with a similar reputation. To allow the Black Belt to disintegrate would scatter the Negro population. To allow it

and collective power, find it remedied in ways we may not care for." (June 26, 1938.) The *Daily News* suggested that "protection of health in the Negro area means health protection to every citizen of Chicago. . . . Quite aside from the humanitarian reasons, the rest of Chicago cannot afford to let this institution stop or even to curtail its activities." (July 5, 1938.) According to the *Tribune,* "Failure to raise the money will mean a vast amount of needless suffering and it may not be confined to the Negroes." (July 8, 1938.)

to expand will tread on the toes of vested interests, large and small, in the contiguous areas. To let it remain the same size means the continuous worsening of slum conditions there. To renovate it requires capital, but this is a poor investment. It is better business to hold the land for future business structures, or for the long-talked-of rebuilding of the Black Belt as a white office-workers' neighborhood. The real-estate interests consistently oppose public housing within the Black Belt, which would drive rents down and interfere with the ultimate plan to make the Black Belt middle-class and white.

The Race Relations Director of the regional office of the Federal Housing Authority suggested to the Mayor's Committee in 1944 that it "request the Real Estate Board, the Chamber of Commerce, the banks, the City Plan Commission, the Chicago Housing Authority, Chicago Housing Council, and labor organizations to develop a program to house the citizens of Chicago, including Negro families of the South Side, in the immediate postwar period. Request them to join with efforts to abolish restrictive covenants. Point out to them that the abolition of restrictive covenants will not involve the influx of any large number of Negro families to any predominantly white neighborhood, any more than free access to the purchase of automobiles will encourage all Negroes to purchase Cadillac or Ford cars. Request these groups to support public housing for the rental market which cannot be served by private enterprise." [12]

The Mayor's Committee itself went on record as being opposed to restrictive covenants and pledged to "continue to work earnestly with other effective agencies to rid the city of arbitrary restrictions on the living space of any group." The Committee chairman stated: "No people can live decently unless they can live freely. The ghetto is a feature of medieval Europe that has no place in America. . . . At present Negroes are confined to restricted areas with bad houses and exorbitant rents. They are confined to these districts by an atmosphere of prejudice and specifically by conspiracies known as restrictive covenants. This Committee has by formal vote declared itself categorically opposed to restrictions of race, creed, or color on the place where any of Chicago's citizens may live." Black Metropolis, remembering similar statements twenty years before by another Commission on Race Relations, remains skeptical.

On June 23, 1945, the *Defender* published an editorial, DANGER: DYNAMITE AT LARGE, which said, in part:

Hate-crazed incendiaries carrying the faggots of intolerance have in the past several months attacked some 30 homes occupied by Negroes on the fringes of the black belt, solely because these colored citizens have desperately crossed the unwritten boundary in their search for a hovel to live in. Buildings have been set afire, bombed, stoned and razed. Their occupants have been shot and slugged.

To date the Chicago Police Department has done virtually nothing to apprehend the guilty.

With the hot summer days ahead, there is dire danger in continued inaction.

Today racial dynamite is scattered about the South side. It needs but a spark to explode.

The *Defender* spoke scornfully of "studies and surveys . . . promises and pledges."* It demanded that the City suspend restrictive covenants by a war emergency order and "post full and complete police protection" for Negroes moving into houses.

The inhabitants of the Black Ghetto grow restless in their frustration, penned in, isolated, overcrowded. During a depression or a war (the periods covered by this account), the consciousness of their exclusion and subordination is tremendously heightened. Within this spatial and social framework morale tends to be low and tempers taut. Anti-Semitic sentiments are latent. Demands for the economic and political control of the Black Belt arise. Resentments assume various organizational forms. The people marshal their economic and political power and make demands for improvements within the Black Belt and for its ultimate dissolution as an enforced state of existence. For, while it is conceivable that many Negroes would prefer to live in an all-Negro community, they resent being forced to live there.

* After declaring its opposition to restrictive covenants, the Mayor's Committee seemed to avoid any further discussion of the abolition of covenants. Evidently the Committee soon realized that it had no power or authority to attack them legally and was hesitant to antagonize the political machine and powerful real estate interests. As in other fields when up against entrenched interests, the Mayor's Committee found itself powerless to act and seemingly reluctant to continue any agitation.

CHAPTER 9

The Job Ceiling

DURING THE WEEK OF MARCH 24, 1940, A BRIGADE OF FEDERAL DOORBELL-ringers descended upon Chicago's 800,000 households to extract the bits of information from which the Sixteenth United States Census was to be compiled. The industries of Midwest Metropolis were just beginning to hum again after limping along for ten Depression years. For the second time within a generation, a war in Europe had caused a stir upon the Midwestern plains. Hope was in the air as the unemployed dreamed of work and pay-checks. But optimism was alloyed with skepticism. Everybody remembered the previous cycle of War—Boom—Collapse. Negroes, particularly, kept their fingers crossed, repeating their widespread aphorism, "Negroes are always the last to be hired and the first to be fired."

Negroes had originally come to Chicago in large numbers to meet a wartime labor demand. Now, after twenty-five years, on this day of enumeration, in the year 1940, their economic plight was not enviable. A new war boom had begun, but they had not begun to share in the upswing. Here was manpower waiting for a chance. The First World War began with a labor shortage; the Second World War began with a labor surplus of ten years' standing—and Negroes made up a large part of this surplus. A fourth of all Negro males above 14 years of age, and over a tenth of the females, were "seeking work" in private industry (Figure 10). They were on relief and WPA or were being supported by friends and relatives.

The Census of 1940 revealed some startling things about these Negroes "in the labor market"—the able-bodied adults who wanted to work—the "available workers." (Figure 11.)

19 out of every 100 Negro men were on Emergency Work Projects.
17 out of every 100 Negro men were seeking work.

12 out of every 100 Negro women were on Emergency Work Projects.
23 out of every 100 Negro women were seeking work.

It was evident that Negroes were suffering at least three times more severely from unemployment than the white population. (Figure 11.)

Figure 10

PROPORTION OF AVAILABLE WORKERS: March 1940

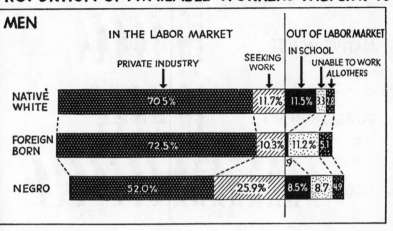

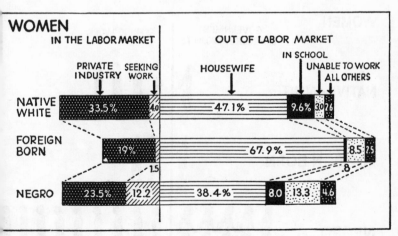

"Seeking work" includes emergency project workers.

The 1940 pattern was nothing new. Five years before, the picture had been even more bleak. The first five years of the Depression had piled up a backlog of over 150,000 unemployed workers of

Figure 11

AVAILABLE WORKERS WHO DID NOT HAVE
JOBS IN PRIVATE INDUSTRY IN MARCH 1940

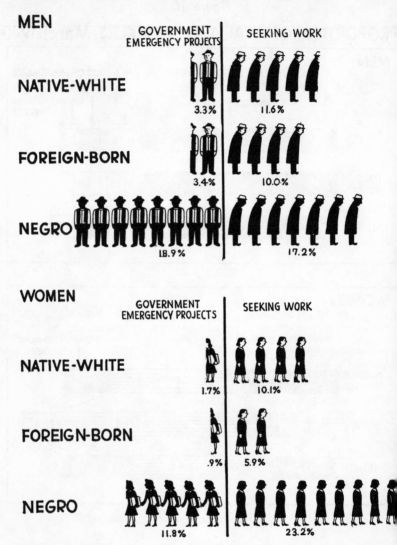

Percentages based on total persons "in the labor market" for each ethnic
group. "Seeking work" refers to persons without regular *or* emergency jobs.

whom about 35,000 were Negroes.* *While Negroes made up only eight per cent of the available workers, they constituted twenty-two per cent of the unemployed.* All along the line, Negroes had been displaced in a ratio of roughly three to one. Almost half of the Negro domestic servants, a third of the semi-skilled workers, and a fourth of the unskilled were unemployed in 1935. (Table 4.)

TABLE 4

UNEMPLOYMENT AMONG NEGROES IN MIDWEST METROPOLIS, FIVE YEARS AFTER THE DEPRESSION BEGAN, COMPARED WITH UNEMPLOYMENT OF THE WHITE POPULATION

(Estimates in Round Numbers) †

Occupation	Race	Number of Persons at Work in 1930	Number of Persons Still at Work in 1935	Number of Persons Displaced	Per Cent Displaced	Excess of Negroes Displaced
Professional, proprietary, and managerial	W	229,000	223,000	6,000	3.0	5×
	N	7,000	5,900	1,100	15.0	
Clerical	W	245,000	230,000	15,000	6.0	
	N	5,000	4,000	1,000	20.0	3×
Skilled	W	236,000	216,000	20,000	9.0	3×
	N	9,000	7,000	2,000	30.0	
Clerical semi-skilled	W	273,000	247,000	26,000	10.0	3×
	N	27,000	18,000	9,000	33.0	
Unskilled	W	134,000	116,000	18,000	14.0	2×
	N	29,000	22,000	7,000	24.0	
Service	W	89,000	78,000	11,000	12.0	2×
	N	46,000	34,000	12,000	26.0	

† Estimates based on tabulations in Estelle Hill Scott, "Occupational Changes Among Negroes in Chicago, 1890-1930," Cayton-Warner Research, and Chicago Housing Authority, "Memorandum on Unemployment in Chicago," 1935. Estimates are based upon the assumption that the major increases in Negro population between 1930 and 1940 began after 1935. This assumption seems to be borne out by the population census of 1934.

* The high-water mark of unemployment among Negroes was probably reached in 1930 and 1931. In January of 1931, the Unemployment Census

Why were Negroes so disproportionately represented in the ranks of the unemployed? The answer is threefold:

1. They were concentrated in the occupations which are the first to feel the results of an economic crisis.

2. As a minority group, they were likely to be dropped first, with white workers retaining their jobs longer.

3. Negroes continued to migrate to Chicago—40,000 of them between 1930 and 1940—fleeing the collapse of the southern cotton economy and discrimination in the administering of relief in the South. There were no jobs for them.

NEGRO WORKERS ON DEPRESSION EVE

To understand the intense feeling within Black Metropolis about job discrimination, it is important to visualize the economic position of Negroes in Chicago on the eve of the Depression, at the end of a ten-year wave of "prosperity." It is obvious from an examination of Figure 12 that Negroes were doing a disproportionately large amount of the city's servant work, a disproportionately small amount of the "clean work," and a little above their "proportionate share" of the "manual labor." The term "proportionate share" as used throughout this chapter is simply a device for comparing the occupational status of Negroes and whites by assuming: (1) that Negroes and whites have the same conception of what constitutes a "good job"; (2) that Negroes, if permitted, would compete for these good jobs; (3) that there are no inherited mental differences between the races; (4) that if competition were absolutely unfettered by racial discrimination, Negroes, being approximately 8 per cent of the workers in 1930, would tend to approximate 8 per cent of *each* occupational group.*

✦

revealed that over half of the Negro employable women (58.5 per cent) and nearly half of the employable men (43.5) were without jobs. These data are summarized in Richard Sterner, *The Negro's Share,* Harper, 1944, p. 362.

* This method of analysis is, of course, open to the criticism that it does not take into account the time factor—that the fifteen years between 1915 and 1930 may not have constituted a sufficiently long period of time for such a distribution to take place. At the rate of speed with which industry was expanding during the Twenties, and with the amount of turnover in personnel which seems to have been involved in the crucial fields of skilled labor and white-collar employment, it seems reasonable to assume that the differentials between the actual proportions

The "Clean Work": Professional, proprietary, managerial, and clerical work was almost a white monopoly on the eve of the Depres-

Figure 12

DISTRIBUTION OF THE CITY'S WORK

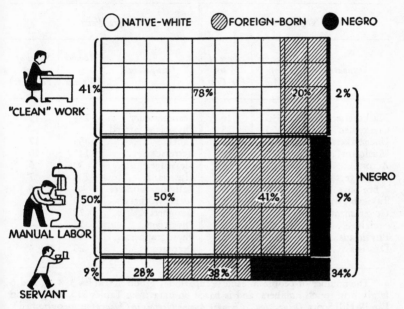

Prepared from tables in Estelle Hill Scott, "Occupational Changes Among Negroes in Chicago: 1890-1930," WPA, 1940. Data for 1930.

sion. Negro representation in Chicago's large white-collar class was very small. Those few Negroes who did "clean work" were almost entirely confined to the Black Ghetto and were dependent upon the

and the theoretical "proportionate share" would not have been so great if barriers had not been placed against the use of Negroes.

The concept of the "proportionate share" has more than theoretical interest, however. During the Depression several Federal agencies reserved a certain quota of jobs for Negroes based on their numbers in the population. Thus, on a job in area where Negro carpenters were 3 per cent of all carpenters in 1930, this percentage of Negroes was hired. In the autumn of 1944, the Communist Party raised the issue sharply within a number of unions as to whether seniority provisions should not be waived during postwar cut-backs in order to let Negro workers retain the same proportion of jobs in the plant which they had gained during the War period. This tendency to think in terms of "quotas" and "pro-

wage-earning masses for a livelihood, or upon the ability of white people to pay for their services as entertainers. (See Table 5.)

TABLE 5 *

THE TEN "CLEAN" OCCUPATIONS IN WHICH NEGROES WERE MOST HEAVILY REPRESENTED: 1930

Negro Men			Negro Women		
Occupation	Number of Men	Share of Work (Per Cent)	Occupation	Number of Women	Share of Work (Per Cent)
Mail carriers.....	630	16	Restaurateurs.....	235	19
Clergymen.......	390	15	Physicians' attend-		
Undertakers......	120	12	ants	55	12
Musicians........	525	10	Actresses	145	10
Actors...........	215	9	Messenger girls...	30	6
Messengers and of-			Musicians........	205	7
fice boys.......	385	6	Religious workers.	45	6
Taxicab owners...	110	8	Social workers....	50	5
Government offi-		5	Designers........	25	5
cials...........	40	5	Physicians........	17	4
Physicians........	265	5	Photographers....	10	4
Dentists..........	130	5	Decorators.......	20	4

* The number of people in each occupational group in Tables 3, 4, 5, and 6 is given in round numbers, and is based on data from Tables 110, 111, 112 in Estelle Hill Scott, *Occupational Changes Among Negroes in Chicago* (mimeographed), Work Projects Administration, 1939.

Servant Work: Over twenty-five out of every hundred employed Negro men and fifty-six out of every hundred Negro women were doing some kind of servant work on the eve of the Depression. This was at least four times their "proportionate share," for Negroes did over a third of all the servant work performed by women, and a fourth of that done by men. *While only twelve out of every hundred white women were in service occupations, over half of the colored women did such work.* The Negro woman's share of the various types of service work is indicated in Table 6.

portions" of Negro workers is admittedly an unsatisfactory approach to the problem of integrating Negroes into the economic life of the country, but some people feel that it is the only method of making sure that Negroes will secure broadened economic opportunity.

TABLE 6

SERVICE OCCUPATIONS WITH HIGHEST PROPORTION OF NEGRO WOMEN: 1930

Occupation	Number of Negro Women	Share of Work (Per Cent)
Laundry work done in homes....................	1,600	55.9
Elevator service................................	200	42.7
General domestic and personal service............	20,000	42.5
Charwomen and cleaners........................	450	20.4
Janitors..	180	9.6
Waitresses.....................................	1,100	9.5

Negro men had a virtual monopoly of some types of service jobs—jobs that depended upon an affluent white population, traveling, spending freely, and passing out tips.

TABLE 7

SERVANT OCCUPATIONS WITH HIGHEST PROPORTION OF NEGRO MEN: 1930

Occupation	Number of Negro Men	Share of Work (Per Cent)
Railroad porters...............................	3,600	94.9
Other types of portering........................	2,100	82.5
Domestic and personal service...................	3,500	82.2
Waiting table on trains, in hotels, etc............	3,000	31.4
General service................................	5,000	26.6
Janitors..	4,000	19.1
Elevator men..................................	5,000	10.6

Manual Labor: Negroes were not overrepresented among the people who did the city's manual labor, but if we go behind the bare figure of nine per cent we find that they were doing a disproportionately large share of the poorly paid and less desirable work. They were concentrated in the unskilled labor categories which suffered heaviest from unemployment. Over half of all the Negro men who earned their living by manual labor were employed in the jobs listed in Table 8.

TABLE 8

MANUAL LABOR JOBS WITH HIGHEST PROPORTION OF NEGRO MEN: 1930

Occupation	Negro's Share of Work (Per Cent)	Number of Negroes	Desirable Aspects of Job	Undesirable Aspects of Job
Garage labor...	58.5	1,860	Easy to get, not monotonous	Low pay, exposure, very dirty
Coal yard labor	40.5	1,525	Easy to get	Low pay, exposure, very dirty
Stockyard labor	34.2	1,640	Relatively good pay	Very heavy and dirty
Labor in stores..	31.8	3,360	Relatively clean	Low pay
Packing and slaughter labor	28.7	1,960	....	Very dirty
Laundry operatives	26.3	1,470	Easy to get	Low pay, extreme heat and dampness
General labor...	25.0	7,500	Easy to get	Low pay, insecurity, exposure
Steel mill labor	15.0	4,000	Relatively good pay	Heavy work, often very hot and hazardous
Railroad labor..	14.0	1,815	Easy to get	Low pay, exposure
Building labor..	13.3	2,850	Fairly well paid	Insecurity and intense competition of foreign-born
Road and street labor	13.0	567	Easy to get	Low pay and intense competition of foreign-born

Total number of Negro men employed..........28,547

About 100,000 women were doing manual labor when the Depression began. Of these about 15,000 were colored women—twice their proportionate share. Some three out of four of the Negro women doing manual labor were employed in the occupations listed in Table 9. All of these were marginal occupations, and the dress industry in which Negro semi-skilled women were concentrated was one of the industries hardest hit by the Depression.

TABLE 9

MANUAL LABOR JOBS WITH HIGHEST PROPORTION OF NEGRO WOMEN: 1930

Occupation	Negro's Share of Work (Per Cent)	Number of Negroes
Laundry operatives..........................	55.4	5,000
Railroad labor...............................	44.3	140
Labor in steel...............................	20.2	80
Clothing factory operatives...................	20.0	3,000
Slaughter and packing operatives..............	21.5	300
Labor in packing............................	17.0	130
Semi-skilled in boarding houses...............	16.2	1,000
General labor...............................	11.5	360

Total number Negro women employed.........10,010

THE JOB CEILING

The Depression began fifteen years after the Great Migration and at the halfway mark between the two World Wars. Despite fifteen years of urbanization during a period of industrial expansion, Negroes had not attained a proportionate share of the skilled and clerical jobs or of the professional and business occupations. They were clinging precariously to the margins of the economy. As former sharecroppers and underpaid southern city workers, they had "bettered their condition"; but they had not made the type of rapid progress which white European immigrants had made in an equal period between 1895 and 1910. This was due primarily to the fact that they had not been allowed to compete freely, *as individuals,* for any types of jobs to which they aspired and for which they were qualified. The result of these limitations was the crystallization of a "JOB CEILING."

The nature of this ceiling in terms of the "proportionate share" is indicated in Figure 13. All other things being equal, Negroes might have been expected by 1930 to approximate eight per cent of each occupational category.

The Job Ceiling also has its reflection in the internal structure of the white and the colored communities. These differences are depicted in Figures 15 and 16. Out of these differences in occupational distribution arise many of the peculiarities of social life within Black Metropolis. Over half of the white workers were doing skilled labor or "clean work." Over two-thirds of the Negroes were doing semi-skilled, unskilled, or servant work.

Figure 13

NEGRO'S SHARE IN SELECTED WORK GROUPS

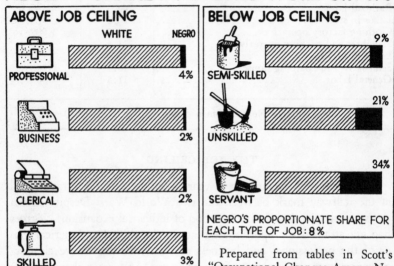

Prepared from tables in Scott's "Occupational Changes Among Negroes in Chicago: 1890-1930." Data for 1930.

EVOLUTION OF THE JOB CEILING

Between the first World's Fair and the Great Migration, Negroes constituted only a minute proportion of the city's workers. (See Figure 14.) As late as 1910 only three out of every hundred workers in Chicago were colored and at no time during this period did these few thousand Negroes offer any significant competition to the foreign-born who did the city's industrial work. Although they occasionally complained of discrimination in the building trades, Negroes, on the whole, tended to bypass skilled and semi-skilled work for employ-

Figure 14

TRENDS IN JOB DISTRIBUTION: 1890-1930

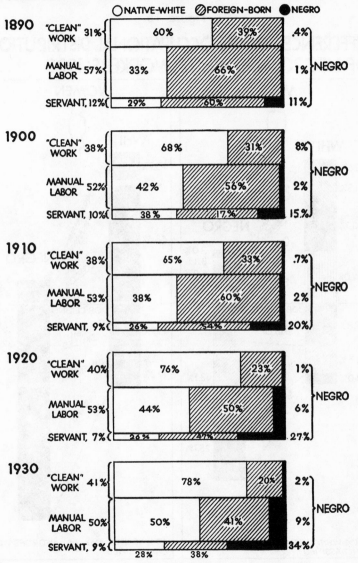

From tables in Scott, "Occupational Changes Among Negroes in Chicago: 1890-1930."

Figure 15

DIFFERENCES IN THE OCCUPATIONAL DISTRIBUTION OF NEGRO AND WHITE WORKERS: 1930

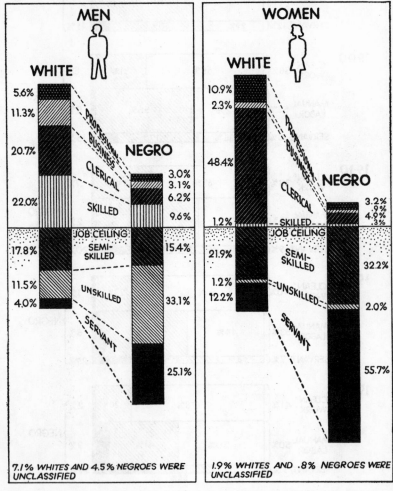

From data in the Fifteenth Census of the U. S., 1930.

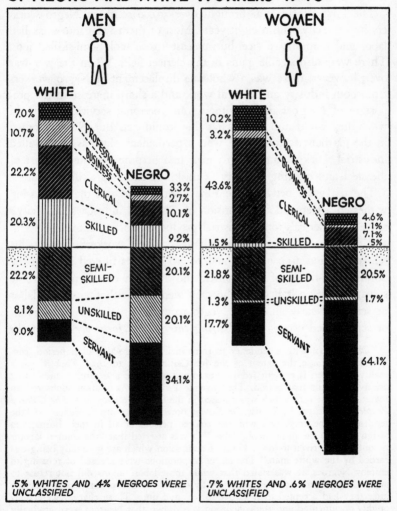

Figure 16

DIFFERENCES IN THE OCCUPATIONAL DISTRIBUTION OF NEGRO AND WHITE WORKERS: 1940

MEN

WHITE

7.0%
10.7%
PROFESSIONAL
BUSINESS
22.2%
NEGRO
CLERICAL
3.3%
2.7%
20.3%
10.1%
SKILLED
9.2%

22.2%
SEMI-SKILLED
20.1%
8.1%
UNSKILLED
9.0%
20.1%
SERVANT
34.1%

.5% WHITES AND .4% NEGROES WERE UNCLASSIFIED

WOMEN

WHITE

10.2%
3.2%
PROFESSIONAL
BUSINESS
43.6%
NEGRO
CLERICAL
4.6%
1.1%
7.1%
.5%
1.5%
SKILLED

21.8%
SEMI-SKILLED
20.5%
1.3%
UNSKILLED
1.7%
17.7%
SERVANT
64.1%

.7% WHITES AND .6% NEGROES WERE UNCLASSIFIED

From data in the Sixteenth Census of the U. S., 1940.

ment in domestic and personal service.* The unskilled jobs which they held were largely in stores and transportation. A very small business and professional class existed, and a few Negroes held responsible political posts. But neither in the "clean work" nor in the industrial sphere had Negroes yet raised an insistent claim for a "proportionate share" of the jobs.

The First World War brought over 50,000 southern Negro workers into the city within eight years. Most of them went into unskilled labor and domestic service, but at least 10,000 took semi-skilled jobs. There were also sizable gains in the clerical field. When the war was over, however, there was a wholesale displacement of Negro workers from both industry and clerical work and a sharp increase in the proportion of Negroes doing domestic and personal service. They held what they could and took what they could get. But Negro women in the garment factories had won a permanent place as semi-skilled industrial workers, and Negro men had become an integral part of the steel and packing industry as unskilled and semi-skilled laborers.

The ten years between the First World War and the Depression witnessed a tremendous expansion of Chicago's industries. The city's share of America's total industrial production rose to fifteen per cent, and this expansion required nearly 328,000 new workers. During this ten-year period, 64,000 additional Negro workers filtered in from the South. Two-thirds of the women and a fourth of the men became servants. Over a half of all the men went into either unskilled labor or service. Nearly all of the Negro women went into either servant or semi-skilled occupations. *During this period, forty per cent of the*

---

* Old Settlers, with a tendency to romanticize the pre-Migration period, consistently minimize the extent of the Job Ceiling prior to 1914. That it was a reality, however, is evident from an examination of the few careful studies that are available for that period. The Juvenile Protective Association sponsored an investigation in 1913 which was released in the form of a pamphlet, *The Colored People of Chicago*, by Louise De Koven Bowen. There are references to "the tendency of the employers who use colored persons at all in their business to assign them to the most menial labor." It was asserted that "the colored laborer is continually driven to lower kinds of occupation which are gradually being discarded by the white man." The larger corporations were accused of refusing to employ Negroes. It was stated that while most labor unions did not refuse to accept Negro members, some consistently denied work opportunities to Negroes after they had accepted their initiation fees and dues. These charges were thoroughly documented and the conclusion was drawn that Negroes were gradually being "crowded into undesirable and underpaid occupations." (Bowen, *op. cit.*, pp. 1-10.)

*new white women workers went into "clean work," but only five
per cent of the Negro women secured such jobs.* While few of the
migrant Negro women were trained for such occupations it is probable that very few of the trained Negro women already in the city
were "upgraded" to such jobs. (See Tables 10 and 11.) *

TABLE 10

HOW THE BOOM NEEDS OF MIDWEST METROPOLIS WERE MET BETWEEN 1920 AND
1930: JOBS BELOW THE CEILING

Type of Employment	Number of Workers Absorbed	How Negro Labor Was Utilized
Unskilled labor in stock-yards, packing plants, steel mills, stores, warehouses, and wharves	10,000 men 2,670 women	Negroes supplied virtually the whole demand as whites moved up. Virtually no Negro women used.
Servants	28,000 men 14,000 women	10,000 Negro men supplied about one-third of the demand for men. Negro women supplied almost all of the demand. Two-thirds of the Negro women migrants became servants.
Semi-skilled factory workers	36,000 men 11,000 women	8,000 Negro men used: 500 in the stockyards; 2,000 in garages; 1,100 in laundries; others general. 8,000 Negro women used, supplying three fourths of the demand: 5,000 to laundries; 1,100 to garment factories; others general.

In fact, Negroes who were already in the city, as well as the newcomers, found it impossible to secure a "proportionate share" of the
good jobs even when they were qualified for them. They were not
permitted to "advance on the job" or to secure apprenticeship opportunities. Instead, white male workers moved up, and white women
either moved up or left industry to become housewives. Those Negroes
who had entered industry during the Great Migration tended to ad-

* The estimates in Tables 7 and 8 are based on an analysis by Estelle Hill
Scott, *op. cit.*, pp. 217-228.

TABLE 11

HOW THE BOOM NEEDS OF MIDWEST METROPOLIS WERE MET BETWEEN 1920 AND
1930: JOBS ABOVE THE CEILING

Type of Employment	Number of Workers Absorbed	How Negro Labor Was Utilized
Clerical work	35,800 men	Only 2,500 Negro men used, largely within Black Metropolis. A proportionate increase, but not enough to "catch up." At least 7,000 jobs were needed to give Negro men 8.0 per cent of clerical jobs.
	42,000 women	Only 300 Negro women secured such jobs. Ten times as many jobs —at least 3,000—would have been necessary to give Negroes their 8.0 per cent of the new workers.
Skilled labor	19,400 men	4,000 Negro men secured jobs in the building trades, but few in industry.
	2,700 women	Less than a hundred Negro women.
Professional, proprietary, and managerial	53,000 men 16,000 women	3,000 Negroes. 1,800 Negroes.

vance to the level of semi-skilled workers, but no farther. The 64,000 new Negro workers found their place as servants and unskilled workers. (Tables 10 and 11.)

Had competition been entirely free, with advancement upon individual merit; had Negroes been integrated and promoted in accordance with principles of seniority and at the same rate as white workers, the difference between the jobs the Negroes secured between 1920 and 1930, and the approximate number of jobs they might have been expected to get is illustrated in Figure 17.

A continuously expanding economy might conceivably have operated to give Negroes their share of jobs above the ceiling, although this could have happened in the skilled and clerical fields only if there had been such a phenomenal increase in available positions as to create an actual shortage of white labor. There were signs, however,

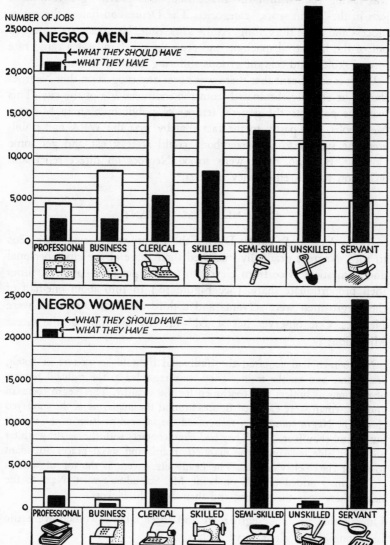

Figure 17
NEGRO'S "PROPORTIONATE SHARE" OF JOBS

NUMBER OF JOBS

NEGRO MEN
← WHAT THEY SHOULD HAVE
← WHAT THEY HAVE

25,000
20,000
15,000
10,000
5,000
0

PROFESSIONAL | BUSINESS | CLERICAL | SKILLED | SEMI-SKILLED | UNSKILLED | SERVANT

NEGRO WOMEN
← WHAT THEY SHOULD HAVE
← WHAT THEY HAVE

25,000
20,000
15,000
10,000
5,000
0

PROFESSIONAL | BUSINESS | CLERICAL | SKILLED | SEMI-SKILLED | UNSKILLED | SERVANT

From tables in Scott, "Occupational Changes Among Negroes in Chicago: 1890-1930." Data for 1930.

that a Negro business and professional group catering to Negroes was taking root within the Black Belt, thus providing a few more jobs in the "clean work" categories. The Depression halted the entire process and froze the ceiling. At the same time, Negroes were squeezed out of the industrial machine and onto the relief rolls at a rapid rate —semi-skilled and servant groups suffering most severely.

But it is significant that there was never any suggestion that Negroes should be entirely eliminated from the industrial life of the city. This was due partly to the general temper of public opinion in Midwest Metropolis, and partly to the fact that by 1934 the WPA had stabilized the system so that everybody could at least eat and get some clothing. By 1940, there were 20,000 Negroes on direct relief and 40,000 on various emergency projects.[*]

THE NEGRO AS SERVANT

Negro Men as Servants: During the twenty-year period from 1890 to 1910, Negroes gradually increased their share of the city's personal and domestic service from eleven to twenty per cent—over six times their proportionate share. (See Figure 16.) In 1910 about one-half of the Negro men were servants and a third of all male servants were Negroes. One observer has stated[1] that by the time of the Great Migration:

Negro men had acquired the traditional right to be waiters in hotels, restaurants and on the trains. They were regarded as the rightful holders of positions as butlers and coachmen for the wealthy. The Negro footman and houseman were expected figures around the mansions of the moneyed class. The Negro community recognized the favored position of the waiter, butler and chauffeur. . . . They had close contacts with the wealthy whites and were able to acquire the manners, polish and social graces attendant to upper class behavior. . . . The headwaiters were at the top of society. . . . A man prided himself on being Mr. So-and-So's valet. Next to the headwaiters were the porters, and then came the barbers.

During this period, Negro men and foreign-born women were the backbone of the city's servant class.

The First World War tripled the proportion of Negro workers in

[*] The Illinois Emergency Relief Commission reported in 1939 that 44.9 per cent of all "general relief" cases were Negro—a term embracing families without a wage-earner and all "problem" families.

industry. Enough migrants poured into the city, however, to allow for an increase in the proportion of servants at the same time. The migrant men tended to go into industry while the women streamed into domestic service. This is dramatically illustrated by the 1920 Census returns. The proportion of all Negro men doing servant work fell from 45 per cent to 25 per cent and remained down. The proportion of Negro men in industry rose from 40 to 65 per cent and stayed up. (See Figure 18.)

Women as Servants: The proportion of all Negro women who were servants had been gradually falling from 1890 through 1910. The First World War added a large number of semi-skilled women workers who further reduced the proportion. Although the number of Negro women in industry increased from 1920-1930, female migrants from the South continued to supply the servant demand. Post-war cut-backs also eliminated large numbers of both Negro and white women from industry; by the time of the Depression, therefore, the proportion of all Negro women doing servant work had begun to rise again. (See Figure 18.) It fell again with the outbreak of the Second World War, as Negro women left domestic service for war work.

Despite the industrialization of Negroes in Chicago, 21,000 men and 24,000 women were working as servants when the Depression began. The servant situation was virtually the same in 1940 on the eve of the Second World War. The Negro's share of the servant work, too, has been continuously increasing. (See Figure 16.)

"NEGRO JOBS"

In the remaining sections of this chapter we shall examine first those jobs in which Negroes predominate (the so-called "Negro Jobs"), then those in which they make up a very high proportion but are not dominant, and finally the "White Men's Jobs." In discussing the first two types of jobs—predominantly servant occupations and semi-skilled occupations—we shall examine briefly the part played by labor unions in restricting or expanding economic opportunity.

Very few occupations in Chicago can be called "Negro Jobs," although the concept of "Negro Jobs" is not new. As early as 1885, a

Figure 18

TREND IN NEGRO EMPLOYMENT TOWARD
INDUSTRIALIZATION: 1890-1930

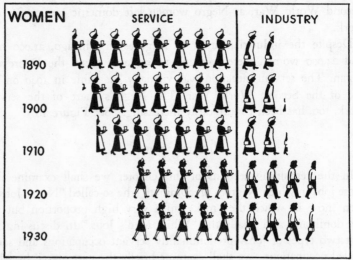

EACH FIGURE REPRESENTS 10% OF TOTAL EMPLOYMENT INCLUDING WHITE-COLLAR
OCCUPATIONS. WHITE-COLLAR WORKERS ARE NOT SHOWN IN PICTURE.

From tables in Scott, "Occupational Changes Among Negroes in Chicago: 1890-1930." (Percentage of Negroes in white-collar occupations not shown.)

prominent colored woman was deploring the fact that Negroes were beginning to lose their monopoly in certain fields: [2]

It is quite safe to say that in the last fifteen years, the colored people have lost about every occupation that was regarded as peculiarly their own. Among the occupations that seem to be permanently lost are *barbering, bootblacking, janitors in office buildings, elevator service,* and *calcimining.* White men wanted these places and were strong enough to displace the unorganized, thoughtless and easy-going occupants of them. When the hordes of Greeks, Italians, Swedes, and foreign folk began to pour into Chicago, the demand for the Negro's places began. One occupation after another that the colored people thought was theirs forever, by a sort of divine right, fell into the hands of these foreign invaders.

By 1930, there were only three servant fields in which Negro men had a monopoly and none in which Negro women had a monopoly.

The two most important "Negro Jobs" are the occupations of Pullman porter and Red Cap, in which 94 and 85 per cent respectively of all the workers employed are Negroes. Both of these groups reveal the manner in which relatively well-educated Negroes, forced by the Job Ceiling to accept such positions, have tried to organize the workers in these occupations for immediate and long-range ends.

PULLMAN SERVICE

"George," the Negro Pullman porter, is an American institution. In 1930, there were 9,000 porters in America, of whom about 4,000 lived in Chicago. Since the days when the enterprising George Pullman began building sleeping cars in Chicago, Negroes have had a monopoly of these jobs. In 1925, an editorial appeared in a Chicago Negro weekly [3] expressing disapproval of such a monopoly (the italics are the authors'):

DANGERS OF MONOPOLIES

Much has been said about the Pullman porters and the fact that our Race has maintained an unquestioned monopoly in that particular field of labor. Efforts are now being made by the porters and outsiders to perfect an organization whereby this monopoly will become permanent. And in this step lie great dangers, not only to the Pullman porters themselves, but to laborers in every other branch of American industry.

For years we have fought against just such steps as this. We do not believe we should have a monopoly on Pullman porter service any more than that white people should have a monopoly on Pullman conductor service, or that Irishmen should have a monopoly on police and fire departments. We cannot hope to break down the bars that keep us from other fields of endeavor if we are going to start movements that will automatically bar others. We believe there should be black and white porters, and that there should be black and white conductors, all employed according to their abilities and not according to their race. We believe that they should all work together along all lines and not in separate contingents. . . .

We want all workers of all races to start at the same place together and work up together with only their ability determining their progress. Monopolies are dangerous if formed along race lines.

Ten years later, however, Pullman portering was still a Negro monopoly, but after a strenuous fight, the Brotherhood of Sleeping Car Porters (AFL), under the leadership of A. Philip Randolph, had secured a contract which placed porters upon a "living wage." Prior to this they had existed largely on tips. The organizational campaign which centered in Chicago was a bitter one involving frequent charges that civic leaders and ministers were being bribed by the Pullman Company to oppose union organization.

The leaders of the Pullman porters have used their all-Negro union as a nucleus around which to organize pressure against the Job Ceiling both within and without the railroad industry. The broader philosophy of this leadership was revealed in a statement by the national president in 1931:

We hold that union organization is desirable from the point of view of workers of both races, as a low-paid, unorganized group of one race is inimical to keeping up the standards of workers in another race.

Preachers, lawyers, social workers of our race are co-operating and meeting with us for discussion of such problems as unemployment. We believe we discern a change in the attitude, formerly hostile, of Negro thinkers and professional people toward labor organizations.

Randolph has carried the fight against discrimination within the AFL to the floor of the national conventions annually, though without any marked success.

Using his union as a base, this same leader emerged in 1941 as the outstanding fighter against racial discrimination in war industries and the army and navy. As has been said earlier, the March-on-Washington Movement which he fostered was primarily responsible for the institution of the FEPC.

THE RED CAPS

Tradition has it that on Labor Day in 1890 a Negro porter at the Grand Central Station in New York tied a bit of red flannel around his black uniform cap so that he could be more easily identified in the crowd. As a consequence of this strategy he "cleaned up," and set a style which became the emblem of an entire occupational group —America's Red Caps.

In 1940 there were about 600 Red Caps carrying luggage and otherwise assisting passengers to board and leave trains, buses, and airplanes in Chicago's various depots and stations. Of these 600, over 400 were Negroes.

Red-Capping has been a typical service occupation, in which both the earnings and the prospects of advancement are dependent upon cheerful and, if necessary, ingratiating service. Until 1935 most Red Caps were entirely dependent upon tips for their income. They were not recognized as railroad employees, although some stations paid nominal wages of from $10 to $40 a month. Yet, in prosperous years, an enterprising Red Cap who had advanced to servicing Pullman cars on crack express trains could average as much as $150 a month. Even very well-educated Negroes did not scorn such jobs.

Organizing the Red Caps: During the Depression an income from tips became an extremely precarious one. Stations, moreover, that had formerly paid a nominal wage now ceased to do so. Chicago's station porters turned to union organization in order to demand recognition as "bona fide employees" of the railroad stations. They sought a minimum wage and bargaining rights under the Railway Labor Act, and within two years, after a series of bitterly contested hearings before the Interstate Commerce Commission, they were so classified. In 1944 they were receiving a basic wage of $4.56 a day. The railroads charge travelers a fixed sum for each item of luggage handled, and the money is pooled. Any amount in excess of the basic wage is prorated among the men. If the pool does not meet the basic wage, the railroad company makes up the difference.

The organization of the Red Caps was begun in 1936, during the period of the nationwide union organizational drives conducted under the sanctions of Section 7-A of the National Recovery Act. Officials of the union report that some of the railroads maintained spy systems and occasionally utilized older employees with a "big banker" complex to intimidate younger porters. Reprisals against men who would not join company unions consisted in depriving them of choice trains or penalizing them for attending union meetings. One railroad company even offered its men a salaried status if they would abandon union organization. Despite these difficulties, a union official reported that, after several months of organizational activity, "at one station 60 of the 80 Negro Red Caps were organized; at another, 67 out of 90; and at one station, 103 white Red Caps. One company was threatening to replace the Negroes with whites if they joined a union."

The Chicago Red Caps began as a Federal local of the AFL. Later the Brotherhood of Sleeping Car Porters (Negro) and the Union of the American Railway Clerks (white) both claimed jurisdiction over this young union. The Red Caps eventually broke their ties with the AFL and functioned as an independent union for five years. Finally, in 1942, the organization brought its 12,000 members into the CIO.

White Men in a Negro Job: At the Red Caps' first national convention, held in a downtown hotel in Chicago, a Negro was elected president; a white man, treasurer; a Negro, secretary; and another white man as general organizer. (The Negro president, Willard S. Townsend, who has remained head of the organization to the present time, is a graduate of the Royal College of Science in Toronto.) A reporter of the Chicago *Daily News,* writing of this first convention, observed that "it's Bill and Joe and Harry among the white and Negro porters. . . . The color-line in labor relations was smashed." One of the Negro officials was also enthusiastic over the prospects of Negro-white unity at the time, and said:

"This is a mixed union. There is no discernible difference between the white and the Negro Red Caps. There is no advantage in separate locals. Lack of association between racial groups isn't conducive to solving the race problem. This ticklish question will best be solved by association and the resultant understanding of their common problems. They will discover that prejudice is based on ignorance. Together they will find that prejudice is absolutely unfounded.

"All of our social affairs have been 'smokers.' Both whites and Negroes attend. Last month we held one at the Century Club here on the South Side and it was well attended by both groups. We plan to have a big dance at the Savoy. All of the locals in the international plan to hold big dances in other cities on the same night."

But this official added that some of the Negro Red Caps in other cities had refused to affiliate with the international if the white minority controlled the General Executive Board.

The honeymoon period of Negro-white relations was short. Even at the first national convention, disagreements crystallized along racial lines in relation to every controversial issue that arose. In one argument, the president of a white local in the organization was accused of double-crossing the Negroes by appealing to the Railway Mediation Board in the following terms: "The assistance we ask of you is only for the white boys at our depot." He defended himself on the ground that he thought this good strategy in establishing a test case, since the Board was more likely to render a favorable decision if it thought only white workers would benefit.

The struggle for racial control which arose almost immediately within the union was made more bitter by the difference in educational status between the Negro and the white Red Caps. One Negro official commented on this situation at the time:

"The Negroes in our union are the best informed on parliamentary procedure. Whites lack this knowledge because the economic condition of the white man doesn't usually make for an educated man becoming a Red Cap. The educational status of the whites in the union is lower than that of the Negroes."

The official of another local insisted that 72 of the 90 Negroes at his station were college men, including two practicing physicians! It was his impression that "in the last fifteen years, there hasn't been a Red Cap there who hasn't finished high school." He was equally sure that at least half of the white Red Caps had never been to high school.

Because of the Job Ceiling, an educated Negro suffers no disastrous loss in social status within his own community by working as a Red Cap, although a white employee of similar status in such a job is likely to be insecure and "on the defensive." This is suggested in the remarks of a white union official to a white investigator:

"You may wonder why I went into this kind of work. You know, I'm a college graduate. One of my brothers studied neurology for three years, and another one studied psychology for two years, and another one is a doctor. I could teach high school in Pennsylvania if I wanted to—I've got the political pull. You might wonder why I'm a Red Cap. Well, when I got out of college, I decided that I wanted to help the masses."

Trouble between white and colored union members continued, and finally, after a conflict involving charges that a white union official had made dishonest use of union funds, the white minority in the union withdrew and went back into the AFL. The white group then adopted a constitution which prohibited Negroes from holding office in their union, but providing for the organization of Negro Red Caps in a separate local! An official of the new white union defended this action as follows:

"Us and the colored fellows used to be one organization. Now there are two separate organizations. We've made a rule that no colored person can hold office in our organization. The trouble with colored men is that they want to run things. They just want to boss the whole show. White people ain't like that, but the minute a colored man gets into the organization, he wants to be an officer and run things. Now you've got to have white people running things if you want to get anywhere. I ain't like some. I don't see no difference between a colored man and myself, except that he's black and I'm white; but all the same you have to have white people for officers. Look at that union what's all colored fellows—the Pullman Porters' Union or something like that. They're right where they were eight or nine years ago. Oh, they did get something or other, I forget what, a little while ago. But look at the union at our station—they've got everything they want. I ain't got no objection to colored people. I like them all right, and I've got a lot of Negro friends that I think a lot of . . . [but] they have been trod down so long that when they get a little power, it goes to their heads."

Another member of this white union voiced similar sentiments:

"At the beginning, when we first planned to form an organization with the Negroes, the rest of the boys didn't like the idea of teaming with Negroes, but they trusted my judgment because I have so much more education. It doesn't do for white and black to be in the same organization. The whites have no respect for the Negroes and the Negroes have no respect for the whites. And a lot of employers refuse to negotiate with a Negro at all. When we formed this organization, we had our officers—

first a black one, then a white one, then black, then white, and so on. That was all wrong. If you had real equality, you wouldn't take special care to see that Negroes were elected, you would simply elect the men who were the best qualified for an office."

The comments of these white workers indicate that they felt out of place in a predominantly Negro union. One man was far less calm about the matter than the men quoted above. His remarks included the following diatribe:

"I know what Negroes are like. I spent seven years, the best years of my life, down South and I know. Give a nigger a finger and he will take a whole hand. I suppose Jack has told you the trick Tom pulled on us?

"Tom won't show his black face around here. He's afraid of me. He knows I'd break his neck if I saw him. There's only one good one around here and that's Hank. He knows his place. He's all right. There's one way a Negro is all right—that's in his place.

"Employers don't want to deal with Negroes; a lot of them refuse to do it. When Hank wants anything, he sends for me and I go over and talk to the management. The boss has told me that he wouldn't *have* a Negro sit down in his office. It would drive him wild."

Other white Red Caps felt that Negroes were *too* influential. The blending of social and economic insecurity which gave rise to these contradictory sentiments was further revealed in a conversation between two white Red Caps seated in the rear of a union hall.

Harry: "Tom [a Negro] gets pretty nearly everything *he* wants over at the station. He is real sirupy to the bosses, always yesses them. He's a regular stooge, that's what he is. He gets what he wants. And you know, there are some people who are just naturally *nigger-lovers.* You know what that is? They just naturally love niggers. There used to be white Red Caps, too, at that station, but they're all Negro now. Some official in the railroad was a nigger-lover, and he done it."

Jack: "Yeah, that's right. The Court Street station is the only one we've got left." (This was not true—white Red Caps were employed in three stations at the time.)

Harry: "The railroad I work for doesn't like us, either. If they had a chance, they'd throw us out just like that [snapping his finger]. They'd rather see *niggers* there than us."

Jack: "So you see we've got to watch our step. We can't antagonize them too much." (I.e., the Negroes in the union.)

Negro Job—Negro Union: After the white members withdrew from the union, it became for all practical purposes a Negro organization, although it continued to include a few white persons and Japanese-Americans. As early as 1937, the president of one of the locals stated:

"Personally, I think the condition of the white Red Cap is worse than that of the Negro. The Negro takes pride in his job and feels no 'let-down' because he is performing what is considered menial labor, whereas the white considers himself above such 'menial' labor; and thus when they are forced into this occupation, they feel they are working under pressure. They make little effort to *dignify their jobs.*

"The average Negro Red Cap stays in the service a lifetime, because it is fairly lucrative and a fairly steady occupation, and somehow it 'gets' you. Come down some time and wear a uniform and cap for a week, and you'll understand what I mean. We Red Caps actually take great pride in our work and *have brought more dignity to it than you probably think.*"

Eventually the union began to consider organizing all unorganized Negroes in the railroad industry into this new union, as well as those in Jim-Crow auxiliaries of lily-white railroad unions. These interests resulted in a change of name from the International Brotherhood of Red Caps to the United Transport Service Employees of America.

Two years after the union became an affiliate of the CIO, its president, Willard S. Townsend, was elected to the national executive committee of that organization. In this capacity he has been able to use his union as a pressure bloc against discrimination within all CIO unions and to stimulate the formation of a CIO Committee Against Discrimination within that body. In the eyes of Negroes he ultimately became a prominent *Negro* Leader, as well as a bona-fide labor leader. And the Red Caps' union, like the Pullman porters' union before it, has become a weapon for fighting the Job Ceiling.

IN THE WHITE FOLKS' HOUSES

In 1940, almost half of the women who did domestic service in Chicago were Negroes. Many of the Negro women who came to Chicago between the First and the Second World Wars were accustomed to working in the homes of white people as cooks, maids, nurses, and laundresses. It was inevitable that they would tend to replace the foreign-born, who were securing better jobs, and the Negro men who were leaving service for industry. (See Figure 18.) With some 40,000 white women entering industry and commerce between 1920 and 1930, it was not surprising that 10,000 additional Negro women were utilized as domestic servants.

Domestic service is not a money-making job.* During the Boom Years, wages for "day's work" tended to hover around $2 and for "week's work" at $20. The impact of the Depression on the white family budget was reflected in the widespread dismissal of Negro servants and in the drastic lowering of wages for those who remained. Yet, throughout the Depression, Negro women continued to supplement their relief checks by surreptitious "day's work." The State Employment Service reported its largest volume of Negro placements (and its highest turnover) throughout this period as temporary assignments for domestic work. Competing with these Negro women for such jobs were some 10,000 white women.

Hard Folks to Work For: Out of the servant-employer relations of the Depression period grew bitter and caustic expressions of antagonism toward white employers, often tinged with anti-Semitic and anti-foreign sentiments. The following diatribe is typical of the frustrated Negro domestic's complaints:

"You see, I am only employed regularly half-days, so in order to meet expenses, I have to find other work.

"I am supposed to work for Mrs. Carter from 2:00 P.M. on, do all the work. Both she and her husband are employed—that is, they have their own business.

"They only have three and one-half rooms in a large apartment building, yet I find plenty to do. I do all the laundry, which is plenty, and cleaning and cooking. I get so disgusted, for she always waits until she gets home before telling me what she planned for dinner and then sends me to the store.

"Tonight she made me real mad. After I had finished dinner dishes, she asked me to wash the woodwork around the windows, as she wanted to put up new drapes. She could have told me the night before, but they

* Of course, during a war, when servants become scarce, the wages for such work begin to approach those in industry. This is a temporary situation, however.

never think of your time, and too, I was so tired. I had done a day's work.

"Once a week I do all the cleaning for a Jewish couple. It is supposed to be half-day work but I never get through until 8:30 and 9 P.M. I have to get on my knees and scrub up every floor. Since I only go once a week, the house gets very dirty, and the kitchen is terrible. They have money but are too stingy and she doesn't like to work either; in fact, she doesn't do anything, only cook. She has a daughter thirteen years old and you would think she would have her clean the bathtub and bowl, but I always find a dirty rim around both, and foodstuffs that have been dropped on the floor have been walked on.*

"I never eat anything there either, for she spits in the sink if she happens to be in the kitchen. I just get $1.50 and she tries to get a week's work done, but since I only make five dollars and carfare on my regular job, I have to do it.

"I also have another place where I clean in the mornings weekly for $1.50, but her floors are all carpeted and it isn't so hard. I can't say Mrs. C. isn't nice to work for. She doesn't bother me, yet there just isn't enough money; I prefer working all day. I have been trying to leave her for some time, but some little while ago she loaned me money and I have been making so little that I haven't been able to pay her. Sometimes I just think I will leave and send it back to her. No, she doesn't even ask me for it, I guess she realizes I have had such a time. This is the fourth time I have lost my furniture. I am trying to pay out my radio and I sold some of my furniture for little or nothing."

Most domestic servants, like the woman just quoted, drew a distinction between "nice people to work for"—who pay over the usual wage or do not overwork them—and "hard people to work for."

Nice Folks to Work For: Most Negro domestic servants work for ordinary middle-class white families and do not have the intimate personal ties which characterize the few situations where the white family can afford a permanent retainer who lives on the premises and is almost a member of the family.

"Staying on the premises" is not the rule in Chicago. Most domestic

---

* The statements of Negro servants about middle-class Jewish employers reflect all the derogatory anti-Semitic stereotypes which exist among white people. Yet, many of these same servants will praise Jewish employers for being "less prejudiced" than other white employers. At least two-thirds of some 150 domestic servants who spoke of Jews thought that they treated Negroes "more like equals" than other employers but "paid less."

servants travel to and from the Black Ghetto and their work places outside of the Negro community. Yet there are Negro women who express a great deal of loyalty to specific families. These are either women who have considerate employers, or those who have not abandoned the southern Negro attitude toward white employers. One fairly well-educated Negro woman describes a "nice family."

"The Bradleys are lovely people. He being a minister and she working in the church keeps them away from home all day Sunday.

"They have two darling little girls; Baby is seven and Milly is four. That is the only confining thing about this job—they expect you to stay with the children; in fact, I almost take charge of everything. Mrs. Bradley is in her early twenties and evidently has never been used to much. She is on the go all the time. She is more particular about caring for the children than the cleaning of her house. I do all the housework except the window-washing. Neither do I take care of the laundry; that is sent out."

Another servant's comments indicate what Negro domestics consider "nice" working conditions:

"At the Darnells' I have a very nice room and bath, well furnished and cozy. I like the job very much. Of course I knew before accepting that it would be confining.

"When I went on my vacation last year, they presented me with a beautiful leather traveling bag. I imagine I will be with them the rest of my life.

"I was born in Cleveland, Ohio, and completed a high school course there. Then I finished college, later taking up musical work. Jobs seemed hard to get at this time, and not having any close relatives to whom to turn, I had to take the first job I could get, which was housework.

"I started working with the Van Lorns when they lived in New York. I had only worked for one other family. I didn't like them at all. No one could get along with her; she was so very crabby. Nothing ever pleased her, I don't care how well it was done. A friend who had formerly worked for the Darnells was leaving town and recommended me. I took the job and have been with them ever since. I began at twelve dollars per week, now I get fourteen.

"Each year I have gotten a two weeks' vacation with pay, but not until they have visited her mother for two months. She stays there until I have returned and cleaned the apartment."

Such cases of Negro servants as a "part of the family" were exceptional. Many Negro women were so desperate for employment during the Depression that they actually offered their services at the so-called "slave markets"—street corners where Negro women congregated to await white housewives who came daily to take their pick and bid wages down. One experienced stenographer who was forced to offer her services for $3 a week at the West Side "slave market" described her situation as follows:

"It is an area on the West Side of 12th St. near Halsted. A large number of girls go there daily and hire themselves by the day to the highest bidder. The more enterprising would solicit—others would wait to be approached. Many days I worked for 50 cents a day and no carfare—one meal was given. I then applied for relief. After suffering more embarrassment and humiliation I was refused relief because I could now and then get jobs at the 'slave market.' Having no references it was hard for me to get a good job."

Domestic workers often expressed the hope that their children would be able to find other types of work. Typical of the attitudes of many domestic servants with daughters were those expressed by one woman:

"I have not told you much about the life of my two daughters for, as you know, each of them has a work life of her own. My life as a maid had been brief—until I married I did office work. Only after my second husband and I separated did I begin work as a maid. My oldest daughter is quite bitter against what she calls the American social system and our financial insecurity. I hope they may be able to escape a life as a domestic worker for I know too well the things that make a girl desperate on these jobs."

Colored girls are often bitter in their comments about a society which condemns them to "the white folks' kitchen." Girls who have had high school training, especially, look upon domestic service as the most undesirable form of employment. It is not surprising that with the outbreak of the Second World War, middle-class white housewives in Midwest Metropolis began to complain about "the servant problem." Negro women had headed for the war plants or were staying at home.

During the Depression, several sporadic attempts were made to unionize domestic servants. The very nature of the occupation makes organization overwhelmingly difficult. If the domestic servant is not a casual worker, the relations between employer and employee are so personal as to form a psychological barrier against organization. If the domestic servant is not emotionally involved with the family it seems much easier to find someone else to work for or to find another type of work than to join a union. The physical conditions under which domestic servants work—each in a separate household—does not generate the kind of social solidarity that arises among a factory group. It is almost impossible to use the strike as a bargaining weapon. And most important, there was always a surplus of women seeking a few pennies to supplement their relief checks. All efforts to organize domestic servants in Chicago during the Depression failed.

The organizers of domestic workers were themselves caught between a desire to organize all domestics to fight for higher wages and better working conditions, and a desire to train a small group of women so that they could demand higher wages on the basis of more efficient work. One of the most experienced and energetic organizers stated in 1938:

"Our organization has grown but the membership fluctuates. At present the association is at a standstill as far as actual organization work is concerned, but the encouraging thing about it is that a Citizens' Committee has been organized, composed of Negro and white members who have pledged their financial and moral support in carrying out our training school project. I am primarily interested in union organization but in order to maintain it there must be a program. The training school will be that program. It will establish standards in this field, which are sadly needed, and will have an appeal to employers. It is a necessity. Maids *do* need training, and on this basis, financial backers may be interested."

A young colored Communist criticized this woman's efforts, as well as her own, in the following terms:

"I started a domestic workers' group of about 125 members who we picked up in the park. First, I think our discussions were wrong. We didn't take up the problems of the girls. We took up the problem of inefficiency and would criticize the girls for untidy appearance, dirty nails, and such things. This antagonized the girls. You've got to talk to workers about how mean the boss is, if you want to keep them interested. Such problems as long hours should have been talked about more, rather than runs in the girls' stockings. Second, I think girls should be taught that domestic work is an occupation and not a profession.

WHISK-BROOM, MOP, AND SERVING TRAY

Much of the personal service done by Negro men and women in the city is not in private homes, but in the hotels, lodging houses, houses of prostitution, athletic clubs, and similar institutions. In these situations where Negroes and whites often work side by side, labor unions have arisen that include both Negro and white members. One of these, the Miscellaneous local of the Hotel Employees' Union has 4,000 white members and 5,000 colored. The white business manager states that, on the whole, the Negro women take an active part and that both Negroes and whites attend the occasional social functions given by the union.

Before the Great Migration, Negroes had a virtual monopoly as maids at houses of prostitution. With the closing of the Red-light District in 1912, they have still maintained a large share of these jobs. One woman now in the less lucrative field of domestic service looks back with nostalgia at her employment in a North Side "resort" as she talks with a union organizer:

"Ever since the death of my husband, eight years ago, I acted as personal maid to a couple of prostitutes who lived in a hotel. I made good money then, for I had a chance to make tips. I never made less than $25 a week for they catered to the rich men, bankers, and other high-class people.

"This hotel was full of those women, and it ran wide open until party politics was changed. It was soon after a clean-up drive was begun that they were raided, so naturally I lost my job. Then the Cohens, through my mother, asked me to come and work for them. They both have nice personalities, and seem to think a great deal of me, but I am still a maid to them. I only make seven dollars a week. That is clear money but I can't do much with it.

"No, I haven't heard of the union, but I imagine it is a good thing. Maids really need helping, for those white people will certainly take advantage of you. When you first start with them you are only supposed to do so much, but the longer you remain with them, the more they expect and the longer the hours. I am so tired in the evening. I don't feel like reading—in fact, not doing anything but getting away from the house, even if it is only across the street. I have to wash all the little girl's clothes too. If I leave, I shall have more time. Then I will be able to learn more about this organization and perhaps attend a meeting. I have become rusty in everything. I don't even get to see my friends often.

Today is the first time I have visited in months and then I didn't get here until after 3 P.M. I had to prepare something for dinner before I left.

"I don't have to get back for dinner, but I must be there for seven o'clock breakfast, and the ride is quite long. I have to leave here early, for it is quite dark out there. I am disgusted with the job, yet I know I have to work for my living."

Negro men and women also serve in a variety of personal-service positions, as valets, personal maids, hotel maids, washroom attendants. Negroes and whites are thus thrown together in large numbers in this rather specialized relationship of menial service. Such contacts contribute to the confirming of stereotypes about the characteristics and "place" of Negroes. They also tend to produce, within the Negro servant's personality structure, a mixed attitude of obsequiousness and hostility.

WASHING CLOTHES—OLD STYLE AND NEW

In the South, the colored "washwoman" is a familiar figure; but in Chicago in 1930, there were only about 3,000 women who earned their living by washing clothes in the homes of their employers or by taking laundry to their own homes. Of these over half were Negro women. The average wage for such work near the end of the Depression period was $2.50 a day. Charges of exploitation were frequent, and often contained an anti-Semitic note, as in the case cited below:

"The Jewish woman that I work for tries to get a colored woman to do all of her work for as little as $2 a day and pay her own carfare.

"She is expected to do all the washing, including the linen and towels as well as all the clothes for the five members of the family. She is supposed to finish the work—that is iron the entire wash—and then clean the house thoroughly—all for $2. Because there are some women who will do all of the work for that amount, this Jewish woman feels that a colored woman who demands more is silly to think that she can get it. She says that she doesn't understand why, if some colored people can get along on that amount, all can't do the same. I know one woman who does all this work. This woman is an 'Uncle Tom' type of person who says, 'Yes, ma-a-am!' and grins broadly whenever the woman speaks to her. The woman prefers this type of servant to the more intelligent type."

Most of Chicago's laundry is done in large commercial enterprises. It takes about 15,000 workers to keep the city's clothing clean, and the mechanical laundry has replaced the "washwoman." This type of work still has menial implications, however, and wages have tended to be low. Negroes have been hired in large numbers, and in 1930, 55.4 per cent of all the women working in laundries were colored, as were 26.3 per cent of the men working as semi-skilled operatives in the industry. The nature of the work has been such as to make it more favorable for union organization than domestic service, and the laundry workers' union affiliated with the AFL, in the late Depression years, included about 2,000 white members and 8,000 Negroes.

In a union of this type, Negroes have become familiar with the processes of collective bargaining and union participation with white workers. The more personal servant-employer relationships are absent. The brief observations at a union meeting cited below indicate the manner in which Negroes and whites co-operate in a laundry union, with Negroes, in some instances, displaying leadership:

The meeting was very orderly. The crowd was made up of Negroes and whites. Negroes comprised about one-third of the total. There was no discrimination, workers from the same laundry sitting together in groups in some instances and carrying on conversations. It was clear at the outset that the rank-and-file members were gathered in order to hear a report on the negotiations that had been carried on by the union officials. The business agent had just presented a contract which did not seem to satisfy the members. A Negro laundry operative wanted to know why they couldn't "tell the laundry owners to take it or leave it." He slowly walked to the front of the room [he was seated in the front row] and rubbing his hand over his head began in a slow drawl:

"I ain't satisfied with that contract there. Why is it that we let them bring us a contract and tell us to sign it? [Cheers.] Why don't we take *our* contract to *them* and tell *them* to sign what *we* want? For three years I've been working like a dog and I don't even make a living for dogs. I had greens last night for supper—I had greens today for lunch—and tonight I had greens for supper! Why? 'Cause I can't afford anything else."

The audience was laughing loudly because of the humorous picture that he was presenting, and the manner in which he spoke and gestured. He began again:

"Don't laugh now. Listen to what I'm saying. If you want to make a thief out of a man you just give him nothin'. I've got a wife to take care of, and how ya goin' to do it on $15 a week? [More cheers and laughter.] You tell those birds to *hell* with that contract. I don't want nothing those birds got in it, and if they don't take ours, they kin git out of business."

He took his seat amid long and loud applause, accompanied by laughter. The chair next recognized a young colored girl about twenty-two years of age.

"Mr. Chairman," she said, "you made no mention of wages for curtain stretchers. In my laundry I am the one who watches the curtain stretcher. It stretches and then finishes them. What about curtain stretchers, Mr. Chairman? I notice no mention was made of them. We got thirty cents by our own efforts. We asked the boss for a raise and when he refused, we struck by ourselves. He gave us thirty cents an hour. We joined the union because we don't think thirty cents is enough and want to get more. If the union can't get us more than thirty cents we might just as well get out and fight our battle alone." [She sat down amidst thundering applause.]

Another colored girl was given the floor.

"In my factory we already get thirty cents an hour. We struck ourselves and our employer said sure he'd give us that. Now thirty cents an hour is all right for them [gesticulating with her thumb to some girls back of her], but we don't work for nothing less than thirty cents an hour in our place now and thirty cents isn't doing us any good. We're already getting that. We want more and *we're going to get more!*" [Applause and cheers.]

She sat down and said softly, so that just those around her could hear.

"Yes, we are going to get it—thirty cents ain't nothing for us—we don't want to take it." Then she lighted a cigarette and gradually calmed down, only to rise up two more times and say about the same thing in different words. On the row in front of her were seated white girls who worked in the laundry with her. Behind was a white woman co-worker. They would tell her to "go ahead get up and tell them" and remind her of things to say. Then they would just laugh, and applaud her. Finally she asked, "Why is it that we've got to dicker and dicker and dicker with the employers? Why can't we just let them take it or leave it!"

The new Negro "washwoman" and "washman" are industrial workers, quite different from the older social types, and unlike domestic workers they have been drawn into the typical urban pattern of relationships with white employers and workers.

NEGROES AS UNSKILLED WORKERS

Until the Great Migration, Negro men and women seemed on the whole to prefer personal service in an atmosphere of relative cleanliness to the backbreaking and dirty labor of the stockyards. They preferred the heat of kitchens (where one could at least be sure of a meal) to the heat of the steel mills. There were always some Negroes in Chicago, however, who did unskilled and semi-skilled labor. (See Figure 16.)

Since the First World War, Negroes have found little trouble in securing more than their share of the jobs which expose them to dirt, grease, grime, and low pay. In the last year of prosperity, Chicago used about 170,000 workers to do the heavy lifting and heaving, the sweeping, tinkering, and furnace-tending. At least 35,000—twenty in every hundred—of these workers were Negroes. (Tables 8 and 9.)

JOBS ABOVE THE CEILING

As has been said, there are very few jobs in Chicago that can be called "Negro Jobs." There are numerous pursuits, however, which for all practical purposes are "White Men's Jobs." Custom has operated through a long period of years to restrict most Negro workers to the level of servants and unskilled laborers, although the years between the two wars witnessed the wide use of Negroes as semi-skilled operatives. On the eve of the Second World War the presence of Negroes was extremely rare on five occupational levels: (1) Control and Policy-Forming Groups in finance and industry; (2) Higher Supervisory and Technical Personnel; (3) Lower Supervisory and Technical Personnel; (4) Clerical Workers and Salespeople; (5) Skilled Labor. There are wide differences in the proportions of Negroes employed in these various types of jobs within the following fields: (1) Transportation and Communication; (2) Commerce and Trade; (3) Manufacturing; (4) Government. In general, the ceiling is "highest" in Government and "lowest" in Transportation and Communication. (Figure 19.) This is illustrated, for instance, by the fact that while no Negroes serve on the boards of directors of major public utility corporations,,

Figure 19

THE JOB CEILING IN GOVERNMENT AND PRIVATE INDUSTRY

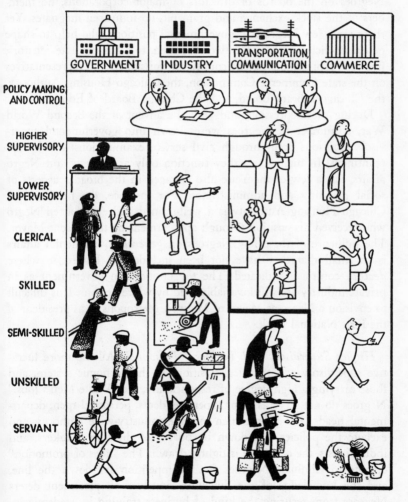

there have been Negroes on the Illinois State Commerce Commission, which has supervision over public utilities.

Control and Policy-Forming Groups: One of the most striking evidences of the Job Ceiling is the fact that there have never been any Negroes on the boards of directors of major corporations, no members of the stock exchange and grain pit, no industrial magnates. Yet there are a few Negroes in governmental positions who help to shape general policies, such as the two aldermen, two Illinois state senators, five state representatives, one county commissioner, and representatives on the state Commerce Commission, the Chicago Housing Authority, the Chicago Library Board, and the Chicago Board of Education.

During the Depression, and with the advent of the Second World War, a number of Negroes were drawn into governmental supervisory positions both through civil service examinations and by appointment. In many cases they function only as "experts" on Negro affairs, but a few of them are also engaged in the broader aspects of social planning and administration. For instance, the head of the Chicago Housing Authority is a well-trained and experienced Negro who received his position through appointment by the present Mayor. The influence of these few Negroes on *general* governmental affairs is so small that they have not been included in Figure 19 where *decisive* control is indicated. The *top* positions in government as in private industry are still invariably held by white persons. It is difficult to envision a Negro as Mayor of Midwest Metropolis or as president of the First National Bank.

Higher Supervisory and Technical Personnel: All the more lucrative supervisory and technical positions in the economic system, and those carrying a high degree of responsibility, are "White Men's Jobs." Negroes do not serve as plant superintendents, personnel men, departmental heads, etc. Where men exercise industry-wide authority and execute the policies laid down by boards of directors, bankers, and industrialists, the color-line is tightly drawn. The "lines of promotion" operate to eliminate Negroes from competition far down the line, and the knowledge of the difficulties involved in placement deters Negroes from securing the kind of business training in academic institutions that would qualify them for such positions if these were, by chance, made available. Even the free courses which were inaugurated during the early war period for training higher supervisory and technical workers had few Negro applicants. This was due partly to the fact that, lacking previous experience, few Negroes could meet the entrance requirements, and partly to the reluctance of institutions to train personnel which might be a "drug on the market."

The governmental structure is flexible enough to allow Negroes to serve as supervisors of some local social agencies, as principals of schools (in Negro neighborhoods), and as functionaries in the United States Employment Service, the Office of Price Administration, and similar agencies. But there are frequent attempts to bar them from such positions, even when they have passed civil service examinations. In one recent case, for example, a Negro passed an examination with a grade that would have made him the logical appointee for heading a major governmental office in the heart of the city. He was persuaded, finally, to remain in a less prominent position in a Negro neighborhood.

There are individual cases in which Negro technicians have been hired by private concerns. A colored man was for some years the chief air-conditioning engineer for the Pullman Company; another is an industrial chemist for a paint company; one is head chemist at a large commercial establishment; a few are mechanical and civil engineers. The general lack of opportunity for Negro technical workers in industry, however, has been reflected in the reluctance of Negro students to take technical training at public schools and in private institutions, since they feel that they would be wasting their time. The Second World War resulted in a marked increase in the employment of Negro technicians, but their use is by no means considered a permanent change of policy.

Negro accountants, architects, or civil engineers are employed from time to time by governmental agencies, but they are rarities. Certain other types of technical workers occasionally fill governmental positions, as in the case of one or two lawyers, who are experts on the traction problem, or the Negro who is considered the outstanding authority on the Illinois election laws.

Lower Supervisory and Technical Personnel: Negroes have an even smaller proportionate representation among lower supervisory-personnel and technical workers in private industry than in the group just discussed. Higher supervisory-personnel and technical workers are recruited from technical and business schools as well as from the ranks of the working class. A Negro may therefore take a short cut *via* education and thus make himself available. The lower supervisory-personnel and technical workers are largely recruited through promotions based on seniority and performance in skilled labor and clerical positions. Competition is very keen, favoritism plays a large part in promotions, and the individual prejudices of foremen are often decisive. The road up is tortuous even for white workers. Since a tight bottleneck on the skilled labor and clerical levels has prevented Negroes from securing such positions in private industry, they are usually not in strategic spots for promotion into the next highest brackets of employment.

Even in the Black Belt it is unusual for a colored man to be placed in a managerial position in a store owned by white persons, and the first Negro who secured such a position (in 1928) was widely publicized among Negroes, and thought of himself as a "pioneer." There were more than 10,000 foremen "bossing" Chicago's industry in 1930. Of these, only 140 were Negroes, and this figure included those persons in public and quasi-public employment. Even the Second World War did not open the ranks of foremen and supervisors, set-up men and minor technicians, to Negroes to any important extent.

The number and proportion of Negroes employed in minor supervisory capacities by governmental agencies fluctuates. In 1930, there were 161 colored policemen, 120 schoolteachers, and some 400 colored social workers and their activities were confined largely to the Negro community.

In general it may be stated that it is definitely not the policy in industry to place Negroes in positions where they give orders to white persons, hire and fire them, recommend them for promotions, or function as expert technicians. Competition for such positions is rigidly limited by those who do the hiring, by white competitors, and, to some extent at least, by the attitudes of the general public.

Clerical and Sales: An industrial city such as Chicago employs a host of white-collar workers—the backbone of the so-called "new middle class." These are the functionaries who do that mass of paper work upon which the complex commercial and industrial structure rests. They make out and collect the bills; they write and distribute the copy that persuades the public to buy this or that product; or they personally present the merits of rival companies and their wares to customers in stores, to retail outlets, and to housekeepers wherever they can effect an entrance by persuasion or guile.

In 1930 almost 100,000 people in Chicago were involved in "selling," and nearly 60,000 were serving the needs of commerce and industry with notebook and typewriter. *Negroes were employed in these capacities in a proportion of less than one in a hundred!* Wherever Negro members of this small group were found, if they were not in government positions they were usually working in Negro neighborhoods.

The political system has operated to place a relatively large number of Negroes in white collar and clerical positions in local government. During the Thompson administration Chicago's City Hall was dubbed "Uncle Tom's Cabin" because of the large number of Negroes employed there. The civil service lists and the payment of political obligations have spotted Negroes about in the city's libraries and governmental offices in increasing numbers, as did the shortage of clerical help during the Second World War.

Clerical and sales positions in Midwest Metropolis have been held, in the main, by people "on the make"—girls temporarily employed until they find a husband, men and women who hope to make a career in business and to advance on the job, and individuals of both sexes from working-class families who have made the first step away from back-breaking, menial or dirty work. Competition for advancement and raises, and for the personal attention of employers and personnel officials, is always keen.

Such positions, even when the pay is low, have been glamorized, and are surrounded with an aura of folklore. The myths surrounding secretary and boss, and the popular stories of the intimate activities of traveling salesmen and the escapades of "the Fuller Brush man," have invested such work with overtones of sexual as well as economic competition. Also, the large number of young women employed in clerical and sales work results in the elaboration of cliques on the job, oriented around the sharing of gossip about "boy friends," and a sort of ritualized primping and mutual admiration of clothes and physical attractiveness. Moreover, since an enterprise tends to be judged by its white-collar personnel, businessmen are reluctant to risk "goodwill" and profits by experimenting with types of workers with whom they feel the public is not familiar. The color-line, consequently, is very rigid in this area. Until the Second World War, Negroes found it almost impossible to secure acceptance, or even trial, in private white-collar employment, because it had become associated by custom with so many goals other than merely earning a living.

Figure 20

HIGH SCHOOL AND COLLEGE ENROLLMENT AMONG CHICAGO NEGROES : 1930 AND 1940

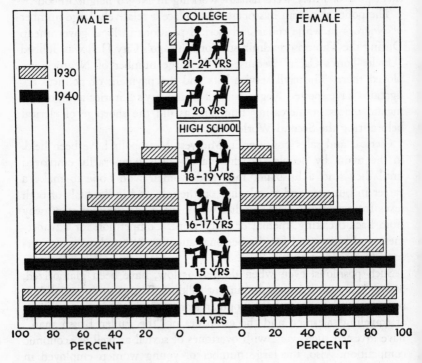

From tables in Fifteenth and Sixteenth Census of the U. S., 1930 and 1940.

Most of the colored women in clerical and sales work, prior to the Second World War were employed in the Black Belt and there were less than 1,500 of them. Clerical work elsewhere (except in Civil Service) has become the preserve of native-born white women. Negro girls, however, in increasing numbers during the last twenty years, have been attending high school and college. (Figure 20.) But the outlook for permanent white-collar employment has remained extremely bleak, despite temporary war gains. Figure 21 lends eloquence to a colored

Figure 21

ECONOMIC OPPORTUNITY FOR WOMEN

OF EVERY 10 TEEN-AGE WHITE GIRLS 5 ARE IN HIGH SCHOOL

OF THESE 6 CAN EXPECT WHITE-COLLAR JOBS

OF EVERY 10 TEEN-AGE NEGRO GIRLS 5 ARE IN HIGH SCHOOL

OF THESE ONLY 1 CAN EXPECT A WHITE-COLLAR JOB

Estimates based on data from the Sixteenth Census of the U. S., 1940.

school girl's mournful statement: "Teacher said not to take a commercial course because there were no jobs opening up for colored. So there's nothing but housework and cleaning left for you to do." *

✦

* The estimate of "economic opportunity for women" in Figure 21 is based on an analysis of 1930 and 1940 Census data, and on the assumption that most of the war-time clerical jobs held by Negro women are only temporary. Not more than 3 per cent of the Negro women held bona fide clerical and sales jobs in 1940. The saturation point for employment had been reached in Black Belt stores and offices. Yet, the high schools were continuing to turn out girls with "white-collar aspirations."

Skilled Labor: Prior to 1943, Negro skilled workers operated at a very great competitive disadvantage. Skilled workers have been ordinarily recruited largely from the ranks of the semi-skilled through apprenticeship service. A few were trained from trade schools and by plant-training programs. Until the outbreak of the Second World War all of these doors were closed to Negroes. In only one skilled labor category—as foundry men—did Negroes make up any appreciable number of the workers. Here the work is heavy and hot, and Negroes secured a priority on these jobs.

Craft unions, particularly those of the carpenters, steamfitters and plumbers, machinists, electricians, motion-picture operators, and street car employees have even restricted the competition of whites by constitutional provisions, high initiation fees, and demands for sponsors who were already members of the unions. Special barriers were erected against Negroes. The closed shop contracts and the political influence of the American Federation of Labor, have reinforced this closed circle, and even extended the influence of craft unions into the public trade schools and government employment.

Until the advent of the war, some unions, such as the machinists' brotherhoods, barred Negroes either by constitutional provision or sections of the ritual which stipulated that initiates were to be "white men of good moral character." Other unions used devices such as the refusal by members to "sponsor" Negroes. Where Negroes were permitted to work they were sometimes organized into separate locals without full membership privileges and were assigned specific areas of the city outside of which they were not permitted to work. Other unions used somewhat more subtle, but equally effective methods of barring Negroes.

Open shop employers who utilized Negro labor, or closed shop employers who wished to use them, were at a definite disadvantage. In the former case they ran the risk of actual intimidation and violence; in the latter case they had no influence over union rules with respect to race. Also, those employers who did not wish to employ Negroes could justify themselves by citing union restrictions. During hearings held in Chicago by the Illinois State Commission on the Condition of the Urban Colored Population in 1940, and by the Fair Employment Practices Committee in 1943, representatives of several unions and firms that refused to hire Negroes were summoned to testify. In a few cases they definitely defended a policy of discrimination. More typically, there was considerable "buck passing" backward and forward between the unions and management as to the responsibility for the Job Ceiling with a general admission that discrimination against Negroes was "un-American."

Unlike the other areas of government employment, Negroes have not penetrated the Job Ceiling in the skilled trades. This has been due primarily to the fact that the craft unions wield considerable political power and in some cases actually give the civil service examinations. One case was verified in which a Negro who had finished an engineering course in steamfitting and plumbing at a midwestern university and who had passed two state examinations with high marks, failed several times to pass an examination prepared by the Chicago Civil Service Commission. The union gave the examination!

Even within industrial plants in which there are no unions, it has traditionally been very difficult for Negroes to advance upward in the hierarchy beyond the semi-skilled level, since the foremen are the key men for rating workers, and as a general rule, they do not recomment Negroes.

THE UPS AND DOWNS OF COMPETITION

Losing Out: Between the Depression and the Second World War, there were a number of fields in which Negroes felt they were "losing out." These were occupations, which, although not Negro Jobs, had once been freely open to Negroes. With increased white competition, their hold upon them was being broken. Among these were jobs as cooks, waiters, maids and servants in institutions such as restaurants and hotels.

At one time it was traditional in Chicago for Negroes to hold a variety of jobs in most of the major hotels. Before the Great Migration, there were frequent complaints that Negroes were being "pushed out" of these fields by the foreign-born, and the labor unions were accused of aiding in the process. In 1930, colored men made up less than 30 per cent of the waiters in hotels and restaurants, and they were meeting strong competition from white men and girls. During the Depression years, several large hotels replaced Negro waiters with white girls, and there was bitter editorial comment about the matter in Negro newspapers.

✦

Holding Their Own: Between the First and the Second World Wars, Negro men held their own as common laborers and semi-skilled operatives in the mass production industries and commercial establishments. Negro women held their own as semi-skilled workers in canning factories, paper and pulp mills and cleaning and pressing establishments, and in the garment industry.

Breaking the Job Ceiling: By way of summary, it can be said that the competitive process has become organized in such a way that the Job Ceiling for Negroes tends to be drawn just above the level of semi-skilled jobs, with the skilled, clerical, managerial and supervisory positions reserved for white workers. There has been considerable conflict for jobs between white and Negro workers for semi-skilled and skilled jobs throughout Chicago's post-Migration history, and it is only within the last ten years that Negroes have become an integral part of the labor movement in the mass production industries, accepted as individuals subject to promotion on the basis of seniority.

The perpetuation of the Job Ceiling is basically related to the "lines of promotion" during "normal" years. It is expected that a certain proportion of individuals will "advance on the job." Advancement usually comes as a result of recommendations by minor supervisory personnel, or through the operation of union seniority rules. Insofar as Negroes have not been able to secure such recommendations, or have been refused admittance to unions, the Job Ceiling is reinforced. But the Job Ceiling is occasionally broken. Chapter 11 deals with the major factors that cause rifts in the Job Ceiling, but before analyzing that process we should understand the general forces which cause shifts in the color-line.

CHAPTER 10

The Shifting Line of Color

THE COLOR-LINE IN MIDWEST METROPOLIS FLOUTS THE BASIC TENETS OF American democracy, Christian brotherhood, and the "Chicago Spirit." Most Chicagoans, if pressed, would probably admit this. They are acquainted with the lofty declaration that "all men are created equal." Most of them, as children, have pledged allegiance to the flag—"with liberty and justice for all." Abraham Lincoln is an Illinois hero, praised frequently and loudly because he "freed the slaves." Nearly everyone, too, has been exposed to the words of priest, minister, or rabbi preaching the doctrine of "the Fatherhood of God and the Brotherhood of Man." And Chicago's civic boosters never tire of presenting the city as "the land of opportunity." These ideas are conserved and transmitted by churches and schools, press and radio, as well as by organized labor and various political parties and sects.

The most important agencies molding public opinion in Midwest Metropolis have supported the Negro's claim for democratic rights ever since the Flight to Freedom. There has always been, too, a small minority within the city that has militantly espoused the rights of Negroes, and a much larger number of people who, for reasons of political expediency or economic necessity, have welcomed the participation of Negroes in various sectors of city life. The majority of the residents of Midwest Metropolis have probably had no strong feelings one way or another about the place of Negroes. Except in crisis situations, they seldom think of Negroes. They have a policy of "live and let live." *

An analysis of the speeches made at the Mayor's Conference on Race

---

* No adequate statistical studies of the opinions and attitudes of white people in Midwest Metropolis toward Negroes are available. This chapter is based upon miscellaneous reports of interviewer-observers connected with the Cayton-Warner Research; the report of the 1919 Commission on Race Relations; a mass of data collected by the Illinois State Commission on the Condition of the Urban Colored Population (1940); and the memoranda and published reports of the Carnegie-Myrdal study, "The Negro in America." A poll conducted by *Fortune* for the Myrdal study also contains breakdowns of attitudes by section of the country, and some tentative generalizations may be drawn from its findings for the East North Central States including Illinois.

Relations in 1944 indicates the manner in which the status-bearers of the city—the political leaders, the industrialists, the labor leaders, the higher clergy, college professors, and administrators of private and public social agencies—are verbally committed to the ideal of equality of opportunity for Negroes. The first meeting was opened with an address by the Mayor, a man with a national reputation as the boss of a reputedly corrupt political machine. Practical and hard-boiled, he announced that this was "not a meeting of idealists and dreamers to sketch a panacea." Yet, proud of anything that makes Midwest Metropolis a "first," he boasted for the record: "I appointed, last July, with the approval of the City Council, a Committee on Race Relations. Chicago's pioneering in this realm started a widespread movement. I am informed that since last July, 137 similar committees have been appointed by Mayors, Governors, or civic and religious bodies from one end of the country to the other." Out of the Mayor's address emerged the main outlines of the official, public doctrines about the rights of man, which, along with the demands of economic necessity and political expediency, help to shape events as well as rationalize them. All of the speakers echoed these basic ideas.

The Mayor emphasized the *virtue in variety*—"Our people trace their origin from almost every country on the globe, representing more than thirty-two different nationalities and sixty-two dialects. . . ." He stressed the *fact of interdependence* with an epigram: "Benefits to any one group can result in advantages to all." The *primacy of civic harmony* was driven home: ". . . to avoid friction and to promote co-operation among the many great groups that make up this city. . . ." The Mayor also revealed his *faith in planning:* "Only recently have we begun to realize that it is as important to plan for human relations as for material needs."

Belief in the *primacy of civic harmony* and *faith in planning* led most of the speakers to emphasize education and "good-will" as the desirable mechanisms of social change. *Tolerance* was constantly emphasized as the cardinal civic virtue, ideological trimmings being thus given to the more mundane imperatives of city life—a state of affairs in which bankers and pickpockets, preachers and prostitutes, artists and gangsters not only inhabit the same city, but are inextricably tied together in a web of political and economic relationships which is real although usually hidden and denied.

The Negro is automatically included within this framework of optimistic dogmas based on the realities of urban life. One speaker, a member of the editorial staff of the liberal daily, the Chicago *Sun,* reminded the conference, however, of the *moral* imperatives which should guide their deliberations: "There are many reasons why the community cannot shirk this responsibility—reasons of expediency, reasons of fair-play, reasons of long-range social prudence—what we might call self-interested social insurance for the future. But in the end none of these surpasses the basic reason that underlies them all. To act against discrimination is right, morally right; we know in our hearts it is right. We know that equality is indivisible and cannot be split by a color-line."

Equality was the master-slogan of the Mayor's Conference. The head of the city health department boasted proudly that, in the venereal disease clinics, "there is no distinction because of race, sex, creed, or nationality." The Commissioner of Relief testified that in his department, "the needs of all persons have been treated alike without regard to race, color, or creed." A district police captain, solicitous for equality before the bar as well as at the relief station and the VD clinic, stated that "men who will judge others by merit and not by the yardstick of color, creed, or nationalities should be the only persons placed in executive positions." The Subcommittee on Employment, composed of sixteen leading industrialists, went on record as being opposed to the Job Ceiling by suggesting that employers "regard each Negro employee as an individual, with potentialities and limitations, who takes his or her place in your firm on the basis of merit as a worker and not on the basis of belonging to any special racial grouping." The AFL spokesman, in a contrite mood, referred to "race and sometimes religious barriers that all of us know are contrary to the spirit of our country." The CIO representative proclaimed "the moral righteousness of treating all Americans with complete equality regardless of the pigment of their skins." The Chairman closed the conference with a reminder that "full victory will come only if we put aside our petty prejudices and, in the Chicago spirit of 'I will' make up our minds that regardless of race, creed, or color, we are going to treat all people on the democratic basis of individual merits."

These profuse expressions of belief in equality led the president of a YMCA college to admonish the conference: "We have all the ideals we need to solve this problem. We know what democracy is and we all know what the Christian ideals for human associations are. We all know them, whether we live by them or not."

BELIEFS MEN LIVE BY

With nearly everyone in Midwest Metropolis verbally committed to a belief in democracy, freedom, equality, fair play, and similar civic ideals, why does a color-line persist? The answer lies partly in the fact that these are not the ideals men live by, however much they may believe in them. Side by side with the official doctrines about men's relationships to their fellows are the "folk-beliefs" that influence human behavior far more profoundly than do any political or religious dogmas. These folk-beliefs and attitudes become set at a very early age within family and play groups, where they are acquired by imitation and unconscious absorption long before the other institutions get to work on the child's mind. Adult associations and cliques preserve them. The folk-beliefs and the behavior pattern associated with them are difficult to change.

The most basic of these reaction-patterns is the habit of reacting to people in terms of *inequalities*. Children learn early that social differences *are* important—that income, education, language, eating habits, skin-color, and a hundred and one other things must all be weighed in determining a man's intrinsic worth or his acceptability as an associate. In our Western European culture the basic categories of invidious distinction are *group* differences—of religion, nationality, and socioeconomic status. In countries with an Anglo-American tradition, "race" —as denoted by skin-color—is an additional marker. We have already seen how the competition between such groups has been the thread upon which the history of Midwest Metropolis is strung.

Since the early days of the slave trade, dark skin-color has been considered a mark of inferiority—social, economic, and political—in the Anglo-American world. Africa has become the master-symbol of benightedness and savagery, its people being thought of as lowest in the scale of culture and civilization—perhaps even not fully human. A vague belief permeates the society that Negroes are "closer to the apes." Folk-thought invests them—the descendants of African slaves—with an aura of "primitiveness." They are considered impulsive, childlike, overemotional, oversexed, and short on brains and initiative. They are thought to be docile, easily frightened, incredibly superstitious, but gifted with a sure sense of rhythm (perhaps in compensation for lack of gray matter). These basic beliefs are reinforced by the objective fact that, the world around, the darker peoples are predominantly "backward" when judged by Western European standards.

The low cultural and economic status of Negroes in America seems to confirm this estimate. Quick judgments arising from limited contacts with Negroes, and from the picture of Negro life presented by the press, radio, and screen, perpetuate the stereotype. Epithets like "nigger," "darky," "shine," "smoke," "spade," "dingy," exist in the culture and may be used as short-cut symbols to express all the contempt concentrated in the popular estimate of the Negro. Kinky hair, thick lips, and dark skin become the esthetic antithesis of straight hair, small lips, white skin, and these physical traits are thought to be correlated with all of the unsavory characteristics indicated above.

Negroes in America are only eighty years out of slavery. As described in the early part of this book, less than a hundred years ago, the slave-catchers were chasing fugitives through the streets of Midwest Metropolis. In the South, Negroes are still living in the backwash of slavery—floundering in a morass of poverty, ignorance, and disease. Periodically, the South debouches a flood of these "backward" people into the northern city streets, and always there is some seepage through the ramparts of the Mason and Dixon's Line.

As the center for the formation of attitudes about the Negro, the South keeps alive the belief in the Negro's differentness and inferiority and, in doing so, depends not only upon derogatory propaganda, but also upon a caste system which effectively limits the chances for Negroes to change their status. The situation thus becomes circular: Negroes are deemed unfit for citizenship or full equality; they must be kept in their place; through being kept in their place they cannot show whether they are fit for citizenship and equality. These southern attitudes exist in a watered-down form in Midwest Metropolis, as they do throughout the North.* Negroes in the mass are poor and still display

---

* Eugene L. Horowitz, discussing "Attitudes and Sectional Differences in the United States" (*Characteristics of the American Negro*, Otto Kleinberg, *ed.*, Harper, 1944), presents the results of a poll which included small samples

many of the rough edges of conduct that come from their southern background and their social isolation. They are quarantined behind the color-line. But—and this is the crux of the matter—this quarantine intensifies their differentness and curtails their chances for improvement. Negroes become the victims of circular reinforcement.

Not only does folk-thought deal with Negroes as a separate and inferior group. It also brings to bear upon the Negro problem all of the superstitions about "blood," and the half-truths about heredity, which are a part of our general culture. It is assumed that "Negro character traits" are passed on from generation to generation, that somehow "blood will tell." The smallest drop of colored blood will "taint" the white stock. As Negroes sometimes jocularly phrase it: "Negro blood is powerful. One drop will make you whole." It is necessary, therefore, in order to preserve the "purity" of the white race to see to it that persons with Negro blood will mate with Negroes only and not "infect" the white race. The obverse side of this argument is that any Negro with white blood has had his undesirable traits diluted and thus becomes a little more civilized than a pure black. Such people must stay on their side of the fence and breed with "their kind." It will take centuries to submerge the Negro traits; meanwhile mulattoes, octoroons, quadroons serve as a leavening force for the black people. This theory of blood magic, in a general way, is a widespread feature of folk-thought.

But nowhere in America have caste tendencies ever been so strong— even during slavery—that *some* Negroes did not find an opportunity to exercise intelligence and skill and to display talent and initiative.

from various sections of the United States. It suggests some of the sectional differences in folk-thinking about Negroes:

	East South Central and South Atlantic States (Per Cent)	East North Central States (Per Cent)
1. Belief in intellectual inferiority of Negroes	72.5	70.4
2. Heredity alone accounts for this inferiority	52.5	38.0
3. Environment alone accounts for inferiority	20.3	40.2
4. Some Negroes surpass white average of intelligence..........................	75.3	90.7
5. Negroes are "improving"...............	29.2	25.9

The Christian-humanitarian tradition and the demands of economic necessity and political expediency have consistently weakened the will, wherever it existed, to keep *all* Negroes, everywhere, in a subordinate economic, political, and social status. The beliefs in the inherent intellectual inferiority of all Negroes were contradicted by the facts long before the mental-testers ever got the statistics down on paper.* The dictum that Negroes were animal-like and incapable of assimilating Christian morality was challenged by the growth of stable family elements even before the bonds of chattel slavery fell. The early emergence of a class system among Negroes made it impossible for anyone to miss the fact that *some* Negroes were interested in "getting ahead" just like their white neighbors.† Faced with these facts, it was necessary to take refuge in certain dodges: "Of course, there are exceptional Negroes"; "Most exceptional Negroes have some white blood"; "The best of them are niggers underneath; culture and education are just a veneer"; "Education spoils the simple Negro and makes him restless and unhappy"; "If they get too far ahead they'll start wanting social equality."

These racial doctrines are not taught in any systematic fashion in Midwest Metropolis, nor do they form an integrated ideological framework. Rather, they are picked up by children from adult conversation and are mediated through play groups. They are strengthened through contact with southerners who come to Chicago and northerners who travel in the South. In a very unorganized fashion they get reinforcement from caricatures and cartoons, newspaper stories and movies, and statements here and there in textbooks. When the Great Migration began it is doubtful whether the masses of foreign-born workers and their children had any clear beliefs about Negroes such as they had about Jews and Poles and Italians and other European ethnic groups. Confronted by thousands of Negro migrants they were forced to

---

* A Public Affairs Committee pamphlet by Ruth Benedict and Gene Weltfish, *The Races of Mankind,* summarizes the results of intelligence tests given to whites and Negroes as a part of a general discussion of the conflict between the folk-ideas about race and scientific findings.

† Social and economic stratification among Negroes in the United States began very early. One Anthony Johnson, member of the first group of Negroes imported at Jamestown in 1619, had obtained his freedom and become the master of indentured servants within twenty years after he landed. Colonies of free Negroes existed in all southern cities throughout the late seventeenth century and subsequent years. In Chapter 2 we have described the emergence of the class system among Negroes in Midwest Metropolis.

hammer together a set of attitudes and opinions from a disjointed mass of folk-prejudices. And groups with axes to grind helped them.

THE ROLE OF ECONOMIC INTEREST

The frequently heard statement that "the race problem is economic," has become a platitude. Although this is only a half-truth, color-caste did have its origin in economic interest. Plantation owners in the West Indies and North America needed labor to grow the cane and cotton, indigo and tobacco, upon which the fortunes of the New World were built. They first tried the Indians, and then turned to a vast reservoir of indentured servants from Europe and Negroes from Africa. The early traffickers in slaves often justified their business because it "brought the heathen to Christ" as well as in terms of economic necessity. The doctrine of inherent biological and racial inferiority grew slowly throughout the seventeenth century, and seems to have been partly due to the Puritan streak in English thought. How could Christians enslave their fellowmen? Only if they were not *really* men. (As one scholar has phrased it, "Negroes suffered because of the white man's virtues as well as because of his vices.") But the circumstances that finally riveted the chains upon Negroes sprang from the conflict of interest between white landlords in the southern United States and white indentured servants. So long as there was free land to the West, no English workers, with the traditions of relatively unlimited freedom behind them, could be bound permanently to the soil of the plantation. Planters, unable to hold white labor tied to the soil, were forced to keep Negroes in a position of chattel slavery bound in perpetuity to labor. Every resource of religion, propaganda, and violence was utilized to justify this enslavement of millions of Africans.[1]

White indentured servants, having the advantage of cultural kinship with the overlords, sharply dissociated themselves from the African slaves and buttressed their privileged position by stressing the importance of the color of their skins. By keeping the Negro bound to the plantation, the lowly white man protected his claim to the free lands of the West and his opportunity to rise from indentured servant to apprentice to journeyman to master artisan in the South and East. (Further, he accepted the doctrines of inherent biological inferiority in order to square things with his Puritan conscience and his democratic idealism.)

By the turn of the nineteenth century, however, it was becoming evident that the southern landed aristocracy was ambitious to extend its system of slavery even to the free lands of the West, and thousands of southerners and ex-southerners in the border states began to turn against the planter class. Northern capitalists and artisans became the spearhead of an attack upon a slave system that threatened to hamper the growth of an industrial society, and menaced the free yeomen farmers in the West. The result was civil war. By this time the racial doctrines had become a part of the folk-thought, and, although the white workers in North and South alike hated slavery, they did not love the slave. In fact, the freeing of the slaves threw millions of potential competitors into the struggle for jobs and the scramble for western lands. This competition did not become serious, however, until the period of the First World War, for the southern landlords had no intention of letting their labor supply walk off to the North and West. Whatever interracial stability existed in the North between the Civil War and the First World War was directly related to the southern caste system which "protected" the North and West against an influx of Negroes.

Once the folk-beliefs about Negroes had come into being to justify the privileges of southern white laborers and to rationalize the economic interests of the planters, they kept going under their own power. Today, they often exist independently of economic interest. But in Midwest Metropolis, as elsewhere, there are still many situations in which the folk-beliefs about Negroes and economic interest reinforce each other. Among industrial laborers, for instance, there has been, since the days of the Flight to Freedom, the fear that employers would use poverty-stricken Negro labor from the South to keep wages down and to break strikes. This fear has been frequently justified. The traditional reaction of white workers has been to lash out blindly at the Negro as the source of the trouble, and to seek to limit his competition by refusing to admit him to membership in unions, by stressing his alleged incompetence and unreliability, and by attacking him physically when he got in the way. Even today two of the strongholds of anti-Negro sentiment in Midwest Metropolis are a group of AFL unions in the skilled trades and a group of railroad brotherhoods.

The main focal point of anti-Negro sentiment in Midwest Metropolis, and by far the most important one, is a loose association of neighborhood property owners' associations aided and abetted by the Chicago Real Estate Board and the Chicago Title and Trust Company. In Chapter 8 we have seen how the generally low cultural status of Negroes and the folk-prejudices against them, excite fear of a decline in property values when Negroes move near, or into, middle-class neighborhoods. Even middle-class Negroes are thought of as a "taint" or "blight" in a middle-class white area. When these propertied interests fight to preserve the residential color-line no holds are barred.*

The small property owners, as we have seen, are aided and abetted by the large real-estate interests and the banks. This is due partly to concern about their mortgages in middle-class white neighborhoods, but it is also a reflection of the fact that these larger interests stand to make quick profits from the high rents which they can charge in Negro areas since the Negroes can't get out. When a high official of the Chicago Real Estate Board can say at a public hearing, "I know that restrictive covenants are undemocratic; but my first duty is to the property holders I represent," we can understand the power of economic interest in holding the color-line tight.

Much of the incidental discrimination in public places is directly related to economic interest. An individual proprietor may, himself, have no objections to Negro patronage, but if even one customer objects, or if he thinks one will object, he is likely to become panic-stricken and discourage Negro patronage if he can. An employer may honestly mean it when he says, "I'd like to employ that attractive Negro girl in the office, or that aggressive colored salesman, but what can I do when some customer says, 'I don't want to do business with a nigger'?" The economic argument can always work the other way around, too. An employer or proprietor who has strong feelings against Negroes can cover his prejudice, salve his conscience, or hoodwink Negroes— as the occasion demands—by pleading that consideration for Negroes may hurt his pocketbook.

In a northern city like Midwest Metropolis, if only a tiny fraction of the white population is aggressively anti-Negro, the color-line may be reinforced. A proprietor or an employer can never be sure that a preju-

---

* The influence of the real estate interests in buttressing and extending segregation extends far beyond the Negro community. In 1945, some officials of the larger real estate associations who were also members of the board of the Chicago Y.M.C.A. demanded that a study be made of the proportion of Negroes and Jews attending the Central Y.M.C.A. College with an eye to restricting their attendance. The President of the College and over half of the faculty resigned in protest.

diced client will not close his account, cease his patronage, or create a scene. Whenever there is the possibility that a black face will drive business away, a hitch is taken in the color-line.

THE ROLE OF SOCIAL STATUS

Economic considerations, while extremely important, alone cannot account for the persistence of the color-line. One of the most powerful factors implementing it is the concern for the preservation and enhancement of social status. In the life-history of the individual he is constantly seeking approval and psychological support from various groups. First, the immediate family circle dominates; later, teachers, fellow-pupils, and the play-group; still later, courting cliques and various types of formal associations. Adults are responsive to the pressures of their work-associates, recreational groups, formal associations, and to the standards of any higher social stratum to which they aspire. These groups (or one's conception of them) act as controls upon individual behavior. In addition to these primary groups, the individual is also under the constant scrutiny of the larger public which he meets on the street and in public places. Whatever "private" attitudes an individual may have are influenced by public opinion.

There is considerable evidence to indicate that very young children react to differences in skin-color mainly in terms of curiosity. They have to be taught the facts of social life. They learn quickly, however, under the impact of a restraining hand here, a little heart-to-heart talk there, a lifted eyebrow, a stare, a frown, and gossip.* During the critical period of adolescence, if white youngsters are in contact with Negroes of the same age-group, sensitiveness to the color-line becomes sharpened, and behavior toward Negroes tends to crystallize into an

---

* Eugene L. Horowitz, in an article "Attitudes in Children" (*op. cit.*), summarizes the research findings on the development of race attitudes in children and presents case materials to illustrate the force of social pressure. The following is a typical response: "There is like a wall preventing the Negro and white people from being sociable. If you even try to be sociable with Negroes the rest of the people lift their eyebrows and say, 'Aw—that's awful.' When I meet them in the hall I say hello to them. All the other children look at me like it would be a crime to be sociable with them." (From a sixth-grade white boy in Cincinnati, Ohio.) A young Jewish child said: "I wouldn't want a Negro for a chum either. It wouldn't seem right. Everybody would be talking about me if they saw me going around with a colored person."

action-pattern for adult life. Many white persons in Midwest Metropolis, however, grow up without any close contact with Negroes. The problem of how to react toward Negroes confronts the average white person in a piecemeal, disjointed fashion. Usually he acts toward them as he would toward white persons of equivalent socio-economic status, unless his economic interests or his personal prestige seem menaced. In fact, it seems likely that there are hundreds of people in Midwest Metropolis who have very little strong race-consciousness and no particular aversion to social relations with Negroes of a similar socio-economic status. Social pressure, however, effectively keeps them in line.

The doctor in suburban Glencoe may actually wish to invite to his home for dinner the brilliant young surgeon that he met at the Negro hospital; but he is effectively deterred by the thought of what the neighbors will say when a black man and his mulatto wife get out of a Packard and go up his front steps.

The businessman in a Loop office may have no objections to a colored stenographer referred to him by the U. S. Employment Service; but could he stand the jokes that his cronies might level at him? His fear of a ribbing keeps the Negro girl taking care of his children instead of pounding his typewriter.

The white stockyards laborer at a union dance may have no aversion to dancing with that attractive brown-skinned girl who works in the smoked ham department; in fact he'd like to learn a little "rug-cutting" the way they do it in Black Metropolis. But none of the other white fellows are dancing with colored girls, and one of his buddies just can't stand these "smokes"—even ridicules him for going to a place where they let them dance on the same floor with white people.

The waitress at the restaurant thinks the colored bus-boy is a swell guy. They are always joking together in the pantry. But to walk into the Oriental Theater with him (as he half-jokingly suggested once), with all the white people staring and with the chance that some of her crowd might see her—that just isn't worth the risk. She wouldn't marry a Negro, and no white fellow would marry her if he knew she had dated a colored boy. Over to Club DeLisa in the Black Belt? Well, she'd gone with him once, but her heart was in her mouth all the time. And she couldn't let him escort her all the way home. Never again!

THE NEXUS OF SOCIAL CONTROLS

The intimate tie-up between strong folk-prejudices, economic interest, and social status is so intricate that it is difficult to unravel the threads. Negroes and whites seldom marry, not because it is illegal, but primarily because of strong folk-prejudices. Yet people without strong folk-prejudices don't do it either. Social pressure is too great and they might jeopardize their jobs. Negroes are confined to a Black Ghetto primarily because of the economic interests of property owners; but land values wouldn't be affected if folk-prejudices did not exist. And the whole problem is complicated by middle-class emphasis upon maintaining a relatively high social status. The Job Ceiling is primarily an economic device, but it reflects the reluctance of white people to lose prestige by working under the supervision of, or beside, Negroes in certain situations. It also reflects some deep-seated beliefs about the incapacity of the Negro to hold down certain jobs.

If we take a situation in which the law supports the Negro's demand for the abolition of the color-line, we can see how all these factors operate to produce incidental examples of discrimination here and there. Any given case of refusal to serve a Negro in a public place may have any or all of the following elements in it:

a. Traditional neighborhood hostility toward Negroes.

b. Fear of a Negro "invasion" by a neighborhood or establishment.

c. Fear of economic loss if customers object.*

d. Expression of an individual proprietor's own attitudes.

e. Expression of an individual functionary's or employee's attitude, sometimes in violation of established policy of the enterprise.

f. The assumption on the part of an employee that his employer wishes him to discriminate even though policy has not been defined. (Often a carry-over from previous work situations.)

---

* The fear of customer objection does not seem to have so much basis in reality as most proprietors assume. The Committee on Racial Equality, a group of young Negro and white people connected with churches and Socialist organizations has for three years been systematically visiting establishments that discriminate against Negroes. It reports that the general attitude of customers seems to be one of indifference. Even when an argument arises between a proprietor and the group asking to be waited on, other customers rarely join the dispute. The experimenters have never been beaten or otherwise attacked, and occasionally a white patron has sided with them.

g. Interpretation of the situation as "private" or "social" and of the Negro's demand for service as an unwarranted invasion of an "exclusive" situation.

The net result of this loose system of social controls is to make white behavior almost unpredictable, and to create a feeling of insecurity and tension among Negroes in their dealings with white people. In contrast with the South where the racial etiquette is rigidly defined, the Negroes of Midwest Metropolis can never be quite sure what will happen. It has been noted by some observers that Negroes experience a "gain" in psychological security in the South. Most of the Negroes in Midwest Metropolis would probably say that they prefer "insecurity." Within this loose nexus of controls lie the seeds of social change.

THE SEEDS OF SOCIAL CHANGE

The color-line in Midwest Metropolis is not static. The Job Ceiling is sometimes pierced and broken. Negroes occasionally find homes outside of the Black Belt, and the Black Belt does expand. In fact, Negroes are continually expressing surprise at some new "gain" made by The Race. Despite the Negro's impatience and the white man's fears, there is enough change to generate a vast amount of optimism among Negroes and progressive whites. This optimism was evident throughout the discussions at the Mayor's Conference on Race Relations. The participants, all interested in some relaxation of the color-line, seemed to define the problem in the following terms:

1. Creating a favorable public opinion toward the aspirations of Negroes.
2. Reducing the cultural difference between Negroes and whites.
3. Securing a larger measure of equality of opportunity without abolishing segregation in clique, church, and associational life, exciting a social-equality scare, or precipitating a race riot.
4. Ignoring the long-time perspective, thus avoiding commitments on intermarriage or amalgamation.

In pursuing these ends everyone seemed agreed that education and counterpropaganda were necessary to combat folk-prejudices; that increased friendly and co-operative contacts between Negroes and white people were desirable; and that considerations of economic necessity and political expediency should be exploited to set new social situations in which the status of Negroes could be changed. The summary of the conference (*City Planning in Race Relations*) assumed that social change in race relations could be controlled.

The Place of Education and Counterpropaganda: There is widespread belief among many Americans that "prejudice comes from ignorance." It is assumed that if both Negroes and whites can be educated they will learn to co-exist harmoniously (education usually meaning the verbal reiteration of certain ideas). Those who stress education start out with certain things in their favor. In the first place, Midwest Metropolis is already half educated. The absence of a slave tradition and the widespread profession of the ideals of democracy mean that most people are willing to concede at the outset that Negroes have rights which should be respected and that they are entitled to increased opportunity. Side by side with the belief in the inherent inferiority of Negroes there exists a tendency to accept the proposition that Negroes are "evolving" and that education will speed up the process. The following comment by a white drugstore owner during the Great Migration illustrates a mishmash of ideas [2] incorporating both folk-prejudices and democratic idealism:

"I have nothing against the black man as a black man. He comes into my place of business and I sell him. Not many come in, as there aren't a lot of colored people around Sixty-third and Woodlawn or Dorchester. But I don't want to live with niggers any more than you or any other white person does. People who say, 'I like the colored people and don't see why others can't get along with them' don't talk practical common sense. Theoretically, all this talk is all right, but you get a white man of this sort to come right down and live with a nigger and he won't do it.

"Niggers are different from whites and always will be, and that is why white people don't want them around. But the only thing we can do, it seems to me, is make the best of it and live peaceably with them. The North can never do what the South does—down there it is pure autocracy, I might say like Russia. That might have worked here in the North from the start, but it can't be started now, and we wouldn't want such autocracy anyway. They are citizens and it is up to us to teach them to be good ones. How it can be done, I don't know—it will have to come slow and no one can give an offhand solution. Everybody says, 'We don't want the niggers with us.' Well, here they are and we can't do anything. Must let them live where they want to and go to school where they want to, and we don't want to force their rights away."

This co-existence of folk-prejudices with a belief that Negroes should have a chance to develop (if they can) was expressed, during the same period, by a number of white community leaders. The pattern of responses is indicated in the following analysis of the opinions of four persons who wrote out their attitudes toward Negroes: [3]

Beliefs About Negroes	Attitude Toward Extension of Opportunity	Attitude Toward Negroes' Demands
1. Distinctly inferior mentality. 2. Deficient moral sense. 3. Shiftless. 4. Good-natured and happy disposition. 5. So different from whites that the two races can never be amalgamated.	"If surrounded by good living conditions and given a proper education they would be good citizens."	"I believe in educating Negroes, although I am not sure what it will lead to. . . . Probably many of their demands should be granted." (Believes in segregation only if Negroes consent.)
1. "Evolutionally" handicapped. 2. Childlike qualities: carelessness, improvidence, loyalty, imitativeness, affection, receptiveness.	"As a race have never had a fair chance for their finest development." "Their education should not be curtailed but enlarged." "Have the right to expect and demand justice in opportunity to develop industrial, social, and spiritual growth."	"Their demands should be granted if not incompatible with the common good."
1. Sluggish mentality. 2. Somewhat low moral character. 3. Seem to have more of the animal in them.	"They need education and the help that comes from association with those who are farther along in the polite amenities." "Deportation unchristian and unwise." "Complete segregation unjust and impractical."	"Regrettable that a minority cannot expect complete justice." (Thinks they should be settled in a separate state in the South, but not by force.)
1. "I have a strong prejudice."	"All Negroes should be educated as highly as possible. They have a right to it because they are Americans."	"If demands follow this education, it is right they should be granted." (Prefers colonization of Negroes in Africa.)

One of the main sources of racial tension in Midwest Metropolis is confusion and apprehension about what social change will mean. A very small minority probably feel that the ultimate result of the Negro's rise in status will be amalgamation.* A larger number feel that Negroes and whites will continue to remain socially separate. Very few people think that it is possible to deport Negroes, or that they will voluntarily leave the country.† *The general hope seems to be that Negroes will remain segregated socially and in separate neighborhoods, and will be content therewith; that they will not force the pace of breaking the Job Ceiling to the point of precipitating violence; and that they will use their political power "wisely."* Few people have consciously thought out any such position, but when the Negro issue is raised, or when

---

* Liberals and progressives try to avoid discussion of amalgamation as a possible outcome of their efforts to secure equal opportunity for Negroes. At the same time, however, they propagate the *myth of the melting pot.* For instance, the Mayor's Conference on Race Relations accepted *difference as a fact,* emphasize the *virtue in variety,* but also espoused the *myth of the melting pot.* The Mayor stated proudly, "Of all communities in the world Chicago perhaps can be most appropriately termed the melting pot." Another speaker grew almost lyrical in his reference to "this wonderful melting pot." The President of the Council of Social Agencies referred to Midwest Metropolis as the "melting pot of melting pots." The *myth of the melting pot* implies the eventual disappearance of all ethnic divisions and the substitution of social-class lines for divisions of nationality and race. It also implies the fusing of diverse physical strains into some future American type. The latter implication is found in a speech by one prominent white civic leader who told the conference: "It is highly appropriate that the first permanent resident of this city which is the melting pot of melting pots should be a sort of one-man melting pot himself. Jean Baptiste Point de Saible, who came here shortly after the Revolution, was half Negro and half French. As he had as his consort an Indian woman, he included in his immediate family the three principal races of the world." The Chairman of the Conference prefaced his summary of the findings with this statement: "Chicago has been built by many different kinds of people. The first settler in the trading post that became Chicago was Jean Baptiste Point de Saible, half French, half Negro, and married to an Indian. This cosmopolitan character has continued all through the city's history. . . ." The story of Chicago's Negro founder and his family is taught in Chicago's public schools with the same emphasis upon its symbolic foreshadowing of Midwest Metropolis, the cosmopolitan city.

Superficially it would seem that the men quoted above were advocating amalgamation, or at least sanctioning it. It is probable, however, that the use of the Point de Saible story has a totally different function. By idealizing the past it permits contemporary individuals to feel very liberal. The very fact that it can be used by an official body like the Mayor's Committee is testimony to the confidence which Chicago's civic leaders have that the present-day taboo on intermarriage will not break down.

† These generalizations are based upon interview documents, newspaper analyses, and inferences from the overt behavior of white people in Midwest

some incident focuses attention upon Negroes as "a problem," this is the type of "solution" that seems to crystallize in the popular mind.* Events, however, are continually forcing white people in Midwest Metropolis to face up to their relations with Negroes. When the problem arises, either in actuality or in conversation, they must choose sides, and the tension between democratic idealism and actual practice demands resolution. When in the throes of such an intellectual and moral crisis, people are susceptible to education and counterpropaganda.† During a strike or a war or a depression, education and counterpropaganda can be very effectively used to point up the necessity for integrating Negroes more fully into American life.

Most of the social engineers in Midwest Metropolis are primarily interested in a long-time program of education and counterpropaganda as a means of changing the folk-prejudices. They see their problem as one of gradually changing the tone of the press, radio, and screen.

Metropolis. The *Fortune* poll confirms these general observations. Horowitz (*op. cit.*) gives the following percentages for the East North Central States in response to a query on what the solution of the race problem was likely to be.

Per Cent

1. Believe that things will remain "about as they are" 37.5
2. Believe that Negroes will remain socially separate but will be treated as equals in all other respects 22.8
3. Don't know 29.8
4. Believe that amalgamation will ultimately result 2.6
5. Believe that deportation is feasible 1.3
6. Believe that Negroes will secure full equality 5

* It is perhaps significant that only 8.4% of the East North Central people queried in the *Fortune* poll thought of the Negro as a "problem."

† Such a moral crisis can also be resolved through an *anti*-Negro action-pattern. Men can strike very brutally when goaded by an uneasy conscience. People can be very stubborn if they feel their efforts to be "fair" are not appreciated. A large number of people seem to consider that Negroes are "on trial"; that they must "prove themselves"; that America has given them a fine chance to do so; that "after all, they've come a long way since slavery." When Negroes dissent from this view, a white person who holds it can become righteously indignant. There is some evidence to suggest that this attitude is widespread. Several surveys of public opinion made in 1944 by the National Institute of Public Opinion Research, Denver, Colorado, indicate that at least half of the white public professes to believe that "Negroes are getting a square deal in this country." Over two-thirds, however, think that "Negroes do not believe they are getting a square deal." In other words, well over half the population seems to feel that Negroes are being unreasonable in raising demands for the abolition of the Job Ceiling and for the relaxation of the color-bar. It could be that these verbal responses conceal an uneasy conscience arising from the knowledge that democratic profession and practice are at variance in America.

They recognize the fundamental necessity of utilizing the schools for incidental intercultural education and the churches for direct indoctrination. But the liberal and progressive forces have only scratched the surface when it comes to using the resources at hand for a planned attack upon the false ideas about ethnic groups in general and Negroes in particular.* This is due partly to a shortage of personnel and funds, but it is also directly related to considerations of social prestige and economic interest. There are individuals and institutions in Midwest Metropolis that definitely do not wish to see any basic changes in the status of Negroes. Yet an awareness of the Negro's aspirations and of the disabilities from which he suffers seeps throughout the city year by year, and increasingly large numbers of people are forced to face the issue, or experience a change of attitude so subtly that they hardly notice it.

The Role of Contact: One Negro speaker at the Mayor's Conference, after admitting the need for education, said, "The education we need most is the education of association." Another speaker, deploring the fact that residential segregation tends to separate Negro and white school children, stated:

"It is tragic that American boys and girls in the most impressionable period of their lives are prevented from having the natural and normal contacts which a mixed school system provides. The separate school system develops hatreds, suspicions, and disrespect which are carried over into our work and play life as we reach adulthood. It is significant that persons who have been taught by both white and colored teachers are more willing to work and play side by side with each other than those who have not had this broadening experience."

This almost mystical faith in "getting to know one another" as a solvent of racial tensions is very widespread. It is undoubtedly true that mere contact is likely to result in some degree of understanding and friendliness. It is equally true, however, that contact can produce ten-

* The Chicago Board of Education has recommended a set of carefully prepared booklets on the Negro for use as supplementary materials in the public schools. There is no adequate check, however, on the extent to which individual teachers make use of these data in the classroom. Officials of both the Mayor's Committee on Race Relations and the American Council on Race Relations have criticized the school board for not introducing a planned program of "intercultural education." Teaching "racial tolerance" is one of the stated aims of the State Board of Education.

sion and reinforcement of folk-prejudices. On the adult level this is especially true if the contact is between Negroes and whites of very different socio-economic levels.* Dr. Charles S. Johnson, the sociologist who directed the study of the Race Riot in 1919 and served as consultant for the Mayor's Committee in 1944, called attention to this fact when he observed concerning migrants that:

"The attention of the public may become focused upon the strangeness of the newcomers, upon the mannerisms and folkways that were developed in their social isolation from the best examples of public decorum. These are given high visibility by the conspicuous features of the Negroes, as well as by their strangeness. Almost invariably this reinforces racial stereotypes which carry unpleasant and even threatening implications.

"The areas of contact and racial intercommunication are wider and still widening in labor groups, in some industrial establishments, in some public conveniences outside the 'black belt'; and in unsegregated transportation. These broadened contacts, while they accelerate the accommodation and assimilation, also create new temporary problems." [4]

If contact is to play any direct part in breaking the color-line it must be accompanied by a "meeting of minds" and must involve people of similar tastes and interests. It is a significant trend of the last fifteen years that an increasingly large number of higher-status Negroes and whites have been getting to know one another, while, concurrently, thousands of Negroes and whites at the working-class level have become organized into the same unions. As we shall see in Chapter 12, this latter development has brought with it wide social and semi-social contacts between Negroes and whites. (Increasing residential segregation has reduced the amount of friendly contact between Negroes and whites of the middle classes who once shared certain neighborhoods together.)

These close contacts result in various types of co-operative action and in the multiplication of individual friendships. It is doubtful, however, whether they play a dominant part in shifting the line of color.

---

* Contact between employers and servants, for instance, may result in close bonds of friendships so long as the servant remains in her place. The stereotype of "the Negro's place" is thus reinforced. If the servant or her relatives become presumptuous enough to seek treatment as equals, tension may result. The same thing would be true if the servant were white, but in the case of a Negro the servant's behavior would be generalized in racial terms. Some studies have indicated that even contacts of Negroes and whites as equals can mean an increase in tension rather than a favorable change in attitude.

There are, for instance, perhaps a score of highly trained Negroes in Midwest Metropolis who have close and friendly relations with the city's influential and wealthy. These relations, although primarily those between philanthropist and civic leader, often have semi-social extensions. While such contacts have undoubtedly done much to influence the tone of the press and to secure some mitigation of the Negro's subordinate status, they cannot effect a major break in the Job Ceiling or the abolition of residential segregation. Economic interest again!

As we have mentioned, the members of the white middle class set the tone of Negro-white relations in Midwest Metropolis. Immigrants and their children see in them a model for imitation as they strive to become Americanized. The basic type of contact that the Negro has with members of the white middle class is economic. He has to do with them as employers, managers, and officials; he is the customer buying from white merchants and salespeople; the debtor facing creditors and collection agents; the client of lawyers, and the patient of doctors and dentists. Large numbers of Negroes are also in competition with the white lower middle class for jobs in skilled labor or clerical pursuits. Even when the Negro confronts middle-class white people in noneconomic relations, he usually does so as a subordinate— as a student under white teachers, a client dependent upon relief workers, a black criminal facing the white law. Such contacts do little to create goodwill among white people, but they do leave a residue of resentment among Negroes. The Negro middle class views the white middle class as its competitor, and the Negro lower class sees it as an exploiter.

The highly charged relations between the white middle class and the Negroes is a force for social change, though in a negative sort of way. Negroes are stimulated to organize their opposition. They fight to break the Job Ceiling, to smash restrictive covenants, to dislodge white people from the economic and political control of the Black Belt. Such activities may disturb the racial peace, but they develop self-confidence among Negroes and play an important part in shifting the color-line.

The almost complete isolation of the Negro middle class from the white middle class, and the organization of their relations in terms of antagonism, will no doubt continue so long as residential segregation and the Job Ceiling remain. Feeble attempts have been made by some of the churches and YWCA groups to sponsor teas, meetings, forums, discussion groups, etc., for bringing Negroes and whites together, but these tend to be artificial and both sides are usually under strain.*

Any major shifts in the social evaluation of Negroes will have to come from their being accepted as equals in a wide range of semi-social situations, and by a break in the Job Ceiling so that a much larger number of Negroes can function permanently in white-collar and supervisory positions. When major shifts in the Negro's status have occurred, it has usually not been as the result of education and counterpropaganda, or of engineered contacts operating in a vacuum; they have come in response to the demands of economic necessity and political expediency.

Economic Necessity: The dictates of economic necessity are primarily responsible for the presence of large numbers of Negroes in Midwest Metropolis. During the First World War the city needed labor. Southern Negroes supplied it. Once in the city they were thrown into competition with white workers, who, themselves insecure, did not hesitate to erect barriers against colored competitors. To white labor, organized and unorganized, Negroes constituted a pool of unorganized, potential strike-breakers. It could not drive them from the city— neither labor's allegiance to the democratic ideology nor the industrialists would permit that. It could not welcome them as individuals, for the folk-habits kept them in a separate category. Time after time, the Negroes broke strikes, and ultimately won a permanent place in the basic industries. They were used, for instance, to break the strikes of stockyard workers in 1904 and 1921; of the teamsters in 1905; and of the workers in the steel and clothing industries during the period of the First World War. When the CIO movement swept the city, Negroes could not be ignored. Once in the unions, they became accepted as "brothers" and were able to utilize seniority rules for an attack upon the Job Ceiling.

Any white men who wish to sell goods or service to Negroes must reckon with the fact that Black Metropolis has been experimenting

---

* The few Negroes who have contact with whites of equivalent status—such as social workers, politicians, lawyers, teachers, and policemen (and during the war skilled laborers and clerical workers)—sometimes form close friendships across the color-line. Such social intermingling is not general, however, and is due partly to the fact that in many cases Negroes consider themselves of higher *social* status than the whites who have the same type of job. This attitude can be fully understood only after an examination of the Negro class system.

with the application of an old political tactic to the economic field, "Reward your friends and punish your enemies." The "Spend Your Money Where You Can Work" Campaign was, as we have seen, a dramatic expression of this tendency. Yet, Negroes have not been able to organize their purchasing power in such a way as to break the Ceiling in stores outside of the Black Belt.

Political Expediency: The demands of political expediency have operated to modify the subordination of Negroes. Politicians need votes and are willing to pay for them with patronage and favors. An astute political leadership in Black Metropolis has been able to bargain for representation and to place Negroes in a number of responsible posts. This concentrated political power has also been used to demand legislation against the Job Ceiling and to provide public sounding boards for the Negro's grievances.

The existence of a political machine based upon the Black Belt reinforces residential segregation, but it also provides a powerful weapon for struggle against subordination. The political process, on the whole, acts as a stabilizing force in Negro-white relations, since it is accepted by white people as a legitimate medium for Negroes to use in seeking changes in their status. Negroes, for their part, since they can see political results, are restrained from more precipitate forms of action.

The pattern of Negro-white relations in Midwest Metropolis since the days of the Flight to Freedom has been characterized by constant, sometimes rapid, social change. The general tone of relationships has varied from period to period in response to the dictates of economic necessity, the imperatives of political expediency, and the fluctuating divergence and coincidence between these factors and the American tradition of Christian-democratic idealism.

Specific economic and political groups within the white population tend to view "the Negro" as a competitor for the rewards and privileges of the city, since it is the custom in our society to organize such competition along ethnic lines. In the fear of economic loss and in the effort to protect their privileged position, such groups have sought to maintain a Job Ceiling and a Black Ghetto. The overwhelming majority of the white residents, whether directly affected by Negro competition or not, have drawn the color-line rigidly at the point of social intermingling and intermarriage. Competition is a constant source of tension.

But employers need labor; white labor needs allies; politicians need votes. Negroes have something to offer. So the color-line bends and breaks here and there as these demands weld blocs of Negroes and whites together temporarily for common action. In those alliances there is usually a certain amount of semi-social contact. Always, too, a spiritual community of interest bridges the color-line—a small but influential fraternity of rebels and dreamers, of individualists and thinkers, and of plain, ordinary people who work or live side by side. Unconsciously, Negroes and whites maintain a moving equilibrium of peaceful interrelationships with conflict muted and competition controlled and ritualized. Sometimes, though, the pattern breaks: both groups become restless, tensions arise—and the color-line becomes a battle-line.

Actual physical conflicts between large groups of Negroes and white people in Midwest Metropolis have been rare. Occasionally, however, when small groups feel that their economic security or their social prestige is threatened, or when groups of Negroes have become aroused to the point of defending themselves or launching an attack against the color-line, violence occurs. Such violence usually breaks out in periods of *general* social unrest as during a war or a depression. Then things settle down and change proceeds at a slower pace.

In the long run, the economic and political factors are probably decisive in effecting major shifts in the color-line. The operation of these factors continuously presents Midwest Metropolis with new situations that cannot be ignored. These processes confront the ordinary white person with changes in the status of Negroes—*faits accomplis*—and he adjusts *mutatis mutandis*. These changes take place within a confused context of attitudes and opinions, of democratic idealism mixed with folk-prejudices, and the white individual is often unaware that he is experiencing a readjustment of attitude.

The last two chapters of this section are devoted to an examination of the manner in which economic necessity and political expediency operate to change the Negro's status.

CHAPTER II

Democracy and Economic Necessity: Breaking the Job Ceiling

THE PRECEDING CHAPTER OPENED WITH THE STATEMENT THAT THE ACTUAL position of the Negro in the life of Chicago contradicts the democratic principles of American society. This is true in many respects. Yet the status of the Negro is not rigidly fixed. Negroes, to use their own terminology, are "advancing," and this "advance" has assumed the form of a separate social and community life resting upon a continually broadening economic base in the larger society. The belief is widespread among Negroes that any further progress is contingent upon breaking the Job Ceiling.

PIERCING THE JOB CEILING

American society places a premium upon individual initiative—that happy combination of skill and nerve which, coupled with "lucky breaks" and a "good personality," is supposed to lift a large number of people from the level of poverty to that of a decent standard of living, and a small number to wealth and fame. Theoretically, all are supposed to have an equal chance in the combined lottery and proving ground of school, industry, and commerce. They are led to expect that, through preparing themselves in school and by showing their mettle in the world of practical affairs, they will receive rewards in the form of a "good living," the approval of their fellows, and "advancement." The hindmost, who cannot stand the pace or who "do not have it in them," have traditionally been left to the tender mercies of these social devils: poverty, charity, the jail, the potter's field.

Some individual Negroes have been able to play the game and rise in the world. Personal skill, luck, and nerve do, on occasion, pierce the Job Ceiling. In Midwest Metropolis there are Negroes who, for instance, function as industrial chemists, physicists, and civil engineers; several Negroes are even employed as professors by the larger universities. But the instances are few; the rule is that Negroes find it much more difficult than whites to rise through individual initiative, although a small professional group is supported exclusively by the Negro community itself.

THE NECESSITIES OF PRODUCTION

During a period of labor shortage, the necessities of production sometimes demand the use of Negroes as workers in jobs that are customarily above the Job Ceiling. This has happened only twice on a large scale in Chicago—during the First and the Second World Wars. The demand for Negro labor during the First World War resulted in the Great Migration and broke the ceiling that had previously confined Negroes to unskilled and service jobs. A similar demand occurred in the early Forties, with the induction of many workers into the armed forces, and the concomitant increase in the total number of employees required for the booming war industries. Shortages in housing, transportation, and other community facilities kept at a minimum the influx of white workers from out of the city. Negroes already in the city were gradually drawn from the relief rolls into industry.

The Second World War broke the ceiling at the level of semi-skilled work and integrated thousands of Negroes as skilled laborers in the electrical and light manufacturing industries, from which they had formerly been barred by custom, and in the vast new airplane-engine factories established in the area. They also began to filter into minor managerial and clerical positions in increasing numbers. Negroes in Chicago have kept their fingers crossed, suspecting that when wartime production slackens they would be rapidly displaced. Even if this happens, however, a residue of workers will probably remain in types of positions which Negroes had not held previously.

PROFIT AS A PROD

Employers customarily hire labor at the lowest possible wage level. If the members of any ethnic group are willing to work for less pay than other people, it is good business to employ them. At the present time, there are probably no large industries in Chicago in which Negroes are paid less than whites doing the same job within a given plant. There were, however, some small plants, on the eve of the Second World War, which employed all-Negro personnel at wages lower than those paid whites for similar work in other plants of similar size. During the first days of the 1939-40 war boom many incidents came to the attention of the authors that involved the use of Negroes as semi-skilled, skilled, and even technical workers at wages considerably lower than those paid whites. Such differential payment was sometimes defended by white employers on the ground that Negro workers were not so productive as white workers, though there is no reliable evidence supporting this contention.* Officials of the FEPC and the War Manpower Commission reported, in 1944, that they knew of no such differentials still existing, and that employers were no longer claiming that Negro labor was unproductive.

That profit is a prod which frequently motivates white employers to hire Negro workers or otherwise break the Job Ceiling becomes especially evident during strikes, when colored workers are used as strike-breakers. Under such circumstances Negroes may for the first time enter a specific type of job or an entire industry previously barred to them. In Chicago this was true in the packing, steel, and garment industries. As the number of Negro employees increased, unions in these industries were forced to accept Negroes in order to prevent their being continuously used as strike-breakers.

In the Twenties, some Negro leaders advised Negroes to underbid white labor systematically in order to secure jobs, and justified strike-breaking where unions refused Negroes admission. Today, few leaders take this position. Moreover, it has grown harder to use Negroes as strike-breakers since their employment in large numbers has made them an integral part of Chicago's mass-production industries, and since they have been effectively incorporated into the CIO unions operating in these industries.

The profit motive sometimes works to the advantage of Negroes in unusual ways. An interesting situation arose in 1939 when many private employment agencies having a backlog of applications, for the first time, began actively to try to place Negroes in war industries.

* Both the Chicago Commission on Race Relations in 1919 and the Mayor's Committee on Race Relations in 1944 report that the majority of the leading private employers agree, also, that Negro labor is as efficient as that of white workers when their training is equal. (See *The Negro in Chicago*, pp. 374-88, and *City Planning in Race Relations*, p. 36.)

As one agent told an applicant: "I get $10 a throw when I get a man a job. What the hell do I care whether he's white or black? I want the ten bucks. And I can't get it with a boxful of cards sittin' up here on my desk. I call these people up and tell them I've got some good Negro boys—why not try 'em?"

THE LAW AS A LEVER

The right to a job has never been established as a civil right in America. Employers have jealously guarded their right to hire and fire on any grounds they chose to cite. Even under New Deal legislation, an employer's right to hire and fire was curtailed only with respect to dismissal of employees for union activities. Despite this fact, Negro leaders have constantly sought legal grounds which could be used to force a break in the Job Ceiling.

The first successful use of the law as a lever arose in connection with Federal and state civil service. The purpose of any merit system is to safeguard the prospective employee from the prejudiced judgments of an employing agent. Ordinarily, civil service rules limit the range of choice to from one to three persons. But Negroes insist—and in the past there has been evidence to support the contention—that their names are often passed over; though in Illinois there is probably a minimum of racial discrimination in the civil service system, particularly in Federal jobs.

Negro legislators have sought to have riders attached to various appropriation bills making it illegal for unions that discriminate against Negroes to work on state jobs. In some cases their attempts have been successful. Another approach has involved the demand for legislation which will make it illegal to use public funds or to grant franchises to institutions that do not extend equal employment opportunities to Negroes. No bills of the latter kind have as yet become law, but their mere presentation has had a salutary warning effect upon the institutions involved.

On the basis of recommendations made by a state commission, and following the lead of New York and Indiana, the Illinois State Legislature in 1941 passed a bill making it a misdemeanor for an industry engaged in war production to discriminate, in hiring, against an applicant on the basis of race, color, or creed. Through May of 1945 there had been no convictions under this act.

The Second World War brought into being a number of Federal agencies bound by law not to discriminate against Negroes in their employment policy, and obligated to see that private employers with whom they work do not do so, among them being the War Manpower Commission and the President's Committee on Fair Employment Practices. The United States Employment Service, too, in filling manpower needs has been officially committed to a policy of "no discrimination." There have been no cancellations of war contracts, however, for the failure of an industry to hire Negroes.

In March of 1945, Senate Bill 254 was introduced in the Illinois General Assembly "to prohibit discrimination in employment because of race, religion, color or national origin; to make equal opportunity to seek employment a civil right; to declare certain employment and labor practices as discriminatory and unfair; to establish a Board of Fair Employment Practice; to prescribe its functions, powers and duties; to prescribe penalties for violation and to make an appropriation for administrative expenses." The Bill provided for an appropriation of $250,000 for "ordinary and contingent expenses incident to the administration of this Act."

The bill provides for a five-man board to receive complaints, hold hearings, and to hand down orders requiring employers or labor unions "to cease and desist from such discriminatory practices and to take such affirmative or other action as will effectuate the policies of this Act." If its orders are defied the Board is empowered to petition the circuit court in the county where the discrimination occurred to see that the order is enforced. The bill has teeth—"Any person, employer or labor organization who, or which, shall wilfully resist, prevent, impede or interfere with any member of the Board or any of its agents or agencies in the performance of duties pursuant to this act, or shall wilfully violate any order of the Board, shall be guilty of a misdemeanor, and upon conviction therefor, shall be punishable by a fine of not more than $500.00, or by imprisonment in the county jail for not more than one year, or by both; but procedure for a review of any order of Board shall not be deemed to be such wilful conduct." The Bill does not depend entirely upon punitive measures, however, but provides for "a comprehensive educational program" utilizing the public school system and private agencies to educate the public to the importance of establishing and maintaining a truly democratic form of government free from discrimination against any citizen because of race, religion, color or national origin."

Civic leaders in Chicago were mobilizing public opinion throughout the spring of 1945 to secure passage of the Bill, but were not too sure that the forces of democratic idealism could be mobilized in those parts of Illinois where Negroes wield little political power. In Midwest Metropolis political expediency and the efforts of liberals, the CIO and various church groups assured the support of the Chicago legislators.

GOVERNMENT AS AN EXAMPLE

Throughout the history of Chicago, Negroes have been able to use the political machinery to lift the Job Ceiling. They have occupied civil service, elective, and appointive positions, both high and low, and the city has become accustomed to seeing colored people in such situations.* Negro leaders are able to point to such positions as proof that Negroes are competent employees and acceptable to their white fellow-workers. Government policy in some respects sets a pattern.

According to the results of one careful investigation, approximately 6½ per cent of all employees in the classified service in the city of Chicago in 1932 were Negro—which was almost their proportion of the total population. But less than a quarter of the 1,908 Negroes constituting this group were in the clerical, professional or commissioned personnel; more than three-quarters were janitors, laborers or temporary employees. An examination of the kinds of jobs held by Negroes employed by the city reveals that the Job Ceiling, although less rigid and probably higher than in general, exists in this area, too. Only in the Department of Health, the Bureau of Parks and Recreation and the Bureau of Water and the library services did Negroes come near to their population ratio in positions which are largely clerical and professional. (Negro city employees were concentrated in these departments; they tend to be under-represented in most other city departments.) The proportion of Negroes in jobs as janitors, laborers, etc.,

---

* In the investigation for The Juvenile Protective Association made in 1913, Louise Bowen reported that over ten per cent of all the Federal employees in the city were Negroes although they were only three per cent of the population. She stated also that "the negroes [sic], however, do not fare so well in local government." They were less than two per cent of the total workers. The growth in the Negro vote within the next five years greatly increased their representation in city government.

considerably exceeded their representation in the population in all city departments.[1]

The same situation is clearly evident from a consideration of the Negro's share of governmental jobs of all types, as shown in Table 12. Negroes are somewhat over-represented in certain relatively choice jobs—as social and welfare workers, probation and truant officers, and chemists on the professional level, as firemen (except locomotive and fire department) and as mechanics. But still two-thirds of all porters and cooks are Negroes, as compared with two or three per cent of the policemen and lawyers, and one per cent of the firemen in the Fire Department and officials and inspectors.

The postal service is frequently cited as an example of what Negroes, given an opportunity, can do by way of proving their ability. In this service, positions are secured through competitive Federal civil service examinations, and reputedly without political influence. Consequently, Negroes have flocked into postal jobs, and in 1930 Negroes comprised one-quarter of all of the postal employees in Chicago. But even in this case, where Negroes are considerably over-represented in many relatively desirable types of positions, traces of the Job Ceiling remain. Contrast, for example, the types of positions—porters, elevator tenders, janitors—in which Negroes hold eight or nine out of every ten jobs, with such positions as foremen and overseers, of which Negroes are only five per cent; stenographers and typists, of which they are four per cent, and managers and officials, of which they are but one per cent. (See Table 13 on p. 295.)

Despite the existence of a Job Ceiling in government employment the fact remains that, until the Second World War, it was only in government offices that Negro men and women were given a chance to show what they could do as clerical workers, and Negroes were able to use these government white-collar Negroes as examples in educating white employers.

MASS PRESSURE

The Depression and the Second World War both created much restlessness and dissatisfaction among Negroes, each emphasizing sharply their subordinate position in the economic system. Applications for employment during these periods sometimes revealed discriminatory hiring policies. Reports of refusal to hire Negroes circulated widely in the community. At first there was grumbling; there were spontaneous and

TABLE 12

THE NEGRO'S SHARE OF SELECTED PUBLIC SERVICE JOBS, CHICAGO, 1930 *

	Number of Negro Workers	Per Cent Which Negroes Were of All Workers
Porters and cooks	16	66.1
Janitors and sextons	116	27.0
Mail carriers	631	16.0
Messengers, errand and office boys	8	17.4
Social and welfare workers	5	11.9
Garbage men and scavengers	42	11.7
Mechanics	10	11.5
Charwomen and cleaners	3	10.7
Firemen (except locomotive, Fire Dept.)	20	9.5
Other laborers	384	9.5
Probation and truant officers	17	8.8
Chemists, assayers and metallurgists	6	8.5
Elevator tenders	5	8.2
Trained nurses	8	7.5
Marshals and constables	3	7.1
Agents (not elsewhere classified)	14	6.9
Chauffeurs and truck and tractor drivers	35	5.7
Draymen, teamsters and carriage drivers	13	5.3
Officials and inspectors (U. S.)	43	5.2
Clerks	185	4.9
Plumbers and gas steamfitters	8	4.4
Advertising agents and others	43	3.9
Guards, watchmen and door keepers	20	3.8
Lawyers, judges and justices	9	3.6
Cranemen, deckmen and hoistmen, etc.	1	3.3
Housekeepers and stewards	2	3.3
Sheriffs	14	3.1
Bookkeepers and cashiers	7	2.9
Stenographers and typists	29	2.7
Officials and inspectors (city)	48	2.5
Office appliance operators	1	2.4
School teachers	452	2.3
Officials and inspectors (state)	6	2.2
Policemen	152	2.1
Oilers of machinery	1	2.0
Detectives	13	1.9
Engineers (stationary)	9	1.7
Soldiers, sailors, marines	4	1.6
Accountants and auditors	3	1.4
Street cleaners	8	1.2
Civil engineers and surveyors	5	1.0
Firemen (Fire Dept.)	27	1.0
Officials and inspectors (county)	3	.8
Carpenters	1	.8
Electricians	3	.6
Total	2,433	4.5

* Taken from H. F. Gosnell, *op. cit.*. Table XIX, p. 377. There were no Negroes in 621 public service occupations.

TABLE 13

NEGRO WORKERS IN THE POSTAL SERVICE IN CHICAGO, 1930 *

	Number of Negro Workers	Per Cent Which Negroes Were of All Workers
Porters	23	95.8
Janitors	35	87.5
Elevator tenders	12	85.7
Laborers	369	69.5
Charwomen and cleaners	9	69.2
Chauffeurs and truck and tractor drivers	42	41.6
Other occupations	28	46.0
Clerks	1,825	28.0
Compositors, linotypers and typesetters	3	27.3
Mail carriers	631	16.0
Mechanics	7	13.7
Messenger, errand and office boys	10	12.3
Machinists	1	8.3
Foremen and overseers	6	4.5
Stenographers and typists	2	4.3
Guards, watchmen and doorkeepers	1	4.3
Inspectors	1	3.7
Managers and officials	2	1.2
	3,008	25.2

* From H. F. Gosnell, *op. cit.*, Table XV, p. 304. Not listed in the above table are some 69 skilled, clerical and supervisory jobs in which Negroes were not represented at all. An examination of these jobs showed that most included only two or three workers, and, therefore, Negroes would naturally be under-represented, or they were types of jobs in which the political influence of certain craft unions was undoubtedly manifesting itself.

violent verbal outbursts against employers or employees. The net effect of such unorganized restlessness is to make the larger community aware that "something is wrong" with the Negro population. Then Negro leaders and the leaders of white liberal and political groups together appeal for increased recognition of the Negro's claim for equal job opportunities. When these appeals are not immediately successful in some measure, organized mass protests often follow.

Organized mass pressure usually follows from spontaneous mass pressures. Sometimes, however, it is deliberately planned by organizations devoted to advancing the interests of Negroes. In 1931-32, for instance, the "Spend Your Money Where You Can Work" Campaign, was started in a fairly deliberate and organized fashion, as were various picketing and boycott episodes that occurred throughout the Depression and in the early years of the Second World War.

CATASTROPHE AS A CATALYST

During periods of sudden or rapid social change, the Job Ceiling, like everything else, is altered. A war or a depression, a devastating fire or a flood, may so disturb organized social relations that, for a time at least, new patterns are permitted to arise. Catastrophe acts as a catalytic agent in social change. The First World War attracted thousands of Negroes into industry and significantly altered the social composition and occupational distribution of the Negro population. The Depression of 1929-40 worked in two directions. On the one hand, large numbers of Negroes in marginal positions were pushed out of industry; on the other hand, white-collar workers found employment in clerical and minor supervisory positions on relief projects and in the relief administration. The Depression also resulted in mass action to force white business people in the Black Belt to employ Negroes. The industrial union movement, gathering momentum during this period, swept thousands of Negroes into organizations that accepted them as equals and actively sought to enforce seniority rules and promotion on merit, without reference to color.

The Second World War not only brought the demand for the full utilization of man power, but also resulted in the training of thousands of Negroes for semi-skilled and skilled jobs. Where difficulties in securing employment were experienced, Negroes, operating within the framework of the stated goals of the war, demanded jobs. Mass pressure forced the establishment of the FEPC, and the "law" became a very useful lever in raising the Job Ceiling after President Roosevelt issued his Fair Employment Practices order. Government set an increasingly strong example as Negroes flocked into Civil Service. More important still, the needs of war industries and government bureaus exhausted the supply of trained white-collar and clerical personnel and opened opportunities in these and other fields hitherto barred to Negroes. Colored girls, for instance, became salespeople in a few Loop stores, and colored Western Union messengers appeared on the streets of Midwest Metropolis for the first time. Negroes cropped up in many unusual spots.

EDUCATING THE WHITE FOLKS

All of these processes, seen in the widest perspective, result in what Negroes call "educating the white folks"—the white employer and the white worker, as well as the public. A part of this educational process is unconscious and beyond the effective control of individuals or organizations. The necessities of production, the desire for profits, the coming of catastrophe—all upset the established order and make men act as they have not previously acted. But a part of the process is deliberate, as when an individual sets his eye upon a position and achieves it, when the law is used as a lever, or when mass pressure is organized. Negro leaders and friendly whites try to manipulate the impersonal forces to the deliberate end of lifting the Job Ceiling.

Educating the Employers: One of the most important aspects of the educational process concerns employers. Employers in Chicago give a number of reasons for their failure to extend full job opportunity to Negroes. A few employers (these seem to be a minority) have stereotyped conceptions of what the Negro can and cannot do. A larger number do not question the Negro's capacity, but still feel that he should permanently occupy a subordinate place in the economic life of the society. Most employers, however, do not seem to have any clear-cut, articulate convictions on the matter one way or another. They are simply hesitant to make innovations that might curtail production, cause trouble in the plant, or otherwise jeopardize their profits or prestige. Under normal conditions the hold of custom is heavy everywhere.

But when employers have been successful in integrating Negroes in a plant, they are often very proud of their feat and sometimes wonder why they had not thought of the idea before. The following case is not at all atypical. A nationally known company that manufactures electrical equipment had never employed Negroes. A personnel official told an investigator from the War Manpower Commission that it would be impossible even to hire Negro matrons for washrooms, because, if this were done, the white girl employees would refuse to use the facilities. In 1942, this firm was persuaded to employ several hundred Negro workers of both sexes and at all levels of skill. Not only has there been no significant friction between white and colored workers at any time, but the work of the Negro employees has been highly satisfactory. The plant management is now very much pleased with this record.

Employers in general maintain that they are not responsible for discrimination against Negro labor—almost always they tend to assign responsibility for the policy to their employees. Some employers contend further that the education of white workers to accept the upgrading of Negroes is primarily a job for the unions. This was the tone of the responses reported by the Mayor's Subcommittee on Employment, and also, apparently, the official attitude of the Committee itself. This same committee, however, recommended to management that before Negro workers are first hired, a company should be sure that its *supervisory personnel* is completely won over to the new policy. Incidentally, it is to be inferred from the contents of this report that probably the principal reason why many establishments that had never before hired Negroes began to hire them relatively early during the Second World War was fear of, or at least a strong wish to avoid, investigation by government agencies on charges of discrimination. Government, too, can be a most effective prod. Employers are educable—but such education in Chicago has included mass picket lines, petitions and protests, public hearings and legislation, as well as sweet reasonableness on the part of Negroes.

Educating White Workers: Negroes are often irritated at what they feel is conscious "buck passing" between employers and labor. Employers say, "We would hire Negroes if employees did not object." Labor unions say, "Not us—the employers." The truth is complex. Doubtless there are situations in which employers honestly fear that white workers would cause trouble if Negroes were hired, but in which actually nothing at all would happen. There are other situations in which white workers are absolutely and bitterly opposed to the employment of Negroes. In Midwest Metropolis, as we have said previously, the center of such opposition is in the AFL craft unions and among the railroad brotherhoods. Though there is less evidence of organized opposition on the higher technical and supervisory levels, there is enough to indicate that the prestige concern of many white employees in these positions operates to exclude Negroes from them.

The education of the white worker has often proceeded in a very blunt fashion. Negroes have simply broken strikes and underbid white labor. White employees in the packing, steel, and garment industries have apparently learned their lesson, for Negroes are now included in their unions.

A marked difference prevails in the attitudes of the AFL and the CIO toward the incorporation of Negroes into both industry and unions. The industrial unions of the CIO, since their appearance in 1935, have uniformly and actively tried to recruit Negroes into the unions and to have them admitted into industry on an equal basis with white workers. The leaders have fought prejudice wherever it has existed: among employers, among employees, and upon occasion, among members of their own unions. The older AFL craft unions, on the other hand, have traditionally excluded Negroes. Where Negroes have been admitted to unions, they have frequently been organized into Jim-Crow locals and denied full membership privileges. This is still the general situation, despite some recent moves in the direction of liberalization, stimulated on the one hand by competition from the CIO and on the other by pressure from government agencies, particularly the FEPC.

The difference of attitude between the two organizations was evident even in the official remarks of the representatives of the AFL and the CIO unions at the Employment Session of the Mayor's 1944 Conference. The AFL representative stated that there was no justification for discrimination by unions against Negroes, but that the problem could only be solved through a long term program of education. Laws would do no good, and the AFL could not force member unions to reform because part of the "democratic" tradition of the AFL was the "autonomy" of local unions, which would refuse to accept "dictation" from above. The position of the CIO representative, who favored law as well as education, is apparent in the following statement (quoted from the report): "The CIO has been, is now, and always will be committed to a policy of complete equality for all workers, regardless of race, color, or creed, and always will militantly champion a fight to realize that complete equality. The record, too long and too extensive to cite now, will testify to the truth of the existence of that policy."

Despite these efforts to have Negroes upgraded strictly in accordance with seniority considerations, much remains to be done, even in the most advanced CIO unions and the industries where they have contracts, before the Job Ceiling will be completely removed.

✦

Educating the Public: Employers often "pass the buck" (consciously or unconsciously) to the public, instead of, or as well as, to their employees: "Educate the public to accept Negroes in the better jobs and we'll hire them," they say. "We can't risk losing our customers." It is, however, virtually impossible to predict accurately the public reaction to the widespread employment of Negroes in unfamiliar fields.

The manpower shortage produced by the Second World War resulted in the use of Negroes (at least temporarily) as bus drivers, operators, and motormen on the surface and elevated transportation lines, as clerks in stores, waitresses in restaurants and at soda fountains, and in a variety of other situations where they had not been seen previously. Before the war, it would have been considered impossible to employ Negroes in some of these spots. Yet these colored employees have apparently been accepted, without serious incident, by both their white fellow-workers and the public. A concerted campaign to have Negroes employed as saleswomen in the downtown department stores was conducted during 1943 and 1944, but met with little success.

It seems probable that the public's reaction to Negroes in new or unusual job situations goes through three phases. First, there is surprise—perhaps shock. Second comes curiosity, and "definition of the situation" (either acceptance or criticism), with or without further overt action. Third and last, there is complete acceptance.

Little effort is made to help the public over the first and the second hurdles toward acceptance. A sporadic editorial or occasional radio comment may stress the necessity of treating minorities justly or the need to utilize our manpower fully—but that is all.

EDUCATING THE NEGROES

The process of lifting the Job Ceiling is not entirely one of educating the white folks. It involves also the problem of educating the Negro—educating him to want the job, to get it, and to keep it.

Negroes have for so long had a subordinate "place" in American life that many find it hard to conceive of themselves or other Negroes except in that place. The initial reaction of many Negroes to a Negro locomotive engineer or a colored streetcar conductor is one of surprise, coupled with expressions of doubt—made jokingly, yet half-serious—as to whether the Negro is capable of holding the job. This attitude is soon replaced, ordinarily, by intense pride that "one of our boys made it."

A low ceiling results in low horizons. Social workers and vocational counselors report a real problem in encouraging Negro youth to "raise their sights." They have to fight always against a legacy of self-doubt and the acceptance of "place."

Almost all Negroes think that they and other Negroes should be given any job for which they qualify. But many of them have no idea how to prepare for and secure the better jobs. Social agencies, therefore, are continually urging Negroes to prepare themselves even when there are no jobs open to them, so that they will be ready if opportunities are created. Thus it is probable that, during the Second World War, more colored girls could have secured skilled office jobs had more possessed the training for such positions when the war commenced. There is also the problem of selling oneself to an employer. Negroes have to acquire a technique in such matters. In particular, colored job applicants have the special problem of learning how to "go back for more" when they have been rebuffed.

Many Negroes, especially recent migrants to Chicago from the South, not only are untrained for any specific job, but are often completely without previous experience in any kind of business or industrial work. They are unfamiliar with the discipline of a steady job in an urban factory or office. According to the Mayor's Committee survey, most firms stated that the Negro worker produces fully as well as the white when selected on the basis of equivalent training and experience; and that, although most of the Negroes lack a background of training for skilled work, they respond to training as well as white workers do when it is given to them.

Negro leaders in Midwest Metropolis are greatly concerned over whether Negroes will be able to hold any of the economic gains secured during the Second World War. The advice of these leaders includes everything from urging Negroes to mind their manners, to advising them to join the union. A nationwide movement, the "Hold Your Job" Committee, has been sponsored by both the Urban League and the National Council of Negro Women. The committee conducts educational campaigns in factories and in the Negro community to urge Negroes to so work and act that employers will have no legitimate excuses for discharging them after the war. Negro newspapers carry articles urging Negroes to be quiet, clean, orderly, and reliable, so that

The Race will not acquire an unfavorable reputation. This preaching sometimes irks the Negro. A packing-house worker remarked to a union official: "Why 'n the hell do these big Negroes have to always tell us how to act? I'll admit that we hurt ourselves sometimes. But the thing that burns me up is how the white man lets one Negro break all our necks. Why don't they let us break our necks for ourselves, individual?"

It is generally agreed that the problem of training Negroes both for specific jobs and for urban industrial life in general (including the problem of proper "conduct" in the urban setting) can be solved only through training, experience, and—above all—equal opportunity.

The processes through which the Job Ceiling is lifted and broken in places could be illustrated in the history of any industry in which Negroes are now employed in large numbers. Since, in Midwest Metropolis, meat packing is an industry with a long history of employing Negroes, it is perhaps most appropriate to select it as a case in point.

NEGROES AS HOG BUTCHERS FOR THE WORLD

The story of the integration of Negroes into Chicago's slaughtering and meat-packing industry provides a dramatic illustration of the interplay between the forces of democratic idealism and the economic and political forces outlined above.

According to local tradition, the first Negroes to work in the packing industry in Chicago were a beef-boner and a butcher, who secured jobs in 1881. Although Negroes and whites are today organized together in a union affiliated with the CIO, where Negroes share positions of leadership with white workers, the slaughtering and packing industry was once a racial battleground.

Between 1881 and 1894, a few Negroes filtered into the stockyards and packing plants without any apparent opposition from the foreign-born white workers who predominated in the industry. During the Pullman Strike of 1894, when the stockyard workers walked out in sympathy with the American Railway Union, a large group of Poles were employed as strike-breakers. A few days later, Negroes came into the yards in a similar capacity, and union resentment was focused on them to such a degree that a Negro was burned in effigy. After the strike a few Negroes retained their positions, and although they were numerically unimportant, their presence in the yards was interpreted as a threat to the labor unions. In employing Negroes, management had tapped an almost inexhaustible supply of cheap labor from the South and simultaneously secured a labor force that seemed very resistant to union organization.

The next large influx of Negroes into the yards occurred during the strike of 1904. When the strike began, Negroes constituted about five per cent of the labor force. Their numbers were immediately increased, and hundreds of Negroes were smuggled into the plants on the same day that the white workers downed their tools. So large a number were employed that for a time it was thought that Negroes would predominate in the packing industry. The more extravagant estimates placed the number employed as high as ten thousand.

In this dispute, the role of the Negro worker differed from his role as strike-breaker in the 1894 strike. In the earlier dispute, Poles had been numerically more important, and, in spite of the publicity which attended their activities, Negroes played only an incidental part. But in 1904 their importance as strike-breakers was immediately recognized and an even more intense resentment by union men resulted.* After the strike had been settled, a small number of colored men retained their positions. The rest were discharged or displaced by returning union men. The packers were no longer in need of Negro workers, so they were loaded into special trains and sent back to the South.

Four years later, there were about 500 Negroes in the industry, and a small but steady stream of black workers continued to flow into the yards. Then, in 1917, because of the war labor shortage, the packers again tapped the southern labor pool, sending their agents into the Deep South to recruit Negro workers by the hundreds and even thousands. By 1920, one packing plant employed over 5,000 Negroes, more than a quarter of its total labor force. The peak of Negro employment was reached in 1923, when 34 out of every 100 workers in the two largest packing establishments were colored. From 1922 until the De-

---

* "To the striking union men no scabs were as loathsome as the Negroes who took their jobs. Easily distinguishable, they were conspicuous among the strike-breakers and suffered the animus which is vented upon all scabs. They were jeered if they emerged from the plants under police escort; chased and attacked if alone. Pistol shots invariably brought the assaults to a close. Among the first of the strike-breakers to be hired, they were among the first to be asked to leave at the conclusion of hostilities." (Alma Herbst, *The Negro in the Slaughtering and Meat Packing Industry in Chicago,* Houghton Mifflin, 1932, p. 28.)

pression, the proportion of Negroes among all packing-house workers remained about 30 per cent.

Negroes and the Old Unions: After the strike of 1904, the packing-house union was so weakened that its membership dropped from 34,400 in 1904 to 6,200 in 1910. With the sudden increase in the number and proportion of Negroes in the industry, the Amalgamated Meat Cutters and Butcher Workmen (AFL) began an organizational drive in 1916-17. The packers granted an increase of twenty cents an hour to unskilled workers, but the union continued to grow, and in 1917 the Stock Yards Labor Council was formed by the united action of all the craft unions with jurisdiction in the stockyards.

The problem of establishing a policy with respect to Negroes in the union organizations soon became pressing. Twenty of the various craft unions in the council drew the color-line sharply. The union officials appreciated the importance of organizing Negroes, and realized that a union organization could not succeed without them. Nevertheless, unanimity of opinion regarding a solution of the racial problem could not be achieved. Some union leaders urged that colored men be admitted to all the unions, but in some cases this was prohibited by constitutional provisions; in others, the racial prejudice of union officials had the same effect. A typical AFL solution was suggested—the organization of Negroes into separate locals. The Amalgamated Meat Cutters and Butcher Workmen, one of the craft unions involved, followed its traditional policy and admitted Negroes, but complications over racial matters soon developed.

Many Negroes joined unions, but on the whole the organizers were disappointed in the response of the colored workers. It was estimated that among northern-born Negroes 90 per cent became union members. Few southern-born Negroes joined, however, and at the height of the drive only about a third of the Negroes employed in the yards became affiliated with any union organization.*

At the beginning of the 1917 campaign, approximately 12,000 Negroes worked in the stockyards in Chicago. The number increased in direct ratio to the success of the unions in organizing the white labor-

* Perhaps it should be pointed out explicitly that no one union existed in the yards at this time. There were as many different AFL craft unions represented as there were crafts in the packing industry. The largest union was the Amalgamated Meat Cutters and Butcher Workmen.

ers. Not only were the colored workmen regarded by management as almost immune to organization, and unreliable union members when they did join, but also the unions had no consistent policy toward Negroes.

The packers, realizing that their hope of defeating unionism depended upon holding the allegiance of colored workmen, inaugurated a policy of increasing the number of Negroes in their plants, at the same time influencing them against unionism. In this connection, packing-house management made use of a colorful Negro promoter, Richard Parker, who was hired to organize a Negro union. A most enterprising person, Mr. Parker started his activities by distributing about 20,000 handbills warning Negroes not to join the "white man's union" but, instead, to affiliate themselves with his organization, the American Unity Labor Union. The argument was twofold: Negroes should not join white unions because the unions would not admit them on a basis of equality, and, secondly, white employers preferred non-union help. The following is a typical advertisement [2] appearing in the Negro press at the time:

GET A SQUARE DEAL WITH YOUR OWN RACE

Time has come for Negroes to do now or never. Get together and stick together is the call of the Negro. Like all other races, make your own way; other races have made their unions for themselves. They are not going to give it to you just because you join his union. Make a union of your own race; union is strength. Join the American Unity Packers Union of the Stock Yards, this will give you a card to work at any trade or a common laborer, as a steamfitter, electrician, fireman, merchants, engineers, carpenters, butchers, helpers, and chauffeurs to drive trucks down town, delivering meat as white chauffeurs do for Armour's and Swift's or other Packers. A card from this Union will let you work in Kansas City, Omaha and St. Louis, or any other city where the five Packers have packing houses.

This union does not *believe in strikes*. We believe all differences between laborers and capitalists can be arbitrated. Strike is our last motive if any at all.

Get in line for a good job. *You are next. . . .*

It was this Negro leader's proud boast that he had brought more Negroes to the city from the South than had any other man in Chicago. Parker's organization introduced considerable confusion into the union situation in the stockyards, and thus further weakened the AFL unions.

When a strike seemed imminent in 1917, a Federal arbitrator was appointed. The Stock Yards Council enjoyed some temporary success in recruiting Negro workers by telling them that the government would see that they got a raise if they joined the union. The Council planned a special drive to attract Negroes: [3]

To this end a "giant stockyards union celebration" was planned for July 6. A workers' parade which was to include both races was scheduled. . . . On the morning of the event, the packers asked the police to revoke the parade permit lest a race riot be precipitated. As the workers were not permitted to march together, two parades formed, a white and a colored, and marched to the Beutner playgrounds, where a Negro and white audience was assembled. The marchers were greeted by cheers from the colored workers who lined the streets. . . . One of the placards which dotted the procession read:

"The bosses think that because we are of different color and different nationalities we should fight each other. We're going to fool them and fight for a common cause—a square deal for all."

In addressing the meeting, the secretary of the Stock Yards Labor Council [who some years later became the state chairman of the Communist Party] said:

"It does me good to see such a checkerboard crowd—by that I mean all of the workers here are not standing apart in groups, one race huddled in one bunch, one nationality in another. You are all standing shoulder to shoulder as men, regardless of whether your face is white or black."

But this attempt to develop solidarity among the packing-house workers was abortive, partly because of the outbreak of the Chicago Race Riot in 1919. Probably one of the underlying causes of the Riot was the conflict between union members and packing-house employers for the allegiance of Negro workers.

Each group laid the responsibility for the riot upon the other. The riot resulted in a barrier to further union organization among Negroes and brought to an abrupt end the drive to enlist Negro packing-house workers.

On the Sunday afternoon when the Race Riot started, and throughout the week, there were sporadic clashes between whites and Negroes in the packing-house area. On Monday, union members were notified by management that arrangements had been made for the militia to protect the workers in the yards. A militant colored unionist proposed that rather than send for troops, the employers should recognize the closed-shop plan, and that the union would then assume responsibility for the conduct of all workers in the yards. Needless to say, the proposal was turned down by the employers. The employees refused to work under the guns of the soldiers, and thousands of them struck. After a few days the troops were withdrawn, and the workers were notified to return to the yards. Approximately 600 laborers, both white and colored, delayed a day and were dismissed.

The union organizations connected with the stockyards labored incessantly to maintain order during the two weeks of the riot. Editorials in union papers expressed not only sympathy for Negroes, but also a concern for the future existence of the union. One editorial observed:[4]

Right now it is going to be decided whether the colored workers are to continue to come into the labor movement or whether they are to feel that they have been abandoned by it and lose confidence in it.

The friendly attitude of union officials apparently brought some of the colored workers closer to the union. It was reported that "the white and colored union men sustained each other in the main and ministered to the stricken. The financial aid and moral support which the union colored men received during the riot and immediately following it served to bring them to the headquarters of their organizations and to keep them 'out of the packers' bread line." It is to be remarked that both the packers and the union tried to aid the Negro workers—by feeding them and in other ways.

Under the circumstances, however, it was extremely difficult for Negroes to remain loyal to the union. The employers had replaced many staunch Negro union men with non-union Negroes, first when they refused to work without protection during the riot, and later when they refused to work under the guns of the militia. Negroes returning to work in the yards after the riot were glad to obtain employment under any terms and rapidly abandoned the union organizations.

Two years after the riot, another strike was called and lost in the yards, and the Amalgamated Meat Cutters and Butcher Workmen became a completely feeble organization. While the 1921 strike was brewing, Negro leaders expressed fear that the unorganized Negroes in the yards might become the target of another race riot. Thus the Chicago *Defender* wrote:[5]

There is a phase to the situation which cannot be overlooked, and that is the possibility of recurring race troubles. Many of our people are employed at the yards. They are not members of the union and will not be inclined to leave their employment. The fear of being supplanted by white workers will hold them at work. Naturally, they will become the targets of pickets and strike sympathizers while going to and from their employment. Clashes under such circumstances are inevitable.

Negroes and the New Union: Between 1921 and the Depression, the so-called company unions were dominant in the stockyards and packing plants. With the advent of the Depression, the AFL unions were revived, and a new union, the Packing-house Workers Industrial Union, also appeared on the scene. The latter union called several strikes in 1933 and 1934, but none of them were successful. Before the NRA, there had been fewer than 200 Negro members in the entire international organization of the AFL packing unions; but in the campaign that followed the passage of the blanket code, Negroes came into the union with the rest of the packing-house workers in large numbers. By January of 1935, there were more than 5,000 Negroes enrolled in Chicago locals alone.

Most of the Negro members, however, were highly suspicious both of the wisdom of defying the packers' will and of the white workers' good intentions. When the union showed the first sign of weakness, many colored workers dropped out. Because of the half-hearted way in which the Amalgamated dealt with the problems arising out of Negro participation in the union's social, political, and economic affairs, Negro workers became increasingly suspicious of this AFL union, but the Packing-house Industrial Workers Union, which was Communist-affiliated, never succeeded in making significant inroads among the workers, either colored or white.

When the CIO was formed in 1935, it immediately set itself the task of organizing the packing industry and breaking the hold of the company unions. Negroes responded enthusiastically to its appeal. Plant after plant was organized, until contracts had been negotiated with all of the major packers. Negroes and whites were organized together in the locals, and many Negroes were elected as officers. White workers under CIO leadership gave a convincing demonstration of solidarity with their colored fellow-workers, and Negroes responded by giving the union their confidence and loyalty.

A prominent Negro labor leader in 1937 described the relations of Negroes to the new union as follows:

"In the yards, the dominant group is the Poles. They constitute 40 per cent of the workers. Negroes are 38 per cent. The rest are Lithuanians, Germans, Italians, and Croatians. The Negro is best informed on union procedure and is most articulate. The foreign groups understand, but aren't articulate because of language difficulties. We have our union literature printed in several languages so they will understand even though they can't speak English.

"The best proof that the Negro is the best union member is that we have more Negro stewards and officers in our locals than any other group. And these were elected in mixed locals. In one local we have a Negro president. Local #6 is completely organized and a Negro is president of that local, too. The other officers are almost evenly distributed between Negroes and whites. The president of the local is white. The secretary is a Negro.

"Negroes and whites in the same departments get practically the same pay. Of course, cleaner jobs go to white workers. There are more Negroes in the wool, glue, and sausage departments because this is dirtier work. Negro women are in the dirtier departments, too. These things will have to be ironed out after the union has agreements in all packing houses."

Testimony to the effectiveness of the union in improving Negro-white relations in the industry was offered by a rank-and-file Negro member, a stockyards laborer, who said to an interviewer in 1938: "Now the union come and we has a friendlier feeling 'mongst us—we feels all together, 'stead of working 'gainst each other. That's a long ways from the time we was all fighting each other back in 1919 during the race riots. Then we was afraid to go to work for fear we would be kilt."

CAN THE CEILING DISAPPEAR?

The Job Ceiling has been rising, although slowly, in recent years. This has been especially true since the Second World War began. Perhaps the best way to give some idea of the extent to which Negroes have been incorporated into the industrial life of Chicago, to date, is to present a brief summary of the findings of the Subcommittee on Employment of the Mayor's Conference on Race Relations, in February, 1944.* The findings were as follows:

* The survey on which these findings are based covered 94 firms, employing half a million workers, of which one-tenth were Negroes, and included all types

1. By January of 1944, only an insignificant number of manufacturing and business establishments in Chicago did not employ Negroes in any capacity. A majority of the firms, however, had employed Negroes only during the last two to four years—i.e., only since the beginning of the Second World War.

2. Most of the rather large number of firms that had employed Negroes for from ten to thirty years stated that they first employed Negroes during the First World War, and because of the labor shortage. But most of the firms that had employed Negroes only since the coming of the Second World War gave the requirements of government contracts as the reason for first hiring colored workers. The labor shortage and "pressure from organized groups" were the other important reasons indicated.

3. Most of the firms that hired Negroes during the First World War employed them only in the capacity of unskilled laborers. On the other hand, plants that first engaged Negro labor during the Second World War claimed to have originally hired them in semi-skilled as well as unskilled jobs, and also maintained that Negro employees on all levels were constantly being upgraded. Virtually all colored girl employees in offices, however,* held unskilled jobs.

4. As for continuing Negro employment after the Second World War, we quote: "The one concrete opinion that came out of the survey was that, unless maximum employment continued, the operation of seniority contracts would work heavily against Negroes, who for the most part are recent employees." [6]

Gains during the Second World War would appear to be substantial, *if* Negroes can hold them. But even before this war—indeed, throughout the period since the First World War—Negroes have composed an integral part of the labor force of mass-production industries in Chicago. Although extremely limited, some occupational mobility did occur between 1920 and 1940. The occupational status of Negroes was not purely static even during the Depression. The advent of the CIO represented a gain in and of itself. The CIO has pledged itself to fight to attain equal rights on the job in all industries—which in its most significant aspect means an equal opportunity for occupational

of industries and businesses. There can be little doubt that the sample was representative—with the possible exception of very small plants.

* In private industry, that is, since civil service positions were of course not included in the survey.

advancement. Not only have most CIO unions fought for the upgrading of Negro workers on the same basis as white workers, but some have addressed themselves to the special problem of post-war Negro employment. One possible solution that has already been tried, at least once, is described thus:[7]

The United Electrical Workers, CIO, in one instance where a cutback took place, proposed that the proportion of Negro and white workers that had been achieved in the industry be retained and that there be a proportionate layoff in order that seniority would not adversely affect those who had been denied opportunity of employment in industry heretofore. This was the proposal of the union and it was carried into effect.

In the past, the Job Ceiling has been significantly raised only during periods in which a labor shortage existed. But, even given economic necessity, this has occurred only after white employers and workers, in some sense or another, were educated to accepting colored workers in higher jobs. Were that education to become a part of a permanent outlook—if democracy in the realm of occupational opportunity were completely extended to Negroes—the Job Ceiling might not only become independent of the undulations of the business cycle, but disappear completely.

CHAPTER 12

Democracy and Economic Necessity: Black Workers and the New Unions *

THE STRUGGLE BETWEEN CAPITAL AND LABOR HAS BEEN A DOMINANT MOTIF in the life of Midwest Metropolis since the Eighties; some of its more dramatic episodes have been described in the Introduction. By the time of the First World War, the building trades and various other crafts were strongly organized, and the Chicago Federation of Labor included some twenty-nine autonomous AFL unions. All attempts at organizing the basic mass-production industries, however, had been unsuccessful. When the great steel strike of 1919 was broken, and the packing-house and stockyards strikes of the early Twenties failed, the union movement in these industries was effectively scotched for a decade to follow. But, as we saw in the preceding chapter, the craft unions remained strong during the Twenties and wielded considerable political power. The mass-production industries, with the exception of the garment industry, remained unorganized until the CIO appeared on the scene in 1935, and swept the majority of the workers in these industries into the new industrial unions.

During the five years preceding the Second World War, the workers in the mass-production industries—steel, packing, farm equipment—selected CIO unions as their bargaining agents. The organization of these unions took place within the legal framework provided by New Deal legislation, but the process of actually building the unions has required strenuous effort on the part of union leaders. Between 1935 and 1938, the dominant organizational tactic for union recognition was the strike. After the establishment of the National Labor Relations Board, machinery was available for choosing or rejecting a bargaining agent without recourse to conflict. Unions, however, still found it neces-

---

* The title of this chapter is taken from a study of Negroes and the CIO movement made by Horace R. Cayton and George S. Mitchell, *Black Workers and the New Unions* (University of North Carolina Press, 1939). The chapter is based on some materials in this book and on additional data gathered in the Cayton-Warner Research.

sary in some cases to call strikes in order to force an election or to put themselves in a favorable bargaining position. Strike activity continued, therefore, until the outbreak of the Second World War, when a no-strike pledge was adopted generally throughout industry.

From the outset, the leaders of the new unions made a deliberate effort to win the allegiance of Negroes, for economic necessity demanded their inclusion in any industrial union movement. The approach to the Negro was not dictated solely by expediency, however, for the CIO was, in a sense, a crusading movement also—in the tradition of the old Knights of Labor. Belief in racial equality was a component part of its ideology, and was kept constantly before the membership by a vigorous left-wing minority within the CIO. Formerly skeptical of "the white man's union," both the Negro workers and the Negro community became pro-CIO. Even conservative Negro leaders who professed shock at the "radicalism" and deplored the "violence" of the new unions, praised them for their stand on race relations. An analysis of Negro participation in the new union movement during the stormy organizational period reveals the interplay of democratic idealism and economic necessity—an interplay that resulted in making the Negro an integral part of the CIO movement.

ORGANIZING THE NEGRO WORKER

In view of the long history of conflict between Negro and white workers in the basic industries of Chicago, it has been necessary for the new unions to employ special tactics in recruiting Negroes during organizational campaigns, and in educating white workers to accept them. The appeal of the CIO was both idealistic and practical. The approach was often carefully planned and executed, with the leaders stressing equality between black and white workers in addition to class solidarity.

Negro organizers who have been employed have sometimes attained important positions of national leadership. CIO leaders have usually insisted upon the election of Negro officials to responsible positions in local unions. Negro stewards and members of grievance committees, often in unions with an overwhelming majority of white workers, discuss wages, hours, and working conditions with the representatives of powerful industrial concerns. Attempts have been made to break the Job Ceiling by utilizing seniority rules.

The techniques used by CIO unions to attract Negro members throughout the organizational campaigns that were conducted from 1935 until the advent of the Second World War may be summarized as follows:

1. to employ Negro organizers who could talk to Negro workers in terms of their group experiences, special apprehensions, and general attitudes;

2. to see that Negro workers in unions with a large Negro membership were represented on grievance committees and in the official hierarchy of the unions;

3. to treat Negroes as equals at all social affairs and to avoid scheduling meetings or social affairs at places where they are barred or might be embarrassed;

4. to fight consciously for the rights of Negro workers, in relation to promotions, seniority, pay, working hours, etc.;

5. to protest against segregated washrooms and eating places;

6. to respect the special sensibilities and grievances of Negro workers; and

7. to support community drives for better housing, etc., and the broad fight against discrimination.

Probably none of these approaches would have been successful, however, had not Negroes, as well as the white workers, been assured by union leaders and the course of events that the Wagner Act provided protection against reprisals by employers.

The CIO organizing campaigns in packing, steel, and related industries had by 1940 been successful in organizing the majority of both the colored and white workers employed in these industries. One stockyard laborer expressed the basic argument for interracial co-operation which appeared during the organizational campaigns:

"Colored people has woke up to unionism now. He won't accept the boss-man's telling him, 'You don't want to be with the white man—even if you're not making as much now, you'll get more soon.' And then this same boss will tell the white people, 'Don't get together with the colored people—they'll work for less than you get.' That's how he separates the white from the Negro and the Negro from the white. The average Negro makes a good union man. 'Course, one of them told me when I asked him to join: 'What do I want to belong to a CIO union for? It's a white man's union.' But I told him, 'It's a poor man's union.'"

Another Negro laborer described the tactical approaches to packing-house workers in 1938 as follows:

"One of the men got together about twelve or thirteen men all working at the Bruno Beef Company one Sunday at a friend's house. About half of the people present was white men and we had a good discussion and all of us wanted to have the CIO.

"The reason that we did not want the AFL is because they would separate us—put the whites in one local and the colored in another. We all wanted to be in the same local. After that meeting we all pledged that by the time of the next meeting, which would be held two weeks from that Sunday, we would bring one or two with us. So we all went to work on our friends working beside us in the plant. It so happened that I was working with a foreign-born Polish man and he did not know much English. I had a hard time, but he agreed to go with me to that meeting."

The effect of these assemblies at homes and of the recruiting in factories was strengthened by frequent mass meetings that tended to generate intense enthusiasm and high morale among the newly unionized workers, and to inspire in them a feeling of identity with their fellow-workers. Something of the élan that characterized these new recruits is revealed in the statement of one Negro worker:

"Our whole gang went into the union—every one of us. Now there's Joe who lives on South Parkway; he was the first to join. We all saw that if we wanted to protect our interests we would have to join. Then there's Lupe, the Mexican; that guy is one of the fightenest guys you ever saw. He put his button on the first day he got it. Yes, all our gang is a good bunch of union men, and will stick together. If we could get the whole plant to stick together half as well, we would have a strong union and things would be better for us."

Sometimes the CIO unions were competing with an old-established company union or with a recently organized independent union—organizations likely to appeal strongly to Negroes who distrusted white workers. Also, no doubt many Negro workers, accustomed to the paternalism of employers in the South, felt more secure in a company union. One Negro defended such unions with these observations:

"It protects us against any other union because when you are a member of the Security League that shows that you are satisfied with your employer—that you don't want any other union to come in and make trouble for you. Fifteen cents a week guarantees you the right to have your own spokesman for your group. That means that every six months you elect a representative."

Another packing-house worker described the advantages of belonging to a company union in terms of the welfare program:

"The members pay ten cents weekly as dues; this was put into the general fund and was used for the benefit of the group. For instance, we could borrow money in case of sickness, and if there was a death in the family we received $3 death benefits; this could not do much good as a burial fund, but at least we were assured of flowers. Two years ago we, through the main club, started a Christmas Saving Fund, and last year the members cashed checks amounting to $7,000. This year the amount is expected to reach around $35,000. The members of the various clubs have also been given the opportunity to buy shares in the business."

The rise of the CIO weakened the company unions, and by 1938 these had ceased to constitute an important force in the mass-production industries. Negroes followed the trend into CIO unions. The following are typical of the objections to company unions voiced by Negro workers:

"It is just something in name, but it don't mean a thing to the men working there because the way things are run there, it can't do any good."

"We have our own representatives from the different departments and they meet together and work out something and take it up with the manager, but they don't get anything but promises."

"We did not get a raise until the Wagner Act went into effect, and we have the same speed-up we have always had. In brief, the company union is no good. All the men are hollering about it."

"It is no good to the men who have to work because the representatives are so afraid to say anything about conditions that they let anything happen, and they don't say anything unless the men don't be working fast enough for them when the big boss is around. Then they come around and tell you that if you don't work faster you will never get a raise. That makes the men go as fast as they can, so they can get a raise, but that don't help at all."

The active participation of Negroes in the labor movement broke the stereotype of Negroes as strike-breakers and a source of cheap labor. Once Negroes become unionized, they must depend on the union to protect their rights through seniority rules and active opposition to the Job Ceiling. They can no longer rely on personal contacts with the employer for security. It is natural for some who have previously secured advancement, or favors, to view the union with suspicion, and to generalize that unions are detrimental to racial interests. Some Negro workers, like their white fellows, felt that their chances for advancement were better if they were not "mixed up with unions." For instance, a steel chipper who had worked for one company for seventeen years, said:

"The New Deal is linked up with the CIO. I don't believe in the CIO. Organized labor is against the Negro. I believe each plant or company should have its own independent union. That is the way we have it at the Crux Steel Plant. I worked all the time during the last strike. The colored and white are treated alike in my plant. There is no discrimination—no segregation in washrooms or restaurant."

On the other hand, there were "successful" workers who, although they would not join the new union, were not hostile to the CIO. An assistant foreman in a steel plant, for instance, first cited reasons why he had preferred not to join the CIO.

"I was approached by men from both unions, but as I felt fairly secure in my position, I saw no need to join. I've worked for the company long enough so that I have a right to my job as long as the company operates. . . . I wouldn't join the union before the contract was signed, and there was no need after it was signed." But he added, "I am not opposed to unions."

Moreover this man, despite his non-union status, seemed proud of the fact that "before the contract was signed, in my department we had the strongest union representation of any unit in the plant. . . . After the contract didn't force all men to join the union, the men began to drop out because they couldn't see any advantage in paying for the same things that non-union men got."

Still other Negroes who have acquired preferred positions in industry have nevertheless embraced the union. Sometimes the action resulted from recognizing that unions can "make the way hard" for a person who has the reputation of being timid or of being a stool pigeon. More commonly, however, the men in question had been nursing grievances of long standing against the establishments for which they worked, and the union provided a means of expression for such grievances. One worker, for example, felt that he had a "lifetime job" at the mill where he worked, but he nevertheless entertained numerous grievances against the company. He joined the union, and at the time that the following interview was taken, he was a leader in a predominantly white union. He explained his union affiliation thus:

"Let me tell you a thing or two about the plant. I know, too; I've worked there thirteen years—since I was twenty years old. You know, I'm doing highly skilled work. It took me a year to learn every part, its number, where it is to be sent, where these parts are kept, how much is to be sent out each month. But what is my occupational classification? I'm assigned as a 'porter.' They can't stand the idea of a Negro being classified as a skilled worker.

"Let me tell you a thing. There are only six of us colored men. We're all classified as porters, and all of us are doing some kind of skilled work. You see how they get us this way. When we ask for a raise according to the work we are doing, the boss says, 'Why, you're getting more than most porters now.'

"Of course, I've been there so long, and it would be so hard to train another person to do what I'm doing, that they pay me more than most white workers, $27, but they'd fire me in a minute if they thought anyone else could do my job.

"Let me tell you something. I was called into the office and the boss said to me, 'Bobby, it grieves us very much to see you a member of this harebrained outfit. Haven't we always treated you fair? That outfit isn't doing anything for you.'

"I told him that I worked hard and well; that what I did off the job was *my* business; that I had worked thirteen years for them, and it took the CIO to get a vacation for me. They kind of threatened me, but I wasn't bluffed so easy, and I'm still working. What's more, I'm shop steward; I'm on the Grievance Committee; I'm the sergeant-at-arms at my lodge, too."

When an organizing campaign begins, or a strike is imminent, Negro workers must face the possibility of running afoul of management on the one hand, or of their fellow-workers on the other. Undoubtedly, in such situations, many individual workers would prefer not to join a union, but they operate in a social milieu which forces them to choose sides and to assume the consequent risks. Many persons who first "choose" the union under such circumstances subsequently become deeply interested in union activities and wish to be members.

One of the most significant aspects of the contact between Negroes and whites in the labor movement has been the emergence of Negro leaders who have won the loyalty and respect of both colored and white workers. During an organizing campaign, both Negro and white leaders are used. Appeals are made to Negroes on the basis of their individual economic interest, opportunities for "racial advancement," and the broader philosophy of class solidarity. As the union becomes more highly integrated, the appeal to class solidarity becomes more pronounced and effective. The organizing campaign, especially in initial stages, may make use of special appeals to Negroes as Negroes, but fundamentally and ultimately the appeal is to economic self-interest and the doctrine of working-class solidarity.

THE STRIKE

A strike is a crisis situation in which the state of Negro-white relations may constitute a decisive element. Negroes, as a consequence of the fact that they have been used as strike-breakers in the past in Chicago, have been stereotyped as potential "scabs." It is relatively easy, therefore, for antagonism toward "scabs" to be focused with double intensity upon Negro strike-breakers. On the other hand, where Negroes have been organized into unions with white persons, class solidarity is likely to soften racial antagonism even when other Negroes are used as strike-breakers. The symbols and slogans of the class struggle serve as doctrinal support for Negro-white co-operation against the "bosses." A strike is a conflict—a conflict often freighted with emotion and meaning for those who participate in it. A strike serves to weld workers into a class-conscious and temporarily unified action group. The following speech by a Negro strike leader, delivered during the "Little Steel" strike in 1937, illustrates the manner in which class solidarity is stimulated:

"Two thousand marching CIO miners will lay down their picks, and Girdler needs coal to blast his furnaces! Thousands of auto workers from the CIO will stop using any steel made in Republic, and Girdler must fill his contracts with the auto companies. Thousands of longshoremen will stand idle, and Girdler needs their help in transporting steel. Thousands of railway employees will let Girdler's steel sit on the tracks, and Girdler needs the railroads to carry on any business. Girdler needs them all. Girdler needs them all, and John L. Lewis knows it. They say they'll make steel anyhow. Where will they send it? When it piles so high that Girdler can't see over it, he'll sign. He'll sign."

The picket line drew Negroes and whites together in common and dangerous activity. Struggle gave real content to the doctrine that union men must "stick together as brothers." Between 1935 and 1940, a number of important strikes involving both Negro and white workers occurred. The Republic Steel Strike of 1937—one of the most dramatic of these disturbances—illustrates to an unusual degree the operation of factors that create solidarity between Negro and white workers—as well as certain other factors which impede this development.

The Republic Steel Strike: In May, 1937, approximately 20,000 workers of the Republic Steel Company, situated in South Chicago, walked out on strike. The principal demands of the workers were for union recognition and a wage increase. The strike was effectively broken in a relatively short time, though it dragged along for many months. This strike is significant because it was the setting within which the nationally famous "Memorial Day Massacre" occurred.

On Sunday, May 30, 1937, a crowd of some 5,000 people—strikers, their wives and children, and union sympathizers—were assembled near the plant for purposes of mass picketing and demonstration. During the afternoon a disturbance occurred and the police fired into the crowd. Ten workers were killed, and nine more persons were injured. The police were severely and widely denounced for unprovoked and excessive brutality. They claimed that they were "attacked," but impartial evidence assembled at the time contained nothing to justify their conduct.

When the Steel Workers' Organizing Committee (SWOC) called the strike at Republic Steel, more than half of the Negroes in the plant were union members, and these walked out with the white workers. (At the time, about 25,000 men were employed in the plant, of whom 17,000 were white and 8,000 were colored.) Some Negroes did not leave work, however. A striker interviewed at the time reported:

"Since the strike there are about twenty-five or thirty Negroes who stayed in. . . . I think those guys would come out, but they are ashamed. They don't even come around to any of the places where strikers hang out."

A Negro striker reported on his efforts to bring out all of the colored workers:

"We went around and talked to the men that stayed in because it put Negroes in a bad light. Even though many whites stayed in, we colored men felt that those staying in would give Negroes a black eye in the union. You know the first thing white union men think is that Negroes will scab and break strikes. We didn't have any success. The men said they needed the money. Most of them were scared of losing their jobs, and some are just ignorant."

At one point in the strike, strike-breakers—both white and Negro—were imported by the company. Since most of the colored employees had come out on strike, the union was able to handle the situation in a highly effective manner. One observer told this story:

"The Republic Company had hired a lot of Negroes as strike-breakers, and in order to create racial friction these Negroes had been sent out to break up the picket line—but only when there were all white workers on the picket line. The situation got pretty tense at strike headquarters. There were murmurings of 'Niggers are always scabs'; there were little tussles among some of the men.

"However, the situation was cleared up in a clever way. All of the Negro strikers stayed near the picket line and waited for a skirmish. When the Negro scabs came out to beat up the pickets, the Negro strikers were let out and gave them such a beating there was never a recurrence of the trouble."

Strike leaders exerted every effort to draw Negroes into full participation at public meetings. The emphasis thus placed upon Negro-white solidarity served to counteract the unfavorable impression created by the Negroes who were acting as strike-breakers. An observer described one of these meetings in terms of Negro participation:

"At 2:30, 'Spike' Smith, the Negro organizer, announced that a brother from the United Mine Workers of America was there to speak. Another report was made by Jack Ross, a Negro molder. . . . His appearance was greeted with cheers and applause. He has been very active in the South Chicago area. He owns an automobile, which is placed at the disposal of the strikers at all times.

"After the speeches, the Negro organizer announced that they had just received a call for a blood transfusion to aid a brother who was in the hospital in a serious condition. [He had been hurt on the picket line.] He asked for volunteers. At least ten men, two of whom were Negroes, went up to the table without hesitation. They were all sent to the hospital. Later Spike announced that a group of children were going to present a little program. Twelve Negro children marched in, carrying violins and banjos. . . . Another announcement was made concerning relief for strikers. The men were told to report to the organizer, Spike."

Other methods, too, were used to checkmate racial antagonisms. At one meeting Spike addressed a mixed audience, and denounced "the ignorant Negro who held a gun on the workers," citing this as "an old company technique to incite racial prejudice." He cried out, "A scab is a scab, black or white, and should be scorned by all union members, black and white!" He insisted that today "workers refuse to bite at the racial bait-line." Whistles and cheers followed his speech.

A special effort was made to involve Negro women in strike activities, and one observer noted: "Several of the wives of the Negro members went to the strike headquarters and worked in the kitchen where meals were prepared for the pickets. It was felt that this pleased the union members because the general opinion was that the Negroes could not be depended upon in a crisis."

The climax of the Republic strike came with the "Memorial Day Massacre." Of this affair, one Negro participant commented: "I have been in three strikes. I was in the 'Memorial Day Massacre' and I can't find words to express the horror of it. In the World War, both sides at least had an equal chance."

Another Negro striker, who subsequently testified before the La Follette Committee during that committee's investigation of the "massacre," gave a dramatic account of the police attack:

"On that Sunday we marched out of the plant with signs. Lots of us were singing songs and laughing. I was in the front line. All of a sudden the cops started shooting. When they started, I ran to my extreme right, then west, then I made an 'L' turn to the south. All the time, bullets were going right past my face.

"When I looked up I saw a guy right on top of the plant training his gun on us. I couldn't tell whether it was a machine gun, 'cause I was anxious to get out of the line of fire. I could see the police in my path, the way I was running, so I turned around toward Sam's Place. I ran to a car and started to duck in it. A bullet whizzed by and lodged right above the right fender. Boy, I shake now when I think that if I hadn't ducked I'd have been shot in the head. I finally made it into the car and was driven to Sam's Place."

The CIO regards the men who died that day as martyrs to the union cause. Among the ten men killed was one Negro. After being shot, he was beaten by the police and taken to jail. Later his wife had him removed to a private hospital, where he died. She seemed bewildered by this outburst of violence resulting in her husband's death. This is how she talked about it:

"He was told to go to the meeting that Sunday. He was on the front line and was one of the first to get hurt. I have his clothes here. You can see where he was shot in the back. His hat is bloody. He sure was beat terrible. His life was really lost for the CIO, whether he understood it or not. I do hope his loss will help others who live."

Her feelings toward the union were mixed, uncertain:

"He never said nothing much about it. He just told me he was joining a new union. He did say he was joining because it was beneficial. We didn't talk about those things much. I don't think he understood it either.

"I ain't never thought much about it before. I guess a union's all right, but when people have to lose their life it ain't so good. 'Course, in war, men lose their lives for freedom, but this is a little different. The union caused me to lose a very good husband. They seem to want to drop me so soon. I don't expect them to take care of me forever, but I do feel they should help till I can see my way out."

Toward the police, however, her attitude was one of unmitigated bitterness:

"They wouldn't let me in to see him until the Saturday before I had him moved to St. Luke's. They treated me all right, but they wouldn't let me see him. I saw others going in, but I couldn't tell whether they were visiting in the hospital or in the jail.

"I was let in on June 13. He'd been in since May 30. They thought he was dying that Saturday night, so they sent two policemen to my home to bring me to see him. He was so glad to see me he could hardly talk. He kept asking why I hadn't been there to see him. He cried and I cried and told him they wouldn't let me in. He said they hadn't taken the bullet out and infection had set in. He was so sick! I wouldn't let him talk, but he kept saying over and over, 'Police sure treat a man dirty; they kicks 'em and beats 'em.' He almost screamed at times.

"I thought they [the police] would tell him how I came out two and three times a day, and how I called every day, but he didn't know nothing about it. Every time I'd call, they told me he was getting along fine, until they was scared he was dying. Then they sent for me."

Those Negro members who continued to support the union after the "Memorial Day Massacre" felt that the CIO was fair to them as Negroes, and that the strike was justified. The following interview is typical of this view:

"Though Republic Steel paid all workers the same wages for the same kind of work, they did not treat the white and colored employees alike in other respects. The Negro employee was restricted to certain departments. There were no colored foremen, and no possibilities of promotion for the colored employees.

"The AFL did not attempt to organize the workers at Republic Steel. The AFL did not organize many Negro workers. I think the AFL should kick into the CIO. I feel the CIO is far the better organization for Negroes. I like the union fine. The union is 100 per cent for the colored man. There is no discrimination in the CIO."

In November, some six months after the Memorial Day affair, an observer visited the union headquarters. The strike had been broken. Men were trickling back to work. Gone were the morale and enthusiasm of former days, though some residue of the solidarity created by the strike between Negro and white workers seemed to remain.

And, through the strike, the union had gained new and loyal members, Negro as well as white. At union headquarters, one such recruit told his story to the interviewer—in the presence of a Mexican and five white unionists.

"I came to Chicago in 1922. I started working in Republic Steel in April, 1923, and was there steady until the strike was called on May 26, 1937.

"I have four boys . . . so you see it was pretty hard to walk off from my job not knowing how I'd make a living for them. I didn't know anything about unions before, but I did know that I wanted organization and a contract to stop the company from pushing the men around and to stop the speed-up. You know the company could tell you if you didn't like it you could take it or get the hell out.

"Negroes only had certain places to work in Republic. Even in the washroom, Negroes were told to use one side and whites the other side. The washroom is just one big room, yet Negroes had to stay on their side of it. I believe, from the way they talk, that there is no prejudice in the CIO.

"Negroes spend ten or fifteen years in Republic and can't get higher than chippers. They never get to be on the cranes, never get jobs as engineers or firemen. That's why I wanted organization. I understand that without organization a person can't get any place.

"While we were organizing our department, the company gave us shorter hours and only two or three days a week, and let the other departments do steady work. That was the company's way of bringing pressure on us union men.

"Once the boss said to me: 'You fellows are nothing but a bunch of Bolsheviks.' I asked him what the hell that was and he walked away. I realized that I spoke too quick. I might have got more out of him if I had waited.

"I saw some of the preparations for the strike. While I was in the storeroom one day, I saw a big delivery truck back up to the door. It had a lot of big packages on it. One of them had a hole in it where the clubs had punched through, and I could see several club handles about the size of a kid's baseball bat. I didn't say anything about it, but I certainly remembered it that Sunday in May." (Here a white union member added that he, too, had seen clubs stacked in the back room of the credit union office.)

General discussion of the strike followed; then the Negro worker concluded: "I'm a union man, from now on. There isn't no way out for us, except the union. Maybe we'll lose this time. But the day will come when we will win."

The Republic Steel strike demonstrated that in a time of crisis white workers would not only struggle side by side with Negroes, but would also follow them as leaders and honor them as martyrs. As it became a part of the traditions of the area, the incident strengthened the position of Negroes in unions, as well as the hold of unions over colored workers. The strike had shown that some Negroes, acting on the basis of their class alignments, would subordinate racial loyalty even to the point of criticizing and fighting Negro strike-breakers. It was also evident, however, that such behavior was not yet common enough to be accepted as entirely normal by many workers—white and colored.

DAY-BY-DAY RELATIONSHIPS

During the excitement of an organizational campaign or a strike, both racial antagonisms and class solidarity across race lines are at their height. Once a contract has been signed, the day-by-day routine of workers is broken only by occasional elections and grievances. Those unions in which the leaders are concerned with improving race relationships make use of these situations for further impressing upon Negro and white workers the necessity for fairness, co-operation, etc. Such interim periods bear dividends when crises arise.

Labor unionists contend that membership in a progressive union is reflected in the day-by-day relationships of Negro and white workers. The colored shop chairman in a small plant with fewer than a dozen workers described the improved atmosphere in his plant: "Well, I'll tell you what the CIO has done. Before, everyone used to make remarks about 'that dirty Jew,' 'that stinkin' black bastard,' 'that low-life Bohunk,' but you know I never hear that kind of stuff any more."

Both white and colored workers who take their labor unionism seriously are in a position to remind the less zealous that they must not jeopardize class solidarity by exhibiting racial antagonism. One colored steel-worker cited an incident involving another colored worker: "'Course, not all prejudices are wiped out right away. The other day I was working on a gang with another colored man and two white men. The colored man tried to get me to give the white men the hardest part to do, but I told him off on that, and later he came back and told me he realized we must *all* do the same amount of work."

Such incidents as those just cited may be exceptional, but it seems that organization of Negroes and whites together in the mass-production industries has resolved many of the antagonisms and suspicions that in the past contributed to widespread insecurity on the part of both white and colored workers.

SHARING POSITIONS OF CONTROL

Some of the AFL locals have separate colored locals in which Negroes occupy all of the positions of leadership. The CIO, on the other hand, does not sanction separate locals, but seeks to integrate Negroes and whites together in the same plant and local organization. The philosophy underlying this practice was outlined by a steel worker:

"In 1921, company stooges split the union by advising Negroes to meet in their own section and whites in theirs. This worked up destruction on both sides. Negroes met on 43rd Street some place—I believe it was at Forum Hall. This plot was quite successful. The packers were clever in bringing the proposal. Their agents told the Negroes it would be more convenient for them to meet close to home, and the plan sounded feasible. The whites met on Loomis Boulevard. This set-up made it easy to play one group against the other and built up animosity. Insidious propaganda was injected at the meetings by telling each group that the other was not to be trusted."

Where Negroes and whites are organized in the same locals, it has been customary for Negroes to insist upon some representation among the officers, executive committees, etc. White workers have become accustomed to following the leadership of Negroes.*

Out of the ranks of the workers have arisen individual Negroes who function on grievance committees, serve as shop chairmen, and act in other capacities that throw them into contact with management as spokesmen for the union. Here the personal nexus with the employer has been entirely broken and the Negro individual abandons any semblance of currying favor or depending on his relations with management.

All lodges of the CIO steel unions with Negro members have some Negro officials. There are a number of Negro shop stewards in the locals who direct grievance committees, collect dues, and deal with the management. They also appear before the NLRB when necessary. A middle-aged Negro migrant from Georgia, in answer to a question about how Negroes and whites get along in his local, replied: "Fine, as far as I know. We have both Negro and white officers in our union and nobody seems to mind."

Labor leaders believe that Negroes have a distinct advantage over the foreign workers, since the first-generation immigrants have lan-

* It is not to be inferred that all AFL unions, by any means, organize Negroes into separate locals, or that Negroes have never attained positions of leadership in mixed AFL locals. As a matter of fact, the pattern of organization characteristic of the CIO emerged first in certain AFL unions. In Chicago in 1920-21, this pattern—including Negro officers in mixed locals—was well developed in several Chicago unions, most notably perhaps, in the International Ladies' Garment Workers' Union, the Hod Carriers' Union and the Flat Janitors' Union. The last-named organization had Negro officers from the time it was first organized, and in 1920, 1,000 of the 5,000 members of the union were Negro. (See *The Negro in Chicago*, pp. 412-416.)

guage difficulties. Negroes are more vocal and can become leaders easily.

In the ranks of lesser leaders, both in the unions proper and in the women's auxiliaries, there are many Negro officers. One Negro president stated: "I was elected by unanimous vote. The fellows had been telling me that they wanted me as president when they held the election, and I had told that I didn't want the presidency. I resigned after they elected me, but they ignored my resignation and re-elected me, so I've been serving ever since."

The president of one local in the packing industry thus described the situation in his plant just before the war boom:

"The CIO is the greatest thing that could have happened to Negroes in packing. Before that they were outside the labor movement, mostly, and could be used as strike-breakers by the bosses. I'm happy to be president of the local, and I work hard at it to bring in as many Negroes as well as whites as I can into the union.

"The shop stewards are 50-50, white and Negro among the men; there is no friction—the white workers are willing to have a Negro shop steward head the Grievance Committee. In the meetings of the local, the Negro members feel free to go up on the floor—they make good speeches and usually talk to the point."

Stimulating Participation by Negroes: Because Negroes do not have a long tradition of union participation there are frequent complaints from both white and Negro officials that they do not participate so actively in union affairs as they might. The Negro financial secretary of a local, in a plant about one-third Negro, described relationships in his plant as follows:

"We have 621 members; 198 are Negroes. Only about fifteen Negroes come out to meetings, and we're doing good to get that many out. The whole department has only about 1,500 men. Fifty per cent of the Negroes pay dues but are not so good in attendance. Those Negroes who come out are very active and pay good. One thing, it has been easier to collect from Negroes than other races. The Negro realizes that he has a real chance to join an organization with the rights of other races. I think they're all faithful union men, though for the time being it's hard to get them out. Especially with the CIO leaders, the Negro has a chance to fill any position where he's capable. I believe the policy of the CIO is against discrimination."

Occasionally, a Negro labor leader will voice a complaint similar to that of an organizer in the fur workers union:

"There is no Negro on the Executive Board now. This is not the fault of the union. One Negro woman was nominated at the last election. There are fifty-five Negroes in the local, thirty-two of whom are eligible to vote. Only nine came out to vote, yet this woman lost by only seven votes, which proved that she was more acceptable to the white workers than to the Negro workers who didn't even come out."

The colored shop chairman of a steel local reported:

"Attendance isn't as good as it should be. Most of the boys are young; they don't really have the union at heart. They saw what the union did for them, and so they pay up their dues, but it's hard to get them out to the meetings. I notice that the men who have family responsibilities like myself are the most active members."

Labor leaders continually emphasize the fact that when Negroes are active participants in the day-by-day affairs of the union, and when they attend meetings regularly, it is possible for them to secure positions of control within the local union organization. One steel worker made the following comment:

"One thing that I have tried to get the Negro to understand and do is to join in such large numbers that they will be a power from a voting standpoint so that when the union has an election of officers they can vote some of their own into office. If the Negro would learn to pick the person best fitted for office, and quit putting a dumb person in simply because of friendship, then we should be able to meet, plan, and scheme with the other fellows and would not only be a floor member."

The very realistic attitude of the more astute Negro union leaders is revealed in the comment of a packing-house worker during the organizational drive of 1937:

"I am chairman of the —— local and Secretary of the Industrial Council. I was given one of the fourteen offices in the local. Negroes are taking a leading part. When some of them say the Negro will get a dirty deal from the CIO like they do in the AFL, I preach to them to get in when the policies are being formed and help form them. I tell them that workers themselves form union policies when they have enough sense to get in on the ground floor and take part in shaping policy.

"They seem to understand better now and they are getting in on the ground floor in the CIO. We have ten locals in the yards. Four have Negro presidents. At one plant only about ten per cent of the employees are Negroes. But a Negro has one of the elective positions out there; this is encouraging."

Protecting the Rights of Negroes: Negro workers share in whatever economic gains a union brings, but they also expect their union to protect their rights to promotion, office holding, and treatment as union brothers. The day-by-day problems arising in the plant and at union meetings provide union officials with an opportunity to use both persuasion and pressure for enforcing the union program of equality. The Negro president of a steel local explained the procedure in his shop as follows: "The person in question would be called before the executive board where the disadvantage of prejudice would be explained to him. He would then be given another chance, and if the difficulty arose again he would be expelled."

The colored trustee of a local in the meat-packing industry said, "There's no prejudice at all," and then explained: "We have by-laws and constitutions, but there is no rule covering prejudice. I'm pretty sure if a case occurred, everyone would embarrass the person to death."

SOCIAL EXTENSIONS OF ECONOMIC CONTACT

Labor unions are not concerned entirely with economic problems. They depend on dances, picnics, parties, and similar social events to raise money and to maintain *esprit de corps.* Such social and quasi-social events often involve the attendance of Negro members. During the organizational drives in the mass-production industries in 1937 and 1938, such affairs were very frequent, and the more enthusiastic union members reported their experiences in glowing terms:

"Our lodge gave a dance in September. It was a free social to try and encourage men to come out. It was very successful, and quite a few Negroes came out. They socialized with the others and seemed to feel that we're all one race."

"At the social events, one sees mixing of the groups. Both Negro and white drink beer together. More and more there is an intermixing between both races and sexes in the dancing."

"One thing can be said for the SWOC staff and lodge officers: They stress Negro participation in social affairs. This gives a sort of education in race relations."

After the first novelty of the new CIO movement had worn off, social participation, while less frequent, was also less commented on. Today, the presence of Negroes at a union dance or party is not a matter for remark except in certain special situations.

A crucial point in this social participation has been interracial dancing. A young Polish Communist commented during the organizational drives of 1937: "If everybody felt like me, we wouldn't have any trouble running dances and other affairs. That's the struggle we got to fight now, so that Negroes won't be scared away from our affairs." The common pattern was described by a trustee in a predominantly Negro shop: "There was a large attendance of both white and colored. There were no colored and whites dancing together. Some stayed in groups by themselves, mostly whites. There was no friction, they just didn't dance together. They all talked and laughed together." At one dance on the South Side attended by more than 1,000 persons, only ten or fifteen white men and women came, though the manager said, "A lot of tickets were sold to whites who didn't come."

That many Negroes do not adjust easily to interracial dancing is suggested by the complaint of an organizer who said: "Certain indications point to the strong influence of the idea of not mixing, in the form of Negroes' limiting themselves. I was the only one who danced at this affair. The rest of them drank and talked with the whites, but they didn't dance."

Many Negro workers use the test of social participation as one measure of the white worker's sincerity. This attitude was illustrated by an incident in which a Negro member came to the local headquarters to report a rumor which, as he phrased it, "was causing some confusion in his lodge." It seems that a white official, in referring to a dance which had been planned, stated that it was being held in a neighborhood unfriendly to Negroes. Some of the Negroes interpreted this as a gentle hint that they were not wanted, and the Negro union member said: "I felt that I should come right to you so that the rumor can be stopped. The men are kinda touchy and if it gets around it will have a bad effect on the colored members of the union." The union official was quite anxious to straighten out the matter, assured the member that he would bring the grievance up at the council meeting that night, and stated that he could "easily see how they might have felt that it was intended to discourage Negro attendance because that's the approach used by persons who actually don't want Negro attendance. I think I made a mistake when I apologized for having the dance at a place inconvenient for Negroes. I should have told the members that if they disapproved of the place, we'd get another where Negroes wouldn't be molested. We'll make it clear tonight."

The more conservative Negro members take the position of a colored worker who said: "We work together and we understand each other better when we socialize and find out that we're all alike, and especially the white ones find out that the Negroes don't bite. I like to dance but I prefer dancing with colored girls. I think we can show solidarity without dancing together."

The strength of the general social taboos against dancing with Negroes is indicated by the comment of an Italian president of a steel workers' women's auxiliary to another white woman:

"We used to have a lot of colored fellows in the lodge, but they're all gone now, every one. We even had two of them officers. But they've all left now. When they were in, we used to try to get their wives to join, but now they've gone.

"Of course, as my husband and I have said to each other, you give them a foot and they'll take a yard. If you ask them to your dances, they'll come and they don't just dance with each other but some of them will try to dance with white people. If they do, the white women will just stop going to the dances. There's something about colored men that just makes you *afraid*. I don't know what it is, but you have a certain *fear*. I don't feel that way at all about the girls, but the men are different —I don't know what it is, exactly, but it's fear. At a dance we had here a while ago, a Negro man actually came up to me and asked me if I would dance with him. I didn't know what to say, but I wasn't going to dance with him, so I told him that I had promised that one to someone. With a colored man, I just feel afraid. I don't know what it is. The girls are different, but I don't feel that way about them. A Negro woman has been a good friend of mine for years, but the men are different.

"I know that Negroes *are* workers, and I suppose that, really, they *are* human, but there's just something about them—that black skin— I guess the trouble with us is really that we're not liberal enough. You know, the thing is that you would like to be nice to them yourself personally, but other people don't feel that way. Perhaps if you were just with a colored person away from the eyes of everyone, you would act quite different; but with the eyes of everyone on you, you don't feel that way."

On the level of informal social participation, friendships sometimes arise between Negroes and whites which involve taking a beer together, visiting in the home, and participation in private parties. Such behavior is not widespread, but it has undoubtedly been made more general by the union movement. The president of one SWOC local related an incident which occurred in the South Chicago area which indicates the type of relationships that develops:

"This community was not neighborly. A year and a half ago Negroes could not walk in some of the streets out here. The change is due to the union and the intelligent part the Negro has played out here. Since the union campaign, I have been there on many occasions to different union members' homes. I knew these same people before the campaign started, but I was never invited to their homes. It is much different now. On June 11, my wife's birthday, the white women of the East Side gave her a surprise party at a white woman's home. It was a fine party. There were about thirty people present, and only four of us were Negroes. There were so many flowers, I thought someone had died. They called me to come over and we didn't know what it was all about. The party was at the home of Joe Petronio. He's an Italian. He's financial secretary of the union."

The secretary of one steel local, a white Virginian, said: "We occasionally have just a few cases of objections to the colored members in the union. And there is some partiality. The colored members attend the union's social affairs and dance the same as the whites. There is a complete intermingling at our social affairs. Of course, some conflicts are to be expected. Workers as a whole are still uneducated."

UNIONS AND THE JOB CEILING

The Job Ceiling in the mass-production industries has been maintained by a combination of factors. In the first place, Negroes entered industry as untrained workers at the bottom of the occupational hierarchy. But this consideration is not sufficient to account for the fact that twenty years later Negro workers have not risen in appreciable

numbers into the ranks of the skilled, white-collar clerical and supervisory occupational categories. Before the advent of industrial unionism
in these industries, the exclusive policy of the craft unions and the
reluctance of employers in both union and non-union plants to advance
colored workers were the principal factors in the lack of occupational
mobility among Negroes.

The interplay of these two factors is revealed in the testimony of
experienced and reliable workers, both colored and white. A highly
skilled Negro worker in a packing plant who was a member of the
CIO union blamed the company for discrimination existing in 1938:

"In the plant Negroes work in most departments but are definitely
excluded from the bacon department. This work is done by women
and is the cleanest department in the whole plant, being the one that
is most often shown visitors. No Negro women are allowed here, it
being said that the public objects to black hands touching the bacon.
The union does not approve of this and fights against it."

There is a tendency among union members to blame the corporations for the absence of colored workers in the better jobs in the plants,
while Negro non-union workers blame white workers.

The lack of opportunity for occupational advancement is the most
prevalent grievance expressed by Negro workers.

A union trustee in a plant in which Negroes have exceptional opportunities said: "Negroes can advance up to supervisor and timekeeper.
We got a new timekeeper the other day—a Negro. Of course, Negroes
don't advance as fast as whites and they don't intend to give Negroes
proportional representation on boss jobs."

A Negro steel-worker blamed management: "I never had any boss
trouble, but they never promotes us Negroes."

Another steel-worker said: "Most Negroes does common labor. They
ain't no Negro bosses and no Negro electricians. Only white men has
them jobs. . . . The company keeps the Negro down."

Another colored worker remarked in the same vein: "Though the
company paid all workers the same wage for the same kind of work,
they did not treat the Negro the same in other respects. The Negro
employees were restricted to certain departments. There were no
colored foremen, and no possibilities of promotion for the colored
employees."

A Negro skilled worker who had been able to advance within his
plant said:

"Mexicans and Negroes don't get breaks like whites get. I haven't seen any Mexicans or Negroes on cranes or in the electrical department. We have one Negro craneman now in plate mill yards. He's been there since 1919. You know why—he stayed in during the strike. . . . Plenty of us coulda done skilled work after the strike, since many of us did it during the strike. The whites say Negroes can't do skilled work. We can do anything we get a chance to do—and sometimes better than whites, because Negroes know they have to be twice as good as anyone else to get and keep a job."

A colored worker in an open-shop steel mill maintained that the company was responsible for the exclusion of Negroes from the electric department:

"The company definitely excludes Negroes from the electric department. At one time the white workers circulated a petition to get a Negro electrician who was an expert on a job in the electric department. It was signed by all the workers in the department, yet the company turned it down."

A white chemist in a packing plant confirmed the role of company policy in maintaining the Job Ceiling, and incidentally revealed the dilemma of a friendly white worker who objects to discrimination in industry:

"They just don't hire them, but I don't see any reason for it. I have been friends with the colored people a long time and I find them just as capable as the whites. The company could get some colored to do that job if they wanted to, but I haven't heard any discussion on the question at all. I have wanted to raise it, but I was afraid that they would take the wrong attitude towards me and I wouldn't get my promotion. Although I have many friends among the colored people there is one thing I do not understand about them. They take anything or whatever condition is imposed upon them and will not put up a fight for their rights; that is, I have seen one at a time try to stop something, but it's never effective that way. And another thing, in our own shop some of the whites try to be friendly with the colored, but they seem to keep away from them as much as they can, although one or two visit me and I visit them. But on the whole there is a lot of room for improvement on the part of all."

A left-wing Polish worker was equally insistent that the company was responsible for not promoting Negroes: "Generally the management considers the Negro less able than the white. I don't understand why they permit them to do skilled work in someone else's place if they consider Negroes so dumb. They won't promote Negroes as rapidly as whites."

It is very difficult to secure expressions from employers as to why the Job Ceiling exists. The prevailing tendency is to blame the unions or to allege that advancing the Negroes would cause trouble in the plant. Occasionally, however, an employer will reveal personal attitudes that operate to reinforce the Job Ceiling. Thus one steel executive observed:

"Negroes are nice, simple people. I don't approve of using them for skilled work—not that they couldn't do it, but we have enough competition within the skilled groups. Let the Negroes scramble for the unskilled jobs. It used to be possible for Negroes to be used as strikebreakers. The CIO has lots of them now, and sometimes it's harder to get them. The CIO fools them with parties and social gatherings so that they get the idea they're as good as white people."

In general it can be said that plant policy is formulated with a view to uninterrupted production. Anything that might cause trouble is avoided. Minor supervisory personnel is undoubtedly a decisive factor in the promotion policy of many plants. The tendency in many large industrial organizations is to put into foremen's hands such personnel questions as the employment policy toward Negroes. There is a widespread feeling among Negro workers that foremen are largely responsible for the failure of colored workers to advance. Since many foremen are first- or second-generation Americans, of foreign ancestry, the Negro's verbal attacks on foremen are likely to be tinged with anti-foreign sentiments. A colored Baptist minister, working in a steel mill, gave vent to his feelings in the following words:

"Of course there's discrimination. . . . A couple of times I know that my foreman has given me some raw deals. He's a lousy Polack. They're the worst."

So long as the skilled jobs in the basic industries were under the jurisdiction of AFL craft unions, it was difficult to judge accurately whether management or the unions were primarily responsible for maintaining the Job Ceiling. With the advent of industrial unions, the situation has changed. All of the CIO unions have been and are committed to a non-discriminatory policy and union contracts embody clauses calling for the promotion of workers strictly on the basis of seniority. In such situations it is possible to determine clearly whether management or labor is at fault. If a union does not "go to bat" for a Negro, the blame can be squarely placed. If the union does support the colored worker's claim to advancement, and management balks, the situation is equally clear.

The policy of the CIO on this issue is clear cut and has forced many AFL unions to change their attitude toward Negro workers. One AFL organizer said: "My union does not practice discrimination against Negroes. I will admit that some time ago that was a practice, but this union don't carry any of that policy now."

Another AFL organizer recognized that the CIO was responsible for this change of policy: "We make special efforts to recruit the Negroes, because we know how they feel toward the AFL, but we try to explain to them that this is not the old AFL, [that] we have a policy to organize the unorganized. Whenever they join we make them feel at home where they belong. This was not the policy of the union until the CIO was started. Then the International saw that the workers wanted the CIO because of its method of organizing. Since our locals have adopted a militant program, now the workers will join the AFL."

The official position of all unions, then, is increasingly in the direction of demanding equal rights for Negroes. But whether or not a specific union local actually breaks the Job Ceiling in a given plant depends on several factors. First, a new position (or positions) must be open. Secondly, a Negro whose skill or seniority qualifies him for the position must be available in the plant. Given these, the local union must be willing to fight for the advancement of the colored worker, if management or individual white workers oppose the move. The union's weapons in such a situation are persuasion and economic pressure.

The three Depression years between 1937 and 1940 did not offer a favorable situation for measuring the power of unions to break the Job Ceiling. New jobs were few; labor turnover was slow. The period 1940 to 1942 did not provide too good a test situation either, because the labor shortage that attended the coming of war resulted in increased employment opportunities for Negroes without pressure from the unions. However, the Job Ceiling has been rising, and the CIO unions have certainly hastened the process. The question is whether the unions could not have been even more aggressive with respect to this issue.

Both Negro and white labor leaders continually point out that unions are only a tool which Negroes may use, and that colored workers must raise the issues within their own locals. One colored international organizer for a CIO smelters' union said: "Our people don't push hard enough for their rights under the union contracts. They've got to make the union abide by its contracts. They've got to speak up for jobs that belong to them."

Union strategists are now inclined to advise progressive white workers to initiate action in the matter of promotions of Negroes. In this way, they contend, Negro workers will not feel isolated, but will be encouraged by the presence of white allies. In locals in which white unionists do take the initiative, a friendlier feeling than usual seems to prevail between white and colored workers. Negroes in such unions frequently make comments similar to that of the steel worker who said:

"Of course there is the problem of removing the prejudice of bosses, or perhaps I should say, the technique of keeping the Negro out of certain jobs by playing on the prejudice of the white workers. Little by little white workers are learning that they must include the Negro and demand his promotion on the basis of merit. They are not being fooled so easily as in the past."

In the final analysis, white workers must become habituated to working with Negroes in skilled pursuits, and accepting them in supervisory capacities if the Negro Job Ceiling is to be broken. Even the more thoughtful and progressive workers may face an adjustment problem in this connection. A white steel worker, who said that he believed white and colored workers should have the right to work at the same jobs, answered when asked if he would work under a Negro foreman: "I tell you the truth, at first I wouldn't like a Negro boss even if he was smarter than anybody in the plant. Maybe later on, I would get used to him. Then I wouldn't care. I think the CIO will get us away from thinking so much about color."

Any sober estimate of the influence of the labor movement on Negro-white relations must avoid the overenthusiastic claims of partisans, or the disillusionment exemplified in the comment of an elderly steel worker, who said bitterly: "The white men get up and talk about unity, about how a black man is just as good as a white . . . but I never notice any of the colored men, CIO or not, go to any of the white brothers' homes."

A white CIO leader gave that organization's answer: "People seem to forget that the CIO didn't just come along and wipe out prejudice like a wet sponge on a plate. It is doing much toward establishing better race relations and some day prejudice will be brought to a minimum."

Union members, themselves, frequently size up the situation accurately. One white union member—though his explanation of the roots of prejudice is too simple—nevertheless senses the operation of processes that may overcome it: "A union doesn't eradicate prejudices the minute it makes its appearance, but successful negotiations through a union of Negroes and whites working together against a common enemy cannot but result in breaking down prejudices built up by employers."

Negro union leaders also view changing Negro-white relations as a long-term process. One organizer of packing-house workers, after commenting on the former role of Negroes as strike-breakers, said: "Race prejudice will only be overcome through a sustained campaign of education. It will take years to do this. We need the universities, the radio, the press to help us."

That the attitudes of individual white workers are affected by contact with colored workers in the union is suggested by frequent remarks like those of the steel-worker who stated:

"I learned a lot from that fellow [a Negro organizer]. He woke a lot of us up by showing how the company built up race hatred by playing on our sense of superiority. It'll be a lot different when steel is organized one hundred per cent. I never thought much about colored men before I joined the union. Of course, I knew there was discrimination against Negroes, but I just didn't think about it in my department. There were no Negroes there when I got the job, and I never gave it any thought until I began attending union meetings."

Labor union activity in Chicago during the Depression resulted in an increasing propensity on the part of white workers to accept Negroes as equals in the competitive process, and as joint participants in conflicts with employers. With this acceptance of Negroes as *economic* equals, there has developed a rather general acceptance of them as social equals in such semi-public situations as union dances and picnics. But there is little evidence, thus far, that the basic patterns of separate Negro and white family, clique, and associational relationships, other than union relationships, have been much affected by these developments.

The demands of a war economy broke the Job Ceiling at various points, though it is a matter of conjecture how extensive and permanent these changes will prove to be. In this process of breaking the Job Ceiling, the new labor unions have played a perhaps subsidiary, but nevertheless very important, role.

Within the new labor movement, a new Negro leadership has emerged which speaks not only for Negroes but often for white workers as well. The Communists have played an important part in promoting this leadership, as well as in developing the general favorable policy toward Negroes within the CIO—but these developments are now a part of the official policy of the organization.

With the appearance of this new union leadership, other Negro leaders of all class levels (including the preachers) began to lose their skepticism and fear of labor and to praise the CIO. For the first time Negroes seemed to have found a large mass of white people who not only welcomed them as allies in a struggle but also accepted them as friends; who added *fraternity* to liberty and equality.

A Bronzeville Negro—Willard S. Townsend—became the first colored man to sit on the national executive board of the CIO and soon after his appointment, he helped to persuade the organization to establish a committee for the investigation of possible discrimination within CIO unions.

The AFL, faced with CIO competition, has been forced to face the Negro issue more squarely. This was apparent in certain events of the 1944 AFL convention, held in New Orleans. At this convention the spot-light was turned on the race issue in a manner unprecedented in the history of the organization. Three spokesmen for the Negro attended the convention—two in addition to A. Philip Randolph who at previous conventions had carried the ball alone. Twenty other accredited Negro representatives were present. Eleven sweeping resolutions against racial discrimination were introduced during the course of the meetings. Although only the traditional, weak resolution was passed, the extensive discussion of the subject indicated that certain elements within the AFL were increasingly aware of the issue. Almost unprecedented also was the lack of segregation in the seating of white and colored members at an AFL meeting in the South.

At the same time that the AFL met in New Orleans, the CIO convened in Chicago. Numerous resolutions against race discrimination were presented and the strong anti-discrimination resolution unanimously passed by the convention delegates pledged the CIO to a ceaseless fight against racial inequalities and recommended that all affiliated unions include non-discriminatory clauses in their contracts. In supporting this resolution, President Philip Murray stated, in part:[1]

"I think that this . . . provides an opportunity to invite, through the medium of this convention, all Negro workers eligible for membership in trade unions to promptly seek affiliation with CIO organizations. . . . I do really believe that the eventual economic emancipation and political emancipation of the colored people lies in their willingness to associate themselves with organizations such as are affiliated with the CIO. . . . God help the Negro in America, and God help the minority groups of America, were it not for the splendid work that is being done by this great institution of yours and mine. We don't confine ourselves to the mere adoption of resolutions in meetings of this kind; we make those resolutions effective and workable. . . .

"I regard this work, this particular work of protecting and advancing the cause of the Negro, as a holy and a noble work, the kind of a work that all right-thinking citizens, regardless of their status in life or their affiliation with other groups, should dedicate themselves to."

It is this kind of talk that has made most Negroes in Chicago, regardless of social class, look toward the labor movement with some hope. But while they accept the overtures of the labor movement they still do not dismantle their *racial* organizations. Rather they increase their demands for racial solidarity. They believe that their bargaining power *within* the labor movement will be strengthened if they stick together. Many feel that they have been wooed by the labor movement primarily because in the past they have demonstrated their strength.

CHAPTER 13

Democracy and Political Expediency

THE SOUTHERN NEGRO COMING TO MIDWEST METROPOLIS DURING THE
Great Migration was not welcomed by white Chicagoans either as a
neighbor or as a fellow worker. But there was one group which, if
it did not welcome him, at least did not disdain to work with him
and even assist him in adjusting to northern urban life—the politicians.

Politicians, especially those connected with the political machines
of our great cities, are realists. The politicians of Midwest Metropolis
may have had their own private deprecatory attitudes toward Negroes
and may have resented their coming to the city, but they realized that
the Negro had a commodity in which they were interested—the vote.
Politicians are concerned with winning elections, and they were therefore willing to organize Negroes into the political machine, as they
had done before with the Poles, the Irish and the Germans. It was
necessary to learn new methods of appeal and, to some extent, a new
vocabulary, but this presented no great difficulty to a group of worldly-
wise persons who knew intimately the polyglot peoples of Midwest
Metropolis. So the Negro vote was organized. The peasants from
Mississippi and Alabama became a part of the body politic of the city.

The Negro entered the struggle for political power in Chicago with
many disadvantages. As one student has observed, individual success
in politics depends on access to large campaign funds, on the support
of the daily newspapers, on a certain measure of social prestige, and
on political experience and insight. The Negro had none of these
advantages. The southern migrants who came streaming into Chicago
during and after the First World War were poor and without property. They were a minority—and an unpopular and disliked minority.
Not only did the press fail to present a sympathetic picture of their
struggle for status and power, but as a rule it reported the most unfavorable aspects of their behavior. Moreover, the Negro migrants
were totally inexperienced in the jungle politics of the city slum.

But the stakes for which the Negro was playing were high, and
not even a background of frustration and failure, such as many

brought with them, could daunt them as they faced the challenge of political emancipation. Through politics the Negro hoped to obtain justice in the courts; police protection and protection against the persecution of the police; the chance to get administrative jobs through civil service; and a fair share in playgrounds, libraries, sewers, and street lights. To win these and the many other benefits which political action offers to a socially subordinated group, the Negro overcame many of his difficulties with remarkable ingenuity. If he did not have enough money to finance his own campaigns, he made connections with rich white people—whether real-estate barons, bootleggers, or utility magnates. When he did not get support from the daily press, he utilized his own weeklies to foster community solidarity and political awareness. Though Negroes lacked experience, the more alert of them soon found their way around in the maze of city politics. They took over, and even improvised upon and improved, the techniques for getting out the vote, for organizing and controlling a political machine, and for trading and bargaining with candidates.

Politics became an important, perhaps the most important, method by which the Negro sought to change his status. It was often the only avenue open for struggle against caste tendencies. This struggle invested his political behavior, even when corrupt, with an importance and a dignity that similar behavior could not command in any other portion of the population. To paraphrase Lincoln Steffens, the Negro favored *representative* government, even if it was not always *clean* government.

EARLY NEGRO POLITICIANS

The political history of the Negro in Midwest Metropolis did not begin with the Great Migration. As far back as 1837, one George White, a Negro, served as the town-crier, doubtless by political appointment. As fugitive slaves began to gather in the city they were immediately caught up in the political whirligig. John Jones was elected county commissioner in the Forties. In 1876, J. W. E. Thomas, a native of Alabama who had come to Chicago at the age of twenty-six and started a grocery business, became the first Negro to sit in the State legislature.

While Negroes have traditionally supported the party of Abraham Lincoln, the colored vote of Midwest Metropolis was sought by the Democrats throughout the pre-Migration period. The famous Mayor

Carter H. Harrison I, a Democrat, was one of the first white politicians to win the support of a large percentage of the Negro electorate. Indeed, it was his administration which first attracted some Negroes to the Democratic party, and during his period of tenure the Colored Democratic League of Cook County was formed.*

Not until 1894, however, did the first powerful Negro politician emerge—Edward H. ("Ed") Wright. In that year, at a meeting of the First Ward voters, he urged his hearers to support the straight Republican ticket. The response was surprisingly favorable. The ward's support of the Republican candidate for mayor, George B. Swift, contributed greatly to his election. Since the delivery of Negro votes from Wright's ward was directly attributable to him, he became an important political figure over night. He managed to have a Negro, Theodore W. Jones, nominated for county commissioner at the Cook County Republican convention of 1894. As Gosnell has stated, "These were the days of the caucus, the convention, rough-and-tumble politics, 'boodle' aldermen, and public utility scandals." (In the 1896 Cook County Republican convention over one-third of the delegates were saloon-keepers.) Wright, with a capacity for hard work and keen insight into traction problems, not only played the rough-and-tumble game, but also became an expert on city problems extending far beyond the confines of the Negro community. In 1896, having dictated the appointment of other Negroes to important jobs, he now engineered his own election as county commissioner, and thus became the third colored man to hold that office. With his election he was established as the most forceful leader of the Negro electorate.

Wright's political shrewdness is illustrated by the method he used

* One of Harrison's biographers points out that although there were only 3,000 Negro voters in Chicago in 1890, Harrison carefully cultivated them. He was "one of the few Democrats who could make any headway with this race. . . . In one of his campaigns he sent out a circular in which his love for the dark-skinned race was painted in highly tinted colors, and the 'man and brother' was exhorted to cast his ballot for Harrison. In the election which followed, the *Inter-Ocean* estimated that at least half of the colored vote went for the former Kentucky planter [Harrison]." On one occasion when Harrison had been claiming that the blood of a half-dozen ethnic groups flowed in his veins, everyone was eager "to see whether he would slight the Negroes by neglecting to claim kin with them or scandalize his family by claiming such kinship. He did neither. He said that he was a southern gentleman, born in Kentucky, and that he was proud to state that he had been nursed by a Negro 'mammy,' and that (quickly twisting a bit of hair on his finger) he had a little kink in his hair." (Claudius O. Johnson, *op. cit.*, pp. 98, 196.)

to win the presidency of the county board. He told each member of the board, privately, that he would appreciate a vote for the presidency as a mark of recognition for his people. All the votes except two were cast for Wright; each man thought that he was just giving a token vote to Wright. Another instance of his political skill was manifested when he refused to authorize an appropriation for the office of State's Attorney Charles S. Deneen until that official fulfilled an earlier promise to appoint a Negro as assistant state's attorney. Deneen appointed Ferdinand L. Barnett, and the appropriation was granted.

In 1897 Carter H. Harrison II was a candidate for mayor. Capitalizing upon the reputation of the elder Harrison as the source from which Negro Democrats had received their first inspiration, his son won considerable Negro support. Shortly after his election, Harrison appointed S. A. T. Watkins assistant city prosecuting attorney, and Robert M. Mitchell was given an appointment of like importance. In spite of the Negro's Republican tradition, young Harrison expressed the belief that "the Negro will divide his vote if the proper intelligence is displayed in seeking it." Harrison continued in office until 1905 and was supported by a large portion of the Negro vote.

Throughout this period Negroes were active in the Republican party also. In 1894 John C. Buckner, a Republican, was elected to the Illinois House of Representatives. Little is known of his background before his election except that he had worked as headwaiter at private parties and had participated in the establishment of the Ninth Battalion, a Negro unit of the State Militia. In 1895 Governor Altgeld accepted the application of this body for transformation into the Eighth Regiment of the Illinois National Guard, with Buckner commanding it as major. He served a second term in the legislature from 1896 to 1898, representing the Fifth Senatorial District.

Following Buckner, William L. Martin, a lawyer, was elected to the legislature in 1898. Martin has been characterized as "just a half-wit wonderfully bright along some lines." His record in the legislature was undistinguished.

The continuity of Negro representation in the Illinois House of Representatives, unbroken since 1882, was maintained in 1900 by the election of John G. Jones. The next Negro member, Edward H. Morris, was so vigorous a personality that the Republicans made him floor leader, "to keep the Speaker out of trouble."

By 1904, the Black Belt's most colorful politician had emerged—Oscar DePriest, later to become a Congressman. He was then holding office as county commissioner. The Chicago *Tribune* smugly charged that DePriest was "a low-grade Negro politician" with no standing in the community; but DePriest, along with Buckner, was a main assistant to Martin B. Madden, the powerful white political boss on the South Side. DePriest's ability as an organizer had attracted the attention of Congressman Madden, and he was placed on the Republican ticket for the office of alderman in the spring of 1904, when the question of representation of the Third Ward came up for discussion in the Republican caucus. DePriest lost, but at least he had been allowed to run.

In 1906 the first Negro made a bid for the office of judge of the Municipal Court. Ferdinand L. Barnett, previously mentioned as editor of the *Conservator,* who had been appointed assistant state's attorney by Deneen, was endorsed by the Chicago Bar Association. Barnett was defeated by white Republicans, who stated openly that they would not support a Negro candidate for judge. He was the only Republican candidate defeated at the polls, losing by 304 votes. Twenty years went by before a Negro secured a judgeship.

In 1910 Edward H. Wright ran against a field of white candidates for alderman of the Second Ward. He, like DePriest, was defeated; but he had demonstrated that a militant Negro leader could attract Negro votes in an area that was rapidly becoming race-conscious. Thus ended the first chapter of the Negro in politics in Chicago.

"BIG BILL"—LITTLE LINCOLN

As we have mentioned in Chapter 6, Negroes became a powerful political force in Midwest Metropolis during the first administration of William Hale Thompson ("Big Bill, the Builder"). Thompson was elected for his first term in 1915, served until 1923, was voted out of office and then returned for a four-year period, 1927-31. The Republican party was riven with factionalism and Thompson needed a solid bloc of votes on which he could depend. The thousands of Negro migrants pouring into the city—poor, feared and despised by large sections of the white community—were welcomed by Thompson as a potential source of votes. He cultivated them, and thus drew the fire of a wide circle of enemies. Of Thompson, Gosnell has said: [1]

As mayor of the city . . . , he was hailed as "Big Bill, the Builder," Chicago's greatest booster, the defender of the weak, the champion of the people, while at the same time in certain newspapers the word "Thompsonism" came to be a symbol for spoils politics, police scandals, school-board scandals, padded pay-rolls, gangster alliances, betrayal of the public trust, bizarre campaign methods, and buffoonery in public office.

But this was not important to the Negro voters, for in Thompson they had at last found someone who valued their friendship and gave them jobs, protection, and, above all, the recognition for which they hungered. In the four primary elections at which Thompson was a candidate for mayor, he received over 80 per cent of the total Republican primary vote cast in the Second Ward, the ward with the largest proportion of Negro votes. In fact, he obtained such a hold over the Negro voters that in 1923, when he was not a candidate, he was able to deliver to William E. Dever, a Democratic candidate, 60 per cent of the Negro vote in the rock-ribbed Republican Second Ward, as a gesture to spite the Republican faction which had dropped him from the ticket.

What was the secret of Thompson's popularity among the Negro voters? [asks Gosnell, who then proceeds to analyze the appeal of "Big Bill."] Thompson's showmanship, bombastic style of oratory, ready platform wit, geniality, and practical ethics appealed to many Negroes as well as to many whites. . . . He was "Big Bill," the mayor, who did not hesitate to stand up for their rights. . . . His opponent was a southern "cracker"; he discriminated against Negroes; he was supported by "the dirty lying sheet, the Chicago *Tribune*." . . . There was clearly a friendly feeling between the chief executive of the city and his listeners. To have a friend in the powerful position who could wrest benefits from a hostile community. That was something worth having. Who else was more deserving of their support? [2]

Another factor that helped Thompson to hold the Negro voters during the postwar period was the hostility of the Democrats. When Thompson promised Negroes jobs and protection, the Democrats used the promise as a means of stirring up race feeling among whites. Calliopes playing "Bye, Bye, Blackbird" were sent through the streets, and leaflets were circulated displaying a trainload of Negroes en route from Georgia with Thompson as pilot of the train, and the caption: "This train will start for Chicago, April 6, if Thompson is elected."

The answer of Negro leaders was: "Elect Big Bill or it's going to be 'Bye, Bye, Blackbird' in Chicago."

But Thompson's popularity was based not alone on his satisfying the Negro community's need for recognition and even for protection. His Honor also gave out jobs. He gave out so many jobs to Negroes that some of his opponents called the City Hall "Uncle Tom's Cabin." Moreover, the Mayor gave Negroes responsible and conspicuous positions. Two of the most important appointments were that of E. H. Wright as assistant corporation counsel and of the Reverend Mr. Archibald Carey to an equally prominent post.

Thompson's rise to political power was coincident with and perhaps partially due to the Great Migration, which lasted from 1915 to 1925. The 1910-20 increase in the Negro population of Midwest Metropolis (from 44,103 to 109,458) amounted to 148 per cent. The following decade it rose by an additional 114 per cent—to 233,903. Most significant politically, however, was the *distribution* of the Negro population in Midwest Metropolis. The trend toward the greater concentration of Negroes in a single area was evident by 1910. At that time the areas with the greatest colored population were about 50 per cent Negro. These were located in wards one to four, the heaviest concentration being in wards two and three. The Black Belt spread till two wards became nearly completely Negro, and in three others the colored group was an important factor. Although the community had always contained persons of widely divergent interests and backgrounds, its compactness had facilitated economic, social, and political solidarity. Because of this, Negroes were able to elect two aldermen to the City Council, two representatives and a senator to the state legislature, and finally a congressman. While Negroes have generally been able to elect colored candidates on citywide tickets, without such rigid residential segregation few of these could have been elected, except in cases where the candidate was not known to be colored or had the staunch backing of the machine in power. As a prominent newspaperman stated in connection with a movement to break down segregation: "It's okay to break it down in principle and get a few Negroes over the line. But we want the majority to stay here so they can vote in a bloc."

This increase in the colored population of the city and the movement to force Negroes into a Black Ghetto were accompanied by much friction and even open violence, as witness the race riot of

1919. All was grist to the mill of Thompson, who with each new difficulty proved to his most consistent supporters that he was "a friend of The Race."

Each new wave of Negro migrants was recruited by the precinct captains, who were diligent about introducing them to the process of voting. Most of the migrants were closely attached to the Republican party, or, because of their southern background, were at least predisposed toward the party of Lincoln and Frederick Douglass. The dramatic appeals of the leaders knitted the community into an almost homogeneous political unit.

During the ten years that followed Thompson's rise to power Negroes made a number of gains. Oscar DePriest was elected to the city council, thus becoming the first Negro alderman. Because of an indictment just before the primary in 1917, DePriest refused to run for re-election, and Louis B. Anderson was nominated and elected with little opposition. Anderson served successive terms in the council for the next sixteen years. In 1918 Major R. R. Jackson, who had served three terms in the General Assembly, was elected alderman of the Second Ward; and when the ward lines were redrawn in 1921 he became the alderman of the Third Ward, in which capacity he served for twenty years. The number of Negroes in the state legislature rose to a peak of five in the lower house in 1928. In the state senate, the first Negro was elected in 1924—Adelbert H. Roberts. Finally, as the acme of achievement through Thompson's assistance, Oscar DePriest was elected to Congress, representing the First Congressional District. An even more difficult achievement, since it necessitated citywide support of a Negro candidate, was the election of Albert B. George as municipal court judge.

In appointive offices, too, Negroes advanced. They were well represented in the law departments of the city and state—in the offices of the city prosecutor, state's attorney, and corporation counsel. The peak of recognition of Negro lawyers came in Thompson's last administration, when six assistant corporation counsels, five assistant city prosecutors, and one assistant state's attorney were appointed. This recognition was due in part to the strategic position of Negroes in the Republican primaries, a factor employed to great advantage by the Negro political leaders in bargaining for places on the ticket and for organizational support. These favorable circumstances also allowed the Negro community to build up one of the smoothest-functioning machines in the city. It was during Thompson's regime that the machines in the Second and Third Wards were taken over by Negroes.

The first evidence that Negroes were strong enough and experienced enough to take over the ward machines was the election of Edward H. Wright as committeeman of the Second Ward in the primary of 1920. This was also the first indication that they had been really admitted into the inner councils of the Republican party, for the ward committeeman was the party's ward representative who distributed the patronage and had the power to nominate certain judges and to send representatives to party conventions. Already the recipient of several appointments at the hands of Mayor Thompson, Wright, although temporarily eclipsed by Alderman DePriest, was the outstanding Negro Republican. When he received the backing of Thompson for ward committeeman his election was assured. He remained the recognized spokesman of the dominant Republican faction for a period of six years.

In the next few years Wright built up one of the strongest ward organizations in the city. He kept a card index of his followers, whom he rewarded with positions or money in accordance with their delivery at the polls. He was able to wrest important jobs and favors from white politicians, and by threatening to vote for white candidates forced other ward committeemen to support his candidate. It was thus that he engineered the election of Judge Albert George in 1924. Later he was able to say, with substantial accuracy, "Every conspicuous political appointment of a colored man or woman in Chicago and Illinois from industrial commissioner and Illinois commerce commissioner down has been brought about by the Second Ward Republican organization under my leadership." Further, through his organization Wright was able to influence legislation. (He even won from the state legislature an act placing a statue in honor of Negro soldiers on one of the boulevards.) When testifying at the hearing of the Senate committee investigating campaign expenditures in 1926, Wright was asked about the Crowe-Barrett group in his ward. He answered: "Well, there isn't any Crowe-Barrett group in my ward . . . I am the group."

Through a factional fight, Wright lost control over the Second Ward soon after this, but the ward organization continued under the leadership of Daniel Jackson, who, it is alleged, was the head of a gambling syndicate. He was never the forceful leader that Wright had been, but he too kept the Second Ward organization a powerful factor in city politics with which all ward leaders had to deal.

In 1923 Mayor Thompson decided not to be a candidate to succeed himself, and William E. Dever, a Democrat, was elected Mayor. (During the "closed town" administration that followed in 1928, Dan Jackson was indicted for protecting gambling.) In 1927, however, Thompson again ran for mayor, receiving 94 per cent of the Republican primary vote and 91 per cent of the general election vote. The end of this term closed the reign of Big Bill Thompson.

If Thompson was not a "second Lincoln," as enthusiastic supporters sometimes called him, at least he had treated his Negro followers more fairly than they had ever been treated before. If he had allowed the community to be corrupted and had put into power Negroes connected with the underworld, he had nevertheless given recognition to the entire Negro population and offered it a hope for the future. If for the entire city he had been a buffoon and a corrupt politician, for Negroes he had made possible their own organization into ward machines which could and did demand concessions in return for support.

THE DEMOCRATS COME INTO POWER

In the mayoralty contest of 1931 Negroes again lined up behind their patron saint, Bill Thompson. Charges and invectives were hurled by Thompson against his opponent, Anton Cermak: "Your mayor is building playgrounds, Cermak is building jails." "Thompson is a public servant; Cermak is a public master." "Cermak fights for the multimillionaires." And Thompson's friends echoed: "Thompson is much poorer now than when he went into politics. Cermak has held public office twenty-eight years, starting as a poor boy, and is now worth seven million dollars." "I earned my money," answered Cermak; "Thompson was born with millions." He further accused Thompson of inciting race prejudice.

Other Republicans on the ticket promised more and better jobs to Negroes: "I will do everything in my power to appoint a Negro to the school board." "If elected I will appoint a colored man deputy coroner." "I will give colored people jobs of responsibility." Still other Republicans promised fair treatment in the courts. One judge said, "If elected judge I will ask to be placed at the Forty-eighth Street Station [in the heart of the Black Belt]. Anyone brought there will get justice." Another suggested: "If any one of you gets into trouble, see me or one of the boys here." Still others made straight party appeals: "This election means more than the election of Thompson. It means the salvation of the Republican party. When it's sunk, you're sunk." In great enthusiasm another white candidate, closing a speech endorsing a Jewish candidate, exclaimed: "With the Jews, Irish, and Negroes together we are going to give them a good licking."

This vigorous campaign with its not too subtly injected race issues succeeded in giving Thompson an overwhelming lead in the Negro wards. Cermak received his lowest relative vote in these wards. But Cermak was elected; and, not having received the support of the Negro community, he was under no obligation to reward it. Numbers of Negroes in important positions and any number who held temporary civil service appointments were dismissed. Although Negroes did not know it, they were facing a national change in political parties which would last for twelve years before the Republicans could make even local inroads.

In 1932 the presidential election was before the community. Again the majority of the Negro voters supported the Republican ticket. Hoover had not altogether pleased them, but they felt that they could take no chance with a Democratic candidate such as Roosevelt, who had served in the Wilson administration, especially as his running mate was "Cactus Jack" Garner of Texas. "Hoover," declared one orator, "is like Booker T. Washington, a man of God who has borne the sorrows of the world." Perhaps a more telling argument was, "If Roosevelt should die you would have 'Cactus Jack' Garner for president." Roosevelt received only an estimated 23 per cent of the Negro vote.

With that election there was a temporary eclipse in the influence of the Negro vote in Chicago. The power of the Second and Third Ward machines was no longer felt, as they were in the wrong column. Without patronage the ward machines began to disintegrate. On the other hand, without patronage—for that matter, without leadership—Negroes could not immediately build up a Democratic machine. The ward committeemanship in the Second Ward was in the control of a white man through a "rotten borough" system. However, one group —the policy men—were quick to shift their allegiance to the new party. Political protection was necessary for them to carry on their business.* By 1933, after a series of raids by the police, the "Jones Boys," who were among the largest operators, found it expedient to join the Democratic party.

Many Negroes were offered jobs and other favors to leave the Republican party. This led to demands for colored candidates on the Democratic ticket in 1934. "Mike" Sneed, who had won the committeemanship in the Third Ward in 1932, began to build a Negro Democratic machine in that ward. In the Second Ward Joe Tittinger, a white man, began to organize his area. With the election of Arthur W. Mitchell to Congress on the Democratic ticket in 1934, the shift to the Democrats was well on its way.

After Cermak's death Edward J. Kelly became mayor. He adopted a conciliatory attitude toward the Negro community. Not only did Mayor Kelly appoint Negroes to positions which had been given them by Mayor Thompson but in addition placed a Negro on the school board, made a Negro captain of the police, and gave still another the chairmanship of the Chicago Housing Authority. Kelly also had a Negro put on the ticket and elected as judge of the municipal court. With the election of William Dawson, a former Republican, as committeeman of the Second Ward to displace Tittinger, the transformation was complete. With less ballyhoo and bombast, Kelly had performed the same feat that Thompson had once performed. The Negro community was as strongly Democratic as it had previously been Republican. However, it remained for the national election to give the final blow to the old saying, "The Republican party is the ship, all else the sea."

WHAT THE NEW DEAL DEALT

Although for years the choice between the Republican and the Democratic parties was for the Negro largely a choice between Tweedledum and Tweedledee, with the coming of the New Deal some very definite issues arose on which Negro and white Democratic candidates could capitalize. The popularity of President Roosevelt is shown by the fact that he performed the miracle of transforming a large proportion of Negro voters from staunch Republicans to zealous supporters of the Democratic ticket. While in 1932 only an estimated 23 per cent of Chicago's Negro vote went to Roosevelt, 49 per cent

* See Chapter 17.

supported him in 1936, and 52 per cent in 1940. Perhaps one of the most important factors in that shift was the WPA. One of the "blues" recorded during that period eulogized this Federal agency:

> Please, Mr. President, listen to what I've got to say:
> You can take away all of the alphabet, but please leave that WPA.
> Now I went to the poll and voted, I know I voted the right way—
> So I'm asking you, Mr. President, don't take away that WPA!

One Negro preacher is reputed to have told his flock, "Let Jesus lead you and Roosevelt feed you!"

The Democrats were not slow in learning to use this appeal to Negro voters. "I want the WPA to stay—this is a fight for your jobs," stated one white candidate. Another argued: "Prosperity is here now. A living is what we all want. If the government spends millions, why should we worry? Riches come from the toilers—what does it matter if it is taken from those who accumulated it from the sweat and toil of the masses?" Against these powerful and persuasive arguments the Republicans had but a feeble answer to their job-hungry constituency: "The present administration is trying to make rich men poor and poor men poorer. The New Deal takes from those who have and gives to those who have not. There is no brotherhood in the present relief set-up." But who was looking for brotherhood when he could get a good WPA job?

One realistic Negro candidate was more adroit in attacking the Democrats. He said: "Fifty per cent of Negroes are out of work. We are the last to get jobs, and we have inadequate relief. Some Negroes who get on WPA are removed for white men. My platform is: jobs, security, better housing, higher wages, cash relief, old-age assistance— thirty dollars or more per month." This candidate decided to steal the Democrats' thunder by ignoring the fundamental differences between the two parties and outbidding the New Deal. Negro Democrats, too, were direct and realistic in exploiting the gains of the New Deal. "I hope," explained an ardent colored Democrat, "that if you are a WPA worker or a relief client, and vote against Roosevelt, the food you get will give you indigestion!"

Thus the policies of the national administration aided Mayor Kelly in his successful attempt to pry loose the Negro vote from the hold which the Republican party had had on it since Emancipation. Roosevelt, Kelly, and the WPA accomplished more with the Negro vote than had Thompson in spite of all the odds in his favor.

DR. WIN-THE-WAR AND HIS BLACK PATIENTS

In the spring of 1942, the President of the United States, in an effort to unify the country behind the war program, held out an olive branch to the conservatives and announced that Dr. New Deal was dead and that Dr. Win-the-War had taken his place. Negro Republicans were jubilant. They had found a chink in the Hero's armor and they let the arrows fly. The remnants of the once powerful Second Ward Republican machine, dreaming of the days of Thompson and Oscar DePriest, launched an attack upon the Democrats which seemed to make sense. "If the New Deal is dead," they argued, "it means that Roosevelt has sold out to Rankin and Bilbo and his gang of lynchers." Precinct workers and Republican leaders began to amass the evidence to document their case. Has the President spoken out against segregation in the army and navy? Has he supported the anti-lynching bill? Has he rebuked southerners who abuse Negro soldiers in uniform? Has he forced factories to employ Negroes on an equal basis with white people? Can Negro women become Lady Marines, Waves, Spars? In 1942 they were able to answer every one of these questions with a resounding NO! Meanwhile a champion arose on the national scene—Wendell Willkie. Without compromise, in straightforward language, and with a vigor that a man out of office could easily afford, Willkie supported a straight frontal attack on army Jim-Crow and on undemocratic practices wherever they existed. Black Metropolis began to listen to the Republicans with renewed interest.

During the four years preceding the presidential election of 1944, Republican hopes were high. Negroes were drifting back into steady jobs. They didn't have to vote for WPA any more. Time after time, southern Democratic Congressmen spewed forth their contempt for Negroes on the floors of Congress. It seemed likely that Negro voters would soon feel that it was time for a change. Republican hopes were raised tremendously by a perceptible drift away from the Democrats in the Illinois congressional elections of 1942 and 1943, and by the city aldermanic and mayoral elections of 1943. It looked as if the good old days of Negro Republican regularity might return. Many

Race Leaders felt that this was a good sign. If Democrats wanted to keep the Negro vote, let them show it by making some wartime concessions.

The first evidences of a swing away from the Democrats came in the congressional elections of 1942. Dawson, Negro Democratic incumbent from Black Metropolis, was fighting to retain the seat in Congress first captured by Republican Oscar DePriest. The Black Belt Republicans had a weak candidate opposing him, but they decided to campaign on the issue of "Why support a party dominated by Rankin and Bilbo?" Then, while the campaign was on, a lynching occurred in Duck Hill, Mississippi. It was one of those particularly horrible episodes in which two Negroes were not only hanged but were also fried to a crisp with blow-torches applied by white hands. Immediately thousands of leaflets flooded the Black Belt depicting the two Negroes hanging from a railroad trestle. Over the picture was a caption to the effect that "if you vote Democratic, you help pull the rope." In addition to this racial appeal, Dawson was bitterly attacked as a "Republican renegade" and a "tin-horn Hitler" who was trying to be a dictator in the Black Belt. Congressman Dawson weathered the storm, but his plurality was several thousand less than it had been before. A white senatorial candidate running on the Democratic ticket with him lost the Black Belt. The swing-back had begun.

In the winter and spring of 1943, the Democratic grip on the Black Belt was further weakened. There were two colored aldermen in the city council. One was a popular lawyer with a citywide reputation as a progressive leader. The Kelly-Nash machine feared him, however, because he was hard to handle. The other colored alderman was a "regular" Democrat, but he had been displaying an alarming amount of independence and was actively seeking CIO support. The regular Democratic machine was not anxious to see either of these men returned to the city council. In a bitterly fought primary campaign the "progressive" lost the nomination to an intelligent but pedestrian organization man. The other alderman managed to squeeze through. The Republicans, aware of this factionalism within the Democratic party, saw an opening and skillfully exploited it in the period between the primaries and the general election. They assailed the Democrats for "dictating the election of a man the Negroes don't want." They invited the defeated liberal to return to his "original home—the Republican party." They hinted that they might run him for Congress eventually. In the other ward, they played a trump card by prevailing upon the old warrior, Oscar DePriest, to emerge from his retirement to run again for alderman as he had first done in 1915. The magic of the DePriest name bowled over the Democratic opponent. Thus, on the local scene, the Republicans succeeded in defeating one Democratic alderman and in destroying the confidence of many Negroes in the sincerity of the Kelly-Nash Democratic machine. All through the campaign they hammered home the fact that southern Negrophobes dominated the national Democratic party.

In the spring of 1943 Midwest Metropolis prepared to elect a mayor. Kelly was very popular and Democrats appealed to Negroes to support their "best friend since Big Bill Thompson." They spent hundreds of dollars reminding the Black Belt of the housing project he had sponsored, the scores of persons he had appointed to various jobs, and his friendly, democratic, unprejudiced attitude toward Negroes. The Mayor himself stressed the fact that he was making plans for plenty of jobs when the Negro soldiers should come home. The Regular organization plugged the straight racial line.

For the first time a new political movement appeared in the Black Belt. Anticipating the organization of the National Citizens Political Action Committee and the CIO Political Action Committee by over a year, the liberal and labor forces in Midwest Metropolis began to experiment with independent political action. The liberals called off their traditional fight against "corrupt machine politics" and supported Mayor Kelly in order to checkmate the isolationist Republicans. The labor unions agreed to forget such incidents as the "Memorial Day Massacre" and to support the pro-Roosevelt Kelly as against the anti-labor Chicago *Tribune* Republicans. Both groups appealed to the Negroes on a broad basis of patriotism and progressivism. Though suspicious of these new allies, the Democrats needed them, and for the first time in Midwest Metropolis a broad coalition of liberal-labor leaders began to appeal to Negroes as political allies.* Black Metropolis be-

* In the light of the charges made a year later that labor political action was dominated by Communists, it is interesting to examine their role in this election. The Democratic party and the CIO frankly accepted the aid of Communists in organizing the electorate for this campaign and depended upon them for much of the onerous detail work, of canvassing and getting out the vote. It would be inaccurate, however, to say that the Communists "dominated" this political activity.

came a sort of experimental laboratory, and the labor action groups set up a headquarters with their card files and canvass books ready to prove that they could swing some of the Negro precincts behind the Democratic candidates.

Mayor Kelly carried the Negro vote, but by the narrowest margin he had ever received in the Black Belt. Without the labor action groups he might have lost it. But local political analysts are inclined to attribute the victory to a piece of clever work by the Regular organization. On the Saturday before the election, the Chicago *Defender* hit the streets with an enormous front-page facsimile of a restrictive covenant which the Republican candidate for mayor had signed barring Negroes from residence in his neighborhood. The exposé was a bombshell. The next day, Sunday, the Republicans sent several hundred thousand copies of a leaflet into the Black Belt implicating Kelly in a restrictive-covenant mess. They entrusted these to a white real-estate man who was a known defender of restrictive covenants, and asked him to deliver them to Oscar DePriest. As he walked up the steps of DePriest's home a strong-arm squad grabbed him and hustled him off to the police station, demanding that he be arraigned on a charge of bringing leaflets into the Black Belt designed to incite a riot. The Monday dailies carried front-page stories reciting the episode in detail and deploring the fact that one of the city's most respected white citizens had been "kidnapped by a band of Negro Democrats." But, in carrying the story, they naturally revealed the contents of the pamphlets and thus advertised the issue—RESTRICTIVE COVENANTS. Hardly a Negro voter could escape reading or hearing about the "kidnapping" of a white real-estate man by Negro Democrats. The Democratic machine denied complicity and dutifully denounced this lawless act. But, on Tuesday when the Negroes went to the polls, many Republican precincts voted against the candidate who had signed a restrictive covenant against Negroes. Kelly was in again, but he knew that his hold on the Black Belt was weakened.

The Democratic machine came out of these three elections somewhat battered. Meanwhile a national election was in the air. The Republicans began to oil up the machine for the great contest. The fact that the Republican convention was to meet in Midwest Metropolis lent added zest. But the Negro Republicans' ardor cooled considerably when it became evident that their champion Wendell Willkie would not be the party standard-bearer. They set to work, however, to build up Dewey as a friend of the Negro and to wait for a Democratic blunder.

Before the Republican hullabaloo had died down, the Democrats were in town for their convention. The Negro Democrats, too, had a champion, the vice-presidential candidate for nomination, Henry A. Wallace. For years the Negro press had reported his every speech and move, admiring him for his forthright defense of Negro rights. They were demoralized when Wallace was sacrificed in the interests of party harmony to Missouri-born Harry Truman. The Republicans immediately threw them on the defensive, with the query "What will happen to Negroes if Roosevelt dies and Truman of Missouri becomes president?"

Throughout the campaign period, both Republicans and Democrats vied in pinning the anti-Negro label on their opponents' candidates, or at least upon the party. The Democrats warned the party bigwigs that the northern Negro vote was in danger. Congressman Dawson of Black Metropolis was ultimately appointed to the Democratic National Committee to help deliver the vote to Roosevelt, and the fight was on.

The break in Roosevelt's favor probably came during the summer of 1944 when a group of transit workers in Philadelphia struck against the upgrading of Negroes. Roosevelt faced a showdown. His own FEPC had been defied. What would he do? The fate of Negro votes in a half-dozen northern cities hung on this episode. Negro Democrats breathed a sigh of relief when the army was ordered into Philadelphia and the Negroes' right to the jobs was upheld. From then on, Negroes throughout the country began to feel that, in a showdown, Dr. Win-the-War would write the effective prescription for his Negro patients. The clincher came a week before the election at a political rally in Chicago.

President Roosevelt came to Chicago on November 4, and the Kelly-Nash machine and the CIO Political Action Committee had 200,000 cheering spectators out to hear him, one of the largest political gatherings in American history. Negroes waited to see if the President would speak the Word. They were not disappointed. Four times within the speech, he struck the blow they were waiting for: He assailed the poll tax; he came out for a *permanent* FEPC; and twice he said that he believed in equal opportunity for all men regardless of race, creed, or *color*. Black Metropolis was jubilant. Roosevelt had waited until he came to the political capital of Negro America to make his pledge.

The next day, Henry Wallace, the repudiated hero, came to Black Metropolis and told a cheering audience that they could depend on the President to buck the Rankins and the Bilbos. Two days later, Black Metropolis gave the Democrats 65 per cent of its vote—the highest percentage Roosevelt had ever gained there.*

In a sense Chicago Negroes were voting to give the Democrats another chance before continuing their swing-back to the Republicans. But they did so only after Roosevelt had said in effect that he had resurrected Dr. New Deal. It is doubtful whether they would ever have extracted such an explicit pledge if the Republicans had not threatened to capture the Negro vote. Negroes in Midwest Metropolis had displayed unusual political maturity.

BLACK METROPOLIS VINDICATES "THE RACE" †

On January 29, 1901, George H. White of North Carolina, last of the Negro Congressmen elected during Reconstruction, made his farewell speech:

This, Mr. Chairman, is perhaps the Negro's temporary farewell to the American Congress; but let me say, Phoenix-like, he will rise up some day and come again. These parting words are in behalf of an outraged, heart-broken, bruised and bleeding, but God-fearing people, faithful, industrious and loyal people—full of potential force.

Negroes in the South had been disfranchised and there were not enough of them concentrated at any one spot in the North to elect a Congressman.

On December 18, 1929, a tall, rugged man, with snow-white hair, raised his six-foot frame from a seat in Congress to make his maiden speech. It was a plea for the passage of a bill to investigate American imperialism in Haiti, a measure supported by a number of southern Democratic legislators. His words dripped with sarcasm:

* Some political analysts feel that the Negro vote was won on patriotic and progressive economic issues rather than political issues. It is difficult to prove or disprove this thesis. The vigor with which both parties stressed *racial* issues would suggest that they were decisive, although Roosevelt's post-war economic program undoubtedly had an important appeal.

† This section is based on H. F. Gosnell's *Negro Politicians,* Chapters 4 and 9 (University of Chicago, 1935), from which comes all the quoted material on the Negro Congressmen.

I am very glad to see the gentlemen on the minority side of the House so very solicitous about the conditions of the black people in Haiti. I wish to God they were equally solicitous about the black people in America.

The speaker's skin was almost white, but he was a "colored" man—Oscar DePriest. A Negro had come again to Congress—after twenty-eight years—and Black Metropolis had sent him.

The story of how the black migrants from the South gathered their strength to fulfill George White's prophecy is a story of machine politics—Chicago style. It is the story of the way in which the "God-fearing people, faithful, industrious, and loyal people" are yoked with the gamblers, the prostitutes, and the demimonde and are led by forceful personalities to the conquest of political power. It is a typical story of politics in the "slum wards" of Midwest Metropolis, but it involves the destinies of thousands who shudder at the thought of "machine politics." It reveals the relationship between democracy and political expediency.

Oscar DePriest was born in Alabama six years after the Civil War closed. His father was a teamster, his mother a part-time laundress. Members of his family were so active in Reconstruction politics that when Negroes were disfranchised after 1875, they had to emigrate to save their lives. They moved to Kansas where young Oscar attended grammar school and took two years of bookkeeping and business at a normal school. Then, at the age of seventeen he struck out on his own and arrived in Chicago four years before the first World's Fair. He earned a living by painting and decorating, a trade he had picked up from his uncles. Since it was difficult for Negro craftsmen to secure steady work he sometimes passed for white. Eventually he met one white employer who not only gave him steady work in spite of his color, but also encouraged him to enter business for himself.

Soon after the turn of the century, DePriest was introduced to the intricacies of Chicago machine politics. He tells the story himself as follows:

A friend of mine came by one evening and said, "Come go to a meeting with me." I had nothing to do, so I went. It was a precinct meeting and they were electing precinct captains. The vote was 20-20 for rival candidates and I saw right away that a deal could be made. So I went to one of the candidates and said: "Now you're the man who ought to be captain—I'll give you two additional votes if you'll make me secretary."

The man refused. I went to his rival and made the same proposition. He accepted. I was made secretary. I kept at it because it was recreation to me. I always like a good fight; the chance, the suspense, interest me. I never gambled nor played cards so it was fun to me.

DePriest caught on quickly. He learned that each of the major parties had its "machine"—a tightly knit, hierarchical organization extending into every city block. At the bottom are the precincts, each with its captain dealing directly with a few hundred voters. The precinct captains owe their allegiance to a ward committeeman who dispenses the campaign funds provided by the city and county party organization, and who directs the campaign in the ward and is responsible to his superiors for delivering the vote. He is the real "boss" of the local area. All the ward committeemen, sitting as a body, make up the county central committee, whose chairman is the recognized head of the "organization." This body dictates policies, raises and supplies campaign funds, and carries out the line laid down by the State party organization. As secretary to a precinct captain, DePriest soon realized that a "machine" rises or falls according to the ability of individual captains to "deliver the vote." And he drew the conclusion that a group of precinct captains who stuck together could bargain with the higher-ups.

Working in the old Second Ward in the period before the First World War, DePriest became familiar with another political fact— that every community institution is dependent upon the machine in power. For instance, a man wishes to open a small business at a spot where the zoning ordinances forbid it. The precinct captain can arrange with the ward committeeman to "fix" it. Or a man may need to do a little "private business" with the Bureau of Licenses. Payment for services rendered or as "insurance" for future service is made through votes as well as actual cash.* "Donations" in cash and kind

* The proprietor of a small grocery described to an interviewer on the Cayton-Warner researches how pressure is sometimes applied to get out the vote:

"The precinct workers didn't know what party I belonged to, and I was determined to let it remain that way, because although I have a small business I find it profitable to be in the good graces of both parties. I have many Republican customers as well as Democratic, and of course these small-fry politicians take their politics very seriously. If it got around I was voting a Democratic ticket, the Republican precinct captain would tell his people not to trade with me. So I didn't want to vote and I told him he was wasting his time arguing with me

are also given for the machine's Christmas basket fund or for picnics and parties.

Within the ward, too, are various types of "protected" businesses— some illegal and some on the borderline. If they are to exist without continual molestation by the police, they must make their peace with the powers that be. Midwest Metropolis has always been a wide-open town, and the political machines have had rather close connections with these institutions of the underworld.*

Every family in a low-income area finds it expedient to "stay in" with the machine. When someone is in trouble, or if there is a problem of getting a bed in the county hospital or the sanitarium, the precinct captain can be depended upon to "fix" the matter. During a depression the machine is helpful in getting immediate relief. A church may have mortgage problems or need some free baptismal water—the committee-man can lend a hand. A social club may want to use a public park for an outing—the ward organization can arrange it. There is no pay-off connected with these favors. Good politics is the art of laying the

because I wasn't going to vote in the primary. I told him I liked —— and would give him a vote but I was very busy.

"He waited around a while then said, 'I see you are operating without any license.' I told him, 'Well, you are going to force me to vote, huh?' 'No,' he said; 'I am not going to force you to vote, but we need your vote and you have just about half an hour to vote, and we would like to have your vote. You would be wise to vote.'

"I went to the polls and voted. I had no alternative. I knew he was smart to discover my not having a license, and he was trying hard to carry his precinct, and the consequences would be much more damaging than voting; so I voted."

* See Chapter 17 for a detailed discussion of the tie-up between the policy racket and politics. One operator of a small gambling set-up described the po-litical connections with the machine in 1939 as follows:

"If you have any idea of entering any sort of racket your best move is to first get in the good graces of the organization [political] and the syndicate [gam-bling organization]. Let's take this district as an example. You know, C—— is the head of it. He is the first man to see. Then he goes to L—— [ward com-mitteeman], and it's so adjusted up the line except the police. Down at the City Hall they have a list of all the places the organization protects. If a place opens and the organization knows nothing of it, when it's reported to them they do not immediately raid it or close it down. The organization notifies the police captain, who goes to the place in operation. He asks for the operator and when he finds him he tells him only one thing and that is, 'You can't operate this place like this. It is unlawful; you had better get yourself straight.' The operator knows exactly what he means and proceeds to 'straighten' himself with the or-ganization by paying off, and when that is done he has nothing else to fear from the police. Every week he pays off for the operation of his place and feels safe and secure."

voters under obligation so that they will deliver at the polls—the art of creating good-will.

For those who wish to be active in politics, however, there are rewards other than favors. People are paid for working the polls on election day; they are given a few dollars to use for drinks and carfare in getting out the vote. If they are intelligent and ambitious there are minor jobs for them at City Hall. And for the favored few there is the chance to win elective office.

DePriest became an expert in handling these intricate community relations and in organizing the energies of the people to support his own political advancement. His first independent political action was to organize a group of precinct captains for bargaining with Martin B. Madden, the white committeeman of the Second Ward. In 1904 De-Priest got the nomination for county commissioner by assuring the ward committeeman of a bloc of votes he needed at the county convention. DePriest then won the election and served for four years, during which time "he helped educate the Negro poor to avail themselves of the relief resources of the county, and as a member of the building committee he secured some important contracts." In 1908 he got caught on the wrong side of a factional fight between his ward committeeman and a state senator; he was punished by being dropped from the ticket.

For the next six years DePriest concentrated upon making some money from his decorating business. He also began to dabble in real estate and "would take a long lease on a building that had been occupied exclusively by whites and then fill it with colored people. Since Negroes were charged higher rents than the whites, this business was profitable. In this way DePriest built up a private fortune which enabled him to become an investor in real estate, stocks and bonds." One observer justified these deals by saying that "if DePriest hadn't gotten it [money from the high rentals], someone else would have." Although he was not too active in politics, DePriest maintained friendly relations with the powerful ward boss, Madden. Three times when Negroes ran for alderman in the City Council during these years, DePriest supported the white candidate backed by Madden. Meanwhile, on the strength of his role as a leading businessman, DePriest was quietly preparing to make his own bid for the City Council.

By 1914 he felt strong enough to try for the aldermanic post. He solicited endorsements, arranged mass meetings, and built up such a large personal following that he was able to present the white Committeeman of the Second Ward with "the endorsements of thirty-eight precinct captains, the Hotel Waiters' Association, the Chicago Colored Barbers' Association, ministers of the Chicago Baptist Churches, ministers of the Chicago Methodist Churches, women's church clubs, the Physicians', Dentists' and Pharmaceutical Club, and many individual party workers." Madden, impressed by his genius for organization, also endorsed him, and thus he was able to run in the primaries as a "regular" candidate. Using his own money, DePriest put up such an effective campaign that he won by a plurality of 11,000 in a field of four candidates competing for 20,000 votes. His victory electrified the Negro community. The *Defender,* which had not supported him enthusiastically at first, now wrote:

In the Second Ward, where the voters of the Afro-American race in large numbers reside, the excitement was at fever heat. The race had one of its own on the ticket for alderman. . . . They came to the front 11,000 strong for Oscar DePriest, and for the first time in the history of Chicago a member of this race will sit in that august body.

DePriest represented the Negro Second Ward adjacent to the notorious First Ward—the city's leading white "vice area." It was impossible to "represent" such a ward without dealing with hundreds of voters who made their living by shady pursuits. It was almost inevitable that Alderman DePriest would be swept up along with others when the Democratic State's Attorney decided to lift the lid on the activities of the Chicago Republican machine. DePriest, along with several others, was indicted in 1917 for "conspiracy to allow gambling houses and houses of prostitution to operate and for bribery of police officers in connection with the protection of these houses." He was defended by none other than Clarence Darrow, who contended that while there had been a passage of money it was not for "protection" but was merely a campaign contribution for Mayor Thompson's Republican machine. He warned the jury against showing race prejudice when they judged DePriest. The verdict was "not guilty," but the machine suggested that Oscar get out of the limelight for a while, and not run again for the City Council.

DePriest had no intention of committing political suicide. The Black Belt was growing by leaps and bounds. There were votes in those pre-

cincts. With the odor of machine "corruption" about him and six in-
dictments still hanging over his head, DePriest made a test run for the
Republican nomination in the primaries and lost. He then proceeded
to organize a "People's Movement" to sponsor him as an independent
candidate, and so vigorous was his campaign that even without any
patronage to dispense he polled 6,000 of the 15,000 votes that were cast.
Hundreds of people saw him as the victim of a plot to defame a hard-
hitting leader. On the strength of his 6,000 followers, DePriest in 1919
went over to the *anti-Thompson* faction of the party and secured its
endorsement for the City Council post. But, although he delivered his
6,000 votes at the polls, they were not enough to pull him through.
The Race Riot that year unified all the competing Negro Republican
politicians around Mayor Thompson, "the friend of the Negro." De-
Priest, too, came back into the fold, where he remained quietly for two
years. *But he did not disband his People's Movement*—his personal
following of at least 6,000 voters.

The Black Belt was growing fast, and after the Race Riot an adjustment was made in ward lines to make more homogeneous Negro political units. DePriest moved the headquarters of his People's Movement into the new Third Ward and began to gather together a personal following there. In 1923, Mayor Thompson did not run, but in
order to show his strength in the Negro community he called upon his
followers to deliver the Negro vote to the Democrats. That the delivery was made is testimony to the hold of both Thompson and De-
Priest on the imagination of the Black Belt voters. DePriest then
quickly made his peace with the very anti-Thompson faction he had
fought—Senator McCormick's group. He delivered the vote to them.

Confident of his growing power, DePriest decided to run two of his
independents against the Republican "regular" candidates for aldermen of the Second and Third Wards. He dramatized the battle as one
of "the Outs" against "the Ins." He charged the incumbents with responsibility for "dirty streets and alleys, the growth of vice, the misery
brought upon the families of the discharged officeholders, the lack of
adequate police protection, the lack of bathing beaches and recreational
facilities." The People's Movement polled about 6,000 votes in each
ward, but its candidates lost. Four times now the DePriest forces had
been routed, but Oscar kept at it.

At this point DePriest began a "crusade" for the restoration of Big
Bill Thompson to power. Ringing doorbells, visiting gambling dens,

speaking at churches, saying the good word to neighbors, the People's Movement preached the Gospel of the Good Old Days when Big Bill, the "Little Lincoln," ran the City Hall. Patiently, one by one, the De-Priest forces gathered Thompson pledge cards. And DePriest paid for much of this activity out of his own pocket. In 1928 Big Bill was again swept into power on a wave of reaction against the closed-town Democratic administration; but he could never have turned the trick without the Black Belt vote. He rewarded DePriest with the coveted prize of the Third Ward—the post of Ward Committeeman. With all the precinct machinery now in his hands and with plenty of patronage to dispense, Oscar immediately used his power to rally the Negroes behind his political mentor, Congressman Madden, in his fight for re-election.

Madden was opposed in the Republican primaries by a young Negro lawyer, a college graduate, and a World War veteran, William L. Dawson. He appealed to the Negroes to send him to Congress:

Mr. Madden, the present Congressman, does not even live in the district. He is a white man. Therefore, for these two reasons if no others, he can hardly voice the hopes, ideals, and sentiments of the majority of the district.

Thompson came into the Black Belt to support Madden, declaring that

a Negro might go to Congress and after serving there for twenty years *might* become chairman of the powerful finance committee; perhaps he might—*perhaps.*

He was surprised when his hitherto loyal Negro supporters hissed and booed him. Yet DePriest supported Madden. For the time being he put party regularity above "race loyalty." He was playing for high stakes and he didn't believe in pressing his shots too hard.

Then one of those rare accidents happened which often speed up a historical trend. Madden died between his nomination in the primaries and the general election. DePriest struck fast and hard. He was out of town, but he wired all of his fellow ward committeemen (the group that would choose Madden's successor) that he expected their support for the job. He then telegraphed Mayor Thompson. As Gosnell phrases it, "DePriest had the nomination before the other aspirants woke up as to what was happening." Big Bill, who had opposed Dawson's candidacy, said a few years later to a Black Belt audience:

"I used to come to you and say to you that Bill Thompson would be the last one who would put his hand on a Negro's head to prevent him from rising higher. Yet I used to ask you to vote for a white man for Congress—the Honorable Martin B. Madden—not because I was for a white man, but because I was for Martin B. Madden, Calvin Coolidge, Len Small, Bill Thompson. Martin B. Madden was fighting to complete the waterway. Why did we keep him there? Because of the great work Madden was doing.

"When he died there came some Judas from Washington and said to me, 'We don't want a Negro Congressman. You're the man that can keep a Negro out of Congress.' I said, 'If I'm the one man who can keep a Negro out of Congress, then, by God, there'll be one there.'"

When the regular election took place DePriest carried the district by the small plurality of 4,000. Several factors helped to reduce the margin of his victory. A Negro independent ran against what he called "disreputable leadership of the gangster, gambler, grafter type." Also, before the campaign was well under way a Special Grand Jury returned an indictment against DePriest for "aiding, abetting, and inducing South Side racketeers to operate gambling houses and disorderly places and to protect them from the police." Many white voters in the Congressional district refused to vote for him. But, small though his margin was, he had the satisfaction of being elected—the first Negro Congressman from a northern state.

There was still the question whether he would ever be allowed to take his seat in Congress. The eyes of the country were on machine politics in Illinois. Only two years earlier, Senator-elect Frank L. Smith had been denied his seat after it was revealed that power-magnate Samuel Insull had put $150,000 into his campaign fund at a time when Smith was head of the state commission in control of public utilities. A few days before Congress convened, the State's Attorney announced that the evidence against DePriest was "insufficient to warrant the defendant's being brought to trial," and the case was dismissed. But the rumor was abroad that certain southern Congressmen planned to challenge DePriest when he was being sworn in. Mrs. McCormick, widow of that Senator McCormick whom DePriest had once supported in a factional fight, got to work behind the scenes in Washington. When Speaker Longworth swore-in the 1928 Congress he broke precedent and swore-in the whole body at one time. The usual procedure was to swear them in in small groups and to allow challenges from fellow Congressmen. The Party looks out for its own!

DePriest remained in Congress for two terms. Then factional quarrels within the Republican party and the Democratic shift in 1932 unseated him. The Democratic machine was now in power. It, too, ran a Negro, Arthur Mitchell, a graduate of Tuskegee. Meanwhile William L. Dawson, whom DePriest had opposed in 1928 in favor of a white man, had come over to the Democrats. He built a strong unit of the Kelly-Nash machine in his Black Belt ward and became ward committeeman. We have already mentioned the prominent part that he ultimately played in both local and national politics. DePriest, however, remained something of a legendary figure, the pioneer who was first to crash the City Hall, and then the halls of Congress.

Negroes throughout America have come to regard the Negro representative from Illinois as their lone "watchdog" in Congress—and as the symbol of their struggle for status.* DePriest defended Negroes with vigorous speeches on the floor. He fought for larger appropriations for Howard University. He defied all attempts at segregation in the Capital City. He was idolized as a fearless man who did not hesitate to travel all through the South speaking straight from the shoulder. He accepted the role of the national champion and enjoyed it. He especially relished an opportunity to pillory the South, as in following comment on certain habits of some white southern males:

I spoke in Nashville, Tennessee. Someone said I should talk on social equality of the races. But the whites of the South are not an appropriate audience for talk of social equality. The Federal census shows an increase by thousands and thousands in the birth of mulattoes, mostly in the South. They have Jim-Crow theater laws and Jim-Crow streetcar laws, but what they need is Jim-Crow bedroom laws.

Arthur W. Mitchell, the Democrat who followed DePriest, was never a popular Congressman, partly because he displayed little of the dash and vigor which DePriest had developed in the hurly-burly of Chicago machine politics. Dawson, who followed Mitchell, while less colorful than DePriest was more forceful than Mitchell. He carried on the tradition of "the fighting Congressman." Negroes, realizing that

* In 1944 New York elected a Negro to Congress, the Rev. A. Clayton Powell.

one Negro Congressman can wield but little actual power, expect him to make up in vigorous language for his inability to influence legislation decisively.

WINNING THE "NEGRO VOTE"

Political expediency is a powerful lever in obtaining some concessions for the Negro from the larger white society. Perhaps the greater part of what white candidates say on the platform before election will not be followed by appropriate action; but it is important for the community that it be said. This not only gives the Negroes some immediate satisfaction but also builds up their expectations (in spite of their cynicism) and makes them demand and expect better treatment than that they have been accorded.

The appeals that white candidates make to obtain Negro votes are varied. Nothing is too "corny" or sentimental to "pull" on the electorate —especially if this helps them to escape a discussion of actual specific problems. Here are a few examples:

"I'm Your Friend:"
When I look over the railing I don't see black or white or red—I see human souls and others to deal with.

The characteristic gratitude of your race will cause you to support those who have helped you.

I have gotten to be the father of the colored people in Chicago in every way. We are making history—your race and mine [Irish].

We must stick together and not abuse one another—the Jew and the Irish stick together.

I am proud to say that I was elected by the colored vote.

Another candidate referred several times to the fact that one of the Negro leaders had said that "he must have Negro blood in his veins." Other white candidates stated:

Thanks for having been placed on the ticket—I am one of you.

I have been a close friend of your alderman for twenty years.

Every colored man should vote for every colored candidate. If you don't vote for them, nobody will.

I am very fond of colored people. I have a Negro chauffeur and a Negro laundry woman.

I don't go around talking about my "black mammy" like my opponent.

If elected, I will work for the fair distribution of patronage.

If you elect me, I will do all I can to obtain jobs for Negroes.

"Don't Desert the Party:"

Roosevelt asks you to send a Democratic Congressman.

Do not bite the hand that feeds you.

My politics is like my religion—I never change. I am careful about serving the Lord and voting the Republican ticket.

The Republican party safeguards your liberty; Democrats don't even know the Lord's Prayer.

If Lincoln were alive today, he would be a Democrat.

The Republican party is like old-time religion—it was good enough for my father and it's good enough for me.

The Republican party is the party for all, regardless of race, color, or creed.

"Bread and Butter:"

I want the WPA to stay—this is a fight for your jobs.

Relief is leading us back into slavery.

"On My Record:"

I will continue to fight for an anti-lynch bill; I appreciate what you have done for me.

Thanks for the vote you gave me in the primary. This means that I am a good servant.

The Negro does not need a master, he needs a servant. That is what I am going to be—your servant.

I have learned a great deal during the four years I have been out of office. I will be a better judge than ever before.

The extent to which some speakers will go in their effort to court the vote is shown in the following instance. The speaker appeared on the platform with a bundle under his arm which, when unfurled, proved to be a banner about three feet square. On it an acrostic with the candidate's name was printed in large letters:

F for faithfulness
E for earnestness
L for loyalty
D for duty
O for obedience to law
T for truth
T for trustworthiness

"Damn the Democrats:"

The Democratic party is controlled by devils from below the Mason-Dixon line.

The Democrats make apologies for having Negroes working in their offices.

Negro candidates are no less dramatic in their appeal for support. They have, however, an advantage. Being colored themselves, they can criticize other Negroes more freely and be much more specific in their promises and demands. Here is what colored candidates say at election time.

Racial Appeal:

The Republicans of today have deserted the true principles of the party as interpreted by Lincoln.

Negro high-school and university graduates need an opportunity to work. If I am elected, I will work for such opportunities.

How can a Negro be a Democrat, like Mrs. Bethune? She can't even walk the sidewalks in Georgia.

My grandmother was forced to bear babies for a white master. How can I be a Democrat?

Let us purge the colored people of all the old-time, reactionary, do-nothing, handkerchief-headed Republicans.

M—— apologizes for being a Negro. I am proud to be a Negro.

When white men are wrong on the race issue, they are wrong on everything.

We want a man in Congress who will tell southern white men, "I am as good as you are."

The Negro should divide his voting strength between the major parties. Political solidarity is a myth.

When Negroes learn not to knife each other, we can hope to get somewhere.

We in the Fourth Ward are going to vote for the first man to elevate black womanhood.

We are not going to vote for any man whose home town will not allow Negroes to get off the train there.

We want the man who if he was not colored would be president of the United States—that sterling American, Oscar DePriest.

These candidates may prate of brotherly love, but to test them, try eating in the same house.

The Negro has a "place," and that "place" is where the Negro can reach.

Five hundred years from now, black men and women will sit in this Congress. It will be done without making the black race white or the white race any blacker.

They say that if you vote for me you can't play policy. That's a lie. How can I be expected to stop policy? If money should be made from Negroes, let a Negro make it and not some out-of-town outside interest.

We don't want humility—we want someone who will have courage to stand up and speak out against indignity and oppression.

Economic Appeal:
The alliance of the Negro to the Democratic party will make it a poor man's party. New blood will help rectify the evils of the party.

The Republicans' theory is to give to those at the top first. Those at the bottom get what trickles through.

Patriotic and Party Appeal:
It is not important who is on the ticket. Party is the important thing.

I am for the Democratic party and for the President, who is trying to make the country so we will be proud to say, "I am an American."

In their effort to influence the voters of the community to support them, these appeals are made by the formal political organizations and the leaders of the informal and temporary alliances which have been made with business interests, churches, voluntary organizations, and the underworld. The most spectacular method of appealing for the vote is through the political meeting.

THE POLITICAL MEETING

One writer has compared the political meetings in the Negro community to the religious revival or the camp meeting. They are, Gosnell points out,[3] charged with great emotional appeal: A Negro mass audience is attentive, enthusiastic, good-natured, and content to sit for many hours on uncomfortable seats. When a speaker says something which strikes a popular chord, people yell, clap, or wave programs, hats, or hands in the air. Politics is evidently something which is very close to their experiences and their racial aspirations. They act as if their jobs, their freedom, their right to vote, their happiness, their very lives almost are at stake unless their candidates win.

The following is an account of a meeting held at the height of the Depression before Dawson shifted to the Democratic party and displaced Mitchell as Congressman.

The meeting was in a very large room in an old, dilapidated building probably at one time a dance hall. Between 250 and 300 persons were present, most of them workers and precinct captains in Alderman Dawson's organization. They seemed to be a rather poor, forlorn group for the most part, running from middle-aged to elderly, with a few young people scattered here and there. Apparently they were mostly southern migrants who still clung to the old traditional Republican ideology.

The first speaker was an elderly gentleman, a rock-ribbed Republican, a long-time member of the Second Ward organization. He said:

"We are worshiping a great cause. If I were a preacher I would take a text in the Psalms: 'Oh, how well it is for men to dwell together in unity! We need prayer more than anything else on earth. A lot of our folks seem hypocrites because of the misfortune that befell them here in Illinois, the home of Lincoln, who cut the shackles from the legs of your grandparents and made it possible for us to be here above the Mason-Dixon line. We should give some credit to the Republican party. Of course you have a right to be anything—Communist, Socialist, even Democrat; but first you should consult God. We are tired of white people using us as drawers of water and hewers of wood. In this cruel world no one loves anybody. They only crave for dollars. We are not as interested in this fight as we ought to be—there are too many empty chairs.

"I was in Mitchell's [Negro congressman] office and had a talk with him for two hours. He gave me some of his speeches and told me he gave 50 white boys jobs and 50 colored boys jobs. Now I am not prejudiced, but I asked Mr. Mitchell, 'Do you think you are doing us justice?' There are 434 white Congressmen to look out for the whites. We have fifteen million Negroes in America to help. Friends, get your heart in this thing!"

Another speaker took the floor:

"We are leaders of a family. Our family has become separated in the last four or five years. A lot of us cannot stand pressure. Yet it is painful to have a lot of children and they crying for food and bread. People have left their party affiliations—many have gone Socialist, Communist; some have turned their backs on the Republican ticket and turned Democrats because of poverty, hunger, and lack of work. It reminds me of the parable of Abraham just as he was about to sacrifice his son on an altar but a hand stayed him. I thought about that today downtown in the City Hall in the Council Chamber.

"There are many people now on WPA, some making $85 and some $105. All of that money comes from Washington. Send Dawson to Washington to get us more money."

This talk was followed by music. Miss Pitts of the Ninety-ninth Precinct sang "I'll Tell It Wherever I Go."

Dawson then addressed the meeting and introduced Stanton DePriest, son of Oscar DePriest, the first Negro Congressman from Chicago. DePriest said:

"History is repeating itself.

> Lives of great men all remind us
> We can make our lives sublime,
> And departing leave behind us
> Footprints on the sands of time.

You know and I know the dire necessity of having a county commissioner. For thirty years we have been deprived of representation. You all know the slogan on which our government is founded, 'Taxation without representation is tyranny.' The same is true today, and I will be your county commissioner after November 8. The conditions are terrible at the county hospital. It is all the fault of the Democrats. The Democrats never played fair with the black man."

DePriest was followed by Representative Harewood of the state legislature (a Negro), who said:

"PWA, WPA, relief, etc., is here to stay. We need a man who can
get the most for us. We need Dawson to protect us from American
Fascists. We need more men like Dawson in the high councils of the
Republican party."

Evangelist Essie Whitman was called on to sing two original songs she
had composed about Dawson.

Dawson said: "We must have a record made of those songs. I like the
part she sang about Mitchell having to grow up."

Mrs. Keller then addressed the meeting:

"It is up to us to make Mitchell moan and groan. We should give him
the cramps because he has done nothing for us. Dawson is the man of
the people and for the people. He is a friend of his race and the champion
of his people. We need he-men of this black group to represent us. It is
only seventy-five years this side of Emancipation—Lincoln would roll over
in his grave. It is time we woke up our racial pride and sent Dawson to
Congress. We want a fearless man to fight for the black race."

Two solos followed: "The World Is Mine Tonight," dedicated to the
Republican party, and "Without a Song," dedicated to the Democratic
party.

Alderman Robert R. Jackson closed the meeting with these stirring
words:

"We must stick together to get somewhere as a race. Every Jew will
hunt for and vote for a Jew. The same for the Irish and every other race.
The Negro can't find a Negro's name to save his life. Look for his name
until you find it! He's your own flesh and blood, and nobody is going
to vote for him if you don't. We are going into the Second Ward to
help William L. Dawson—by telephone, telegraph, and tell-a-woman, the
great agencies of communication in the world."

The Republicans were not strong enough to send Dawson to Congress, despite their enthusiasm. He shifted his party and the Democrats sent him to Washington!

Much of the political history of Midwest Metropolis has involved
the fight of reform groups against "machine politics." Negroes, as a
low-income group, looked down upon by the white middle class and
feared by white labor, have seldom supported the reformers. They
have preferred to deal with hardheaded realists who are willing to

trade political positions and favorable legislation for votes. A cynical realism has pervaded Black Metropolis which sees democracy as something granted to Negroes on the basis of political expediency rather than as a right. In the past this has meant dealing with "corrupt" machines, and even the clergy have not hesitated to play the game.*

Since 1930, the local Democratic machine has been tremendously influenced by the tone of national "welfare politics" and by the growing influence of the industrial unions. The "sordid" aspects of political life still remain; but, as large sections of the Negro electorate have come under the influence of labor political action groups, the general level of political life has been appreciably raised. So long, however, as Midwest Metropolis is run by a machine, Black Metropolis will reflect, in microcosm, the pattern of the city's political life—in fact, it reflects, and refracts, every aspect of the larger city's life.

* There have been one or two very prominent Negro clergymen closely associated with the Republican machine. One of these, a bishop, was appointed to the Civil Service Commission, and like DePriest became involved in bribery scandals.

Black Metropolis 1961

BLACK METROPOLIS WAS ORIGINALLY PUBLISHED DURING THE LAST YEAR OF the second World War. The final chapter, "Of Things to Come," was followed by "A Methodological Note" by Professor W. L. Warner (See Volume II). Both statements reflect the extent to which sociologists and anthropologists were then stepping out of their professional roles to discuss the implications of their findings for a democratic society, and to state their own values.

Remembering the situation after the First World War, the authors expressed their fear that unless full employment was maintained, there was danger of interracial violence after the Second World War. They listed a number of preventive measures which they felt were essential, including the progressive elimination of discrimination and segregation, and a constant interpretation of the Negro's needs to the wider community. Their view of the future was tinged with pessimism.

Professor Warner, on the other hand, was optimistic. He was convinced that ". . . there are indications throughout the world that important changes are on the way . . . the next generation's principal task will be the hard and painful one of destroying color-caste in the United States."

The period between 1950 and 1960 was one of great prosperity for Midwest Metropolis, and although the Negro unemployment rate tends to be three times that of white workers, Negroes have shared in this prosperity. On the national scene, the decade has marked the opening of the Era of Integration. It is relevant to ask how Black Metropolis has fared during this period.

MIDWEST METROPOLIS—POST WAR BOOM

Midwest Metropolis, still "Hog Butcher for the World," is gradually relinquishing its role as "Meat Packer." Still "Player With Railroads and Freight Handler to the Nation," it prefers now to boast of its Midway Airport which handles a larger volume of traffic than any in the nation, and of the larger airport being built. There is hope, too, that the opening of the St. Lawrence Seaway will make Midwest Metropolis a major port. Chicago's metropolitan region is still a top producer of steel (1955 was a peak production year). But the Midwest Metropolis of today is proudest of its new diversified light manufacturing industries, especially in the electrical equipment field. Dreams for the city's future revolve around the prospect of its becoming a major supplier of industrial products to the markets of Asia, Africa, Latin America and Europe. Leaders in Black Metropolis are deeply concerned over the question of where the Negro fits into this vision of the future.

During the past decade, Midwest Metropolis has placed very heavy emphasis upon "urban renewal." Acres of slums have been cleared and gleaming structures of glass and stone and steel have grown from the rubble. The city has taken full advantage of Federal aid for such improvements. New skyscrapers have sprouted on the skyline. Thousands of new homes have sprung up on vacant prairie lots. A web of new highways and super-highways has been woven across the city's vast expanse to handle the terrifying glut of traffic. These highly visible symbols of unprecedented prosperity have sustained and increased the boastful mood of optimism which has always been characteristic of the city. But there has been apprehension in Black Metropolis.

MIDWEST METROPOLIS HAS BECOME "MORE COLORED"

Rapid expansion and diversification of industry, as well as vast public and private programs of building construction during the 1950–60 decade, demanded a constant influx of new workers. As in the past, Negro Americans came to Chicago to meet that need. The Negro population doubled between 1950 and 1960.

In 1840, when the Flight to Freedom was just beginning and Chicago stood as a City of Refuge for runaway slaves, there were only 53 Negroes in the city. Today there are over 800,000. In 1840, there were only 4,470 people in Midwest Metropolis, and of these only about one in a hundred was a Negro. Today, there are over 3,000,000 residents, and almost one out of every four is a Negro.

The Negro population increased from 492,000 to 813,000 between 1950 and 1960. At least 60,000 were migrants from the South. But not all of the increase in Negro population has come by immigration, for the more Negroes in the city the more the population increases through the excess of births over deaths.

While the Negro population has been increasing, the white population within the city limits of Midwest Metropolis has been decreasing. There were 3,112,000 white residents in 1950. In 1960 there were only 2,713,000. The main factor in this population decline has been the flight to the suburbs. If we take the entire Midwest Metropolitan Region into consideration as a unit we will find that the proportion of people who live in the city, as opposed to the "ring" around it, was about 70 per cent in 1940 and 65 per cent in 1950. It was even less in 1960, about one half of the total population of city and suburbs. Most of the people who moved to the suburbs were white. On the whole, Negroes are decidedly not welcome in Suburbia.

THE JOB CEILING STILL EXISTS

Black Metropolis emphasizes the fact that the occupational distribution of Negroes in Midwest Metropolis has never been so fixed and rigid as in the South, and that through the years several factors have operated to widen the range of jobs available to Negroes.[1] As groups of whites move up into the best jobs, Negroes sometimes get better ones. Constant pressure by Negro and interracial organizations occasionally results in categories of work, formerly earmarked as "white" jobs, being thrown open to free competition. The continuing acquisition of higher levels of education and skill by Negroes makes it less easy to bar them from posts for which they are fitted. The whole process of change is sped up by periodic labor shortages and by the operation of "law as a lever" (e.g., the new Illinois state FEPC law); "profit as a prod" (use of Negro salesmen to entice more Negro customers); "government as an example," (a wide range of federal, state, and municipal jobs are open to Negroes, and political appointments of Negroes have been made to new types of posts); and "catastrophe as a catalyst" (the Korean War and the threat of a Third World War).

[1] Professor Warner, in his Methodological Note (see Volume II), stressed similarities between the social systems of the South and the North. The authors were more impressed by the differences. The theoretical framework which guided their analysis of Negro-white relations in Chicago (as opposed to the internal structure of the Negro community) has been stated in an article by Horace Cayton and Elaine Ogden, "Research on the Urban Negro," in *The American Journal of Sociology* for September, 1941.

It is relevant to ask how effective these forces have been during the past decade in effecting changes in the Job Ceiling.[2]

An examination of the occupational pyramids in Figure 21a reveals that Negroes found new opportunities in commerce and industry between 1940 and 1950.[3] The proportion of employed Negro men doing various kinds of "service" work (e.g., cleaning, carrying and cooking) dropped from about one person in three to about one in five. The proportion employed in industry rose. But there was no significant change in the category of skilled labor (craftsmen, mechanics, foremen). One out of every five white men were doing such work in 1950, but only one out of every ten Negro men were. The proportions were relatively about the same in 1960.

The most dramatic and significant change has involved the status of employed Negro women. Between 1940 and 1950, the proportion of Negro women in service occupations dropped from almost two out of three to *one* in three. The proportion employed as semi-skilled operatives in industry increased greatly, while at the same time the proportion of Negro women doing clerical work doubled. But despite these very substantial changes, less than 15 per cent of colored women were employed in clerical and sales work in 1950, while over half of all employed white women worked in these fields. By 1960, the proportion of Negro women doing clerical and sales work had risen to about 24 per cent, but at this slow rate it would take almost thirty years for Negro women to "catch up" with white women in these fields! Differences in degree of training and experience may account, in part, for this striking contrast, but such a wide gap is certainly related also to the fact that the city's offices and stores, by 1950, were not

[2] The concept of the "Job Ceiling" is developed in Chapter 9. See Figures 15 and 16 on pages 227 and 228, in which the proportions of Negroes and whites holding jobs above and below the skilled labor level are compared by means of bar graphs. The Job Ceiling was just below the skilled labor level in both 1940 and 1950. Figure 19 on page 253 attempts to make graphic the fact that there was wider opportunity for rising above the ceiling in government employment than in other fields.

[3] The data upon which the occupational pyramids are based may be found in publications by Otis D. and Beverly Duncan, *The Negro Population of Chicago* (University of Chicago Press, 1957), and a report prepared by these two scholars for the Office of the Housing and Redevelopment Co-ordinator and the Chicago Plan Commission, *Chicago's Negro Population*, 1956. The 1960 census data were not available in time to permit presentation of comparable occupational pyramids, but the text has been revised to include some statistics figured from *U.S. Census of Population: 1960, Illinois General Social and Economic Characteristics, Tables 74 and 78.*

Figure 21a

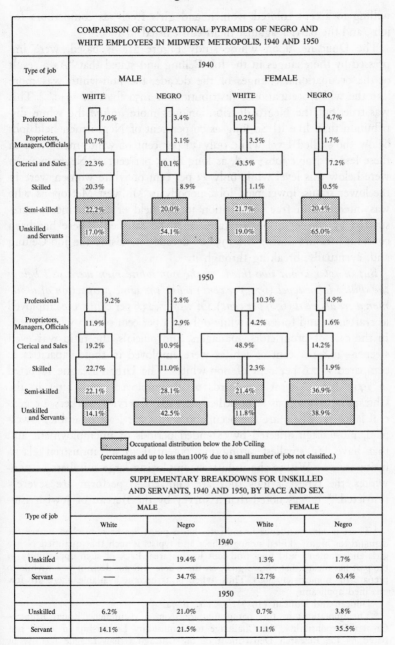

COMPARISON OF OCCUPATIONAL PYRAMIDS OF NEGRO AND
WHITE EMPLOYEES IN MIDWEST METROPOLIS, 1940 AND 1950

1940

Type of job	MALE		FEMALE	
	WHITE	NEGRO	WHITE	NEGRO
Professional	7.0%	3.4%	10.2%	4.7%
Proprietors, Managers, Officials	10.7%	3.1%	3.5%	1.7%
Clerical and Sales	22.3%	10.1%	43.5%	7.2%
Skilled	20.3%	8.9%	1.1%	0.5%
Semi-skilled	22.2%	20.0%	21.7%	20.4%
Unskilled and Servants	17.0%	54.1%	19.0%	65.0%

1950

Type of job	MALE		FEMALE	
	WHITE	NEGRO	WHITE	NEGRO
Professional	9.2%	2.8%	10.3%	4.9%
Proprietors, Managers, Officials	11.9%	2.9%	4.2%	1.6%
Clerical and Sales	19.2%	10.9%	48.9%	14.2%
Skilled	22.7%	11.0%	2.3%	1.9%
Semi-skilled	22.1%	28.1%	21.4%	36.9%
Unskilled and Servants	14.1%	42.5%	11.8%	38.9%

▓ Occupational distribution below the Job Ceiling

(percentages add up to less than 100% due to a small number of jobs not classified.)

SUPPLEMENTARY BREAKDOWNS FOR UNSKILLED AND SERVANTS, 1940 AND 1950, BY RACE AND SEX

Type of job	MALE		FEMALE	
	White	Negro	White	Negro
1940				
Unskilled	—	19.4%	1.3%	1.7%
Servant	—	34.7%	12.7%	63.4%
1950				
Unskilled	6.2%	21.0%	0.7%	3.8%
Servant	14.1%	21.5%	11.1%	35.5%

willing to accept colored women and girls freely as competitors for jobs, and the barrier against them still existed in 1960.[4]

The Duncans, upon whose study Figure 21a is based, were impressed by the changes in the Job Ceiling and stated that "As a result of the occupational changes of the decade, the non-white was more like the white occupational distribution in 1950 than in 1940."[5] This was true, but the Negro distribution was more *unlike* the white distribution than like it! So long as 70 per cent of Negro men held jobs below the skilled level while only 36 per cent of white men were in these less desirable jobs; and, as long as 75 per cent of Negro women were below this level while only 33 per cent of white women were in the lower status, lower paid jobs, nobody in Midwest Metropolis who was interested in free competition in the field of employment, unrestricted by considerations of race, could be satisfied. There has been constant pressure during the 1950–60 decade for raising the Job Ceiling and, eventually, breaking through it.

But in 1960, about two-thirds of the non-white men were still below the skilled labor level (67.3 per cent) while the same proportion of white men were above it (67.9 per cent). Of whites, 23.6 per cent were employed as craftsmen and foremen, while only 12.3 per cent of non-whites were. In the case of proprietors, managers, and officials, the ratio was even steeper—12.8 per cent of whites were employed in these capacities as compared to 2.6 per cent of non-whites. The Urban League reported in 1961 that "Almost two-thirds of all employed non-whites in the Chicago area work as semi-skilled operatives, service workers, or general laborers. These are the occupations that are least desirable, lowest paid, most often affected by extended periods of unemployment and that have the smallest promotion potential in all industrial classifications. . . . Within the industries employing large numbers of non-whites, the types of jobs they are allowed to perform are severely restricted."[6] It was noted that a survey by the Bureau of Jewish Em-

---

[4] There is some evidence to indicate that a point has been reached where the demand for highly skilled stenographers and typists is such that qualified Negro girls and women could now find jobs in this area. Lack of such opportunity in the past has meant that Negro girls, on the whole, did not deem it worthwhile to prepare for non-existent jobs. Thus, when posts become available, there are few qualified applicants.

[5] Duncan and Duncan (1957), *op. cit.,* p. 74.

[6] The quotations in this paragraph are from a pamphlet, "Equal Rights— Greater Responsibility, the Challenge to Community Leadership in 1961" prepared by the Research Department of the Chicago Urban League for use by participants in a Leadership Conference for Fair Employment practices.

ployment Problems of Chicago revealed that "98 per cent of the white collar job orders received from over 5,000 companies were not available to qualified Negroes." The following industries were cited as those which "seriously limit" the employment of non-whites: banking and finance, insurance, airlines, electrical equipment manufacturing, printing and publishing, chemicals and petroleum, railroads and trucking, medical and health services and construction. These are Chicago's most rapidly expanding industries.[7]

Even in those areas where Negroes have secured a sure foothold and some mobility their position is precarious. A fifth of all Negro workers are concentrated in the metal and food production industries and the Urban League reported in 1961 that "both of these industry groups have declined substantially as a proportion of total employment in the Chicago area since 1950. The shift of large packing plants to other cities in the mid-west, the increase in automation, and lack of opportunity for apprenticeship and for retraining, is creating a situation which during periods of unemployment over the past decade has resulted in a Negro unemployment rate three times that of white workers." Some observers feel that unemployment among Negroes may become chronic during the next decade unless pressures from the Federal and State government open up new areas of opportunity.

By 1960, it was almost impossible to find any leading or responsible citizen in Midwest Metropolis who would defend discrimination in employment on the basis of race or creed. There was a widespread tendency to speak of "the high cost of discrimination" as measured in terms of potential skills not utilized[8] and the exacerbation of social

[7] The Urban League, while taking note of the social pressures within Bronzeville to drop out of school early in order to secure the consumption goods necessary for status, as well as to help add to already low family incomes, feels that there is evidence from studies made of high school drop-outs and junior college students to support the conclusion that Negro students "feel little drive to prepare for occupations in which there is little hope of obtaining employment." They state further, that "Many trainee and apprenticeship programs of companies and unions do not admit non-white youths" and that work-study programs under the auspices of the Chicago Board of Education "cannot be extended in any meaningful way to schools with predominantly non-white students because business and industry will not accept these students." (*"Equal Rights Greater Responsibility,"* Urban League, 1961.) The process becomes circular because when students feel they cannot get jobs they will not prepare and thus when jobs do open up there are few Negro applicants who are qualified.

[8] The most militant fighters against discrimination have conceded the fact that individuals are "piercing the ceiling" at an increased rate, but the Urban League stated its belief that the "progress" often referred to with respect to economic opportunities for non-whites reflects placement of a "select few" or "window dressing placement" in the "non-traditional" employment of Negroes.

problems due to low incomes and uncertain employment among Negroes.[9] There was a general feeling, too, that the whole problem should be redefined in *individual* terms, that no one should be denied the opportunity to work at the highest level of his skill and training no matter what people might think of the Negro group as a whole. The result has been some token employment as well as support for legislation to ensure equality of economic opportunity.

A STATE FEPC NOW OPERATES

By 1961, Negro leaders and white liberals in Midwest Metropolis had succeeded in convincing Illinois' powerful Democratic politicians that the Job Ceiling could never be broken without the aid of a state Fair Employment Practices law and that the Negro voters wanted it. FEPC legislation had passed the House of the Illinois State Legislature in 1947, 1949, 1951, 1953, 1955, 1957, and 1959. However, it had always been "killed" in the Senate. But in 1961, a bill passed the Senate as well as the House and added a new weapon to the arsenal of those fighting discrimination.

The campaign for FEPC legislation was led by a statewide committee with an official of a major steel manufacturing company as its chairman. Businessmen's fears were assuaged by pointing out that

[9] Probably no aspect of the life of Black Metropolis has received more publicity in recent years than the small group of unmarried and deserted women who are receiving Aid to Dependent Children funds. It was alleged that these women were making a racket out of "having more and more babies at public expense" and were "supporting lazy boy friends," etc. Eventually a committee headed by a leading white businessman was set up to investigate the problem; its report has emphasized the extent to which the plight of these broken families is bound up with the existence of the Job Ceiling and the Black Ghetto. The report stated in part:

> Racial discrimination in employment was found to be one of the most serious direct and indirect causes of family disorganization, desertion and illegitimacy. . . . Racial discrimination is one of the most serious causes of family breakdown, desertion and ADC dependency. . . . The great majority had unskilled jobs. The last job for 50 per cent of the grantees was in domestic service. . . . 54 per cent were on the last job more than one year and 18 per cent more than 3 years. The median monthly earning on the last job was rather small for these mothers: $162.22. . . . ADC families live in generally substandard housing at high rentals. The rent allowance is the most generous part of the ADC budget, yet ADC families usually live in over-crowded, rundown buildings. Many are ingenious in making the inside attractive, but the outside is most often slum. The rent paid by non-white families for poorer housing is considerably more than that paid by white families. (Summarized from *Equal Rights—Greater Responsibilities,* Chicago Urban League publication, 1961.)

where FEPC legislation did exist in the United States the emphasis was upon "education, co-operation, conciliation, and full hearings" rather than lawsuits and punitive measures. It was pointed out, too, that nineteen states had passed such legislation without any disastrous effects upon business. There was widespread surprise when, in April, 1961, the Chicago *Daily News* carried an editorial, *FEPC GAINING IN ACCEPTANCE,* which advocated passage of the bill. The editorial referred to a very significant fact, namely, that the board of the Chicago Association of Commerce and Industry had "accepted FEPC in principle, although rejecting some provisions of the pending legislation."

Employers who had already opened the door wider to Negroes felt that their more reluctant colleagues deserved a legislative prod. Employers who were inclined to employ Negroes welcomed the FEPC as a stick with which to beat recalcitrant unions. While no one believed that the passage of the bill would work an overnight revolution many hoped that it might be the beginning of the end of the Job Ceiling in Midwest Metropolis.

NEGRO PURCHASING POWER INCREASES

Although the Job Ceiling did not disappear between 1945 and 1960, large-scale Negro unemployment did, and there was also a significant amount of upgrading below the skilled labor level. *Negro family income increased by 50 per cent between 1950 and 1956 while white family income increased by only 28 per cent.* But even with this increase, the median income for Negroes was only $4,200 per year while that for whites was $5,900. The significance of these increases can be measured in the Negro's improved standard of living since *Black Metropolis* first appeared, and in the wider base presented for living the middle-class way of life. Figure 21b suggests the far-reaching implications of changes-in-income levels for the Negro social class structure.[10] By 1960 the median family income for Midwest Metropolis had increased to $7,342; for Black Metropolis to $4,786.

There is evidence that Negroes spend a disproportionately high amount of this income for inadequate housing. One reliable source reports that:

[10] The increase in purchasing power also strengthened Negro publications in their appeal for advertising, and groups bargaining for better job opportunities for Negroes. As early as 1953, a study was published for the benefit of the general business world, Nickolas L. Barnes', *Some Potentialities and Limitations of the Negro Market in Chicago* (T and T Publishing Company, Chicago).

. . . it is clear that non-white families receive less "quality" per dollar spent on housing than do white families; and the relatively high proportion of non-white families in substandard housing can be attributed only in small part to their relative economic disadvantage (i.e., they are able to pay for better housing than they can secure). Non-white families apparently obtain no more space per housing dollar than do white families, but the space which they obtain is likely to be of poorer quality. In Chicago, non-whites are more than twice as likely as whites to be living in substandard housing if they are renters, six times as likely if they are home owners.[11]

Figure 21b

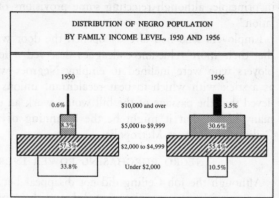

DISTRIBUTION OF NEGRO POPULATION
BY FAMILY INCOME LEVEL, 1950 AND 1956

1950		1956
0.6%	$10,000 and over	3.5%
3.3%	$5,000 to $9,999	30.6%
51.3%	$2,000 to $4,999	55.4%
33.8%	Under $2,000	10.5%

The fact that a much larger proportion of Negroes than whites is still in lower status occupations and in lower income groups tends to perpetuate the image of *The Negro* as being "below" or "inferior to" whites. It also makes much much harder the assemblying by Negro families and community organizations of resources for coping effectively with problems such as crime, juvenile delinquency and family disorganization. The total situation forces whites in Black Metropolis to think of Negroes as "undesirable neighbors." Thus, the Job Ceiling is one factor in creating conditions which lead to the persistence of a Black Ghetto.

THE BLACK GHETTO EXPANDS

Chapter 8 of *Black Metropolis* tells the story of how a "Black Belt" came into existence, and how Negroes were kept within it by the operation of restrictive covenants. Less than three years after the book was published, the Supreme Court of the United States declared re-

[11] Duncan, Beverly and Hauser, Philip M., *Housing a Metropolis* (The Free Press, 1960), pp. 193, 196 and 207.

Figure 21c

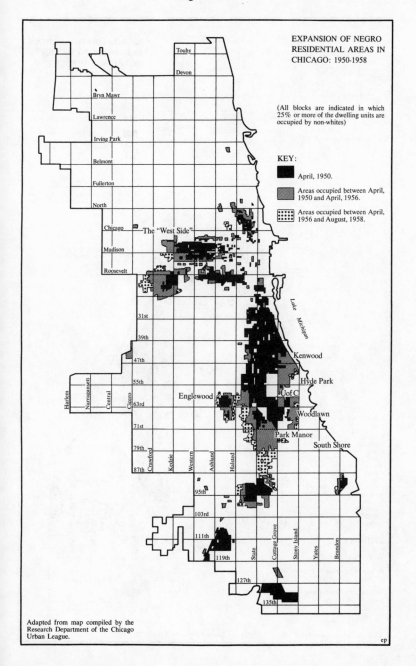

EXPANSION OF NEGRO
RESIDENTIAL AREAS IN
CHICAGO: 1950-1958

(All blocks are indicated in which
25% or more of the dwelling units are
occupied by non-whites)

KEY:

■ April, 1950.

▨ Areas occupied between April,
1950 and April, 1956.

▦ Areas occupied between April,
1956 and August, 1958.

Adapted from map compiled by the
Research Department of the Chicago
Urban League.

Figure 21d

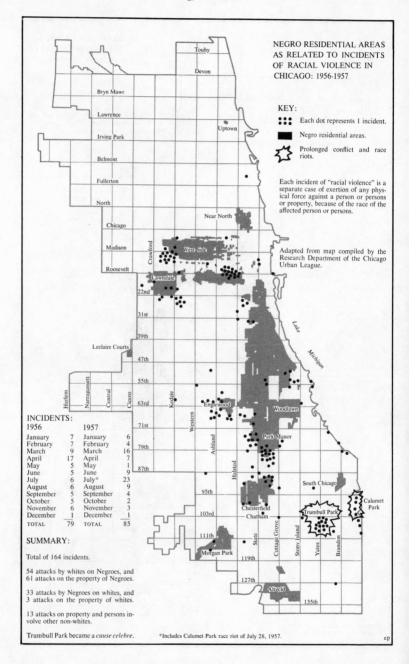

NEGRO RESIDENTIAL AREAS
AS RELATED TO INCIDENTS
OF RACIAL VIOLENCE IN
CHICAGO: 1956-1957

KEY:

••• Each dot represents 1 incident.

■ Negro residential areas.

✦ Prolonged conflict and race riots.

Each incident of "racial violence" is a separate case of exertion of any physical force against a person or persons or property, because of the race of the affected person or persons.

Adapted from map compiled by the Research Department of the Chicago Urban League.

INCIDENTS:

1956		1957	
January	7	January	6
February	7	February	4
March	9	March	16
April	17	April	7
May	5	May	1
June	5	June	9
July	6	July*	23
August	6	August	9
September	5	September	4
October	5	October	2
November	6	November	3
December	1	December	1
TOTAL	79	TOTAL	85

SUMMARY:

Total of 164 incidents.

54 attacks by whites on Negroes, and 61 attacks on the property of Negroes.

33 attacks by Negroes on whites, and 3 attacks on the property of whites.

13 attacks on property and persons involve other non-whites.

Trumbull Park became a *cause celebre*.

*Includes Calumet Park race riot of July 28, 1957.

ep

strictive covenants unenforceable in the courts. Covenants were still legal but now had to be enforced by private action. In some areas of Midwest Metropolis the action was violent, but neither frantic appeals to "Keep This Neighborhood White" nor violence prevented the expansion of the Black Belt. Figure 21c shows how the Negro population spread out between April of 1950 and August of 1958.[12]

The expansion took place in three main directions: (a) on the West Side where a small Negro settlement grew rapidly as Negroes of all social classes began to occupy houses and apartments relinquished by a predominantly Jewish population which moved northward and to the suburbs. Scattered violence accompanied this shift; (b) toward Lake Michigan to the east and south, as the Negro population filtered into Kenwood and Hyde Park and then made a jump around the University of Chicago into Woodlawn. Here, there was very little violent resistance; and (c) directly southward from the tip of the 1950 "Black Belt" and west into Englewood. Here the white population fought a bitter rearguard action with fire and bomb as the main weapons, and gang and mob harassment as a supporting measure. Figure 21d indicates the extent of the violence during a two-year period, 1956 and 1957.[13] There were 36 additional attacks upon Negro property in 1958, but the amount of violence began to diminish after that year.

Rapid expansion of the Black Belt after 1948 was due to the Negro's willingness—and ability—to pay inflated prices for property and to the awareness of real estate men (Negro and white) that larger profits per unit could be made from renting to Negroes than from renting to whites.[14] Many white owners were willing to sell or to move away

---

[12] Cf. pp. 62–64, "Black Lebensraum."

[13] Cf. with map on p. 63. Note that the patterning of violence against Negroes remains the same after 40 years.

[14] The Duncans (1956) state that ". . . there is some evidence that non-whites are forced to pay higher prices than whites for comparable dwellings. For example, in 1947 and 1948 in the Woodlawn area, it has been estimated that Negro buyers paid 28 to 51 per cent more than white buyers for one and two unit structures." It is now rather generally agreed that there is an upward movement of prices in Chicago when Negroes move in. See E.F. Schietinger, "Racial Succession and Value of Small Residential Properties," *The American Sociological Review*, 16, December, 1951. This knowledge is based upon detailed research by various individuals and groups connected with the University of Chicago. As the reader will note, this matter had not been cleared up when *Black Metropolis* was originally published and the authors accepted the view which was then general that property values were depressed by the moving in of Negroes. (Cf. *Black Metropolis*, pp. 174–175.)

and rent their property to Negroes. Needing living space as they did, plenty of Negroes were willing to run the risk of violence to themselves and their property by entering white neighborhoods. Some enterprising white realtors discovered that they could make a profit at both ends of the transaction—by promising to secure property for whites on the edge of the city or in the suburbs where they would be "safe from Negroes," and by promising to get Negroes into areas formerly barred to them. The expansion would not, however, have been possible had there not been a large amount of new building available to whites but denied to Negroes. (See Figure 21e for an analysis of new construction during the single year, 1956).

The story of the expansion of the Black Belt eastward toward Lake Michigan has historic significance. Here, for the first time, a group of white people in Midwest Metropolis made a deliberate attempt to create "interracial neighborhoods with high community standards," that is, to accept Negroes as neighbors on the basis of their social class position rather than on the basis of race. Very soon after the Supreme Court decision of 1948, the Oakland-Kenwood Association, one of the first groups to introduce restrictive covenants in Chicago, decided to reverse its stand and to substitute "occupancy standard" agreements for racial covenants. But the pressure of the housing shortage doomed this experiment.

Higher status residents directly to the south in Kenwood lived in an area zoned for single family occupancy. As members of the Negro upper and upper-middle class began to buy into this area, a basis was laid for interracial cooperation between Negroes and whites of similar status. Faced with an "invasion" by Negroes, the residents of Hyde Park, just south of Kenwood, organized the Hyde Park-Kenwood Community Conference to prevent the precipitous flight of white people and to form block organizations of whites, Negroes, and Orientals to keep the neighborhood safe, clean, and orderly. Eventually, with support from several philanthropic organizations, they proceeded to draw up a plan for urban renewal and redevelopment in the area.

The University of Chicago, which had been viewing its "encirclement" by Negroes with alarm, took independent action to "protect" its neighborhood by sponsoring the organization of a South-East Chicago Commission, which at first concerned itself primarily with crime prevention. Later, a plan for demolishing substandard structures eliminated both poor housing and congregation points of lower-class Negroes, poor whites and Puerto Ricans. It encouraged rebuilding at

Figure 21e

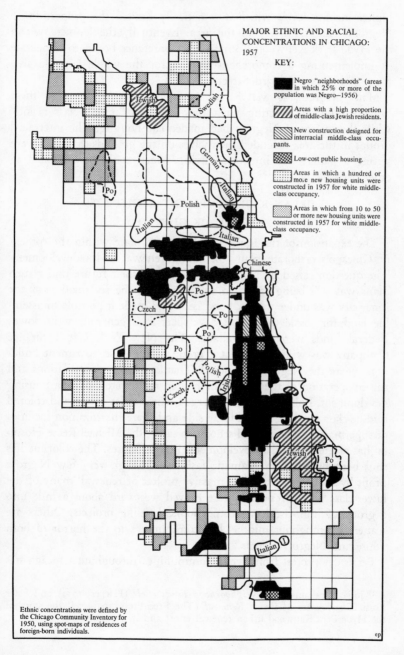

MAJOR ETHNIC AND RACIAL
CONCENTRATIONS IN CHICAGO:
1957

KEY:

■ Negro "neighborhoods" (areas in which 25% or more of the population was Negro—1956)

▨ Areas with a high proportion of middle-class Jewish residents.

▨ New construction designed for interracial middle-class occupants.

▨ Low-cost public housing.

⬚ Areas in which a hundred or more new housing units were constructed in 1957 for white middle-class occupancy.

⬚ Areas in which from 10 to 50 or more new housing units were constructed in 1957 for white middle-class occupancy.

Ethnic concentrations were defined by the Chicago Community Inventory for 1950, using spot-maps of residences of foreign-born individuals.

higher income levels which automatically limited the proportion of Negroes who could live in the area. Eventually the University and the Hyde Park-Kenwood Community Conference began to co-operate in implementing a comprehensive plan for the whole lakeside area from 47th Street to 63rd Street.

Many Negroes, as well as the Chicago *Defender* criticized these organizations for erecting what they called a "middle-class island" while the masses of Negroes had inadequate housing. The interracial groups in the area defended themselves on the grounds that they were setting a pattern for integrated living which could be emulated in other parts of the city.[15]

URBAN REDEVELOPMENT REINFORCES
THE BLACK GHETTO

The expansion of the Black Belt has taken place within the context of Chicago's elaborate plans for urban renewal and redevelopment. The question raised by Negroes in 1945 as to their future under such plans was still being raised in 1961. By 1951, the reclamation of the inner city was under way. A bond issue had made it possible to assemble land for resale to private developers at a generous write-down. Federal funds were also available. The New York Life Insurance Company was willing to erect a group of high-rise apartment buildings where the Negro slums stood. Thanks to federal regulations and the co-operation of the more enlightened real estate circles, a housing development, Lake Meadows, emerged where today white and colored middle-class residents live side by side and share the common facilities of supermart, clubhouse and schools. Nearby, the Michael Reese Hospital has erected a similar development, Prairie Shores. The colorline has thus been breached in dramatic fashion, although very few Negroes profit by it. To carry out this massive project of renewal, many of the lower-class Negro residents were moved westward about a mile into a group of high-rise low-income public housing projects. Others are scattered throughout middle-class communities to the horror of both white and Negro residents.

Persistent protest from white communities throughout Chicago has

[15] Julia Abrahamson, *A Neighborhood Finds Itself* (Harper, 1959) and Peter Rossi, *The Politics of Urban Renewal* (The Free Press, 1961) tell the story of the Hyde Park-Kenwood urban renewal effort and its repercussions.

led the Chicago Housing Authority to adopt a pattern of building most of its new low-cost housing along the western margin of the Black Belt in an undesirable area near the railroad tracks. A five-mile rim of high-rise public housing is gradually going up as a monument to Midwest Metropolis' insistence upon residential segregation. Even this adjustment to the demolition of slums in the Black Belt is resisted in some quarters on the grounds that it is "creeping socialism."

IS THERE ANY PROSPECT OF OPEN OCCUPANCY?

Chicago stands near the top of the list of American cities in the extent to which Negroes are segregated. There is widespread concern over the fact that the Black Belt is now reaching the limits of its expansion without danger of generating wholesale violence or the taking over of the high-income area, Lake Shore, just south of the University of Chicago. Liberals in integrated communities are demanding that other sections of the city "take their share of Negroes." Some realtors, most sociologists, and many social workers feel that unless the Black Belt is thinned out and overcrowding eliminated, and unless its block-by-block expansion is stopped, there will be incessant violence around its periphery as well as increased social disorganization within. These groups have been supporting an "open occupancy bill."

In 1961 when an open occupancy bill was laid before the city council, Negro politicians as well as white "ducked it," for they did not wish to embarrass aldermen loyal to the machine but living in wards where it would be political suicide to vote for open occupancy. The City Council voted to recommend to the State Legislature that it pass such a bill. Although the Chicago *Daily News* had supported FEPC legislation, it now drew the line at residential desegregation by law in an editorial "Discriminating Landlords."[16] The bill did not pass.

THE LINE OF COLOR IS STILL SHIFTING—BUT SLOWLY

The processes by which the Midwest Metropolis color-line has shifted over the years were discussed in detail in Chapter 10. There is still a *"shifting* line of color." Change in Chicago race relations has been hastened by the national trend toward desegregation and "integration," and by subtle, though nevertheless real, pressures emanating

[16] The editorial read, in part, as follows: We do not believe that the 38–7 vote (of the City Council) really reflects the convictions of the citizens of

from the dramatic postwar rise in the power and prestige of the Asian and African nations. On the local scene, considerations of political expediency and economic necessity have also continued to reinforce the efforts of those people, white and colored, who fight against segregation and discrimination because they believe in The American Dream.[17]

The beginning of the ideological assault upon the color-line during the closing years of the Second World War has been described in Chapter 10. The pressure has never been relaxed. The Mayor's Commission on Human Relations eventually became an institutionalized increment of the city government—The Chicago Commission on Human Relations. A coalition between trade union leaders and middle-class liberals functions on the race-relations front through a complex network of voluntary associations and committees in alliance with Negro pressure groups. The Communists are no longer an active component of this "united front." Resistance to change also finds institutional expression through numerous "neighborhood improvement associations" and "white property owners' associations," sometimes operating in a loose alliance with the not-too-respectable groups of the "radical right," such as the now inactive White Circle League. The anti-Negro organizations create a permissive atmosphere within neighborhoods for teen-age violence to express itself. Retaliatory aggression on the part of young Negroes sometimes brings a community to the verge of race riots. But careful police work has prevented the

---

Chicago on such a law, although it is true, and most people know it, that the inability of Negroes to find homes readily outside of a few areas creates one of the city's most serious problems.

We said the other day that the time had come to accept a fair employment practices law. It does not follow however that the case for compulsion in other fields is equally meritorious. . . .

The standards for choosing an employee and for choosing a tenant are not the same. In one, the test is can he do the work? In the other a landlord is rightly interested in obtaining a harmonious group. If he does not achieve it he is creating for himself not only trouble, but possible expense in turnover. . . .

The problem of racial discrimination in housing can and must be solved. We urge the agencies concerned with education in this field to redouble their zeal. And property owners should take note of the strength of the sentiment for compulsion and accelerate their efforts to make it unnecessary while they still have a free choice.

[17] The trends of the past decade confirm the general propositions about the type of social system which organizes Negro-white relations in northern cities, as they were stated in the first edition of Black Metropolis (pp. 756–757).

spread of violence throughout the city, and a press which stands firm for law and order and for racial equality, as well as crusading radio and TV commentators, have helped to create a "climate of opinion" in which the balance is tipped, at present, toward progressive social change in race relations.

Although the Job Ceiling and the Black Ghetto still persist, the color-line is now drawn less tightly in some areas of the city's life. The vigilance of The Chicago Commission on Human Relations and its quiet work of education have almost eliminated discrimination in downtown hotels and restaurants. Negroes now move about in the central business district with a confidence that they have not shown since the Great Migration shattered the structure of the pre-World War I "Golden Age" of race relations in Chicago. Fraternization across the color-line in homes and public places probably occurs with greater frequency and creates less adverse comment than it did fifteen years ago, and mixed couples report that they find people less likely to stare at them in public and more inclined to treat them merely as facts of urban life, while reprisals on the part of parents and relatives seem to be somewhat less severe. The most significant change involves an increase in the proportion of mixed marriages in which the husband is white. Yet, there are still areas of the city where Negroes do not find it safe to walk after dark and where a mixed couple would be risking assault and battery. Beaches are still major tension points.

"Token representation" of Negroes on various boards and committees, and in churches, schools, and business enterprises is becoming fashionable. The seeds of the future seem to be sprouting in a few integrated apartment buildings and interracial churches that have come into being during the last decade. The ritualization of equality at civic banquets and "brotherhood" ceremonies has become routine, and ever-widening circles of white people continuously reaffirm their loyalty to the ideal of eventual complete and total integration.

But Negroes still express impatience with the rate of change. Early in 1962 the NAACP and the Urban League were demanding transfer of children from overcrowded Black Belt schools into vacant classrooms in adjacent white areas. Middle-class Negro mothers were being arrested for conducting "sit-ins" at schools, while college students, colored and white, were sleeping in front of the office of the Chancellor of the University of Chicago in protest against "controlled integration" in Hyde Park. Negroes are taking seriously the *Defender's* slogan, "Race prejudice must be destroyed."

hARPER ✦ ᴄoRChBooKs

HUMANITIES AND SOCIAL SCIENCES

American Studies: General

HENRY STEELE COMMAGER, Ed.: The Struggle for Racial Equality — TB/1300

EDWARD S. CORWIN: American Constitutional History. △ *Essays edited by Alpheus T. Mason and Gerald Garvey* — TB/1136

CARL N. DEGLER, Ed.: Pivotal Interpretations of American History — TB/1240, TB/1241

A. S. EISENSTADT, Ed.: The Craft of American History: *Recent Essays in American Historical Writing* Vol. I TB/1255; Vol. II TB/1256

CHARLOTTE P. GILMAN: Women and Economics ‡ TB/3073

OSCAR HANDLIN, Ed.: This Was America: *As Recorded by European Travelers in the Eighteenth, Nineteenth and Twentieth Centuries. Illus.* — TB/1119

MARCUS LEE HANSEN: The Atlantic Migration: 1607-1860. *Edited by Arthur M. Schlesinger* — TB/1052

MARCUS LEE HANSEN: The Immigrant in American History — TB/1120

JOHN HIGHAM, Ed.: The Reconstruction of American History △ — TB/1068

ROBERT H. JACKSON: The Supreme Court in the American System of Government — TB/1106

JOHN F. KENNEDY: A Nation of Immigrants. △ *Illus.* — TB/1118

LEONARD W. LEVY, Ed.: American Constitutional Law — TB/1285

LEONARD W. LEVY, Ed.: Judicial Review and the Supreme Court — TB/1296

LEONARD W. LEVY: The Law of the Commonwealth and Chief Justice Shaw — TB/1309

RALPH BARTON PERRY: Puritanism and Democracy — TB/1138

ARNOLD ROSE: The Negro in America: *The Condensed Version of Gunnar Myrdal's An American Dilemma* — TB/3048

MAURICE R. STEIN: The Eclipse of Community: *An Interpretation of American Studies* — TB/1128

W. LLOYD WARNER: Social Class in America: *The Evaluation of Status* — TB/1013

American Studies: Colonial

BERNARD BAILYN, Ed.: The Apologia of Robert Keayne: *Self-Portrait of a Puritan Merchant* — TB/1201

BERNARD BAILYN: The New England Merchants in the Seventeenth Century — TB/1149

CHARLES GIBSON: Spain in America † — TB/3077

LAWRENCE HENRY GIPSON: The Coming of the Revolution: 1763-1775. † *Illus.* — TB/3007

PERRY MILLER: Errand Into the Wilderness — TB/1139

PERRY MILLER & T. H. JOHNSON, Eds.: The Puritans: *A Sourcebook* Vol. I TB/1093; Vol. II TB/1094

EDMUND S. MORGAN, Ed.: The Diary of Michael Wigglesworth, 1653-1657: *The Conscience of a Puritan* — TB/1228

EDMUND S. MORGAN: The Puritan Family: *Religion and Domestic Relations in Seventeenth-Century New England* — TB/1227

RICHARD B. MORRIS: Government and Labor in Early America — TB/1244

KENNETH B. MURDOCK: Literature and Theology in Colonial New England — TB/99

JOHN P. ROCHE: Origins of American Political Thought: *Selected Readings* — TB/1301

JOHN SMITH: Captain John Smith's America: *Selections from His Writings. Ed. with Intro. by John Lankford* — TB/3078

LOUIS B. WRIGHT: The Cultural Life of the American Colonies: 1607-1763. † *Illus.* — TB/3005

American Studies: From the Revolution to 1860

JOHN R. ALDEN: The American Revolution: 1775-1783. † *Illus.* — TB/3011

RAY A. BILLINGTON: The Far Western Frontier: 1830-1860. † *Illus.* — TB/3012

EDMUND BURKE: On the American Revolution. ‡ *Edited by Elliott Robert Barkan* — TB/3068

WHITNEY R. CROSS: The Burned-Over District: *The Social and Intellectual History of Enthusiastic Religion in Western New York, 1800-1850* — TB/1242

GEORGE DANGERFIELD: The Awakening of American Nationalism: 1815-1828. † *Illus.* — TB/3061

CLEMENT EATON: The Freedom-of-Thought Struggle in the Old South. *Revised and Enlarged. Illus.* — TB/1150

CLEMENT EATON: The Growth of Southern Civilization: 1790-1860. † *Illus.* — TB/3040

LOUIS FILLER: The Crusade Against Slavery: 1830-1860. † *Illus.* — TB/3029

WILLIAM W. FREEHLING, Ed.: The Nullification Era: *A Documentary Record* ‡ — TB/3079

FELIX GILBERT: The Beginnings of American Foreign Policy: *To the Farewell Address* — TB/1200

FRANCIS GRIERSON: The Valley of Shadows: *The Coming of the Civil War in Lincoln's Midwest: A Contemporary Account* — TB/1246

ALEXANDER HAMILTON: The Reports of Alexander Hamilton. ‡ *Edited by Jacob E. Cooke* — TB/3060

JAMES MADISON: The Forging of American Federalism: *Selected Writings of James Madison. Edited by Saul K. Padover* — TB/1126

BERNARD MAYO: Myths and Men: *Patrick Henry, George Washington, Thomas Jefferson* — TB/1108

---

† The New American Nation Series, edited by Henry Steele Commager and Richard B. Morris.

‡ American Perspectives series, edited by Bernard Wishy and William E. Leuchtenburg.

* The Rise of Modern Europe series, edited by William L. Langer.

** History of Europe series, edited by J. H. Plumb.

¶ Researches in the Social, Cultural and Behavioral Sciences, edited by Benjamin Nelson.

§ The Library of Religion and Culture, edited by Benjamin Nelson.

Σ Harper Modern Science Series, edited by James R. Newman.

º Not for sale in Canada.

△ Not for sale in the U. K.

2

3

History: Modern European